I0836831

CHICAGO IN 1820.

CHICAGO

AND THE

GREAT CONFLAGRATION.

BY

ELIAS COLBERT

AND

EVERETT CHAMBERLIN.

WITH

NUMEROUS ILLUSTRATIONS, BY CHAPIN & GULICK,

FROM

Photographic Views taken on the Spot.

CINCINNATI AND NEW YORK: C. F. VENT.
CHICAGO: J. S GOODMAN & CO. | PHILADELPHIA: HUBBARD BROS.
BOSTON: EDWARD F. HOVEY. AUBURN, N. Y.: F. M. SMITH.
SAN FRANCISCO: F. DEWING & CO.
1871.

STEREOTYPED AT THE
FRANKLIN TYPE FOUNDRY,
CINCINNATI.

CONTENTS.

PART FIRST.

PART SECOND.

ILLUSTRATIONS.

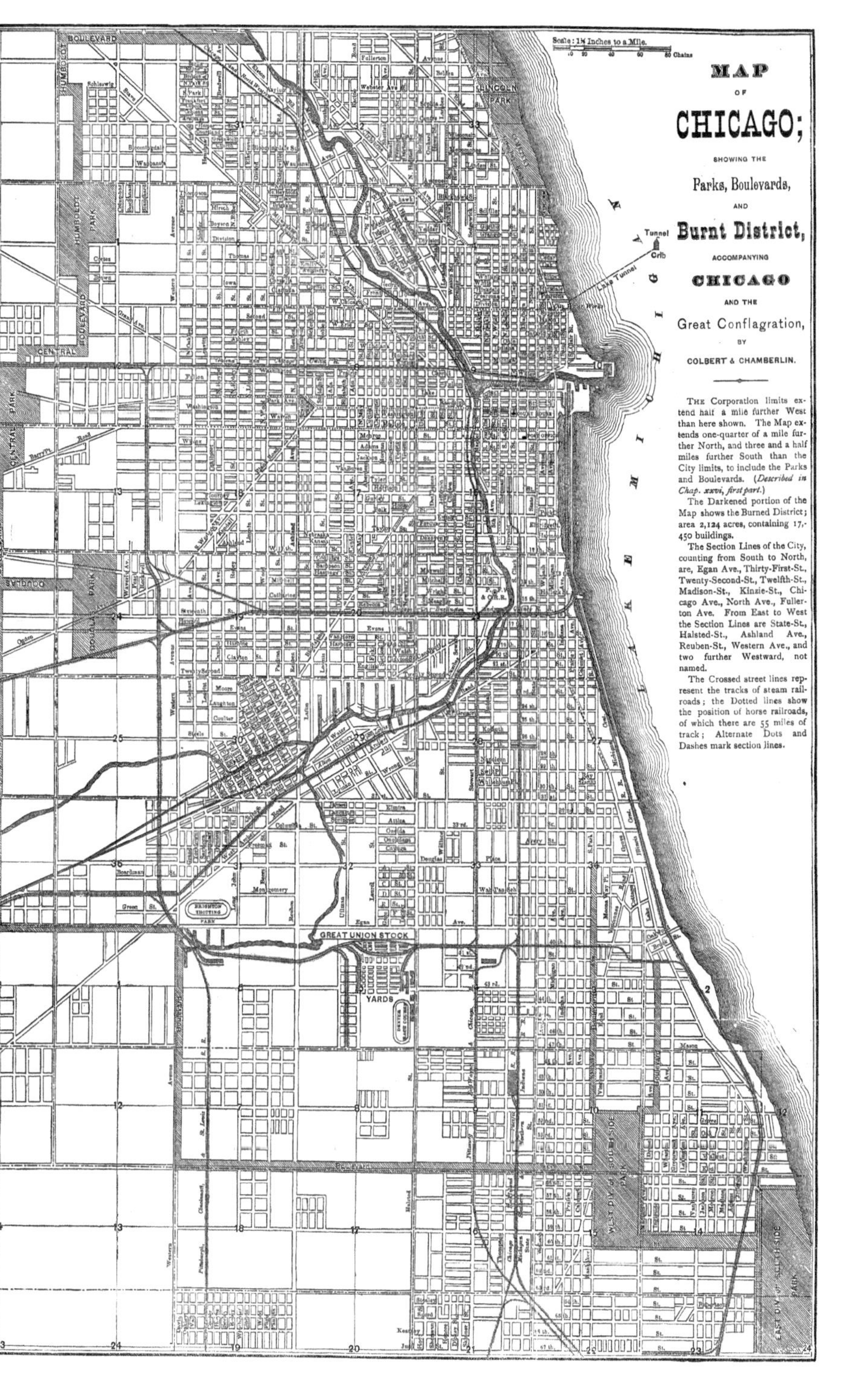
Scale: 1½ Inches to a Mile.
80 Chains
MAP
OF
CHICAGO;
SHOWING THE
Parks, Boulevards,
AND
Burnt District,
ACCOMPANYING
CHICAGO
AND THE
Great Conflagration,
BY
COLBERT & CHAMBERLIN.
THE Corporation limits extend half a mile further West than here shown. The Map extends one-quarter of a mile further North, and three and a half miles further South than the City limits, to include the Parks and Boulevards. (Described in Chap. xxvi, first part.)
The Darkened portion of the Map shows the Burned District; area 2,124 acres, containing 17,450 buildings.
The Section Lines of the City, counting from South to North, are, Egan Ave., Thirty-First-St., Twenty-Second-St., Twelfth-St., Madison-St., Kinzie-St., Chicago Ave., North Ave., Fullerton Ave. From East to West the Section Lines are State-St., Halsted-St., Ashland Ave., Reuben-St., Western Ave., and two further Westward, not named.
The Crossed street lines represent the tracks of steam railroads; the Dotted lines show the position of horse railroads, of which there are 55 miles of track; Alternate Dots and Dashes mark section lines.
Tunnel
Crib
Lake Tunnel
LAKE MICHIGAN
LINCOLN PARK
HUMBOLDT PARK
CENTRAL PARK
DOUGLAS PARK
GREAT UNION STOCK
YARDS
BRIGHTON TROTTING PARK
WEST DIV. of SOUTH SIDE PARK
EAST DIV. of SOUTH SIDE PARK

INTRODUCTION.

THE terrible conflagration in Chicago will long be remembered as one of the most prominent events of the nineteenth century. In the evening of Sunday, October 8, 1871, a stable took fire, and within twenty-four hours thereafter the flames had swept over an area of more than twenty-one hundred acres, destroying nearly three hundred human lives, reducing seventeen thousand five hundred buildings to ashes, rendering one hundred thousand persons homeless, and sweeping out of existence two hundred million dollars' worth of property. Without a peer in her almost magical growth to what seemed to be an enduring prosperity, the city of Chicago experienced a catastrophe almost equally without a parallel in history, and the sad event awakened into active sympathy the whole civilized world.

Such intense anxiety to catch every item of intelligence about the great conflagration, such a spontaneous outburst of liberality in aiding the sufferers, has never before been exhibited, except in times of national disaster. And, indeed, the calamity was universally recognized as affecting every one, not only in the United States, but in other countries. As the greatest primary market for produce on the face of the globe, Chicago had long been regarded as the cornucopia of modern civilization, while the energy and enterprise of her citizens had made her an object of envy to many other cities, and the wonder of the world. Her fame had spread far and near, and not even Solomon, in all his glory, ever excited so much admiration among those who went to see and found that the half had not been told them.

The present volume is intended to supply the wide-spread popular desire to obtain full and accurate information, in permanent form, about Chicago in her prosperity and affliction. It contains a concise *resume* of her previous history; a statement of her condition just before the fire; a graphic account of the great conflagration; a carefully-revised summary of losses of life and property; a description of the aspect of the city after the sad event; a history of the exertions made to aid the sufferers; with a review of the subsequent efforts made to rebuild the city 'mid the ashes of its former greatness.

CHICAGO AND THE GREAT CONFLAGRATION.

I. GEOGRAPHICAL POSITION OF CHICAGO.

CHICAGO is situated on the south-western bend of Lake Michigan, at the head of the great chain of American lakes, and is nearly 600 feet above the sea-level, the height of the lake-surface being 574 feet. What is now the business portion of the city was originally but a few inches above the lake-level, and the surface was often covered with several inches of water for months together. It is only within the past few years that the place has been raised from seven to ten feet by the process of filling in, so as to give a drainage that permits of the cleanliness that is necessary to the health of the inhabitants. The average annual fall of rain is 31¾ inches; the average temperature is about 50 degrees. The Court-house square, which is situated about midway between the north and south limits of the city, and half a mile west of the lake-shore, is in north latitude 41° 52′ 20″. The longitude west from Greenwich is 5h. 50m. 28s. (87° 37′), and 0h. 42m. 17s. west from Washington. The city is surrounded by what is, relatively, almost a dead-level; the prairie stretching away to a distance of several hundred miles south, west, and north, with scarcely an undulation of importance.

With such conditions it is evident that the term "Chicago

River," about which the world has heard so much, is a misnomer. Within the city limits the western shore of the lake runs nearly due north and south, trending about two points to the west of north. One-eighth of a mile north of the Court-house line a bayou strikes westward to the distance of five-eighths of a mile, then divides into two branches, both of which run nearly parallel with the lake-shore for a considerable distance. Near the end of the south branch a canal commences, which extends to the Illinois River at Lasalle, a distance of ninety-six miles. This canal has recently been deepened, so that the waters of the lake flow slowly along the "river" and the canal, into the Illinois River, and thence into the Mississippi. If the bayou at Chicago were a "river," it would furnish an instance of that wonderful phenomenon, "water running up hill." The current flows at the rate of about one mile per hour.

The banks of this river and its branches have furnished the dockage of Chicago, and, at the time of the great catastrophe, all the available space was so fully occupied that large systems of additional docks were being constructed along the lake-shore, outside what was usually known as the "harbor."

In the geographical and topographical position of Chicago, as above sketched, we have the key to the wonderful commercial prominence which she attained in such a short time, that some of those whose all was swept away in the conflagration of October, 1871, were among the earliest settlers in the village that afterward became a mighty city. The belt of only a few degrees in width, that includes the highest type of civilized advancement and the greatest energy in the development of cereal growth, has the city of Chicago situated nearly midway between its southern and northern limiting lines, and the head of the lake system was naturally the point at which the grain and other produce of the great North-west should be unloaded, first from wagons and afterward from railroad cars and canal-boats, to be placed on vessels, where the wind should replace horse or steam as a motive power, and carry that produce forward on its way to supply the wants of a hungry world. The place where the property changed hands was also the place where it would change ownership, as the smaller quantities laid down there would need to be massed into larger amounts for the long lake-journey in great vessels. That fact attracted capital to the spot, and then another point was soon developed: The growers of produce would spend their money in the place where they sold their property, if they could there find what they wanted on as favorable terms as elsewhere. And thus Chicago grew, in her double function of receiver and forwarder of Western produce to the East and to Europe, and of distributor of other necessaries and luxuries to the tillers of the soil and the manifold industries that clustered around them. With this came the establishment of numerous manufactories for the supply of the wants both of the city and of the country beyond, and the adoption of many processes by which the property in transit was better adapted to the wants of the buyer. These built up the city on the foundations laid by nature. The position with respect to the surrounding country established the place as the natural depot for collection and distribution in both directions; the enterprise and energy of the men who were attracted thither by those natural advantages did the rest.

The result of the operation of these two sets of causes, was a rapidity of growth that scarcely finds a parallel in the history of the world. Other cities have grown as rapidly for a few years, but we call to mind none, either in the old world or the new, that has exhibited an almost uniform increase of population at the rate of more than ten and a half per cent. per annum during thirty-five years, with an even greater augment in business volume and property values. That was the scale on which Chicago was developed, from the time of her incorporation as a city, in 1837, till the memorable catastrophe in 1871. And the events of the short period that has elapsed since the calamity tend to show that she will exhibit as great a ratio of grówth in the future. The history of such a wonderful progress can not but be of intense interest to millions of readers.

II. ABORIGINAL HISTORY.

FOR many centuries before Chicago was visited by a white man, it was the home of the Red-skins, and appears to have been successively occupied by several Indian tribes. There can be no doubt that the place was a favorite rendezvous for Indians, as it afforded facilities for fishing, and formed the terminus of a long route of canoe travel, the divide between the waters of the Mississippi and the Illinois River being so shallow as to necessitate but a very short portage. The earliest of these tribes of which we have any record was the Tamaroas, the most powerful of many Illinois families, and who claimed the name Checaqua as that of a long succession of their chiefs, just as Pharaoh was the name of many successive Egyptian kings.

The first white men known to have visited the region were Marquette and Joliet, two Jesuit missionaries, who were there in 1662–3, only three or four years before the great fire that laid in ashes two-thirds of the city of London, England. It was subsequently visited by two other French explorers, Hennepin and La Salle. The first geographical notice of the place is found in a map, dated Quebec, Canada, 1688, on which "Fort Checagou" occupies the exact location of the present city, and the form of Lake Michigan is represented quite correctly. In an atlas, published in 1696, by Le Sieur Sanson, "Geographer to the King," we find the whole Mississippi River, from its origin to the Gulf of Mexico, is named Chacaqua. In other old works it is called the "Chacaqua or Divine River." A manuscript, purporting to have been written in 1726 by M. de Ligny, at Green Bay, and brought from France by General Cass, mentions the place as Chicagoux, and that name is found to occur several times in the official correspondence of the earlier years of the present century.

The name "Chicago" has been variously interpreted to mean "Skunk," or Pole-cat, an animal supposed to have abounded there, and "Wild Onion," after the herb which is known to have grown profusely on the banks of the creek. But the above historical facts tend to prove that the word had a much nobler meaning; added to which, we know that the word *Checaque* was used as the name of thunder, or the voice of the Great Manitou. It has been suggested, however, that all of the above intentions may be harmonized, if we attach to the name the meaning of "strong," as it is well known that the Indian speech contained many more of these incongruous congruities than are to be found in the languages of the present day.

The Indians retained undisturbed possession of the site long after the whites had began to settle in the West. That settlement was principally made from the Southern States—Virginia and Kentucky—from the eastward, and by the French from the south, up the Mississippi. Hence the southern part of the present State of Illinois contained a considerable white population, while the wolf and the Red man only disputed with each other possession of all north of the State capital (Springfield), except in the little patch of ground occupied by the United States at the entrance of the Chicago harbor. Illinois was first organized as a county of Virginia in 1778, and was made a separate territory in 1809, but the territorial lines did not include Chicago; the northern boundary running due west from the southern extremity of Lake Michigan to the Mississippi. In 1815, Hon. Nathaniel Pope, just elected to represent the territory in Congress, procured the passage of an act extending the northern line of the territory to 42½ degrees of latitude, thus giving to the State a most valuable line of lake frontage, which now contains the three harbors of Chicago, Calumet, and Waukegan. The territory was elevated to the dignity of a State in 1818, the capital being Kaskaskia. Shadrach Bond, of that city, was elected as the first governor, in October of the same year.

The influx of settlers from the south was now quite rapid, but the immediate effect of the movement was to cause the different tribes of Illinois Indians to crowd northward, and make the site of Chicago alive with red-skins, who clung all the more pertinaciously to the soil, as the finger of fate pointed to their removal farther west at no distant day. The business of trading for furs became an important one, and traders gathered in the vicinity to purchase their stocks and send them eastward. This traffic was first established about the beginning of the present century, and marked a prominent phase in the history of the location.

III. FORT DEARBORN.

THE year following his first visit to Chicago, Pere Marquette returned, and erected a building for the purposes of worship. The French subsequently formed a plan to extend their possessions from Canada, along the Mississippi Valley, to New Orleans, and thence to sweep the continent eastward. They seem to have built a fort at Chicago, as a link in their great chain of domination. Canada was transferred to England by the victories of Wolfe in 1759, and the fort was then abandoned. After the close of the war of the Revolution the Indians became very troublesome, owing to British intrigue, and only after having been effectively chastised by General Wayne did they consent to a treaty of peace, in 1795, the chiefs of many tribes assembling at Greenville, Ohio, to sign the compact. Among the articles signed we find one recording the first land-sale in Chicago, and furnishing the only clue we have to the first erection of the fort by the French. The Indians ceded to the United States "one piece of land, six miles square, at the mouth of the Chekajo River, emptying into the southwest end of Lake Michigan, *where a fort formerly stood.*"

It has been facetiously remarked that the first white man who became a resident of Chicago was a negro. This first amendment to the copper color (whose race has since risen to the dignity of the fifteenth degree) settled there in 1796. His name was Jean Baptiste Point au Sable. He built a rude cabin on the north bank of the main "river," and laid claim to a tract of land surrounding it. He disappeared from the scene, and his claim was "jumped" by a Frenchman named Le Mai, who commenced trading with the Indians. A few years later he sold out to John Kinzie, who was then an Indian trader in the country about St. Joseph, Michigan, nearly opposite Chicago, on the eastern shore of the lake. Mr. Kinzie was an agent of the American Fur Company. They had traded at Chicago with the Indians for some time, and this fact had probably more than any other to do with the determination of the Government to establish a fort there. The Indians were growing numerous in that region, being attracted by the facilities for selling their wares, as well as being pressed northward by the tide of emigration setting in from the south. It was judged necessary to have some force near that point to keep them in check, as well as to protect the trading interest. Louisiana was purchased from the French in 1803, giving to the United States the control of the entire Mississippi Valley. In 1804 a fort was built by the Government, named "Fort Dearborn," in honor of a general of that name, and garrisoned with about fifty men and three pieces of artillery. Mr. Kinzie removed his family to the place the same year, and improved the Jean Baptiste cabin into a tasteful dwelling. His son, John H., but a few months old at the time of the removal, subsequently became one of the most prominent men of the city.

For about eight years things rolled along smoothly. The garrison was quiet, and the traders were prosperous, the number of the latter having been considerably increased. Then the United States became involved in trouble with Great Britain, which finally broke out into the war-flame. The Indians took the war-path long before the declaration of hostilities between the two civilized nations. On the 7th of April, 1812, they made an attack on one of the outlying houses, and killed and scalped the only male resident, then descended toward the fort, but refrained from making an attack, finding that the soldiers were ready to give them a warm reception. For some months they continued to harass and rob the outside settlers. The Government finally decided to abandon the fort, as it was too remote from headquarters to be successfully maintained in a hostile country. On the 7th of August, 1812, Captain Heald, the commander, received orders to evacuate the fort, if practicable; and, in that event, to distribute all the United States property among the Indians in the neighborhood. He hesitated for five days, knowing that a special order had been issued by the War Department to the effect that no fort should be surrendered "without battle having been given." He then reluctantly decided to comply, as his little force of seventy-five men was evidently unable to cope with the Indians.

On the 12th instant the Indians assembled in council, and Captain Heald informed them that he would distribute among them, on the next day, all the ammunition and provisions, as well as the other goods lodged in the United States factory, on condition that the Pottawatomies would furnish a safe escort for him and his command to Fort Wayne, where they should receive a further liberal reward. The Indians acceded to these terms, but Mr. Kinzie, who had learned the treachery of Indian character by long experience, afterward prevailed on Captain Heald to destroy all the liquor and the ammunition not needed by the troops on the journey.

The next day the blankets, calicoes, and provisions were distributed as agreed upon, and in the evening the liquors were thrown into the water, with all the ammunition, except twenty-five rounds, and one box of cartridges. They also broke up all the spare muskets and gun-fixtures, and threw them into the well. So much liquor was thrown into the river that the Indians drank largely of the water, saying that it was almost as good as "grog."

The next morning Captain Wells, a relative of Captain Heald, arrived from Fort Wayne with fifteen friendly Miamis. In the afternoon another council was held, at which the Pottawatomies professed to be highly indignant at the destruction of the whisky and ammunition, and made numerous threats, which plainly showed their murderous intention, only too well carried out on the ensuing day. On the morning of the 15th (August, 1812), the troops left the fort. Mrs. Kinzie, with her family of four children, two domestics, and two Indians, took a boat, intending to cross the lake to St. Joseph, but remained at the mouth of the harbor during the subsequent carnage, then returned to their home. The military party went southward, intending to march round the head of the lake. They had only proceeded about a mile and a half, when they were attacked by a party of Indians, who were concealed by a sand-ridge, whom they charged and dislodged from the position; but the Indians were so numerous that a party of them were able to outflank the soldiers, and take the horses and baggage. A severe fight followed, in which the number of the soldiers was reduced to twenty-eight; and during that action a young savage tomahawked the entire party of twelve children, who were in the baggage-wagon. Captain Heald then withdrew his troops, and a parley ensued, the consequence of which was that the troops surrendered, on condition that their lives should be spared, and were marched back to the fort, which was plundered and burned the next day. Mr. Kinzie did duty as surgeon, extracting the bullets with his pen-knife.

Accounts vary somewhat as to whether the Indians kept faith in their agreement, some charging that they massacred the children and some of the women after the surrender. We believe the facts to have been as above stated. The total number of killed was fifty-two, which included twenty-six soldiers, twelve militiamen, two women, and twelve children. The prisoners were ransomed some time afterward, the Kinzie family being taken across the lake to St. Joseph and thence to Detroit, a few days after the massacre.

IV. RE-OCCUPATION.

FOR four years the place was deserted by all save the Indians. Even the fur-traders did not care to visit the scene of so much disaster, and Chicago seemed to have been remanded into aboriginal darkness. In 1816, the fort was rebuilt, under the direction of Captain Bradley, and was thereafter occupied continuously by United States troops for twenty-one years, except for a short time in 1831. In 1837, it was abandoned, as the Indians had been removed far to the westward. The fort stood, however, till 1856, when the old block-house was demolished. Its position was on the south bank of the river, just east of the place where Rush Street Bridge was afterward built. One old building, however, remained, almost rotten with age, till the great conflagration swept it away, as the last relic of military rule. It was a small wooden structure that had formed a part of the officers' quarters, and stood almost in the apex of the sharp corner formed by the meeting of Michigan Avenue with River Street.

But the rebuilding of the fort failed to re-establish the *entente cordiale* that had existed between the Indians and whites previous to the spring of 1812. Mr. Kinzie did not return till some time after the fort was reconstructed. Gurdon S. Hubbard, Esq., who is still a resident of Chicago at the date of this writing, visited the place in 1818, as agent of the American Fur Company, of which John Jacob Astor was then president. He came in a small schooner, which was sent there once a year with provisions for the garrison. On his arrival he found only two families on the site of the future city, outside the fort. John Kinzie lived on the north side of the river, nearly on the line of Michigan Avenue; and Antoine Oulimette, a French trader, who had married an Indian woman, resided on the same side, about two blocks further west. J. B. Beaubien arrived about the same time. In 1823, one more white resident appeared on the scene, Archibald Clybourne, who established himself about three miles from the fort, on the north branch. In 1827, he built a slaughter-house and entered into business as butcher for the fort. He has resided in Chicago ever since then, and was alive very recently. In the same year the place was visited by Major Long, on a Government exploring expedition, who drew a sorry picture of the place, which then only contained three families, all occupying log cabins. He said, in his subsequent report, that Chicago presented no cheering prospects, and contained but a few huts, "inhabited by a miserable race of men, scarcely equal to the Indians from whom they had descended," while their houses were "low, filthy, and disgusting, displaying not the least trace of comfort." His opinion of the site as a place for business was equally poor. He spoke of it as "affording no inducements to the settler, the whole amount of trade on the lake not exceeding the cargoes of five or six schooners, even at the time when the garrison received its supplies from the Mackinac." How wonderfully the aspect of the place changed, within half a century from the time of Major Long's visit, has been written with a pen of iron—the record graven so deeply, that not even the great conflagration could efface it.

V. THE CANAL.

THE project to connect the Mississippi River with Lake Michigan, by a canal from the lake to the Illinois River, was the real cause of the up-growth of Chicago. The commercial advantages of the site as the terminus of that avenue of water communication, first attracted attention to Chicago, and led to the gathering of a most important community long before the canal was completed, or even begun. The measure was first agitated as a needed means of connection between the southern part of the State and the Atlantic Ocean, much shorter than that afforded by the Mississippi—a secondary consideration being the great value of a ship canal, connecting the two great water-courses of the continent, in case of another war with a European power. That measure, designed for the benefit of the south, then the only settled part of the State, has resulted in attracting to the northern portion a tide of emigration, and an abundance of capital, that has thrown the southern counties into a comparative shade, though ministering largely to their development.

The canal project was agitated as early as the year 1814, the measure being urged in the presidential message to the Thirty-seventh Congress, and reported on by the military committee, and the select committee on the deepening the great lakes and rivers, the latter body styling it "the great work of the age" for military and commercial purposes. Governor Bond, of Illinois, pressed it upon the attention of the Legislature, in the very first gubernatorial message ever delivered in the State—in 1818. His successor, Governor Coles, also urged its importance in 1822; and an act was passed in February (14) 1823, appointing a Board of Inspectors, who made a tour of inspection in the year following. On the 30th of March, 1822, Congress had passed an act, by which the State was authorized to make the survey through the public lands, and reserving ninety feet on each side of the canal from any sale made by the United States. It was conditioned, however, that if the State did not survey, and within three years direct the canal to be opened, or if the canal should not be completed within twelve years, that the grant should be void. The commissioners surveyed five routes, and made estimates of the cost of the work; the highest was $716,610.

On the 13th of January, 1825, the Legislature passed an act incorporating the Illinois and Michigan Canal Company, with a capital of one million dollars, but no one was found willing to take the stock, and the charter was subsequently repealed. The matter was again taken up by Congress, principally through the exertion of Hon. Daniel P. Cook, from whom was afterward named the county in which Chicago is situated. Congress granted to the State every alternate section in a belt of land six miles wide on each side of the proposed canal, provided that the work should be commenced within five years, and completed within twenty years; otherwise the State should pay to the United States all the money received for lands previously sold. On the 22d of January, 1829, the State passed an act providing for the appointment of commissioners to adopt such measures as might be required to effect the required communication between the river and the lake. These commissioners were directed to select the State lands, and to sell them where they thought proper to do so, and to lay off certain parts into town lots. This was the commencement of the system of land grants, which has since been so extensively adopted in the United States, and upon this action was laid the foundation of the future city of Chicago.

VI. THE TOWN OF CHICAGO.

UNDER the direction of the commissioners, James Thompson proceeded, in 1829, to Chicago, which then consisted only of Fort Dearborn. He made a survey of the site, and the first map of the city was prepared by him; it bears date August 4, 1830.

The canal was not commenced till 1836, and the year 1848 had arrived before it was completed, and then on a much inferior plan to that at first proposed, but the effect was wonderful. The benefits of the measure were long antedated by the enterprising people, who saw that the completion of the work would establish a mighty commercial depot at the head of Lake Michigan; indeed, they, and those who came after them, have always been noted for the rapidity with which they could discount the advantages of an event long before its occurrence. As only one out of many instances of this, we may here note the fact that the expected greater demand for breadstuffs during the war between France and Germany, in 1870, caused her grain-markets to touch a much higher point before the declaration of war than at any time after the event, and the price of wheat in Chicago actually fell almost steadily during the entire time that the war was in progress. So with the canal. The place had grown to the dimensions of a city before the first sod was turned, and fell into the slough of despond long before it was finished. But we anticipate.

The tide of emigration had set westward, to a limited extent, during the agitation of the canal measure, but the settlement of the West was retarded by the hostility of the Indians, who were particularly restless in 1828, murdering several emigrants and menacing the fort with destruction. A large military force, under General Atkinson, restored order. The country was filling up to the westward, as the fertility of the rich prairies became known to the people of the East and of Europe. But the site of Chicago was still as barren and uninviting as when visited by Major Long in 1823. Near the fort, and again near the junction of the two branches with the main river, the land was relatively high; but between those points, and all around, was a low, wet prairie, only a few inches above the lake-level, and subject to inundation with every shower. An early writer says that it "scarcely afforded good walking in the driest summer weather, while at other seasons it was absolutely impassable." Another, who visited Chicago at even a later date, tells how he passed over the ground from the fort to the junction of the river with its branches,on horseback, and was up to the stirrups in water the whole distance. He said: "I would not have given sixpence an acre for the whole of it." For a long time the usual mode of communication between these two points was by canoe, the "road" being too marshy for traveling.

Of course such a site was barren of agricultural promise, and

CHICAGO IN 1833.

required strong faith in its commercial future to tempt the settler to brave the poverty and malarial sickness that threatened to starve him out while waiting for the realization of his hopes. It is no wonder that, in 1829, when Surveyor Thompson began his labors, he found only seven families there, outside the fort. Two of these, Mr. Kinzie and his brother-in-law, Dr. Wolcott, the Indian agent, lived on the north side of the river; John Beaubien lived on the south side, near the fort, and John Miller kept a log tavern near the fork, besides which three or four Indian traders, whose names have not been preserved, lived in what is now the West Division. Mr. Hubbard was not then a resident; he was frequently there for several weeks at a time, but did not locate permanently till 1833.

The first map of the future city (August 4, 1830) only embraced an area of about three-eighths of a square mile, the boundaries being Madison, Desplaines, Kinzie, and State Streets. The ground east of State, since known as the Fort Dearborn Addition to Chicago, was a Government reservation.

The next step in the work of preparation for future occupancy, was the organization of Cook County, March 4, 1831, the limits of which included the whole tract now comprising the counties of Cook, Dupage, Lake, McHenry, Will, and Iroquois. Chicago is nearly midway on the eastern border of the present county. Two companies of troops then occupied the fort. In this year the number of male citizen residents had increased to fifteen, including the Government blacksmith, and Billy Caldwell, the Indian chief, who acted as interpreter for the agency. Not less than three of these kept tavern. Among the new arrivals, those who subsequently figured prominently in the history of the city, were George W. Dole, merchant; R. A. Kinzie, merchant; P. F. W. Peck, merchant; Dr. Harmon, land speculator, and Mark Beaubien, tavern-keeper. Besides these, Russell E. Heacock resided three or four miles up the south branch of the river, and Archibald Clybourne on the north branch.

In this year (1831) emigration set in so vigorously that by midsummer all the available buildings in the city were crowded with families, and several were obliged to seek accommodations at the fort, though many of those arriving intended to proceed further west. So great was the pressure that the infant Court of County Commissioners felt called upon to legislate for the protection of travelers, and ordered that tavern-keepers should only charge twenty-five cents for each half pint of wine, rum, or brandy; twelve and a half cents for half a pint of whisky; twelve and a half cents for one night's lodging, and twenty-five cents for breakfast or supper. No less than four additional taverns were opened that year; licenses were granted to three persons to practice as merchants, and James A. Kinzie was promoted to the dignity of auctioneer. His first official act was to sell, in July, a portion of the ten acres previously deeded to the county of Cook, of which the present Court-house square is a part. He received a county order for \$14.53¾ in payment for his services.

In the latter part of September, 1831, about four thousand Indians assembled in Chicago to receive the Government annuity, which was paid by Colonel T. J. V. Owen. The terror of the residents at the scenes of drunkenness and debauchery that followed the payment, was deepened by the rumor that a deputation of Sauks and Foxes, belonging to the band of the notorious Black Hawk, was present, endeavoring to unite the Ottawas, Pottawatomies, and Chippewas, to join in an invasion of the Rock River country and drive out the white settlers.

Their design was thwarted by the chief, Billy Caldwell, who used all his influence in favor of peace.

The lake commerce of 1831 was quite large, not less than *three* vessels arriving during the year, one of which came to carry away the troops to Green Bay. The others were the Telegraph, from Ashtabula, Ohio, and the Marengo, from Detroit; the former brought a stock of goods, as well as many emigrants.

The fort had been vacated by the soldiers in June, leaving it free for occupancy by the emigrants, of whom about four hundred took up their quarters there in September. Most of these stayed there through the winter, which was a long one, and so bitterly cold that most of the other residents of the place also took refuge in the fort, for the double purpose of companionship and protection—the latter not more from the Indians than from the prairie-wolves, which were very numerous. The only communication they had with the outside world was effected by a half-breed Indian, who visited Niles, Michigan, once in two weeks, on foot, and brought in whatever papers he could procure—there were few letters in those days. The long winter evenings were "improved" by a debating society, occasional dances, and a weekly religious meeting, on the Methodist plan. It is noteworthy that in 1831 the first ferry was established across the river—there were then no bridges. Mark Beaubien filed a bond of $200 to carry all citizens of Cook County across the river free, on condition that he should be permitted to take toll from those not resident in the county.

Early in 1832, Chicago was startled by the intelligence that Black Hawk, with a party of five hundred braves, was advancing on the settlements on Rock River. Soon thereafter, people came flocking in from that district to seek refuge, their houses having been fired, and their stock taken by the

Indians. By the middle of May there were fully seven hundred people in the fort, two-thirds of whom were women and children, many of the men having driven their stock farther south, in search of a more favorable location. A "council" was now called, at which the Indians at first seemed anxious to join the marauders, but finally consented to send out one hundred braves against them, if desired.

In May a force of twenty-five men was organized at the fort, under command of Captain J. B. Brown, to scour the country. They were joined by a force of three thousand militia, and a detachment of regular troops from Rock Island, under command of General Atkinson. The Indians were finally routed, and Black Hawk delivered up a prisoner of war, on the twenty-seventh of August, 1832. In September, a treaty was concluded at Fort Armstrong (Rock Island), by which the Indians agreed to remove west of the Missouri, on condition that they should receive an annuity, and that a reservation of forty miles square should be set off to Keokuk, their principal chief.

General Winfield A. Scott was ordered to proceed to the West, to take part in the Black Hawk war. The cholera attacked the soldiers on the lake, and so many were prostrated that a large number were landed at Fort Gratiot, now Port Huron. The remainder proceeded to Chicago, where they communicated the infection both to the garrison and the people outside. The war was ended by the volunteers before General Scott could take part in the conflict, but he carried back with him such glowing accounts of the place that general attention was attracted to it, and, chiefly through his recommendation, Congress subsequently made the first appropriation for the improvement of the harbor.

The autumn of this year, 1832, witnessed the commencement of the packing trade in Chicago. Mr. Dole erected the first frame building, and immediately afterward began the slaughtering of two hundred cattle, which he had bought on the Wabash River, at two and three-quarter cents per pound. The same winter he slaughtered three hundred and fifty hogs, for which he had given three cents per pound, live weight. This was the beginning of a business, for which Chicago afterward became as famous as for her grain and lumber trade. She surpassed Cincinnati in the total exhibit of hogs slaughtered, in the winter of 1862–3, and up to the time of the great catastrophe had steadily kept in the advance of that city, wresting from her, and retaining, the right to be called the world's Porkopolis.

The year 1832 was marked by a considerable increase in the population and importance of the city. Among the new citizens who afterward became prominent, were Dr. Kimberly, Philo Carpenter, J. S. Wright, G. W. Snow, and Dr. Maxwell. South Water Street was formally extended to the lake, across Government property, from State Street eastward, and a road was surveyed to give communication with the southern part of the State. The first Sunday-school was organized in August, by Philo Carpenter and Captain Johnson, with thirteen children, and Rev. Jesse Walker, a missionary of the Methodist Episcopal Church, built a log hut west of the fort, for divine worship. This place was called "Wolf Point," and an intense rivalry sprung up, about this time, between the dwellers there and those in the vicinity of the fort. The good people never dreamed, at that epoch, that the population of Chicago would be more than enough to make up a respectable sized village, and each place was anxious to become the site of that village, when it should have attained to the dwarfish growth which was the utmost limit of their expectations.

Of course there was then no Court-house. The sessions of the County Commissioners, and of the Circuit Court, were generally held in the fort. The first building erected on the public square was an estray pen, put up in 1832, on the southwestern corner, at a total cost of twelve dollars. It is interesting to note that the total tax list of the entire county was returned by the sheriff this year at $148.29, of which amount $10.50 was uncollectable. The treasurer's report for the year ending April 25, 1832, shows the receipt of $225.50 for licenses, and a balance in hand of $15.93. But though poor, the county was not in debt; those were happy days compared with the present, when the great calamity has piled up an enormous loss on the top of a city debt of fourteen and a half millions of dollars.

The next year, 1833, the place grew apace. An appropriation of thirty thousand dollars was made by Congress for the improvement of the harbor, and work was at once commenced. At that time the main channel was narrower than now, and instead of running in an almost straight line into the lake, it turned short to the southward, round the fort, to a point near the present foot of Madison Street, and there connected with the lake over a bar of sand and gravel, the water on which was about fifteen yards wide, and only a few inches in depth. Vessels arriving at the port were obliged to anchor outside, and discharge or take on cargo by the aid of boats. A channel was cut through the bank, running straight out into the lake, an embankment formed to cut off the water from the former channel, a pier run out to a short distance on the north side of the new mouth, and a light-house built to mark the entrance to the new-formed harbor. In the following spring, a great freshet washed out more sand from the channel than had been removed by the dredges, but at the same time it swept away some six hundred feet of piling that had just been built to protect the south shore. It was now believed that a permanent harbor had been gained, which would never more be choked up. Subsequent experience has shown the fallacy of this hope, as continuous expenditures have been necessitated to keep open a passage for vessels. Further appropriations were made, of $32,800 in 1835; of $32,000 in 1836; and $40,000 in 1838, and work was suspended for a long time after the last-named sum had been exhausted.

This was but one of the many extensions made in 1833. A jail was built "of logs, firmly bolted together," on the north-west corner of the Court-house square, which stood there for just twenty years, when it was superseded by the Court-house. The first regular postmaster was appointed, in the person of J. S. C. Hogan, the keeper of a variety store on South Water Street, though a gentleman named Bailey is reported to have previously officiated in that capacity. Mr. Hogan's office is currently reported to have been graced with a number of old boot-legs, nailed up against the wall, which did duty as private boxes for such of the citizens as were honored with the most extensive correspondence. This year, too, was marked by the establishment of no less than three church societies. The First Presbyterian was organized June 26th, with a membership of nine citizens and twenty-five members of the garrison, by Rev. Jeremiah Porter, who was Chaplain of a detachment of United States troops that came from Green Bay early in the year. The First Baptist Church was organized on the 10th of October, with a membership of fourteen, by Rev. A. B. Freeman, and Rev. Mr. Schaffer commenced the erection of a Catholic church-edifice, which was completed the following year. The Methodists also held their first quarterly meeting in the autumn, with John Sinclair as Presiding Elder.

Another memorable event of 1833 was a gathering of about seven thousand Pottawatomie Indians, on the 27th of September, at which a most important treaty was made. The chiefs met the Government commissioners in council, in a large tent on the north side of the river, opposite the fort, and formally ceded to the United States all their territory in Northern Illinois and Wisconsin, amounting to about twenty millions of acres, for the sum of $1,100,000. They received as first payment about $56,000 in money, and $130,000 in goods; the remainder they were to receive in instalments, covering a period of twenty-five years. It is reported that not less than twenty thousand dollars' worth of the goods were stolen by the Indian traders during the first two nights, after the owners had been liberally saturated with whisky, for which they had paid out a large proportion of the articles furnished them. A letter from a traveler, who witnessed the scenes, was unearthed and published in the *Tribune* in 1869. We are sorry that the destruction of the files of that paper in the great conflagration prevents us from reproducing it. The description there given of the disgusting revels of the red men, and the rapacity of the whites, was almost enough to make one lose faith in human nature.

The great event of the year was, however, the incorporation of Chicago as a town. A public meeting was held August 5th, to decide whether the important step should be taken or not. A total of twelve votes were cast for the measure, and one against it, the negative being our old friend of the South

Branch settlement—Russell E. Heacock. An election was held on the 10th of the same month, at the house of Mark Beaubien, the original Charon of the place, who was also noted as the keeper of two fast horses; and we give the following as the list of voters on the occasion, which probably comprised every legal voter in the place, except one, as Heacock resided outside; about six others had arrived just previous to the election, who were afterward voters: E. S. Kimberly,* J. B. Beaubien, Mark Beaubien, T. J. V. Owen,* William Ninson, Hiram Pearsons, Philo Carpenter, George Chapman, John S. Wright, John T. Temple, Matthias Smith, David Carver, James Kinzie, Charles Taylor, J. S. C. Hogan, Eli A. Rider, Dexter J. Hapgood, G. W. Snow, Madore Beaubien,* Gholson Kercheval, G. W. Dole,* R. J. Hamilton, Stephen F. Gale, Enoch Darling, W. R. Adams, C. A. Ballard, John Watkins, James Gilbert—in all twenty-eight votes. The four marked with a star, and John Miller, were elected Trustees of the Town. Mr. Owen was elected President.

The following statistics of the new-born corporation will be of interest:

Area of the town, about	560 acres
Number of inhabitants,	550
Number of voters,	29
Number of buildings,	175
Valuation of property,	$60,000 00
Valuation of taxable property,	19,560 00
First year's taxes,	48 90

The business of the year included the packing of 500 or 600 head of cattle, and nearly 3,000 hogs, at the slaughter-house of Mr. Clybourne, of which 250 head of cattle and 1,000 hogs were packed by Mr. Dole.

The first important public improvement ordered by the new trustees was the establishment of a second ferry across the river, the point chosen being at Dearborn Street. They next extended the limits of the town to take in an area of about seven-eighths of a square mile. The new boundaries were Jackson Street on the south, Jefferson and Cook Streets on the west, Ohio Street on the north, State Street on the east, from Jackson to the river, and the lake-shore on the north side, from the river to Ohio Street.

Of course so important a place could not exist long without a newspaper, and accordingly we find that John Calhoun issued, on the 26th of November, 1833, the first number of the *Democrat,* which was also the first newspaper ever published in Northern Illinois. The early files of that journal are full of interesting matter; even the advertisements speak volumes, for they tell of the way in which business was transacted in those days. There was not much done, except by way of exchange in goods and produce, while land bought was largely paid for in promises. In the first number the editor strongly advocated the prosecution of the work on the Illinois and Michigan Canal, as the one great means necessary to the growth of the city.

During the summer of 1833 not less than 160 frame houses were erected, and the number of stores was increased from five or six to 25. Among the new buildings was the Green Tree Tavern, by J. H. Kinzie, which was the first structure ever erected in the place for that purpose; its predecessors were simply private residences, thrown open to the public for a consideration. Among the arrivals we find the names of S. B. Cobb, Walter Kimball, Star Foote, S. D. Pierce, Mancel Talcott, John D. Caton, Hibbard Porter, Franklin Bascom, E. H. Hadduck, Thomas H. Woodworth, and J. K. Botsford.

The year 1834 witnessed the establishment of closer commercial relations with other points east and west. The second week in April a schooner arrived from St. Joseph, and two cleared for the same port. On the 30th of the same month the corporation organ announced that emigration had fairly set in, as more than a hundred persons had arrived by boat and otherwise during the preceding ten days. On the 4th of June the *Democrat* announced that arrangements had been made by the proprietors of the steamboats on Lake Erie, whereby Chicago would be visited by a steamboat once a week till the 25th of August. On Saturday, July 11th, the schooner Illinois, the first large vessel that ever entered the river, sailed into the harbor amid great acclamations, the sand having been washed away by the freshet of the spring previous. In its issue of September 3d, the paper stated that 150 vessels had discharged their cargoes at the port of Chicago since the 20th of April preceding. The total number of votes polled in the whole of Cook County this year was 528. The poll-list of Chicago had increased to 111, out of a population of 400, besides 200 soldiers in the fort. It is noteworthy that not less than 13 of the 111 were candidates for office at the August election.

In the spring of 1834, a stage communication was opened up between Chicago and the country to the westward, by means of J. T. Temple's line for St. Louis. The route to Ottawa was piloted out by John D. Caton, who had previously been over the unmarked road on horseback. A bitter storm sprung up, and the driver was obliged to resign his post; he died afterward from that day's exposure to the cold. Mr. Caton, afterward Chief Justice of the Supreme Court of the State, took the stage through to Ottawa, where a better system of roads began, the first settlement of the State having been from the southward, as already stated.

The autumn of this year was marked by two historical events of interest. About four thousand Indians assembled there in October, to receive thirty thousand dollars' worth of goods, as the first annuity paid after the treaty by which they had ceded their lands to the Government. The goods were distributed just west of the river, near the line of what is now Randolph Street. The scene was simply disgusting, and several of the Indians were killed in a drunken brawl. The other event was a grand hunt. A large black bear was seen on the morning of October 6th, in a strip of timber on the corner of Market and Jackson Streets, almost exactly on the spot where the armory was afterward built. He was shot; then the citizens got up a grand wolf hunt in the same neighborhood, and killed no less than forty of those animals before nightfall. It was just at this point, thirty-seven years after, almost to a day, that the flames leaped across the river from the West Division, and thence swept northward to the limits of the city.

In this year a draw-bridge was built across the river at Dearborn Street; active measures were taken to prevent the spread of the cholera, and a committee was authorized to build a cholera hospital outside the town if the disease should make its appearance; the first Sunday liquor law was passed (September 1st); the large sum of forty dollars was paid for repairing bridges; and the town was divided into four wards, by an ordinance intended to prevent fires. Prior to this year all the stores were located on South Water Street; indeed, Lake Street, and all the streets southward of it, only existed on paper. In the autumn of 1834, Thomas Church erected a store on Lake Street, which was soon the busiest in the whole town. The packing statistics of the year show that Mr. Clybourne packed 600 cattle, and more than 3000 hogs; while Messrs.

Newberry & Dole slaughtered some 400 cattle and 1400 hogs in a packing house of their own, recently built on the south branch. The same year Gurdon S. Hubbard packed 5000 hogs, on the corner of Lake and Lasalle Streets.

Among the prominent arrivals of 1834 we note the names of F. C. Sherman, James Grant, A. E. Webster, Thomas Church, Wm. Jones, and Grant Goodrich. The first water-works of the future city was established about this time, the sum of $95.50 being paid for the digging, stoning, and stone of a well, in Kinzie's addition, on the north side.

VII. INFLATION.

THE year 1835 was a most remarkable one in the history of Chicago. It was preëminently the epoch of speculation. Colonel E. D. Taylor and James Whitlock arrived in the spring, and opened a United States Land Office on the 1st of June, over Thomas Church's store on Lake Street. The rush was immense. They sold over half a million dollars' worth of property in the first six months, and the sales were almost as great, correspondingly, through the next year. The extent to which the speculative mania raged, drawing people from far and near, may be inferred from the fact that the first census of the place, a statement of which was published in the *Democrat* of November 25, 1835, shows that the town then contained 3265 inhabitants, and the county 9773. The population had been multiplied by *eight* in a single year. The people were wild during the summer, and the records of the town show that the authorities were almost at their wit's ends, passing huge ordinances, and as quickly repealing them, to meet the exigencies continually presented by such a rapid influx of people to be governed and provided for. In the winter things were worse. There was nothing to do but to talk of the price of corner lots, and this inexhaustible subject was discussed again and again in private houses, and in the hotels, where hundreds of men strutted around like conscious millionaires, but without the where-with-all to pay for a week's board. Every body grew rich—on paper—as the selling prices of real estate multiplied even more rapidly than the population. The whole country was aflame with magnificent schemes of internal improvement, in which the future canal figured only as an item. These schemes were not put into legal shape till a year or two afterward, but the speculators were already at work cutting up the State into little chess-board squares, to be checkered by railroads, every one of which was to bring untold millions of wealth into the great commercial emporium of the North-west, while they and the canal should give employment to tens of thousand of workers. It is due to the projectors of these magnificent schemes to say that nearly every one of them has since been carried out. The great fault was that they wanted to go ahead too fast. They commenced to build before the structure was wanted, and by working a quarter of a century ahead of their generation, brought down untold misery on the heads of millions in the commercial panic that swept over the whole land at a subsequent date.

As the culminating point of most of these improvements, Chicago was the Mecca of speculators—a genuine El Dorado, where every one could make his fortune by simply buying a few lots, and selling out at an advance before the ink had dried with which the first transfer was recorded. Hence, although large quantities of money were attracted hither, it did little good. It was all invested in lots, and most of the cash immediately found its way into the national treasury. And as all these speculators invested the whole of their "pile," they had nothing left wherewith to pay their way. There was really little inducement to invest in business, as, although the country to the westward was rapidly filling up, the farmers had not arrived at the point where they had surplus produce to dispose of for cash, or to exchange for goods. But the speculators saw that the good time was coming, and discounted the situation fully fifteen years ahead.

From June to December, the sales at the United States Land Office aggregated 370,043 acres, for which $505,729 was received, most of the property being in Chicago and its neighborhood. But these figures fail to convey even a faint idea of the magnitude of the land speculation. The lots were sold and resold, each time at a large advance on the former price, every body dealing, and all making money as rapidly as a shoddy contractor in the early days of the rebellion.

The hotel accommodations of the year increased in proportion to the population. Besides the Green Tree Hotel, on the corner of Lake and Canal Streets, there were now three others. The Tremont House had been erected a year previously, on the north-west corner of Lake and Dearborn, and the loungers of that day used to stand on its steps and shoot the ducks on the river, or on the slough that lay before the door. Starr Foote was the first landlord, but he speedily gave way to Ira Couch, under whose management the Tremont soon became head-quarters for the travelers and speculators with which the town abounded. It was burned down in 1839, in the second fire that had visited the place, the first having occurred in 1834. The Graves (log) Tavern stood nearly opposite the Tremont, and the Saganash Hotel offered accommodations for man and beast, on the corner of Market and Lake Streets, the spot where Lincoln was nominated in 1860 for the presidency. At that date the grove of timber along the east side of the south branch was still undisturbed, the north division was thickly studded with trees, a few pines stood on the lake shore south of the harbor, the timber being thickest near the river, and a great pine tree stood near the foot of Randolph Street.

By an act of the Legislature, approved February 11, 1835, all the land east of State Street, from Twelfth Street to Chicago Avenue, was included within the town lines, except that it was provided that the Fort Dearborn reservation, lying between Madison Street and the river, should not belong to the town till vacated by the United States.

In this year (June) occurs the first instance of an attempt to borrow money on the credit of the town. The treasurer was authorized to borrow $2,000, at not more than ten per cent. interest, and payable in twelve months. He resigned rather than face the novel responsibility, and the street commissioner followed suit. A Board of Health was now appointed, with extreme powers in the way of enforcing cleanliness and prosecuting offenders. The new Board of Trustees, elected July 10th, on a poll list of two hundred and eleven voters, prohibited gaming houses, and the sale of liquors on the Sabbath; forbade the firing of guns and pistols within the limits, appointed police constables, and exacted bonds from the officials of the financial department for the faithful performance of their official duties. They also selected ten acres as a City Cemetery on Chicago Avenue, near the lake shore, and sixteen acres for the same purpose near the corner of Wabash Avenue and Twenty-third Street. These sites were both abandoned a few years afterward, and are now covered with buildings. In this year the Chicago *American* entered the field to compete with the *Democrat* for the advertising patronage of the town and its citizens.

Two additional buildings were placed in the Court-house square in 1835—a small brick edifice on the north-east corner, for the use of the county officers and the safe keeping of the records, and an engine-house, costing $220, the latter not being finished till the following year. The first fire engine was bought December 10th, of Messrs. Hubbard & Co., for the sum of $896.38, and a second ordered. The first Fire-engine Company was organized two days afterward, with the following members: S. G. Trowbridge, Foreman; E. Morrison, J. M. Morrison, H. G. Loomis, John Dye, Joel Wicks, H. B. Clarke, William Young, H. H. Magee, Peter Warden, J. S. C. Hogan, R. A. Neff, T. O. Davis, H. M. Draper, J. H. Mulford, Peter Pruyne, Ira Kimberly, W. McForresten, Alvin Calhoun, O. L. Beach, M. B. Beaubien, A. A. Markle, A. V. Knickerbocker, S. W. Paine, S. C. George, E. Peck, H. C. Pearsons, George Davis, William H. Clark, J. C. Hamilton, John Calhoun, D. S. Dewey, Hugh C. Gibson. A Hook and Ladder Company was also organized, as follows: John Wilson, E. C. Brackett, John Holbrook, T. Perkins, S. F. Spalding, Ira Cook, George Smith, J. J. Garland, J. K. Palmer, P. F. W. Peck, T. S. Eells, Joseph L. Hanson, S. B. Cobb, J. A. Smith, John R. Langston, Henry G. Hubbard, Thomas J. King, N. L. F. Monroe, J. K. Botsford, George W. Snow, G. W. Merrill, Joseph Meeker, S. S. Lathrop, Thomas S. Hyde, and Jason McCord. Hiram Hugunin was elected Chief Engineer.

On the 14th of November the Board of Town Trustees resolved to sell the leases of the wharfing privileges in the town for the term of 999 years, binding the board to dredge the river to the depth of ten feet at least, within four years from the sale, and the lessees of the privileges being bound to erect good docks, five feet wide and three feet above the water, within two years from the date of the lease. The sale of those immensely valuable privileges took place on the 26th of November, 1835, at the store of Messrs. Jones, King & Co., and it may be interesting to remember now the "minimum prices" at which owners of lots fronting the river had the privilege of buying. On South Water Street the price was $25 per front foot; on North Water Street, $18.75 per front foot; on West Water Street, $18 per front foot. The men who got rich in buying such property, at such prices, deserve no credit for speculative ability. But the board, on the 18th of November, 1835, offered still further assistance in their new school of "affluence made easy." They then resolved that they would not be bound to dredge the river, in making leases on North Water Street, consequently they lowered the minimum figure to $15 per front foot, in part, and $8.50 per front foot on the remainder of the line. To aid in paying for leases at this rate, the board took secured notes for three and six months, for the first payment of one-quarter of the price, and gave three years in which to pay off the balance. The sale was three times postponed, and while waiting for a sale all the picked lots seemed to have been taken at a minimum price. When the *vendue* did take place, only six lots remained to be sold, and but one of these found a purchaser, at $26 per front foot. The city will have the right to resume possession of these valuable lots on the 26th day of November, A. D. 2834. The "privileges" thus thrown away by a lot of men who ought to have known better, subsequently became matter of much anxious legislation on the part of the board, and with the sale of the magnificent school-lands, made October 21, 1833, on a petition signed by twenty-three citizens, form the two great sores in the history of the city. Both were literally "sold for a mere song." The school-lands, sold for $38,865, have since been worth nearly fifty millions.

The official seal was adopted in November, 1835—a spread-eagle, having three arrows in his claws, and the words "United States of America" surrounding the same.

Prominent among the new residents added in 1835, were, Tuthill King, Alonzo Huntingdon, J. Y. Scammon, W. B. Ogden, C. V. Dyer, C. L. Wilson, George Manniere, and H. O. Stone. Among the departures we note about fifteen hundred Indians, who left the place on the first of October, with forty ox-teams, and traveled forty days toward the lands allotted to them west of the Missouri, by the treaty of 1833. The party included all that remained of the "noble red man" in Northern Illinois, and the State has ever since been unmolested by the Indians.

There were fewer additions to the population in 1836 than in 1835, the total of dwellers in the latter year being only about 4,000. Among the new-comers were, Laurin P. Hilliard, Mark Skinner, N. B. Judd, John Wentworth, M. W. Windette, W. A. Baldwin, B. W. Raymond, Walter Wright, J. M. Van Osdel, E. S. Wadsworth, Julius Wadsworth, Thomas Dyer, L. D. Boone, Isaac N. Arnold, and Dr. D. S. Smith.

But the speculative fever still raged among the people, and they began to aspire to the dignity of a city, which was granted the next year, in answer to their prayer. There were two notable events in the history of 1836. The first was the launch of the sloop Clarissa, on May 18th, the first vessel ever built in Chicago—an event that was celebrated with great rejoicing. The second was the turning of the first sod in the excavation of the canal, which was performed at Bridgeport, the Chicago terminus, on the fourth of July; a loan of half a million dollars for the purpose having been authorized by the Legislature, and successfully negotiated. In July the commissioners advertised for 2,000 men to work on the canal at twenty to thirty dollars per month. Meanwhile the improvement of the harbor was proceeded with so vigorously that vessels could move freely in and out of the river. Another packing-house was also built this year, by Sylvester Marsh, on Kinzie Street, near Rush. He packed hogs there till 1853.

A good deal was effected this year in the way of city improvements, and much more would have been effected but for the fact that the town authorities were snubbed in their efforts to obtain a loan of $25,000 from the State Bank for these purposes. Several buildings were removed from the streets, where they had been located promiscuously, and thus several thoroughfares were brought into line. Plank sluices were constructed across Clark Street to carry the drainage to the south branch. Canal Street was turnpiked as far north as Kinzie, and Lake and Randolph were similarly improved to the distance of several blocks west of the river. Among the improvements prospected and not carried out were the bridges at Randolph and Kinzie Streets, and the establishment of a system of water supply through pipes, by a hydraulic company, incorporated this year. The water wants of the citizens were hitherto supplied by carts, and the same primitive method was continued for four years longer.

The corporation tax on real estate amounted to $8,998 28,

and in this year we find the first mention of lots being sold to make good delinquencies on the tax list.

This year was the last in the township history of Chicago, and we therefore present the following summary of marine statistics, showing the commercial growth of four years:

Year.	Vessels arrived.	Tonnage.
1833	4	700
1834	176	5,000
1835	250	22,500
1836	456	60,000

In the same time the value of the real and personal property of this city had grown from little more than zero to an aggregate of nearly one million dollars.

VIII. THE CITY.

IN 1837 Chicago became a city. It was incorporated by act of the Legislature, passed March 4th, which extended the limits to include an area of about ten square miles. It was bounded as follows: On the south by Twenty-second Street; on the west by Wood Street; on the north by North Avenue; on the east by the lake, except the fraction of section ten, occupied as a military post; it included, in addition, the ground on the lake shore lying east of Clark Street, extending half a mile north of North Avenue, since occupied as the old city cemetery. The city was divided into six wards, each of which was empowered to elect two aldermen.

A school act had been passed in February, 1835, providing for the annual election of school inspectors and trustees, and giving power to enforce a tax of not more than one-half per cent. per annum for school purposes. The act of municipal incorporation constituted the Common Council as commissioners of public schools, with power to appoint a board of school inspectors annually. Under this regime Thomas Hoyne and Calvin De Wolf were engaged as school teachers; but very little was done in the way of tuition till 1840, on account of the general poverty.

The first charter election resulted in the election of the following officers:

Mayor—Wm. B. Ogden.

High Constable—John Shrigley.

First Ward—Aldermen, J. C. Goodhue, Francis Sherman; Assessor, Nathan H. Bolles.

Second Ward—Aldermen, J. S. C. Hogan, Peter Bolles; Assessor, E. A. Tuder.

Third Ward—Aldermen, J. D. Caton, H. Hugunin; Assessor, Solomon Taylor.

Fourth Ward—Aldermen, A. Pierce, F. H. Taylor; Assessor, Wm. Forsyth.

Fifth Ward—Alderman, Bernard Ward; Assessor, Henry Cunningham.

Sixth Ward—Aldermen, S. Jackson, H. Pearson; Assessor, S. D. Pierce.

N. B. Judd was chosen City Attorney.

The following were the principal statistics of the new city:

Population in 1837, July 1st,	4,170
Number of voters,	703
Area of city, square miles,	10
Number of buildings,	492
Taxable valuation (¼),	$236,842
City taxes,	$5,905

The population included 513 under 5 years of age; 831 over 5 and under 21 years; and 2445 persons over 21 years of age; the latter class contained 1800 males and 845 females. In addition to these were 104 sailors belonging to Chicago-owned vessels, and 77 colored persons.

The list of buildings comprised 4 warehouses, 398 dwellings, 29 dry goods stores, 5 hardware stores, 3 drug stores, 19 grocery and provision stores, 10 taverns, 29 groceries, 17 lawyers' offices, and 5 churches. Several of the buildings appear in more than one class.

Among the new arrivals of 1837 were Peter Page, W. H. Bradley, Thomas Hoyne, C. N. Holden, and C. C. P. Holden. The next year witnessed the arrival of E. I. Tinkham and H. T. Dickey. F. A. Hoffman arrived in 1839.

IX. THE COLLAPSE.

FOR a long time this was the culmination of Chicago's greatness. A few months passed in the enjoyment of the newly acquired dignity, and then came the well-remembered crash of 1837, which operated with peculiar force upon the city, as she was largely filled with speculators in real estate, whose hopes vanished when prices began to fall. For two years prices of real estate had mounted upward like a kite in a gale of wind, stimulated by the bidding of the ever advancing throng. Purchases were made, almost universally on time, and when the people's currency went down it was apparent that there was nothing to pay with. The tide of emigration was stopped, and many left the city, while very many other large owners (?) of real estate were unable to pay their board bills, and staid in the city simply because they were too poor to get away. Nothing but ruin stared the people in the face. A public meeting was held in the autumn, at which it was proposed to petition for relief laws against the collection of debts, but the project was, itself, repudiated, and the people were content to owe that which they could not pay.

The direct cause of the collapse was, as already indicated, the fact that the nation had reached out too fast. The Illinois Legislature of 1836–37 had shared in the general mania, authorizing the construction of some thirteen hundred miles of road at once, on which about five million dollars was expended for locating and grading. The moneys borrowed for this purpose, for the canal, and for other schemes, were all spent, long before there was any return. Production was neglected for construction, and the result was that the west was in debt hopelessly, with not even money enough to pay the interest as it became due. The banks had generally been built on the same unstable foundation of credit, and were the first to go under when the first shock came that showed a want of confidence. The second State bank, chartered by the Legislature in the winter of 1834–5, established a branch in Chicago in December, 1835, which flourished like a green bay tree, till the panic came. It then suspended specie payments, but continued to do business till 1841, when it finally suspended; and for the ten succeeding years there was not a bank of any kind in the whole State.

Under these distressing circumstances, Chicago was utterly stagnated for about five years, each succeeding twelve months witnessing a further reduction in pecuniary values, with no augment of population. The work on the Illinois and Michigan Canal was slowly proceeded with, in spite of the financial troubles, and despite also the fact that a terrible fever broke out among the laborers on the canal, and extended to the city, carrying them off by scores. The Canal Commissioners had been empowered, in March, 1837, to sell as many town lots in Chicago and elsewhere, as might be necessary to produce a million dollars. Many sales were made, and the money applied as designated. In July, of the same year, they were further empowered to sell lots to the value of $400,000, and to enlarge the natural basin at the confluence of the north and south branches of the river. The persistency with which the canal project was sustained was probably all that prevented Chicago from sinking back into original nothingness. In 1840, the official valuation of real estate had fallen to $94,437, and the city taxes to $4,722. The next year work was suspended on the canal, and the situation became more gloomy than ever, real estate being offered at less than five per cent. of the price paid in 1836. A general bankrupt act was passed in 1842, and then there was a slow revival till the middle of the century was reached.

The history of the city during the five years succeeding the crash presents but few points of interest, and those all of a melancholy character. Most of the people settled down into a gloomy despondency over the failure of the bright prospect. Yet the great majority even of these showed that the real grit which led them there had not forsaken them. They despaired of seeing Chicago take the position of a great commercial emporium, but they set to work to improve its appearance, making their cottages neater, and cultivating the soil very assiduously, though the site was really in need of drainage. They really made a virtue of necessity in regard to the latter, raising the vegetables and some grain necessary to their sustenance, having no money with which to buy them from others. This was the horticultural era, when potatoe hills, and cabbages, and flower belts, and onion beds, covered whole blocks, since occupied by fine buildings in the very heart of the city. It was during this epoch and the few years succeeding it that Chicago earned the title of the "Garden City," so often applied to it in recent years, with no known reason on the part of those using the term.

In 1839, the year after the canal fever, the city had a population of 4,200 inhabitants, under the mayoralty of B. W. Raymond. The first business directory of the city ever published was brought out in that year by Edward H. Rudd, and contained the names of 278 business firms, including lawyers, etc. It gives a list of six churches.

The *Chicago American* was first issued as a daily, the first in Illinois, April 9th, of this year. We extract from the first few numbers the following names of mercantile advertisers, etc. The list embraces all of those of any moment, except lawyers:

Dry Goods and Groceries—Goodsell and Campbell, T. B. Carter & Co., Paine & Norton, O. H. Thompson (and crockery), Harmon & Loomis (and liquors), B. W. Raymond, Joseph

L. Hansen, George W. Merrill, S. W. Goss & Co., A. D. Higgins, C. McDonnell, C. S. Phillips, H. O. Stone.

Drugs—E. Dewey, L. M. Boyce, W. H. & A. F. Clarke (and seeds), Philo Carpenter, S. Sawyer.

Hardware, etc.—S. T. Otis & Co., David Hatch, Osborne & Strail, L. W. Holmes.

Boots and Shoes—W. H. Adams & Co., S. W. Talmadge, S. B. Collins & Co., Wm. Osborne.

Auction and Commission—Stanton & Black, Marshall & Tew.

Commission and Produce—J. S. Wright, G. S. Hubbard & Co., McClure & Co., Kinzie (J. H.) & Hunter, Dodge & Tucker, Reed Bartlett.

Books and Stationery—Stephen F. Gale, H. Ross.

Lumber, etc.—Newberry & Dole, G. W. Snow & Co.

Provisions—Newberry & Dole.

Day School—Rev. I. T. Hinton.

Clothing, etc.—Tuthill King, Paine & Norton, G. F. Randolph, J. F. Phillips, J. A. Smith & Co. (and hats, caps, and furs).

Engraving—S. D. Childs.

Jewelry—S. J. Sherwood.

Harness, etc.—W. S. Gurnee.

Cabinet Ware—Bates & Morgan.

Liquors—Isaac D. Harmon.

Hotels—Jacob Russel (City), John Murphy (U. S.), G. E. Shelley (Lake), E. Gill (Shakespeare), Saganash Hotel.

Insurance—E. S. & J. Wadsworth, David Hunter.

In this year the work on the harbor was suspended, the last appropriation of $40,000, made in 1838, having been exhausted. Lake Street lots were now selling as low as $600 each, that have since sold at $2,500 per front foot. The general trouble of the epoch may be understood from the following list of persons discontinuing business, as furnished by Hon. Thomas Hoyne, the city clerk, in a memorial to Congress in 1841, praying for a resumption of work on the harbor:

1836—T. R. Martin, dry goods; M. McFarlan, do.; William Hatch, do.; McClure & Co., crockery; Mr. Howard, dry goods; Mr. Bates, do.; Mr. Hogan, do.; Chamber & Benedict, do.; Chauncey Clark, do.; Mr. Freer, do.

1837—Walker & Brothers, dry goods and groceries; Walter Kimball, do.; Kimball & Potter, do.; Jones, King & Co., hardware; Joel Walker, dry goods; Wild, Maloney & Co., do.; Alfred Farley, do.; Beaubien & Boyce, do.; Monroe & Dunning, do.; Guild & Durand, do.; Jenkins & Reynolds, do.; Kinzie, Davis & Hyde, hardware; J. L. Smith, dry goods; Rufus Masten & Co., do.; Mr. Luce, do.; J. B. Beaubien, do.; Rogers & Marcoe, do.; John L. Wilson, do.; J. & T. Handy, do.; Henry King & Co., do.; Walbridge & Jordan, groceries; Cheng & Johnson, do.; Mr. Brackett, do.; Foyke & Wright, do.; Montgomery & Patterson, auctioners; L. Hunt, hats and furs; Hall & Monroe, groceries; Mark Beaubien, dry goods; Caruthers & Co., do.

1838—King, Walter & Co., hardware; Peter Pruyne, drugs, etc.; J. W. C. Coffin, dry goods; Vibbard & Tripp, do.; J. Rayner, do.; Judge Smith, do.; Thomas Duncan, clothing; Wheeler & Peck, grocers; Noble & Rider, do.; Parker & Gray, dry goods.

1839—Mr. Hatch, hardware.

1841—Mr. Berry, dry goods; James Kinzie & Co., do.; Campbell, Wallace & Plumb, do.

It is true, however, and singularly enough, that it was during this very period of depression, Chicago commenced to achieve her manifest destiny as an exporting point. While industry was taking the place of speculative idling, and the masses of the people were adding slowly to their wordly wealth, and a few busy in planning the schemes of improvement that made the city of 1871, there were a very few who quietly put their shoulders to the wheel of commerce. It rolled slowly for awhile, but once fairly started, it acquired an impetus that nothing could resist. It is true that $1,000 worth of hides was exported in 1836, and nearly $12,000 worth of hides, pork, and beef in 1837, but the grain movement, in which Chicago has attained such a world-wide prominence, only commenced in 1838, the year after the panic, with a small venture of 39 bags of wheat, by Walker & Co., in the steamer Great Western, along with $15,000 worth of hides. Absalom Funk shipped $1,000 worth of beef and pork in the same year. The vessel list of 1838 comprised 127 arrivals of steamboats, and 241 of other vessels; total, 268. The steamer George W. Dole was now plying regularly between the ports of Chicago, Milwaukee, and Buffalo.

In 1839 the number of exporters had increased to eight, who sent forward produce to the value of $35,843, including $15,000 in hides, $11,000 in provision products, and 16,073 bushels of wheat, besides corn and flour. In 1840 we have not less than fifteen firms noted as exporters, the material sent forward being flour, wheat, corn, pork, beef, tallow, hams, beans, salt, wool, lead, flax-seed, hides, and furs, with a total value of $223,883. In 1841 the list of exporters had swelled to twenty-four, who sent out 304,212 bushels of wheat and other produce, making a grand total of $350,000. The arrivals and departures by lake this year were 150. In 1842 the flour and wheat shipped was the equivalent of 586,907 bushels of wheat. The following table shows the value of the imports and exports during each year in the period under review. It will be observed that in 1842 the exports for the first time about equaled the imports:

Year.	Imports.	Exports.
1836, ...	$325,203 90	$1,000 64
1837, ...	373,677 12	11,665 00
1838, ...	579,974 61	16,044 75
1839, ... - .	630,980 26	35,843 00
1840, ...	562,106 20	228,883 00
1841, ...	564,347 88	350,000 00
1842, ...	664,347 88	659,805 20

In 1842 the population had grown to 6,590 souls, having increased about 1,000 in the preceding twelve months. The improvement, as compared with 1837, will be better understood from the following table of buildings in the city in 1842:

	South.	North.	West.	Total.
Brick stores, . . .	37	0	0	37
Frame stores, . . .	206	10	3	219
Brick dwellings, . .	28	10	3	41
Frame dwellings, . .	444	278	120	842
Stone dwellings, . .	1	0	0	1
Other buildings, . .	—	—	—	224
Totals, . .	716	298	126	1,364

In November, 1840, the educational affairs of the city seem to have first received systematic attention. A Board of Inspectors of Schools was appointed, consisting of the following-named gentlemen: William Jones (President), J. Y. Scammon, Isaac N. Arnold, Nathan H. Bolles, John Gray, J. H. Scott, Hiram Hugenin. Under this *regime* the following-named gentlemen served as teachers in the Public Schools, at a salary of $33.33 per month: South Division—A. G. Rumsey, H. B. Perkins;

West Division—A. D. Sturtevant; North Division—A. C. Dunbar. It should, however, be remembered that they taught in none of those elegant buildings recently destroyed by the fire. The first Public School structure had yet to be erected in Chicago.

A few sidewalks were put down during this epoch, and several other minor improvements of a public character were erected, but the principal work was that by which the citizens were supplied with water through pipes, instead of being obliged to buy it from peddlers at so much per bucketful. The Hydraulic Company, formed in 1836, with a nominal stock of $250,000, commenced operations in 1840. They built a reservoir at the corner of Lake Street and Michigan Avenue, on the site since occupied by the Adams House, about twenty-five feet square and eight feet deep, elevated about eighty feet above the surface of the ground, and erected a pump, connecting it by an iron pipe with the lake, laid on a crib-work pier, running into the lake about one hundred and fifty feet. This pump was worked by a steam-engine of *twenty-five horse power*. The water was distributed to the citizens through logs, bored at the "works," five inches for the main lines and three inches for the subordinate ones. In 1842 James Long entered into arrangements with the Hydraulic Company to do all the pumping for the supply of the city with water for ten years, without cost to the company, for and in consideration of the free use of the surplus power of their twenty-five horse engine. In a letter read at the formal opening of the Lake Tunnel, in December, 1866, Mr. Long thus refers to the difficulties of the primitive situation: "In winter the pipes on the pier would be disarranged by the heaving of the frost, and I had frequently to spend hours at a time to caulk up the joints by throwing on water and thus freezing up the cracks before we could make the pump available. When the end of this pipe from the pier was first put down, it was three or four feet below the surface of the lake, but in 1842–43 the lake had receded so far as frequently to leave the end out of water, particularly when the wind blew from the south." But it was soon found that a large extension was needed. Long before the above-named contract had expired the twenty-five horse-power engine had become too small, even without doing the extra work expected of it.

X. GROWING AGAIN.

THE growth of the city from 1842 to the middle of the century was slow, as measured by the lightninglike progress of some subsequent years, but it was sure. The people were working on a firm basis, and past reverses had made them so cautious that they were afraid to risk their little capital in many cases that have since proven to be first-class investments. Many city improvements, that had been projected in more inflated but less prosperous times, were now carried out, and, although the horticultural epoch was still in existence, the people were gradually paving the way for an emergence from the crysalis condition. The place had heretofore been really a village, though nominally a city. There were a few who watched the gradual settlement of the country to the westward, and recognized the fact that the magnificent schemes of the people must soon be realized. These labored on in the face of great discouragement, though the city was filling up rapidly. The city was growing, almost under protest; people came, almost without knowing the reason why, and with an increase of population a steady augment of property values ensued. Work on the canal was resumed, and it soon became apparent that the railroad system, which was not wanted a few years previously, was now a vital necessity.

The canal funds had been kept distinct from the moneys borrowed for other improvements, but when, in 1841, the State indebtedness had amounted to fifteen millions of dollars, it was found impossible to proceed, as enough money could not be raised to pay arrears to the contractors, though another loan of four million dollars had been authorized in 1839. Hence the work was suspended in 1842, as already stated, and the next year a law was passed to settle the outstanding claims of the contractors, provided they did not amount to more than a quarter of a million dollars.

But the canal was of too much importance to be long abandoned. In 1843, certain holders of the State bonds made the offer to advance the money necessary to complete the canal, provided the payment of their advances and bonds was secured by adequate lien on the canal, its lands, and its revenues. At the next session of the Legislature an act was passed, providing that if the bond-holders would advance $1,600,000, then the canal, and the lands still unsold, amounting to about 230,000 acres, with several lots in Chicago and towns along the line, should be pledged to the lenders. Accordingly the lands and revenues were placed in the hands of three trustees, two of whom were to be chosen by the bond-holders, and one by the State. A great portion of the loan was negotiated by Mr. Swift, of Boston, with English capitalists.

With the money so obtained, work on the canal was resumed, and the undertaking was completed in 1848, but not on the grand plan originally proposed. The plan, as at first adopted, was for the canal, of ninety-six miles long, from the Chicago River to Lasalle, to have its highest level only three feet above the lake, this highest line extending from Chicago to Lockport. A part of the work was executed on this plan. But when operations were resumed, it was on the shallow principle, the highest level being twelve feet above the lake; from this level a series of fifteen locks provided a descent of one hundred and sixty-six feet between it and Lasalle. The water for the summit level was supplied by pumping.

Very soon after the opening of the canal, its enlargement to the originally designed scale was strongly advocated. Indeed, a convention was held in the city, in 1847, attended by delegates from all parts of the country, at which the importance of the enlargement was referred to. Another canal convention was held in June, 1863, the sessions of which were made memorable by the temporary suppression of the Chicago *Times*, by order of General Burnside, while the convention was in session. At that gathering the leading idea was to provide for the passage of large vessels, and iron-clads, from the lakes to the Mississippi, to aid in the suppression of the rebellion. The commercial needs of the North-west were not forgotten, but they received only a secondary share of attention. It was even proposed to cut down the summit level below the depth originally agreed upon, in order to allow the waters of the lakes to run through the river and the canal, down to the Illinois, and thus convert a stagnant bayou into a living stream. Various plans for improvement were proposed, the estimates for which ranged from eleven and a half to thirteen a third million dollars. Some of these plans proposed a change in the route of the canal, as it is well known that a less amount of excavation would have been required on another line which was not chosen by the locating commissioners, for the reason that the adjacent lands were not available for sale.

The total amount expended by the commissioners for canal construction, under the act of 1836, was $4,979,903, and under the act of 1843, the expenditures were $1,429,606, making a total of $6,409,509. The receipts from sales of lands, and lots donated by the United States Government, were $4,667,718.42, and for tolls, from the opening to the close of 1868, the receipts were $3,997,281.22. The total receipts, from all sources up to that date, were $10,501,195, and the total debt of the State for construction and maintenance was cleared off entirely when the construction bonds of 1843–4 fell due, in 1871.

The canal has since been deepened by the city at a total cost of three million dollars, of which more hereafter. Now that Chicago is the focus of a grand system of railroads, the canal is far more valuable to her as a sewer to carry off her surplus filth, than as a means of commercial communication with the interior of the State. But at that time it was the only artery along which the life-blood of commerce was expected to flow for many years, and it gave a prodigious impulse to the growth of the city.

The following statistics of a few articles transported over the canal during a portion of 1848 (the year it was opened), and the whole of 1849, will show at a glance the immense stimulus given by it to Chicago trade, which had hitherto been dependent on the wagon or the packhorse in that direction. The movement of lumber, etc., was westward:

Articles.	1848.	1849.
Pork, lbs.	683,600	2,783,102
Stone, cu. yds.	——	7,995
Coal, tons, ...	5,416	7,579
Wheat, bu.	451,876	624,978
Corn, bu.	516,230	754,288
Oats, bu.	72,659	61,989
Lumber, ft.	14,425,357	26,882,000
Shingles and Lath, No. . . .	17,899,000	35,551,000
Tolls on Canal, ...	$87,891	$118,376

The receipts of lumber in 1847 were 32,118,225 feet; in 1848, 60,009,250 feet; in 1849, 73,259,553 feet.

In this connection we present the following aggregates of sales at the Chicago Land Office, to the middle of 1847, when the office was closed, and previous to May 28, 1835, at Danville:

Years.	Acres.	Money.
To May, 1835, ...	29,513.44	$ 37,067 73
1835, [Chicago] . .	370,043.38	505,729 75
1836, ...	202,365.96	252,961 78
1837, ...	15,697.27	19,622 35
1838, ...	85,891.39	109,973 34
1839, ...	160,635.70	218,811 69
1840, ...	142,158.20	177,701 93
1841, ...	138,603.16	173,307 20
1842, ...	194,557.11	243,209 78
1843, ...	229,459.70	284,829 01
1844, ...	235,258.36	294,301 78
1845, ...	220,525.08	275,674 32
1846, ...	198,350.41	247,943 17
To June 29, 1847, ...	49,506.53	61,883 12
Total, ...	2,272,565.69	$2,903,016 87

Total, [brought forward] . .	2,272,565.69	$2,903,016 87
To Schools, ...	104,520.00	Donated.
To Canal, ...	236,680.00	
To State purposes, ...	94,782.00	
Total, ...	2,707,547.69	Acres.
Unsold, ...	914,987.31	"
Total in District, ...	3,624,535.00	"
Total in State, ...	35,941,602.00	"

The influence of the canal on the city is very concisely shown by the statistics of population. In 1842 the inhabitants numbered 6590; in 1843 they had increased to 7580, and only to about 8000 in 1844. Work recommencing on the canal in the latter part of the year, the population had increased to 12,088 in 1845, and steadily swelled afterward to 20,923 in 1848. It should, however, be remembered that the last-named total was scattered over a greater area than in 1845. In 1847 the city was increased by the addition of three and a half square miles to its area, making a total of thirteen and a half sections. The city limits were extended west to Western Avenue (three miles from State Street), and took in all east of Sedgwick Street, between North and Fullerton Avenues.

The augment of shipment eastward was not quite so great as the business of the canal, but it was large nevertheless. The exhibit of valuation of city property, in this period, shows the steady character of the growth with equal clearness:

Property.	1842.	1845.	1848.
Real, ...	$108,757	$2,273,171	$4,998,266
Personal, ...	42,585	791,851	1,302,174
Total, ...	$151,342	$3,065,022	$6,300,440
City Taxes, ...	——	11,018	22,052

These valuations were about one-fourth of the price at which the property could have been sold.

Chicago retained her horticultural aspect during these years of improvement, but there was a steady commercial growth quietly wrought out by a few men, that seemed almost to take the world by surprise when communication had once been opened up sufficiently to let that outside world know what was going on. The harbor received some attention, but work done in accordance with the suggestions of George B. McClellan, submitted in 1844, was of little more value than his exertions in the early days of the rebellion. A long line of piling was driven on the south shore outside of the present line of the breakwater, but in spite of it the waves washed away many acres of valuable land. The piling itself vanished subsequently. The river was improved, South Water Street being set back half a block about the middle of this epoch, allowing the bank of the river to be straightened out, while no less than three bridges were built in 1847, viz: at Wells, Randolph, and Madison Streets. These were, however, only floating bridges, like those removed from Clark and Polk Streets very recently. The magnificent swing bridge was a more modern innovation. There was little dock building done till 1848; then a great deal was constructed on the main river to accommodate the increasing trade, brought in by the just completed canal.

Previous to 1844 a few planks had been laid down to serve the purpose of a sidewalk, but the unimproved soil was the only road-bed in the middle of even the main thoroughfares. Ditches had been dug on the edges of a few to carry off the surplus water, but they were found so inefficient that some bright genius conceived the idea of placing the gutter in the middle of the street, which thus became an open sewer. Those who have since rolled luxuriously over the more than fifty miles of streets paved with wooden blocks, that now exist in Chicago, can form but a faint idea of the blessings of traveling through the prairie road, cut up by hundreds of teams, and reduced to a miry slush of half a yard or more in depth. In 1844 the plank road was introduced, and several of the streets were thus improved during the next few years. Yet the improvement was but a sorry one. The planks would wear well for awhile, then break up under heavy loads and spring thaws, making the street even worse than if the natural soil had been left uncovered.

Previous to 1846 Chicago was only a port of delivery, and belonged to the collection district of Detroit. The first arrival registered at the Custom-house is dated April 6, 1845, when the schooner Congress, of 200 tons burden, arrived from Port Huron with a cargo of lumber. In that year we had a total of 331 steamboats, 85 propellers, 116 brigs, 718 schooners, and 70 sloops arriving; total, 1320. The arrivals in 1847, were, 19 steamers, 17 propellers, 36 brigs, and 120 schooners; total, 192, employing 1628 men. The district of Chicago, formed in July, 1846, included Milwaukee, till September, 1850. We note here that the first arrival ever known in the harbor of Chicago, was the schooner Tracy, which brought supplies for Fort Dearborn in 1803.

As late as 1848 the city was sometimes a whole week without the arrival of a single mail. The total commissions of the postmaster for that year were but $9,681.35.

The first school-houses built by the city were erected during this period. The Dearborn, only torn down in 1871, a few months before the fire, was located opposite the place where McVicker's Theater lately stood, and just north-east of the

6

Tribune office. That school-house was built through the persistent effort of Alderman Ira Miltimore, and was long known as "Miltimore's folly," the people believing that there would never be scholars enough in the city to fill it. That was literally a day of small expectations. But the Jones school was erected soon afterward on Clark Street, near Harrison; the Kinzie school in 1845, on Ohio Street, near Lasalle; and the Scammon in 1846, on West Madison, near Halstead. In the last-named year each of these schools had one male and two female teachers.

The Rush Medical College was founded in 1843, with a class of twenty-two students, and two daily newspapers were established during this epoch—both now alive—the *Journal* in 1844, and the *Tribune* in 1847. The Illinois *Staats Zeitung* (German) was first issued as a weekly in 1846. The first theater ever built in Chicago was opened June 28, 1847, on Dearborn Street near Randolph, the proprietor being J. B. Rice, since mayor of the city. J. H. McVicker was a member of his company in 1849.

The number of church societies formed in the years 1842–43 was not less than eighteen; most of them erected houses of worship previous to the close of 1848.

XI. THE EXPECTANT PERIOD.

THE history of the next three years, from 1849 to 1851 inclusive, is really of the same general character as that of the preceding period, yet so important that it merits notice in a separate chapter. It was emphatically a time of reaching out.

The first design to build a canal to the Illinois River was very early supplemented by a railroad project, which was felt to be of almost equal importance. As early as 1836, when there were not more than one thousand miles of railroad in the United States, the Galena and Chicago Union Railroad was chartered by the Legislature. In the succeeding crash the undertaking was killed for the time being, and ten years elapsed ere it was revived. In 1847, the first length of rail was laid on the present line to Freeport, the rail first used being simply one of strap-iron. The whole line of 121 miles, from Chicago to Freeport, was not opened up till 1853, but enough of it was finished by 1851 to prove that the grand scheme of connection was a decided success. The canal gave access to the central parts of the State, the rich bottom lands in the Illinois Valley, and to the trade of the lower Mississippi, while the railroad would in like manner place the city in communication with the wide domain of the upper Mississippi region, and with the untold mineral wealth in the lead mines of Galena. These two great arteries of commerce would bring into the lap of Chicago the trade of the greater portion of the then settled parts of the North-west. This once assured, capital flowed in apace from the East, and the people felt that they could afford to expend money in the improvement of the city, which had hitherto been sadly neglected. Even at this time, however, the importance of railroad connection with the East was but little understood. Many, even of our business men, thought that the lake system was all that was necessary to carry away the accumulated produce of the West, and bring back the merchandise required in exchange. They had not then learned the value of *time* in commercial transactions; the mail and the canal were better than the railroad and the telegraph. A few men were hard at work in the endeavor to open up railroad routes to the East, but they met with most discouraging opposition from those who were most to be benefited by the improvements.

The population increased from 20,923, in 1848, to about 34,000 in 1851, and the growth would have been much greater but for the cholera. That dread disease was brought up the river from New Orleans in the emigrant boat John Drew, the first case being noticed on the 29th of April. The disease spread rapidly, as other emigrants arrived, many of them from various parts of Europe, where the cholera was raging. It was estimated that the total number of persons attacked was about one thousand, of whom 314 died from July 25th to August 28th, inclusive. The greatest mortality occurred in a neighborhood of three squares in the North Division, with 332 inhabitants, principally Norwegians, and scarcely one of the whole number escaped the infection. It was remarked as singular at that time that the ground in that locality was high and sandy, but the secret was afterward discovered that all had used water from the same well into which the drainings of an outhouse had found their way.

The deaths from cholera during the year were 678, one in 36 of the entire population. In the same year Cincinnati lost 4450, or one in 23; St. Louis lost 4297, or one in 21; New Orleans 4000, or one in 37; New York 5122, or one in 79.

The prevalance of the disease was such that it spread to nearly every cluster of dwellings in the North-west, and for a time communication between Chicago and the interior was almost entirely suspended. Business, however, soon revived, and in a short period the cholera seemed to have produced no ill effect on the prosperity of the city, which grew rapidly.

The disease appeared again in July, 1850, but less severely, though the aggregate mortality was much greater. From July 18th to August 31st, inclusive, 613 died, of whom 416 were cholera patients. September only witnessed four deaths from cholera, making a total of 420, or one in 64 of the inhabitants. The cholera came again in 1851 and 1852, but its ravages were slight.

Early in the year 1849, an act was passed authorizing the formation of the Chicago Gas Light and Coke Company, and giving them the exclusive right to supply gas to the city for ten years. The company commenced operations as soon after the passage of the act as possible, locating their works on Adams Street, on the east side of the river. These works were the first to take fire in the South Division, in the great conflagration, and from that point the flames spread over the entire business part of the city. In September, 1850, the gas was turned on for the first time, and the citizens of Chicago enjoyed the luxury of lighted streets at night. By the end of 1852, the company had laid nearly eight miles of pipe, with five hundred and seventy-four meters, and counted five hundred and sixty-one private consumers.

The people now agitated for a better water supply than was furnished by the crooked arrangement described in Chapter 9, but did not succeed in obtaining it till afterwards. The Chicago City Hydraulic Company was called into existence in

February, 1851, and John B. Turner, A. S. Sherman, and H. G. Loomis were appointed as the first Board of Water Commissioners. William J. McAlpine was employed (June 26th) as engineer. The water was not supplied to the houses till February, 1854.

In 1849, the bridges were all swept away by a great freshet in the river, and better structures were afterward provided.

In 1848, the building of wharves was pushed forward with considerable energy, and some two miles in length were completed by 1852. But the great events of the epoch were the formation of the Board of Trade and the birth of the grain elevator system. Grain had previously been bought, and stored, and shipped, but only in the way each individual dictated for himself. There was no system.

The truth being told, it would be necessary to say that the system was instituted some time before it was needed; and it is this fact that marks the period under review—it was eminently one of expectancy. The commerce of the city grew comparatively little during those years. Indeed, the shipments of wheat, and flour reduced to wheat, fell from 2,286,000 bushels, in 1848, to 799,380 bushels in 1851, but the difference was more than compensated by the increase in other grain, the total shipments being 4,646,291 bushels, in 1851, against 3,001,740 bushels in 1848, the total having dropped to 1,830,938 bushels in 1850. In like manner we find the business of the canal to have been nearly stationary, except in the eastward movement of corn, and the westward movement of lumber. The receipts of corn were nearly nine times as great in 1851 as in 1850, and the increase in the shipments of lumber was nearly fifty per cent. The growth of the wholesale trade of the city, in other departments, was somewhat less than in lumber.

Early in 1848 Thomas Richmond and W. L. Whiting discussed one afternoon the propriety of establishing a Board of Trade in Chicago. Mr. Richmond was then in the elevating business, and Mr. Whiting a grain broker—the first who pursued this avocation in Chicago. These gentlemen consulted with other business men, and the result of this consultation was an invitation (published at the time) for the merchants generally to meet together on the 13th of March, 1848, to take the initiatory steps in regard to the formation of the Chicago Board of Trade. The following is a copy of the call:

"Merchants and business men who are favorable to the establishment of a Board of Trade in this city, are requested to meet at the office of W. L. Whiting, on the 13th (March, 1848), at 3 o'clock P. M.

"Wadsworth, Dyer & Chapin,	Norton, Walker & Co.,
George Steele,	De Wolf & Co.,
I. H. Burch & Co.,	Charles Walker,
Gurnee, Hayden & Co.,	Thomas Richmond,
H. H. Magie & Co.,	Thomas Hale,
Neef & Church,	Raymond, Gibbs & Co."
John H. Kinzie,	

At this meeting nothing further was done than to pass resolutions stating that the growing trade of Chicago demanded the establishment of a Board of Trade. A constitution was then adopted, and a committee appointed to draw up by-laws to be submitted at an adjourned meeting, to be held on the first Monday in April following, when they were adopted. All interested were invited to meet daily at the new rooms on South Water Street, which had been rented at $110 per annum. George Smith (the banker) was elected first president, but declined to serve, and Thomas Dyer was then chosen to fill the office. The Board met and resolved, and appointed committees and inspectors of produce, and considered the condition of the river and harbor, but did no business of any account for a long time. In April, 1850, the Board formally organized under an act passed the previous year, and placed the annual dues at three dollars. In 1851 the association consisted of thirty-eight members, but the records show that often for several days together there was not a single member in attendance, and the entry, "No transactions," became a stereotyped phrase, as well as a standing joke.

In 1848 there were three or four so-called grain elevators in existence, but they were very small, the elevating was done by means of a mule on the roof, and all the grain was the property of the man who owned the elevator, he buying it from the farmer, and generally shipping it forward on his own account, though one of them—Orrington Lunt—always sold his grain to a shipper, after his first shipping venture, in which he lost heavily. About the close of the period under review, one steam elevator was erected, and the business of storing grain for others became a recognized feature, though not extensively resorted to. At first the only storers were shippers, who bought the grain from the warehousemen in winter, and paid for the storage till they could move it forward in the season of navigation.

XII. THE RAILROAD ERA.

IN 1852 Chicago took a "new departure." She became the center of a network of railways, which soon branched out to every point of the compass, except the north-east, though those lines have since been extended farther in every direction, save to the eastward. Hitherto a stranger to the iron-horse, she had depended on the wagon, or the slow canal to the westward, and on a circuitous water route to the seaboard. Then she at once took rank as an important center of railroad travel and traffic, becoming what had been dreamed out for her many years previously, but not realized. Even to-day she avails herself, to a considerable extent, of the facilities afforded by water transportation, but it is as a railroad power that Chicago stands preëminent among the cities of the United States, and her commercial importance is in large part due to the connections made in the one year, 1852.

It is remarkable, too, that though Chicago had been for years preparing for the advent of the railroad system, she had no hand in establishing that mighty series of links that now bind her with bands of iron to the world around her. Not only did the city furnish no aid, in its corporate capacity, to the improvements, to which hundreds of other cities and counties pledged themselves, but few of her citizens subscribed money, as individuals, to railroad enterprises. They were the sought, rather than the seekers. Eastern capital saw that Chicago was equally essential to the development of the West, as the West was necessary to the growth of the Garden City. They saw that the wealth of the West must flow through her, as the sand must run through the neck of an hour-glass, and subscribed

7

their money to build those railroads that center in Chicago, not for love of the place, but because, as one of them naively remarked, they "could not get around her," which was true in more senses than one. Hence it was comparatively easy for the city to grow mightily when the time arrived for it. Her merchants and business men needed enterprise and ability; but the harvest lay at their feet, all ready to be gathered in, and the work of preparing the ground, sowing the seed, and tending the growing crop, had all been performed by others, who stood ready to do even more, as they saw profit in it to themselves.

The parent line has been already named—the Galena & Chicago line—commenced in 1847. In 1850 it had reached Elgin, forty-two miles from Chicago, was completed to Freeport in September, 1853 (121 miles), and a portion of the Illinois Central extended the route to Galena, in 1854.

The next important undertaking was the Illinois Central line, projected to extend from Chicago to Cairo, in the extreme southern point of the State, a distance of 365 miles, and from Centralia, on that line 112 miles from Cairo, north-west to the northern limit of the State, making a total of 704 miles of railroad. This road had its origin September 20, 1850, when Hon. Stephen A. Douglas secured the passage of an act by Congress, granting to the State of Illinois every alternate section of land to a distance of six miles on each side of the line of road, to aid in its construction. The original grant of land was for 2,595,000 acres.

On the 10th of February, 1851, the Illinois Central Railroad Company was chartered by the Legislature, and the lands transferred to it on condition that the road should be built within a time specified, and that seven per cent. of the gross receipts of the line should be paid into the State treasury annually forever, after the road was finished. In 1852 the officers of the road obtained permission to enter the city along the lake shore from the southward, and immediately thereafter commenced the construction of the magnificent line of break-water two miles long, and costing three-quarters of a million dollars, that now protects the south shore from the incursions of the lake, and has rescued many acres of ground from the wild waves. The total length of the piling since constructed is 16,459 feet. The inside line of the crib-works, south of Randolph Street, is four hundred feet east of the east line of Michigan Avenue, and was built in the lake for a distance of one mile. Most of that vacuum has since been filled in, and the great Union Depot was built on a portion of the ground thus rescued from the lake.

After this in the order of beginning, but earlier in execution, and equally, if not more, important, was the double connection of Chicago with the East by rail.

The Michigan Central was the first to approach the city. It was projected in 1842, and built in that year from Detroit to Ypsilanti in Michigan, being afterward extended to St. Joseph, which was for some time the terminus of rail travel from New York and Buffalo westward. Travelers generally crossed the lake from St. Joseph to Chicago, and the former point was connected by stage with the moving end of the rail track as it approached from Detroit. In 1852 it was extended into Chicago, the last rail being laid May 21st.

This was not, however, the first eastern road to make the connection. The people residing around the bend of the lake in northern Indiana, were ambitious at some time to have a line of rail running through their section from Toledo, and opposed the Michigan Central project with tooth and nail, as they believed that there would never be traffic enough to maintain two competing lines. When, however, they found that they could not defeat it, they set vigorously to work to organize the rival road, which, principally through their exertions, was completed to Chicago on the 20th of February, 1852, fully two months before its rival, and being the first after the Galena, to connect with the great railway center.

Other roads followed in rapid succession, to which we shall refer presently, but they only helped the work already begun. The two eastern lines opened up channels along which the tide of emigration rolled so copiously that it was almost impossible to keep track of the movement, which was invited by the fact that the whole State of Illinois was also made accessible by rail to the emigrants who now thronged in from every part of Europe. How much Chicago grew under the impetus thus given, is shown in the fact that her population increased from 38,734 souls in 1852, to 59,139 in 1853, a gain of 52½ per cent. in a single year. The official valuation of property, real and personal, exhibited a corresponding augment, being about $10,460,000 in 1852, and $16,841,831 a year afterward.

That the development of the country beyond proceeded with equal rapidity, is proven by a comparison of the produce trade of the city one year later; the soil could not bear fruit till a year after it was first cultivated. The receipts of grain (flour reduced to its equivalent in wheat) were 6,473,809 bushels in 1853, and nearly two and a half times as much, or 15,726,968 bushels, in 1854. And the increase in the receipts of 1853 over those of 1852, were fully 50 per cent. The grain shipments of 1853 were double, and those of 1854 were four times greater than those of 1848, the year when the canal was first opened to traffic.

The business of hog packing was equally stimulated. In the

winter of 1851–2 the number of hogs cut up was 22,036; in 1852–3 it was 44,156; in 1853–4 it amounted to 52,849. And 25,431 cattle were packed in the last-named year.

The lines above mentioned were but a portion of the great system soon to acknowledge Chicago as its radical point.

The Galena & Chicago Union Company had obtained a charter as early as 1848 for a branch of their road to connect Belvidere with Madison, Wisconsin, by way of Beloit. The Illinois & Wisconsin Railroad Company was incorporated in 1851, and these two were soon merged into one, the whole being in 1855 combined with the Fond du Lac branch from Janesville, to form what has since been known as the North-western Road, which in 1864 swallowed up its parent, the old Galena & Chicago Union. The line from Chicago to Milwaukee was built in 1854. This system of railroads opened up to Chicago the trade of the whole of the country then settled north of a line drawn due west from the city.

The Chicago & Rock Island Railroad was commenced in April, 1852, and finished to the Mississippi, 182 miles distant, in February, 1854. Then followed the line from Chicago to St. Louis, the part from Springfield to Alton being built in 1853, and that from Joliet to Springfield in 1854, the track of the Rock Island road being used as far as Joliet till 1857, when an independent line was constructed between the two cities. The Chicago, Burlington & Quincy road was completed to Aurora, thirteen miles westward, in 1852, and to Mendota, on the Illinois Central, in 1853, this line being then consolidated in 1856 with previously independent roads to the Mississippi. The Pittsburgh, Fort Wayne & Chicago road, furnishing a third route to the East, was last on the list. It was incorporated in 1852, but not finished till November, 1856.

It appears, then, that all the main lines which entered the city at the date of the great conflagration, except one (the Pittsburgh & Cincinnati), were built within about four years from the time that Chicago was first connected with the East by rail. And not only this, but in the early part of that period nearly all the extensions and connections, since perfected, were planned, and most of them have been carried out as originally designed. Among those then contemplated it is sufficient to mention the lines now connecting with Minnesota, the three lines across the State of Iowa and their prolongation into the Great Pacific Railroad, and the road across northern Missouri, with steamboat connections on the Mississippi at all points touched or crossed by the iron rail. These four years are pre-eminently entitled to be called the railroad era, and the five years following 1852 were the most prosperous in the history of the city up to that time.

In January, 1852, there was only about 40 miles of railroad connected with Chicago. By the end of 1853 the mileage was 1785. At the close of 1854 it had increased to 2436½ miles, and to 3953 miles in 1857. These figures do not include the length of independent lines connecting with Chicago roads. For instance, the Michigan Southern & Northern Indiana is not measured beyond Toledo.

XIII. COMMERCIAL GROWTH IN THE RAILROAD ERA.

WE have already seen how wondrously the population and commerce of the city grew during the first year after the introduction of the railroad era. That ratio of over fifty per cent. was scarcely sustained through each following year, up to the crisis of 1857, but the growth of the city in every respect was rapid enough during the whole of that period to satisfy the most sanguine.

The grain trade of the city was wonderfully stimulated. In 1852, the united capacity of all the grain warehouses was scarcely more than 750,000 bushels, and the only steam elevator was one built by R. C. Bristol. In 1857 there were no less than twelve elevators, having an invested capital of $3,087,000, with a storage capacity of 4,095,000 bushels, and a capacity to receive and ship of 495,000 bushels per day. The great year for elevator building was in 1854, when Chicago had passed St. Louis in the contest for superiority as a grain market—a position she ever after retained. The receipts at St. Louis in 1853 were 5,081,468 bushels; in Chicago the receipts were 6,473,089 bushels of grain of all kinds. In 1854, the exports of grain from Chicago exceeded those of New York by 3,471,975 bushels, and were nearly double those of St. Petersburg, Archangel, or Odessa, the largest grain markets in Europe.

It is a singular fact that, although the commerce of the city took such rapid strides, the Board of Trade, since the great channel through which the produce business of the city is transacted, was little better than a figure head during the whole of this period. In 1853, the Secretary was instructed to provide a daily set-out of crackers, cheese, and ale, as an inducement to the members to attend; and though this was afterward discontinued, it was judged necessary to revive it in 1855, as an attendance could be obtained in no other way. The Board grew in membership, but its members preferred to transact their business in their own stores, or in the streets, with the parties who came in from the country with produce. They had not yet learned the art of trading with one another, and as every tub then stood on its own bottom, they cared little for that comparison of views without which little is bought or sold at the present day.

We find the Board very useful, however, in another capacity. It was great on resolutions. In 1853 it advocated the establishment of a monster bank, with a capital of five millions of dollars, to accommodate the trade of Chicago. In 1854 it took action on the improvement of the Illinois River, the dredging out of the harbor, building additional piers, erecting a light-house (built in 1855), and instituted a most important reform in the selling of grain by weight, instead of by the half-bushel measure, as formerly. In 1855 action was taken in reference to the Georgian Bay Canal, and the reciprocity treaty with Canada. In this year it was found necessary to employ a doorkeeper to keep out non-members who were attracted by the creature comforts on the table at the end of the hall. In 1856 the Board provided standards for the inspection of grain and lumber into different grades, and had increased in membership so much that it was found necessary to rent rooms on the corner of South Water and Lasalle Streets, at $1,000 per annum.

The following table of the movement of the principal articles of produce, etc., in 1852, '54, and '56, will show the rate at which the commerce of the city grew during this period. The shipments of wheat and flour were greater in 1857 than in 1856, but the exhibit was not so large in other departments:

Articles.	1852.	1854.	1856.
Flour received, bbls.	124,316	234,575	410,989
Wheat " bu..	937,496	3,038,955	8,767,760
Corn " "	2,991,011	7,490,753	11,888,398
Grain " "	4,195,192	15,726,968	25,817,248
Grain shipped, "	5,873,141	12,932,320	21,583,221
Hogs received,	65,158	138,515	220,702
Hogs packed,	44,156	73,694	74,000
Cattle "	24,663	23,691	14,971
Lumber received, M.	147,816	228,337	441,962
Hides " No.	25,893	28,606	70,560
Stone " cu. yds.	40,752	68,436	92,609
Coal " tons,	46,233	56,774	93,020
Lead " "	678	2,124	3,314
Vessels arrived,	[not stated.]	5,021	7,328
Tonnage of do.	"	1,092,644	1,545,379
Population,	38,734	65,872	84,113

In the last named year the live stock trade had increased so much as to necessitate the establishment of the Sherman Yards, at Cottage Grove, containing some thirty acres, and capable of accommodating 5000 head of cattle, and 30,000 hogs. Previous to this, the business had all been conducted at the Bull's Head, on the corner of Madison Street and Ashland Avenue, which was established in 1848. That site is now occupied by the Washingtonian Home for the reformation of drunkards.

The year 1856 was memorable as the one in which the Dean Richmond, of 387 tons burden, arrived at Liverpool, direct from Chicago.

The wholesale trade of the city increased in a ratio corresponding with her produce movement. The railroads and the canal not only brought in grain and the other products of the farm, but they carried out immense quantities of merchandise, and by the aid of a judicious drummer system, Chicago merchants soon supplied hundreds of square miles of territory with goods, from which they obtained only money in return. The drummer system has recently been found fault with as expensive, and abandoned, to a great extent; but whatever its faults, it certainly did much to open up the eyes of the Western people to the fact that Chicago was prepared to compete with New York, both in regard to quality and price, and she soon carried off the palm.

In 1852, the commerce of the city was estimated at $20,000,000; in 1853, at nearly $30,000,000; in 1856, at $85,000,000. Governor Matteson stated in his message in 1852, that there were then 211 wholesale houses in the city. This was not true, however, in the sense we now understand the term. There were scarcely a dozen real wholesalers. In 1856, the number had increased seven or eight fold.

XIV. MANUFACTURES IN THE RAILROAD ERA.

IN 1850 the manufactures of the city were very limited. The total annual product of Cook County, of which Chicago formed by far the largest portion, was returned at $2,562,583 on a capital of $1,068,025 and employing 2081 workers.

In 1852 there was still but little done in the way of manufacturing, but the next year this department of activity assumed large proportions.

In his commercial *Review* for 1853, Mr. Bross mentions the Chicago Locomotive Company, formed in September, 1853, with a capital stock of $150,000, and the completion in that year of the "Enterprise," the first locomotive built here, with two other engines; the American Car Company, which commenced business in 1853, turning out $450,000 worth of work in the first year, and employing some 260 hands; the Union Car Works of A. B. Stone & Co., and the bridge-yard of Stone & Boomer, the work of the two firms in 1853 being 250 freight, 30 passenger, and 10 baggage cars, 10 bridges and 19 turn-tables; the Illinois Stone and Lime Company; the marble-works of H. & O. Wilson, with an annual business of $15,000; the making of three million bricks; the operations of five firms engaged in the manufacture of carriages and wagons, and aggregating a yearly business of $117,000; five furniture factories; the Chicago Oil-mill, with a capital of $25,000; several soap and candle factories; four machine-shops, with an annual business of $270,000; three leather-factories, employing 107 men; two stove-foundries; and two firms engaged in making reapers and mowers, employing 195 men. Besides these, he speaks of hats and caps, clothing, boots and shoes, fur goods, harness, trunks, saddlery, etc. The statement for 1853 was a large one, but it was far exceeded the next year, and each successive twelve months to the close of 1856, when the work of three years previous had been increased nearly tenfold. In that year the value of the manufactures was $15,515,063, turned out on a capital of $7,759,400, by 10,573 operatives. Among these, iron works, steam-engines, etc., took the lead, with 2,866 workers, and a product of $3,887,084. Next came the manufacture of drinks, employing 165 persons, and turning out $1,150,320 annually. Next were agricultural implements, with

575 workers, $1,134,300 worth of product, and then mills for planing lumber and making sash, doors, etc., with 554 workers and $1,092,397 worth of product. We find also the following items: furniture, $543,000; bricks, $712,000; cooperage, etc., $357,250; leather, $432,000, and stone and marble, $896,775.

The general progress was materially aided by the passage of a general banking act in January, 1853, which enabled the issue of bank notes in the State, after a pecuniary interregnum of more than ten years. The Marine Bank (J. Y. Scammon) was the first to organize under the act. The next year there were not less than nine banks of issue in the city, besides eight private bankers. The total bank-circulation in 1853 was $760,000, and in 1854 was $3,759,000, principally based on Illinois stocks. During the next three years the banks were exceedingly prosperous, and the abundance of currency helped largely to stimulate the unnatural inflation of that period.

XV. CITY IMPROVEMENTS IN THE RAILROAD ERA.

WITH such a tremendous forward march in commerce and manufactures, the aspect of the city could not be otherwise than completely revolutionized. The limits were extended in 1853, and again in 1854, the boundaries becoming Fullerton Avenue on the north, Thirty-first Street on the south, Western Avenue on the west, and one mile beyond the lake-shore on the east. From this quadrilateral was excepted Bridgeport and Holston, on the two western corners.

The city had previously been provided with gas in 1850.

The next step was to procure a good supply of water. In April and August, 1852, bonds were issued to the amount of $400,000, from the sale of which $361,280 was realized, and the work proceeded with, though not without opposition from the Hydraulic Company. A timber crib was built out 600 feet from the shore, near the site of the present pumping works, and the water ran thence into a well, twenty feet deep, whence it was pumped up by an engine of 200-horse power to the top of a cast-iron column 140 feet high. A reservoir was subsequently built in each division of the city to hold a night's supply; that in the South Division was erected in 1854. The water was first introduced into the houses in February, 1854. The supply from these works was estimated to be equal to that required by a population of 100,000; the cost of construction was about $335,000.

The next important public improvement was drainage. The city was visited by cholera, in its worst form, in 1854, not less than 931 deaths occurring in July, or one in 71 of the entire population. The mortality of the year was 3,830, or one in 17. It was soon reasoned out that a thorough drainage would probably prevent the recurrence of such a terrible visitation in the future, and since that important work was undertaken the cholera has only appeared once (in 1866), and then in a very mild form. But here a great difficulty presented itself. In the suburbs the soil averaged 11 to 14 feet above the lowest lake-level; but in the more densely-populated portions the water sometimes rose to within three feet of the surface, as in 1848, and any thing like a sloping drain was impossible. The deficiency must be supplied. In 1855 a grade was established raising the surface about four feet, and that grade was afterward raised, the filling in being as much as six or seven feet in some places, above the original level. Even the improved grade has been found fault with, as not giving sufficient basement room, and the burnt district in the South Division has been raised by ordinance two to three feet higher. It will be rebuilt with the sidewalk lines 14 to 15 feet above the low-water mark of 1847.

The first street filling of consequence was done in 1856, the material used being the sand and mud dredged up from the bottom of the river or pared from its banks, as the channel was widened and deepened to meet the needs of a growing lake traffic. Previous to this, the north bank had been a sloping, sedgy marsh. The Court-house square and the neighboring streets were filled to grade in this way. Subsequently the numerous excavations for cellars and basements supplied all the filling required, and left some to spare to make new ground eastward of Michigan Avenue.

About six miles of sewers had been constructed up to March, 1854. After the grade had been established, so that a sufficient slope could be obtained, the work of drainage proceeded more rapidly, and most of the more thickly-settled portions of the city were sewered by the middle of 1857. The work of making good streets proceeded more slowly. About twenty-seven miles of planking had been laid down to the close of 1854, and a little more was added subsequently, but it made a wretched road-way. Even State and Madison Streets were impassable in the spring, the planks having been broken up by heavy loads, and required constant repairs to permit even an empty wagon to proceed. The condition of many other leading thoroughfares was simply detestable. As late as 1857, it was impossible to ride along Dearborn or Clark Streets near Monroe, and the baggage of persons arriving in the city by rail, would often lie in the depot for several days together, because it could not be hauled through the miry streets. About this time the cobble-stone pavement was introduced sparingly; and in 1856 was laid the first square of the wooden-block pavement, which has since been used almost to the exclusion of every thing else as a road-bed.

The dredging out of the river was followed by the improvement of its banks. Not less than five miles of dockage was constructed, while the pier was run out still further, that step being rendered necessary by the continual accretion of sand brought down by the north-east current in the lake, and a light-house was built in 1855, at a distance of 1950 feet east from the point from which the pier was first put down. This pier is on the north side of the channel. The breakwater of the Illinois Central Railroad, previously mentioned, formed an adequate protection to the south shore.

Other city improvements were carried out, in great numbers. Several additional bridges were thrown across the river. The small buildings which had been erected in the corners of the Court-house square, in the earlier days, were displaced by a City Hall, built in the center of the plat in 1853, that was enlarged in 1858, and the old Bridewell building on Polk Street, near the river, was put up for the occupancy of offenders against the peace and dignity of the city. The Recorder's Court was established in 1853, and in 1855 the police force of fifty-four men was first organized for day duty; they had previously been nothing more than night watchmen. They were now divided into three bodies, corresponding to each of the three divisions of the city, and placed in the three market halls—structures long since swept away by the remorseless hand of progress. The South Division Market Hall stood at the north end of

State Street, and was abolished in 1858; the West Division Market stood on West Randolph Street, near Desplaines, and was pulled down in 1864 or '65. The North Market Hall, on Dearborn near Kinzie, stood till the time of the fire, but had long been disused. These three buildings were of brick, and designed to be of great accommodation to the public. They were soon found to be nuisances, and were abolished accordingly.

The educational system of the city was thoroughy reörganized to meet the growing wants of the juvenile population. The Franklin and Washington schools—the fourth and fifth erected —had been established in 1851. The Foster branch, and the Rollingmill school were added in 1855; the Mosely and Ogden were added in 1856; and the important addition was made of a high school for the further instruction of the best pupils in the grammar departments. In 1857 the Brown and Foster were added to the list at a cost of $28,000 each, making a total of eleven schools, with an average daily attendance of 3354, out of an enrollment of 10,786 pupils for that year. The first public evening school was established in the autumn of 1856, in the North Market Hall. At this time it was estimated that Chicago contained about 17,100 children of school age, of which 8306 were enrolled as pupils in the public schools, and 4400 were found in attendance in fifty-six private schools, leaving about 4400 unprovided for.

In 1854, the public schools were first organized by classifying the pupils according to their merits, as ascertained by set examinations. This important step was taken under the rule of John C. Dore, appointed in May, as the first Superintendent of Public Schools. The same year the office of School Trustee was abolished, and the Board of Education took entire charge of the schools. Under the new rule the High School was constructed from the newly discovered marble, found at Athens, in the southern part of the county; it was for some years the most handsome structure in tht city. In March 1856, Mr. Dore resigned, and W. H. Wells succeeded as Superintendent. He was the author of the graded course of instruction which is still in use, with a few modifications, in the schools of Chicago, as well as in thousands of others in the United States. The Board of Education was reörganized in 1857, and the number of members increased to fifteen.

The Chicago Reform School was opened in November, 1856, for the reception of boys who were either without parents, or needed special care to prevent them from becoming vicious men.

A still higher class of instruction was also liberally provided for during this period. The Catholic University (St. Mary of the Lake), established in 1844, was the only one in the city previous to the railroad era. In 1852, the North-western (Methodist Episcopal) University was originated, and removed the next year to Evanston, twelve miles north of the city. The Garrett Biblical Institute was organized in 1855, and also located at Evanston. The University of Chicago (Baptist) was founded in 1855, Stephen A. Douglas donating the land on which the buildings were subsequently erected. The Congregationalist Theological Seminary, near Union Park, and the Presbyterian Theological Seminary, in the North Division, were founded subsequently.

This brings us to the churches, which exhibit an equally surprising increase. In 1852, and the five following years, we find springing into existance the following societies: Methodist, 7 (one African); Presbyterian, 3; Catholic, 7; Episcopal, 3; Baptist, 4; Congregational, 4; Universalist, 1; Swedenborgian, 1; German Evangelical, 2; Swedish Evangelical, 1; Reformed Dutch, 1; Mariner's Bethel, 1. Total, 35.

The Young Men's Library Association was incorporated in 1857, and the rooms, located on Washington Street, formed a much prized gathering place for the intellectual cultivation of its members; the library was a good one. The Mechanics Institute was also organized about the same time, and succeeded in gathering a valuable library, but died out through internal dissensions. The Chicago Historical Society was organized in 1856, with nineteen members, occupying rooms on the corner of Wells and Kinzie Streets. The Academy of Sciences was founded in 1857, and the formation of a museum commenced, on the south-east corner of Clark and Lake Streets.

Rice's Theater, established in 1847, burned down in 1849–50, and reöpened on the 1st of February, 1851, was the only theater in which English plays were presented, till August 4, 1855, when Levi J. North opened one on Monroe Street, near Wells, the building having been undertaken by Mr. N. while he was visiting the place with his circus, in the preceding April. In 1856 the place was rebuilt as an amphitheater, and a year afterward changed back to the theater form. It was finally closed in 1859, having never paid expenses. McVicker's Theater was opened November 5, 1857.

In 1852 the favorite concert-room was the old Metropolitan Hall, on the corner of Randolph and Lasalle Streets. This was soon superseded by a room in the Tremont House, where Adelina Patti sung in 1854, and several other notables afterward. In 1852 a German society opened a small hall as a theater, on West Randolph Street, near Canal, and this being burned down, they took a room over a blacksmith's shop, on Dearborn Street, Washington, in 1853–4, which was for a long time sacred to the combined shades of Thespis and Gambrinus. In 1855 the same society built the German Theater, on the corner of North Wells and Indiana Streets, and there gave the first purely musical entertainment ever presented in Chicago.

Two newspapers were added during this period to the then limited press list of Chicago. The *Democratic Press* was established in 1852 by Messrs. Bross, Scripps & Spears, and was the first paper in the city to give attention to the commercial importance of the place, and open a column in which the markets were reported. In June, 1854, the *Young America* was started, but changed to the *Chicago Times* two months afterward, under the proprietorship of Cook, Cameron & Co. J. W. Sheahan became editor in 1856.

Previous to 1852 there were scarcely more than sixty buildings in the city constructed of brick or stone; nearly all were wooden structures, and grouped within a short distance of the intersection of State and Madison Streets, the two principal section lines. Up to this time the great majority of the inhabitants did not regard themselves as settlers; they belonged elsewhere, and their buildings were of the cheapest kind, made after the pattern of the old balloon frame first raised in 1832. After the introduction of railroads, the people understood better the value of the position, which was brought home to their minds by the fact of a much larger tax list, and they began to make more permanent improvements. In 1854, not less than twenty-five millions of bricks were used, mostly in building, and fifty millions in 1856, while the receipts of stone rose from 19,901 cubic yards, in 1851, to 122,842 yards in 1857. Of course the principal portion of this material was used in the older districts, working a great change in the aspect of the business parts of the city. Lake, South Water, and Randolph Streets, and even

Washington, with the cross streets, as far south as Madison, rapidly took on the more solid phase, while the north side near the river shared in this change. Meanwhile the lumber piles were drawn upon more extensively than ever for the construction of wooden buildings in the outskirts, and all the leading thoroughfares to a distance of two miles out, in each direction from the Court-house, were thickly strewn with the evidences of civilization. Indeed, in 1855, building had become almost a mania, every street being blocked up with bricks or lumber, or with the wooden structures themselves, which were being moved out to the suburbs to make room for more imposing architectural piles in the places where the trade of the city centered. That year, 1855, was the one in which house-moving first became a business in Chicago.

The year 1856 witnessed the erection of 7 churches, 5 hotels, the City Armory, City Hospital, and High School, 145 stores, many of which were five stories high, and several hundred residences, about 2000 of which were in the West Division. The cost of these improvements was as follows: business blocks, $1,781,900; residences, $1,164,190; hotels, $315,000; churches, seminaries, etc., $311,000; other buildings, $1,500,000; city improvements, $427,434. Total, $5,708,624. In 1857 the total amounted to $6,423,518, of which $1,940,000 was for business blocks and buildings; $869,000 for first-class residences; and $204,000 for churches. The cost of the improvements effected in the four years ending with 1857, was $18,306,300, and from 1852 to 1857, inclusive, over twenty millions of dollars.

In 1856 these buildings were lighted with 60,000,000 cubic feet of gas. There were nearly 600 street lamps, and 2500 private consumers.

Of course the selling value of property rose rapidly under this tide of commerce and improvement. At a moderate estimate it increased fully two and three-quarter times, between 1852 and 1857. Indeed, a perfect real-estate mania ensued after the departure of the cholera in 1854, which involved nearly every one in the city, and was almost a second edition of the speculative days of twenty years previously. Nor was the mania confined to the resident population. During that year, and the two following, a large part of the country around the city was sub-divided up by real estate dealers, and plats were exhibited in all the eastern cities, where almost fabulous sums were realized on lots that have not even yet been occupied—some of them under water, out in Lake Michigan, or in the swamps of Calumet. It was enough to say that a piece of land was in the neighborhood of Chicago to make it salable at almost any price asked for it, and thousands of men and women at the East invested their savings in so-called Chicago lots. Such an overstrain could not last long; the true values of real estate were discounted too far into the future.

The following shows the official valuation of property in the city during this period, with the city taxation:

Year.	Real.	Personal.	Total.	Taxes.
1852,	$8,189,069	$2,272,645	$10,461,714	$76,949
1853,	13,130,177	3,711,154	16,841,831	135,663
1855,	21,637,500	5,355,393	26,992,893	206,209
1856,	25,892,308	5,843,776	31,736,084	396,652

In 1856 the area of the city was about 18 square miles; this would give on a one-third valuation a total value of $8,260 per acre, or about $1,130 worth of property to each of the 84,113 residents of the city.

XVI. THE PANIC OF 1857.

IN September, 1857, the bubble burst. A wave of distrust throbbed across the bosom of the hitherto placid sea of universal confidence, and there was a storm that stayed not its course till it had laid thousands of business houses in ruins, and effected an immense reduction of prices and profits, of capital and production, throughout the world.

The full effects of this storm were felt in Chicago, but it is due to her as a city to say that the unstable inflation that resulted in such wide-spread disaster, was not only not confined to that city, but had not even its origin there. The Genius of speculation had o'erspread the whole land with his wings, and the lurid shadow was even deeper at the East than at the West. Even the undue expansion in Western real estate had its origin in the East, and it was the capital of the seaboard that formed the basis on which those values were bid up by dwellers on the Atlantic slope. The great mass of the Western people were nobly doing their duty through that period of inflation, bending all their energies to the cultivation of the soil, or the distribution of its products to those who needed them. A comparatively small number were engaged in the blowing process, which has been unjustly described as peculiarly a Chicago institution. The great break-up began at the East, and was most severely felt there, as its effects were also the most lasting in that region. Indeed, it was the West that ultimately righted the whole continent by its strength, as it had been the occasion, not the cause, of the panic that wrought such wide-spread ruin.

But Chicago suffered—and deeply. The first effect was felt in the value of money. The circulating medium in Chicago was principally based on Illinois and Wisconsin stocks, many of which sunk to seventy cents on the dollar within a week after mutual confidence was destroyed by Eastern failures. The Chicago banks continued to take this currency at nominal par, but their par was never less than ten, and generally fifteen per cent. below the par that would obtain specie on presentation of the paper at a bank counter. St. Louis, like New York, kept up to the gold par, and in so doing blocked the wheels of her commerce so effectually that she occupied several more years than did Chicago in recovering from the shock.

The Chicago banks generally redeemed their circulation in coin, though the Eastern distrust in the wheat-crop (which had been pronounced a failure) caused a very general withdrawal of Eastern currency that had been sent out to move the crops, and left them bare. The Chicago merchants were equally honorable. When they found that they could not get Eastern exchange to pay their indebtedness, they bought the wheat which New York men had refused, sent it East, and thus made exchange for themselves. Chicago business men really stood by each other nobly through that crisis; and hence, though there was wide-spread loss, there was but little failure. The number of Chicago houses that yielded up the ghost was very small, while hundreds of Eastern houses of a century's standing went down with a crash before the howling blast.

But if general business was only staggered, speculation was destroyed. The effects on the real-estate market were fearful, and the building business suffered correspondingly. The depreciation of prices in corner lots was great in the winter of 1857, but it was much greater in 1858 and 1859, as payments matured which could not be met. A large proportion of the real estate in the city had been bought on canal time—the same terms as those on which Dr. Egan used to prescribe his pills in moments of abstractedness—one-quarter down, and the balance in one, two, and three years. They had depended upon a continual advance in quoted values to meet those payments, and found that they could not even sell at a ruinous sacrifice. Great numbers of workers left the city for want of employment, and those who remained were obliged to go into narrowed quarters to reduce expenses. This caused a great many residences and stores to be vacated, and brought about a reduction in rents on those still occupied, which impoverished even those who were able to hold on to their property. Many hundreds of lots and houses were abandoned by those who had made only partial payments, and the holders of mortgages needed no snap-judgment to enable them to take possession.

A stop was at once put to the erection of buildings. Several blocks were left unfinished for years, and some commenced were never finished by the original owners. As an instance of the severe loss entailed in this direction, we may cite the case of Alexander Lloyd, Mayor of Chicago in 1840. He was worth $75,000 in 1857, and on the strength of that borrowed $50,000 to erect an iron-front building on the north-west corner of Lake and Wells Streets. The walls were almost up when the crash came. He was obliged to suspend, lost his title to the land and building, and died, some years afterward, an object of charity. His poor widow was knocked down, in 1871, by a runaway horse in the West Division, and died the next day.

XVII. LIFTING UP.

FROM this time till the breaking out of the war of the rebellion, in 1861, the city was almost stationary. There was a slight increase in the population and in the volume of business, but, as compared with the five or six years preceding the panic, the progress was exceedingly slow. A succession of bad crops made the West poor, and limited its commerce so much that Chicago was nearly at a stand-still.

But though poor, the people of Chicago neither lost faith nor energy. If new buildings were not wanted in great numbers to accommodate an increasing population, the old ones needed to be rejuvenated and replaced by better structures, against the time when all felt there would be a general revival. The people acted, as a whole, like the individual merchant who employs his spare time in taking account of stock, noting deficiencies, and putting his store in order, so that he can attend to business all the better when it does come.

The plan for raising the grade of the city, so as to procure an efficient drainage, adopted in 1855 and pressed forward in 1856 and 1857, was carried out vigorously during the years 1859 and 1860. Three men deserve honorable mention in this connection: E. S. Chesborough, who suggested the raising of the grade, and carried it through in spite of all opposition; Harry Fox, whose machines straightened out the river and harbor, and carried the sand and mud into the streets to change the grade; and George M. Pullman, since better known as the sleeping-car patentee, who began the work of lifting up bodily the buildings that had previously been erected on a lower grade line. Mr. Pullman began in 1859, and soon had the Matteson and Tremont Hotels, a long line of ponderous warehouses on South Water Street, and of wholesale stores on Lake Street, lifted up by jack-screws, and made permanently higher by bringing up substantial masonry or brickwork from below. Other contractors were at work in this direction, but we believe Mr. Pullman was the first to show how a whole block of brick or stone could be lifted up, with all its contents, without even disturbing the operations of business inside, just as well as the smaller wooden structures that had been taken in hand by others.

This wholesale rising up out of the prairie mud gained for Chicago a notoriety equal to that she had attained by virtue of her commercial importance. The journals of the East and of Europe were burdened with descriptions of the wonderful city, which was achieving a feat almost equal to that performed by the man who lifted himself up by tugging at his boot-straps. This, too, was the epoch of uneven sidewalks, about which the Eastern papers used to be as facetious as they were subsequently over the odors of the Chicago River. It used to be reported that when the genuine Chicagoan visited New York he found himself unable to walk on a level surface; he was obliged to turn into the adjacent buildings, every half block or so, and run up and down a stairway, for the sake of variety. It was, indeed, a period of upheaval of the most unpleasant kind for pedestrians, as the single buildings here and there were raised to grade, and the sidewalk in front lifted to correspond, while those on either side were on the old level, a yard or more below. How the drunken men of that epoch managed to stumble home at night without breaking their necks, is a mystery yet unsolved. It took a long time to bring up the buildings to a uniform height in the business portions of the city.

While the greater number of the buildings were simply

raised, a large proportion of the wooden buildings were moved away on rollers to the suburbs, and their places supplied by noble piles of brick or stone, built to the new grade. Meanwhile the streets were gradually filled up and sewered, and supplied with pipes for water and gas; and then the people began to wish for a better roadway than was supplied by the old planking method. Many of the leading thoroughfares were covered with macadam, most of the stone for which was broken by the prisoners in the Bridewell, though a crushing-mill was also used at the quarries near the corner of Indiana Street and Western Avenue. The cobble-stone pavement was tried on several streets, especially Lake and State. The wooden-block pavement was more slowly introduced. A small piece of about 800 square yards was laid in 1856 on Wells Street, between Lake and South Water, and another piece in 1857 on Washington Street, between Clark and Lasalle. The experiment proved a success, and Clark Street was paved from Lake to Polk, in 1858–9; East Lake Street was paved with it in 1861. Since then it has been the favorite, and used on all the principal thoroughfares, as fast as they have been filled and improved.

Previous to 1859 the omnibus was the only available vehicle for those who could not command an exclusive conveyance. In that year the Chicago City Railway Company laid down rails on State from Lake Street south to the city limits, on Madison west to Reuben Street, and on Randolph Street nearly to the city limits. The same year the North Chicago City Railway Company laid rails on north Clark Street from the river to the city limits; also on Larrabee Street and Clybourne Avenue. On these lines horse cars have been run daily ever since, with but slight interruptions for repairs, and several extensions have been made to the system then established.

The wholesale trade and manufactures of the city, grew much more rapidly during this period than did its produce business. The crops of 1857 and '58 were poor, and the farmers had less ability to purchase than heretofore; but the merchants of Chicago were enterprising enough to try to extend their business over a wider area, and by their efforts the city daily grew in favor with the western buyers, many of whom had previously procured all their supplies from New York.

The Custom-house and post-office was built by the United States Government in 1858–9.

The population was about 93,000 in 1857. The next year it had fallen to 80,000, principally owing to the exodus of workers out of employment. In 1859 the depletion was partially recovered from, the population being about 90,000, and in 1860 the census showed a total of 109,263 persons in the city. The valuations of property exhibited about the same proportion of increase, being $31,736,084 in 1856, and $37,053,512 in 1860—an augment of nearly 17 per cent. in four years.

The following table shows the movement of the produce business during this period:

	1857.	1858.	1859.	1860.
Grain received, bu. .	22,327,076	23,972,765	19,805,147	36,390,951
Grain shipped, . .	18,032,678	20,035,166	16,771,812	31,108,759
Hogs received, . .	214,223	540,486	271,204	392,864
Hogs packed, . .	99,262	179,684	151,339	271,805
Cattle received, . .	48,524	140,534	111,694	177,101
Cattle packed, . .	34,675	45,503	51,606	34,623
Flour man'f't, bbls. .	96,000	140,003	165,520	194,668
Lumber received, M. .	459,639	278,943	302,845	262,495
Wool received, lbs. .	1,106,820	1,053,626	918,319	859,248
Canal tolls, . . .	$106,352	$95,184	$81,078	$63,637
Customs, . . .	82,528	24,820	70,820	49,658

The manufactures of the city had equaled a total product valued at $15,515,063, in 1856. In 1860 the United States census gave a total of $13,555,671, employing 5593 workers, on an invested capital of $5,571,025, for Cook County. Of this amount, about $11,740,684 worth of products was manufactured in Chicago on a capital of $5,422,225.

During 1858, and the three following years, a total of sixteen new churches were built, and the Young Men's Christian Association organized, March 28, 1858, which has since been a wonderful power for good. The Newberry and Skinner schools were erected in the North and West Divisions, in 1859, and the same year young ladies were first appointed head assistants in the public schools. In 1860 the graded course of instruction was introduced by Superintendent Wells. The number of pupils enrolled in the public schools at the end of each year was as follows: 8577 in 1856; 10,786 in 1857; 12,873 in 1858; 14,199 in 1859; and 16,441 in 1860, of whom 15,159 were under fifteen years of age. In 1860 there were above 7750 children attending private schools, and it was estimated that not less than 3000 of school age were totally unprovided with instruction.

XVIII. THE REBELLION—CAMP DOUGLAS.

ON the 14th of April, 1861, the first gun was fired on Fort Sumter, which was evacuated by the United States troops on the next day. Quick as the lightning flashed the intelligence over the wires, was the response made in every part of the land, and in none more heartily than in Chicago. From the workshop and the desk, men rushed forth to form companies and regiments for the war, even before the Government asked their services. The scenes in the streets will not soon be forgotten.

On the 19th of April a telegram was received from Governor Yates, by Brigadier-General R. K. Swift, notifying him to raise an armed force as quickly as possible. At 11 o'clock on the 21st, the General left Chicago with a force of 595 men and four six-pounder pieces of artillery. Among these were the Chicago Light Artillery, and Companies A and B, Chicago Zouaves. This force instantly went on guard duty at Cairo, and zealously enough, for their hearts were in the work, but it is nevertheless true that they did much more harm to themselves at first than to the rebels, as many of the men were totally unaccustomed to the use of fire-arms. In May, 1861, the Chicago Dragoons and the Washington Light Cavalry were organized, and the work of recruiting proceeded even more rapidly than was desired by the Government. The Seward idea that the rebellion could be put down in three months, with 75,000 men, was not generally accepted by the people, who believed from the first that all the power of the North must be exerted to end the war. Hence several companies and regiments were raised and tendered to the Government which were not accepted, and the discouragement experienced at that time told forcibly when more men were called for, as it was seen that they were really wanted. On the 17th of June the Nineteenth Regiment was organized; next the Irish Brigade, and the old Hecker Regiment. In August the Yates' Sharpshooters, the Scotch Regiment, and others, were formed, partially in Chicago, and the Twelfth Illinois Cavalry was also accepted in August or September.

In the latter part of the summer of 1861, Colonel Joseph H. Tucker was appointed by Governor Yates to the command of the Northern District of the State, with orders to establish a camp at Chicago for the rendezvous and instruction of volunteers. He immediately selected a site at Cottage Grove, near the University of Chicago, and named it Camp Douglas, in honor of the Senator to whom the ground had formerly belonged. The camp contained between sixty and seventy acres of ground. Here barracks were constructed capable of accommodating about 8000 men, and a large number of troops mustered into the service. In February, 1862, some eight or nine thousand prisoners arrived, who had been captured at the battle of Fort Donelson. They were placed in camp, and guarded by the Federal troops. Soon after this Colonel Mulligan took command of the camp, having been ordered home to reorganize his regiment, the Irish Brigade, after the battle of Lexington, Mo.

Early in June, 1862, two regiments of three-months' men were raised in Chicago for garrison duty in Camp Douglas, and Colonel Tucker reässumed command. Soon after this came the paroled troops which had been captured at Harper's Ferry, and with them Brigadier-General Tyler, to whom had been confided their management. They were supposed to be under orders for the Indian frontier, but remained in Chicago. Then began the exciting history of Camp Douglas. The rule of General Tyler was that of a man of iron, without any of the elasticity of steel, and the men were very much dissatisfied. They did not believe that they had a right to be treated as prisoners, or even compelled to do garrison duty until exchanged. Hence frequent troubles, which culminated in burning of barracks and attempts at escape. The exchange and removal was a work of time, and during that whole period the citizens of Chicago slept insecurely. They felt that a volcano existed at camp which might at any time break forth and overwhelm the city.

These fears were, however, groundless. The soldiers wished not to do more than testify their sense of the wrongs which they believed themselves to have suffered, and when the rigorous discipline was relaxed the burning ceased.

The prisoners were still in Camp Douglas when the call was issued for six hundred thousand troops, and the rapidly augmenting volunteer companies and regiments were quartered outside the camp, presenting the novel sight of tents dotted all over the surrounding region as far as the eye could reach. The three Board of Trade regiments, the Irish Legion, Van Arman's Regiment, the Railroad Regiment, with several battery companies, will be remembered as thus located, and the challenge of their sentinels was heard at every step for the space of several miles. A more permanent exterior was afterward effected when, on the arrival of the paroled troops, it was found that the camp proper was insufficient for their accommodation, and the fair grounds immediately westward were secured. On these grounds barracks were erected, to which were assigned the Ninth Vermont, the One Hundred and Twenty-seventh New York, and another regiment. On their departure most of those barracks that had not been burned, were pulled down and the limits of the camp shrunk down to the original boundaries.

In the autumn of 1862 Brigadier-General Ammon took command, the Harper's Ferry paroled troops departed, and another camp full of prisoners arrived just on the edge of winter. Being used to a warmer climate, they were but indifferently fitted to stand the hardships of barrack life in what was, to them, the far North, and they died off like rotten sheep in spite of the fact that many noble ladies interested themselves in alleviating the sufferings of the prisoners; and their guard, while doing their duty to the Government by insuring their safe keeping, were yet unremitting in their attentions, and suffered themselves, in consequence of the want of proper means for keeping up the animal heat.

In March, 1863, the camp was cleared, save of a few prisoners who were too sick to leave, and enough of Federal troops to guard and attend to them, and keep the post. Two companies of the Scotch Regiment, and a few men of the Ninth Vermont were all that remained of the immense numbers which had so lately trodden the mud of Camp Douglas, and shivered beneath its thin board roofs. Up to this time fully thirty thousand troops had been recruited, organized, drilled, and furnished with equipments at Camp Douglas, besides which, it had served as a stronghold for confining about seventeen thousand rebel prisoners, and for holding about eight thousand of those paroled at Harper's Ferry.

During the latter part of 1863, Camp Douglas was again occupied as a military prison, an average of some five thousand confederates being confined there. Colonel C. V. DeLand, of the First Michigan Sharpshooters, was made post commandant, and improved the camp at a total expense of about $35,000. Toward the close of the year he was relieved by Brigadier-General Orme, at which time there were 1800 Union men in camp. May 2d, 1864, the command devolved upon Colonel J. C. Strong, of the Veteran Reserve Corps, and in July his successor, Colonel B. J. Sweet, arrived from Washington and took charge. Colonel Sweet caused the whole of the prisoners' barracks to be raised several feet from the ground, to prevent the occupants from boring their way out. Many of them had previously escaped in this way. He also made large additions to the number of barracks, and erected warehouses for the reception of stores.

The number of prisoners now increased so rapidly that more barracks needed to be erected for them, and the force of a little over 1000 men belonging to the Veteran Reserve Corps was found too small to keep them safely. They were accordingly reinforced in August, by the One Hundred and Sixth Pennsylvania (100 day) Infantry, and on the approach of the National Democratic Convention, the guard was further strengthened by the arrival of 156 men, composing the Twenty-fourth Ohio Battery, armed with Parrott guns.

On the 1st of January, 1864, there were 5649 rebel prisoners in camp, and nearly 7500 were received during the year, most of whom were souvenirs of Hood's defeats. During the year, 63, including one Cherokee Indian, were released on taking the oath of allegiance. The mortality among the prisoners was high, 1156 during the year; they suffered severely from small-pox, besides other diseases: 11,780 were in camp on New Year's Day, 1865.

In the spring of 1865, the discharge of the prisoners commenced. The others soon followed on the collapse of the rebellion, 8400 being released in May, and returned to their homes. Only about 200 remained in August, and most of these were on the sick-list in the hospital. The camp was finally abandoned about the close of the year.

In its best estate Camp Douglas covered about sixty acres of ground. The number of prisoners confined there at different times was about thirty thousand.

XIX. OUTSIDE CAMP DOUGLAS.

CHICAGO was early made a depot for the purchase of Government supplies during the war. During 1863 about 1500 horses were bought there at a cost of $1,800,000, and some $2,500,000 more was expended for horses during the first seven months of 1864. In the latter year the purchases of the quartermaster's department alone footed up $2,664,038.54, and the other expenditures $916,528.23, besides which nearly $1,000,000 worth of material were bought in the city by other departments. The material transported by the department in 1864, weighed over 41,525 tons, involving a cost of $1,100 per month for drayage alone. The purchases of the quartermaster in 1865 were about $900,000, and the expenditures $500,000.

During the first three years of the war Chicago had sent into the field all the men required of her, and many more than her due proportion, the city having been an active recruiting depot for both the army and navy. On the 4th of July President Lincoln issued his call for 500,000 men; the quota of Illinois being fixed at 16,182, of which number Cook County was required to furnish 4250. This was more than one-quarter of the call from the entire State, and the assigned quota was so manifestly excessive that it was finally reduced by fifty per cent. Then the county authorities authorized the issue of $300,000 county scrip, to give a bounty of $300 to each recruit credited on the quota. Inside the city the people organized and offered additional bounties, but in spite of all this the county was in arrears to the extent of 1650 men, on the 26th of September, and drafting was commenced. The drawing was continued spasmodically for three weeks, during which time

1550 volunteers were obtained, leaving 59 conscripts held to service.

In November, 1864, the people were startled by the rumor that a plot had been formed to release the prisoners in Camp Douglas, and capture and sack the city, on the eve of the presidential election. A large number of men from the southern part of the State had arrived in the city a few days previously, with no ostensible purpose. These were arrested, with several residents who were suspected of being rebel sympathizers. A number of them were afterward tried by court-martial in Cincinnati, but after the close of the war most of them were pardoned and allowed to return home, after an imprisonment of nine months.

Then came the last call—for "300,000 more"—in December. It found Chicago in trouble. The quota of the county was fixed at 5200 men, and of these the city was called on to furnish by far the greatest portion. It was well known that the quota was assigned on the basis of a population composed in large part of aliens who had been attracted from Canada by an unwonted activity in commerce and manufactures, and all these were called upon to go forward and purge the rolls of all names that had no business there. But most of them feared to become unpopular, preferring to prove alienage if they were drafted. Added to this the fact that the flesh brokers were operating through the naval rendezvous to carry off an average of not less than forty persons per day, to be credited to other places which paid a high bounty. It was in vain that the county offered a bounty of $400 to each recruit, and the city and ward committee's additional sums. The draft was ordered, but Petersburgh and Richmond fell, and then no more soldiers were wanted. Cook County sent in all 22,532 men to the Union ranks during the war, with only one partial draft. Of the men drafted, substitutes were procured for all except fifty before the time arrived for departure, and of those who left the city seven were relieved at Springfield. The majority of the recruits raised under the last call were rendezvoused at Camp Fry, near the northern limits of the city.

The following was our estimate of the total cost to the county, made in 1865, a few months after the war had closed:

Cost of Provost Marshal's Department, not to be included in the total,	$77,089
Paid by city for bounties from October, 1863,	$ 119,742
Paid by the county from October, 1863,	2,565,172
Paids by the towns and wards from October, 1863,	734,453
Paid representatives and substitutes,	56,350
Paid by county to families,	166,034
Paid by city to families,	90,809
Paid by Board of Trade to families,	220,000
Mercantile Association to families,	75,000
Total,	$4,027,560

This is the cost inside the county, and irrespective of private charities; the actual cost of the war to the General Government, amounting in round numbers to $3,350,000,000, was borne in part by Chicago, in addition to the above. The share of the payments made by Cook County into the Federal Treasury was, in 1865, in the proportion of 58 to 3,350. Fifty-eight millions of dollars may therefore be assumed as the share of Cook County, to which add the four millions of local expense, and we have a grand total of sixty-two millions as the expense borne or assumed by Cook County for the suppression of the rebellion.

The news that Richmond had fallen arrived in the city on Monday, April 3d, and the people were wild with joy. The previous good news flashed over the wires, of the fall of Petersburgh, the investment of the rebel capital, the successive advances of the Union forces on the doomed city, and the repeated captures of large numbers of prisoners, had all been in turn rejoiced over, as by men who see the morning light breaking after a long night of storm, and had partially prepared all for the grand result. But when that news came, it was as though they had not before heard of a victory. The joyful news was caught up and shouted through the streets until the very walls of the buildings re-echoed the strain, and in the very suburbs of the city was soon heard the glad news "Richmond has fallen." The quick murmur of fire-arm discharges intermingled with the shouts of the people, and soon bonfires threw their lurid glares all over the city, and around them gathered happy throngs, chanting at the top of their voices the "Battle Cry of Freedom," the "Star Spangled Banner," and other popular patriotic songs. It was a night of wild tumultuous joy, a time when every heart throbbed almost audibly, and strong men vented their feelings in tears of gladness. A majority of the buildings in the business parts of the city were illuminated, and many of those in less thickly-settled portions. Large and enthusiastic mass-meetings were held, at which the people shouted their happiness, and the speakers were too much overcome to make long talks. Greater enthusiasm could not have been exhibited; it showed the hearts of the people to have been in the right place after all, notwithstanding the efforts of some men to get up a feeling of sympathy with the South; it showed that the great heart of the people was true to the Union.

The subsequent news of the surrender of Johnston, and the whole of the concentrated portion of the rebel army, was not received with so much satisfaction, as there was a wide-spread feeling that the National honor had not been sufficiently vindicated in the terms of the capitulation. The capture of Davis was the last in the series of Southern events that was celebrated in Chicago.

Scarcely had the first rejoicings subsided, when the nation was shrouded in deep mourning by the news that President Lincoln had been assassinated. Nowhere was the grief more intense than in Chicago. The whole city was draped in black, and the countenances of men wore even a deeper shade of woe. The body of the murdered President reached the city on the 1st day of May, and was borne through the streets in procession, followed by tens of thousands of people. The corpse lay in State in the Court-house during the next day, and through the night and day the people thronged the building in quick, moving column. The body was taken to Springfield, his old home, on Tuesday night, and was there buried. The *catafalque* was one of the many interesting objects burned up in the great conflagration.

XX. AIDING THE SOLDIERS.

NOT the least important phase in the war record of Chicago, was intense sympathy felt for the soldiers, and the liberality with which that sympathy found expression in deeds.

In the summer of 1862, a number of patriotic ladies associated themselves together for the purpose of caring for the soldiers who were arriving in the city, or departing for the field. The building No. 45 Randolph Street was taken for this purpose, but the work grew so rapidly that it was soon found necessary to erect a building near the Central Depot to receive and feed the travelers, while the first-named building was kept for the disabled ones, and called the "Soldier's Home." The year following, the Home was removed to the lake shore, near the grave of Douglas, and a noble building was subsequently erected as a permanent home for the disabled veterans of the war. That building was sold in the autumn of 1871, the few soldiers remaining at that time being removed to the National Home.

The Young Men's Christian Association took the field at an early day, to minister to the wants of the soldier, and the Board of Trade, and other organizations, also sent special messengers to the front with liberal supplies of good things not included in the army rations. Then the Sanitary Commission was organized, and did a world of good all through the war in caring for the brave boys in the field. In 1863, a Sanitary Fair was held in Bryan Hall (since Hooley's Opera House), under the joint auspices of the Sanitary Commission and the Soldier's Home, at which some $30,000 was netted for the soldiers. That hall, by the by, was the scene of most of the war meetings held, and its walls often resounded with patriotic appeals and soul-stirring songs; while many a distinguished patriot's remains went thence to their last resting-place, the list being headed by the corse of U. S. Senator Douglas.

The closing grand public effort for the aid of the soldiers was made in Chicago during the year 1865—the great Northwestern Sanitary Fair. It was at first intended to hold the fair solely for the benefit of the Soldier's Home, but a union of effort was subsequently agreed upon, by which the Soldier's Home and the Sanitary Commission were joint workers, and the Christian Commission was afterward added. Owing to the

MASONIC TEMPLE, DEARBORN STREET.

TRIBUNE BUILDING AFTER THE FIRE.

sudden collapse of the rebellion the fair was not held until after the real close of the war, and the pecuniary results were therefore much less than they would otherwise have been, as many people saw no further necessity for exertion. Nevertheless the fair netted nearly two hundred and fifty thousand dollars, the gross receipts being greatly in excess of three hundred thousand.

The fair was opened, on the 30th of May, by a grand procession and a series of exercises, in the great Union Building in Dearborn Park, the principal features of which were the delivery of an inaugural poem by T. Buchanan Read, and the delivery of an eloquent, soul-stirring address by Governor Oglesby.

One of the most pleasant uses to which the Fair Buildings was put, was the reception of our brave soldiers, thousands of whom were there saluted, and all, from lieutenant-general to high-private, received with a hearty enthusiasm that told how much was felt the debt owed to them. Major-General Sherman arrived on the 8th of June, and a most cordial reception was extended to him by all classes. On the 10th Lieutenant-General Grant arrived, and was received in Union Hall with an ovation perfectly tremendous in extent and enthusiasm.

XXI. CHICAGO DURING THE WAR.

THE war built up Chicago, giving a wonderful stimulus to its commerce and manufactures, but the first effect was disastrous in the extreme. The shock unsettled every one, the experience being so novel that very few were able to form even a faint idea of its influence upon the business of the city. But it is due to the merchants to say that they were unwilling to take offered chances of gain. Immediately on the outbreak of hostilities large sums of gold were sent to Chicago from New Orleans and other Southern cities, requesting that produce should be sent in exchange. The men to whom these orders were addressed, one and all, sent back the money, saying that they would have nothing to do with the sending of supplies to an enemy.

When the war broke out the issues of Western banks were largely based on Southern stocks—there being not less than twelve million dollars worth (?) of that kind of money in the State. Of course it rapidly depreciated, causing an unnatural fluctuation in the price of exchange, and the market value of all kinds of produce. Within a month the case had become so desperate that the newspapers published daily lists of the quotable values, in gold, of the different bank bills, those quotations ranging all the way from ten cents on the dollar to par—very few of the latter. And these quotations fluctuated so widely that no one felt sure in receiving payment that the quotation would be sustained till he could pay it over to some one else. For once in the world's history, nearly every one preferred paying his debts to keeping that "money" on hand. Soon thereafter most of the Illinois banks went out of existence, and within a few weeks all traces of the "wild-cat" had disappeared forever. The subsequent experience in the gradual depreciation of Government currency, the consequent scarcity of small change, the desperate expedients to which the people resorted before the issues of fractional currency, and the general adoption of the National bank-note as a circulating medium, are matters of general history pertaining no more to Chicago than to any other place in the Northern States, except on the Pacific coast, where the people used a metallic currency all through the war.

An attempt was made to arrest the displacement of this currency by the circulation of a document, to which many of the leading business men subscribed, pledging themselves to take the bills of certain banks at par till the close of the war. But they might as well have attempted to stop the torrent of Niagara with a wooden spoon. The resolve was adhered to barely three days, and then the stuff disappeared as if by magic. It was wonderful, too, to see how little embarrassment was caused by the withdrawal of so much currency from circulation. It astonished even those of the East, but they soon knew the reason—learned it in a lesson that only war could teach. The material of the nation's prosperity lay at the West. Cotton was deposed from his throne, and corn and pork thenceforward reigned undisturbed as the grand duumvirate of the United States. The people of the East were obliged to send their money westward if they would receive those prime necessaries of existence—rendered doubly necessary by the enhanced consumption attendant upon grim war.

As the exponent of Western production, Chicago rapidly rose to a much higher position than she had ever before occupied. Agricultural production was wonderfully stimulated by the shedding of blood. Then the soldiers needed equipments. The supply of ammunition was principally drawn from other points, but for food, clothing, saddlery, horses and wagons, and the other etceteras of the march and the camp, Chicago was called upon to the utmost of her resources, the Government establishing an agency there at an early day. The city was really an important base of supply; far enough away from the scene of strife to be safe, and yet so closely connected by rail with every part of the country that troops and munitions could be moved with facility to any point desired.

The enlivened demand at once stimulated production, and Chicago became very busy as a manufacturing center. Thousands of operatives went there, many of them from Canada, as well as from the East, and from Europe, and large amounts of capital were also sent there, especially from the border States, by men who feared to risk it so near the line that divided the two sections. Then the continued demand for produce, with the gradual drain upon the workers to fill up the army, stimulated the use and production of machinery on a vast scale on the farms of the West. The need of supplies, a gradually depreciating currency, and continually growing taxation, caused a rapid augment in quoted values of property, both real and personal.

And thus Chicago became the paradise at once of workers and speculators, and grew mightily. She prospered apace, while the red hand of war was sweeping her (wayward) sister cities as with the besom of destruction. Notwithstanding the drain upon her for men, her population increased from 109,263 souls in 1860, to 187,446 in 1865; her property assets were very nearly doubled in the same period, her borders were widely extended, while her commerce augmented in corresponding ratio.

The city limits were again extended in February, 1863, to include an area of nearly 24 square miles, being carried one mile further south, and taking in the previously excepted western corners, known as Bridgeport and Holstien. The city now contained sixteen wards. The property valuation was as follows:

Year.	Real.	Personal.	Total.	City Taxes.
1860,	$31,198,135	$5,855,377	$37,053,512	$373,315
1862,	31,587,545	5,552,300	37,139,845	564,038
1865,	44,064,499	20,644,678	64,709,177	1,294,184

These figures are instructive. They show that during the first years of the war there was no material increase in values. After that, however, the value of personal property rose rapidly, and mercantile stocks were greatly enlarged. Real estate continued in a depressed condition till near the close of 1862. Then confidence was restored, and for the first time in five years, real estate was in demand, and became steadily active about the spring of 1863. The demand was healthy and legitimate, confined almost entirely to those buying for actual use or occupation, whether for business purposes or for residences. Some few made large purchases for investment and for sub-division, but these were exceptions. Prices advanced moderately and steadily during this period, the principal advance being in those portions of the city rendered easily accessible by the newly extended horse railroads. Throughout the whole of the year 1864, the demand continued steady for active use and occupation. The largest class of purchasers was among the merchants, whose profits in business were sufficiently large to enable them to make investments of their surplus capital in residence property suitable to their requirements and tastes. Many of the lumber dealers, packers, and manufacturers also found their condition so much improved, that they were able to purchase premises before occupied by them under rent. The desire to invest was also stimulated to some extent by the growing volume of the currency, and the large cash balances accumulated during a period of great business prosperity consequent thereon, with a slight feeling of insecurity among a portion of the community in regard to the ultimate value of legal-tender notes. During the year 1864, desirable inside business property advanced in value about 20 per cent. on the average, and good residence property on the street railroad routes about 10 or 15 per cent.

The following figures show the movement of some of the leading articles of produce during the war:

	1861.	1864.	1865.
Flour man'f't, bbls. . .	291,852	290,137	301,776
Grain received, bu. . .	54,038,906	45,952,736	53,613,823
Grain shipped, " . .	50,481,862	47,124,494	53,212,224
Hogs received, No. . .	675,902	1,410,320	1,178,832
Hogs packed, " * . .	505,691	760,514	507,355
Cattle packed, No. . .	53,754	92,459	27,172
Lumber received, M. . .	249,309	501,592	647,146
Wool received, lbs. . .	1,184,208	4,304,388	7,639,749

We have not at hand a statement of the manufactures of 1864 and '65, our carefully prepared records having been burned up. We shall compare 1860 with 1870, in a subsequent chapter.

City improvements were numerous during the war, rendered necessary by the rapid growth of population. In 1864, not less than 6000 buildings of all kinds were erected, at a cost of $4,700,000. These included 9 churches, 2 schools, and 4 halls and public buildings; of the latter, four were worth $100,000 and upwards. Nearly as many buildings had been erected in 1863, and this large number of additional structures almost

* The winter of 1862–3, was the most active in pork packing ever known in the city: 970,264 hogs were packed, a number far exceeding that returned by Cincinnati, and Chicago has kept the lead of that city in hog packing ever since. The number cut in the winter of 1863–4 was 904,659.

doubled the occupied area of the city. In 1860 there were buildings on Clark and State Streets, north and south, and on Madison, Randolph, and Lake, westward to a distance of two miles and a half from the Court-house, and a few streets parallel to those were moderately occupied. But outside of the main thoroughfares, there were few buildings more than a mile and a half out from the business center in either direction, except toward Bridgeport and Holstein. In 1865 the inhabited area had extended to a distance of fully three miles from the Court-house in every direction except to the eastward (on the lake), while along the principal streets houses were scattered, at intervals, very much farther. The settled portions of the city covered about eighteen square miles.

While the number of buildings increased, there was a noticeable improvement in their character. More than ever stone and brick were employed, and in this period we find that the use of stone from other parts of the United States was extensively resorted to, both for the sake of variety, and because of its greater durability. Previous to the war, only one building—the Court-house—had been constructed of stone from outside the originial limits of the county of Cook, and only one other—the Second Presbyterian Church—from any other quarry than those at Joliet or Lemont. In 1862 the South Branch Dock Company began to excavate the row of slips between Halstead and Reuben Streets, on the north bank of the south branch; the clay was found to be of excellent quality, and as it could be had for the trouble of digging, the brickmakers were enabled to offer their wares at prices which more nearly competed with those of lumber. The commerce and trade of the city increased mightily during the war, and the appreciation in the value of goods on hand made many rich, and enabled them to enjoy the luxury of costly buildings. Then stone fronts became the rage, and iron was invested in to some extent also. Principally from that time have sprung up the palatial residences, the imposing warehouses, the princely stores, the costly churches, which have made Chicago equal to any city in the world, in this respect. Prominent among these we may note the Opera House and the rebuilt Sherman during the war, while those erected since its close are too numerous to mention. The progress in the building of smaller residences is also remarkable. There is a marked reform in their character, a notable improvement in arrangement, while in number they have grown so fast that it is difficult even to count them. Especially is the growth observable near the outskirts of the city, where several square miles are now dotted thick with pleasant cottages which four years ago were in the clay-bed, or in the forests of Michigan.

With this extension came other city improvements. The streets were raised to grade, and the old wooden sidewalks were replaced by stone on the principal business streets, and the avenues. The wooden-block pavement was also extensively introduced; it was laid on Lake Street in 1861; South Water and Wells in 1862; the intersections of Clark with Randolph and Madison in 1863, and West Lake Street in 1864. In 1862 the People's Gas Light and Coke Company commenced (June 1st) to supply the people of the West Division with gas, through 15 miles of pipe, which has since been added to, almost indefinitely. The Chicago Gas Light and Coke Company was henceforth restricted to the supply of the North and South Divisions. About 75 miles of sewers had been built up to the close of the war.

In 1863 the city ordered the dredging out of a passage through the bar, which had grown by continued accretions till

METHODIST CHURCH BLOCK.

NEW ENGLAND CHURCH—CONGREGATIONAL.

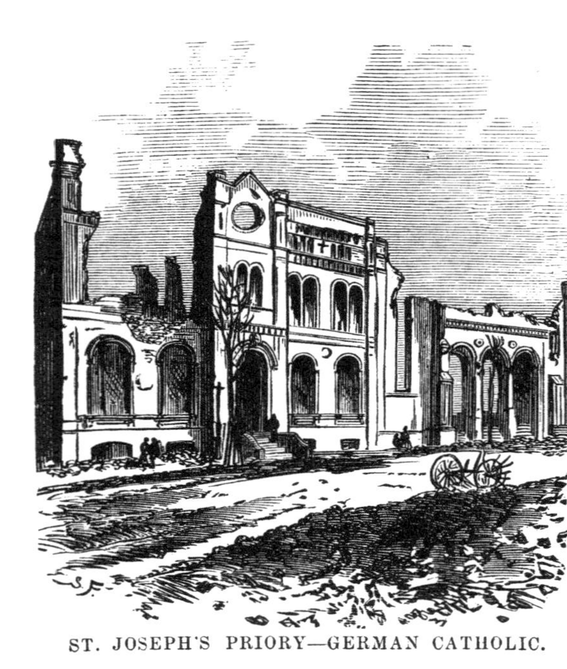

ST. JOSEPH'S PRIORY—GERMAN CATHOLIC.

UNITY CHURCH—DR. COLLYER.

it necessitated a round-about journey of a mile each way to all vessels entering or leaving the harbor. By August, 1864, a passage had been opened to admit vessels drawing 12½ feet of water, 150,000 cubic yards of sand having been removed. The insufficiency of the existing dock room, though presenting nearly ten miles of wharves, induced the digging out of an extensive series of slips on the south branch, and the determination to construct a line of docks outside the harbor on the north shore. The latter project was, however, abandoned till after the close of the war, the first few cribs and piles put down having been washed out in a violent gale.

The greatest internal improvement of this period was the Great Lake Tunnel, undertaken about the middle of the war, though the greater portion of the work was done after the return of peace. The tunnel stretches out under Lake Michigan to a distance of two miles, and is really one of the wonders of the nineteenth century. A large extension of the water-pipe system was in progress from 1862 to 1864, inclusive.

As "it never rains but it pours," so Chicago, having once determined on securing an adequate supply of water by means of the lake tunnel, found herself in danger of having too much of it. The quarries on the then western limits of the city, from which were taken the stones to pave the streets, and to build the Second Presbyterian Church, were permeated with a bituminous material, and some spirit or other was declared to have announced through a medium that oil could be had there for the boring. A company bored down about seven hundred feet only to strike a magnificent artesian well, from which the water has ever since flowed at the rate of half a million gallons daily, supposed to descend along a sandstone stratum from the bed of Rock River, which is 163 feet above the level of Lake

Michigan. Several other artesian wells have since then been put down, with uniform success. One eleven hundred feet deep supplies the Union Stock Yards, on Halstead Street, near the southern limits of the city, and one has been sunk in or near each of the parks in the West Division.

The police force was organized under the metropolitan system in 1861, at which time it consisted of fifty-two men. It consisted of about seventy patrolmen, besides sergeants and detectives, at the close of the war. The first steam fire-engine was introduced about 1859, but the old volunteer force continued to act with their hand-engines till 1861, when the paid system was adopted exclusively, and the old hand-engines went out of existence, with the brawls and feuds attending them.

The Fire Alarm and Police Telegraph, the construction of which was commenced in 1864, was completed in the early part of the year, and formally turned over to the city in the beginning of June, 1865. It consisted of one hundred and twenty-six miles of wire, of which forty-six were in the South Division, fifty in the West, and thirty in the North, which connected one hundred and sixteen fire boxes and stations. The cost was $70,000. Since then continued additions have been rendered necessary by the rapid growth of the city.

We may not pass this period without noting the great impetus given to amusements by the rapid filling up of the city, and the greater abundance of money incident to great activity in every department of trade and commerce. The Museum was opened early in 1863, McVicker's Theater was entirely rebuilt in 1864, and the same year the Opera House was built, and opened only a few days after the evacuation of Richmond.

XXII. PEACE AND PROSPERITY.

THE close of the rebellion staggered the city almost as much as its commencement. The return of the soldiers to their homes caused a large increase in the population, and necessitated much activity in making room for such numbers, though many of them returned to the bosom of their families. But with the return of peace came a tumble in the premium on gold that, added to the withdrawal of an army demand, produced a depreciation in prices that was almost fearful to contemplate, on the part of those who had large stocks of produce or merchandise on hand, however agreeable it may have been to the buyer. The embarrassment was really greatest just before the war ended, as the master finger of capital had detected the weakening in the pulse of the rebellion that foreshadowed its dissolution long before the fact was apparent to the general public. By the middle of April, 1865, the gold premium had dropped from $1.92 to 47 per cent. (from $2.92 to $1.47 per gold dollar), and the quotations on all classes of merchandise fell correspondingly. Farm produce dropped like a hot potatoe from the hands of a boy. Wheat declined from $2.00 per bushel in September, 1864, to $1.00 in May, 1865. In the same time corn fell from $1.33 to 38 cents; oats from 67 to 34 cents per bushel; live hogs from 12 cents to 7 cents per pound; mess pork form $42.50 to $23.00 per barrel, and mixed lumber from $20.00 to $11.00 per thousand feet. These tremendous depreciations in price, on the very large stocks of produce in Chicago and the West, were felt severely, yet no important failures occurred. The loss in mercantile business was relatively less, as the majority of the wholesale merchants had taken note in time, and were carrying very light stocks when the collapse came. The leading politicians, who in the autumn of 1864 were nearly ready to give up the ship in despair, were not half so wise as the mercantile community—the latter felt the coming of the day long before the "darkest hour before the dawn" had lifted its somber veil from the eyes of the people.

And so the prudence that has ever marked the operations of the business men of Chicago, even when they have seemed to be most reckless, carried them safely through this third great crisis. The majority of them had made such liberal profits during the preceding three years, that they could bear considerable loss, and had wisely invested much of their surplus in Chicago real estate, which did not depreciate with merchandise and produce. Indeed, confidence in the future of Chicago was strongest among those who were the heaviest losers by the close of the war.

At the risk of being thought facetious on a grave subject, we digress here to say that it seemed as if nearly all of the returned privates entered commercial colleges to fit themselves for clerkships, while the officers entered upon the insurance business—the generals and colonels as managing agents, and the captains and lieutenants as canvassers. The palmy days of the business college were soon over, when the soldiers found that the diploma earned by five weeks of study and a few more dollars was not a passport to the counting-room. But the insurance business had more endurance. It dated its real life from 1865, and both the life and fire departments had attained to stupendous proportions when the latter was brought to rudely by the Great Conflagration.

The six years succeeding the war formed a period of growth unprecedented, even in the previous history of the city. After about the first year the expansion was almost magical. That first twelve months was active, but unprofitable. Not only did the values of merchandise decline heavily, but the wheat crop of the previous year had been a partial failure, and the important business of packing provisions fell off terribly. But after 1865 had been passed the city took a new lease of prosperity, which, though not limited at the time, proved to be of five years duration.

The population increased from 178,900 in 1865 to 252,054 in 1868, and to 334,270 in 1871, the last total being that obtained by the census enumeration made by Richard Edwards. We append for reference the following figures, which show the ratio of the growth of Chicago in ten years to the county and State:

Population.	1860.	1870.	Per ct. increase.
Chicago,	110,973	299,227	170
Cook County,	144,954	349,786	141
Illinois,	1,711,951	2,537,910	48

A portion of the city growth, however, is due to an extension of territory within the limits of Cook County.

XXIII. COMMERCE OF 1870.

THE settlement of the other Western States and Territories proceeded even more rapidly than the State of Illinois, during this decade, and herein lay the true secret of the continued growth of Chicago. Rival cities were making efforts to catch a portion of her trade, and other routes to the seaboard than those leading through Chicago were constructed, but that city was still recognized as the natural focus of the commercial relations between the Upper Mississippi Valley and the world to the eastward. The more grain was raised in the West, the more passed through Chicago, and the more money was spent in that city in the purchase of articles of luxury or the necessaries of civilized life by the producers of the West. These facts attracted capital and industry to the Garden City, and caused a rapid appreciation in the value of the real estate, as the people of other parts of the world pressed forward to "join in the innumerable caravan" of pilgrims toward the modern Mecca. The following table of aggregates of produce and material received in the city during the year 1870, will show the magnitude of the trade. The last column gives the value of the receipts:

	Receipts.	Shipments.	Values Receipts.
Flour, bbls.	1,766,037	1,705,977	$7,947,166
Wheat, bu.	17,394,609	16,432,585	17,394,409
Corn, bu.	20,189,775	17,777,377	13,123,250
Oats, bu.	10,472,078	8,507,735	4,188,740
Rye, bu.	1,093,493	913,629	798,250
Barley, bu.	3,335,653	2,584,692	2,668,520
Grass Seed, lbs.	18,681,148	6,287,615	840,650
Broom Corn, lbs.	13,688,918	8,405,346	1,230,200
Cut Meats, lbs.	52,162,881	112,433,168	6,522,000
Beef, bbls.	20,554	65,369	266,800
Pork, bbls.	40,883	165,885	981,200
Lard, lbs.	7,711,018	43,292,249	1,079,543
Tallow, lbs.	2,460,157	2,253,030	226,000
Butter, lbs.	11,682,348	6,493,143	2,920,600
D. Hogs, No.	260,214	171,188	5,984,900
Live Hogs, No.	1,693,158	924,453	42,280,200
Cattle, No.	532,964	391,709	21,282,000
Hides, lbs.	28,539,668	27,245,846	3,426,750
H. Wines, bbls.	165,689	176,508	6,627,560
Wool, lbs.	14,751,089	15,826,536	4,300,400

	Receipts.	Shipments.	Values Receipts.
Potatoes, bu.	665,578	42,091	$500,000
Lumber, M.	1,018,999	583,491	15,285,000
Shingles, M.	652,091	666,248	2,445,340
Lath, M.	103,822	56,077	259,500
Salt, bbls.	674,618	571,013	1,349,300
Flax Seed, lbs. . . .	8,691,000	275,000	271,700
Sheep, No.	349,855	116,711	1,050,000
Cotton, lbs.	411,000	431,000	84,200
Tobacco, lbs.	10,093,516	2,080,304	6,056,100
Lead, lbs.	14,445,623	7,855,471	1,400,000
Horses, No.	3,537	3,488	283,000
Coal, tons, ...	887,474	110,467	7,974,900
Wood, cords, ...	144,578		1,230,000
Lake Fish, brls. . . .	78,253		469,500
Total, ...			$182,743,578

To these we may add the following:

	Value.		Value.
Pig Iron, ...	$900,000	Crockery, etc. . . .	$2,800,000
Iron Ore, ...	14,000,000	Jewelry, etc. . . .	5,250,000
Nails, ...	247,500	Groceries, ...	53,000,000
Carbon Oil, ...	650,000	Musical Instruments, .	2,000,000
Building Stone, etc., .	250,000	Cheese, ...	2,100,000
Cedar Posts, . . .	265,000	Miscellaneous, . . .	79,681,922
Telegraph Poles, . .	647,000		
Boots and Shoes, . .	7,500,000	Grand Total, . . .	$399,835,000
Dry Goods, ...	35,000,000	" in 1869, .	412,550,000
Drugs, Chemicals, etc.,	4,000,000	" in 1868, .	397,552,000
Hardware, ...	5,000,000	" in 1860, .	97,067,617
Metals, etc. . . .	3,200,000	" in 1852, .	20,000,000

These figures show a decrease of $13,000,000, or about three per cent. for 1870 as against 1869. But the difference is not real. Taking into the account the difference in the gold values of our currency in these two years, we have an actual increase in gold values to the amount of fully nine per cent. in the receipts of 1870, as compared with those of 1869.

Corresponding to this was an immense impetus to the wholesale trade of the city, as exhibited in the above items of lumber, groceries, dry goods, hardware, drugs, etc., as compared with those of previous years. The wholesale sales of 1870 footed up a grand total of $402,500,000 against $400,000,000 in 1869, or five-eighths per cent., though prices averaged twelve to fifteen per cent. lower in the latter year, giving an annual increase of fully fifteen per cent. in the quantity of goods sold. The reduction was principally in dry goods, the currency received for which, was some $7,000,000 less in 1870 than in 1869.

The business of 1871 bade fair to foot up a much larger total than that of 1870, when it was so ruthlessly suspended by the fire. The receipts and shipments of grain and other produce up to the 7th of October, were far in excess of those for the same time in any previous year, while the mercantile list showed a much more satisfactory business. For nearly two years previous to 1871, except during a short time near the commencement of the war between France and Prussia, the selling values of nearly all kinds of movable property had steadily declined, and no one cared to carry very large stocks, either in city or country. With the 1st of January, 1871, came a long expected reduction in the duties on many foreign goods, and every one felt that the bottom had been reached in prices. Hence those who bought in Chicago were willing to purchase much larger bills of goods than previously, and the merchants were able to extend their trade farther away by the opening of the Pacific Railroad in May, 1870, and the adoption of the bonded-car system in 1871. By the first, the commerce of a large tract of western country was opened up, and a direct communication established with China and Japan, by which the teas of those countries were laid down on the lake-shore so expeditiously and cheaply as at once to stimulate consumption of an article not spoiled by a long sea journey through the tropics. By the second, Chicago merchants were able to import direct from Europe, saving the heavy charges and vexatious delays to which they had previously been subjected in New York. And besides all this, an independent avenue of trade with Europe was opened up in the summer, giving a much more expeditious and cheaper route for goods, by a line of steamers *via* Montreal.

We estimated the sales of foreign goods in Chicago in 1869 at $79,000,000, and at $84,000,000 in 1870. We have reason to believe that the total would have exceeded $120,000,000 in 1871, had the course of commerce been unimpeded by the great calamity of October, as a great many of the leading merchants had made arrangements to buy regularly in European markets. How much this result will be changed by the events of the fire, can not be estimated at the date of this writing.

The wholesale sales of Chicago would probably have footed up nearly $450,000,000 in 1871, had business proceeded through the remainder of the year on a scale commensurate with that of the first nine months. That total may be reached even yet.

The trade of Chicago had spread all over the Western States and Territories. She dealt largely with California, and supplied largely the wants of the people in the vast area between, from Omaha to Salt Lake. Far out into the South-west Chicago goods found a ready market, much of her merchandise going direct through St. Louis. Down South, and up North, her merchants had accounts spreading all over the country, and even to the eastward, great quantities of goods were sent annually into Indiana and Michigan.

We scarcely need pause here to pay a compliment to the energy and enterprise that wrought out such magnificent results within a few years. That enterprise is known to all the world, and even the rivals of Chicago have conceded it; to their honor be it said, they were the first to proffer liberal aid on receiving the news that Chicago was suffering.

To meet the wants of this vast business, the banking facilities of the city included nineteen National banks, of which three were added during 1871, and two during 1870. The sixteen banks made return on the 28th of December, 1870, of $6,550,000 capital stock; $3,041,359 surplus and other undivided profits; $16,774,514 deposits; and $4,906,424 of circulation outstanding. Adding the eight or nine private banks in the city, with an aggregate capital of $3,000,000, we have in September, 1871, a total bank capital and surplus of about $13,500,000. The clearing-house returns show the following as the business of 1870:

	Clearings.	Balances.
Total, 1870, ...	$810,676,036	$80,910,416
Total, 1869, ...	731,444,111	73,831,000
Increase, ...	$79,231,925	$7,079,416

To accommodate the large grain business of the city there were 17 public warehouses (elevators), with a united storage capacity of 11,580,000 bushels. Besides these there were quite a number of small storehouses, with an average capacity of about 50,000 bushels. These were independent of the storehouses for the keeping of flour, pork products, and other articles of produce.

The number of vessel arrivals in the port of Chicago during 1870 was 12,739, with an aggregate tonnage of 3,049,265 tons.

The number in 1862 was 7417, with 1,931,692 tonnage. The number of vessels owned in Chicago in 1870 was 644, with 94,217 tonnage, being nearly one-seventh of all the tonnage owned on the northern lakes.

The number of arrivals in 1870, from April 1st to December 1st was 12,596, and the clearances 12,358, being an average of over 50 per day, including Sundays. This is greater than the aggregate of New York, Philadelphia, Baltimore, New Orleans, and Mobile, during the same time, though the tonnage of sea-going vessels is much larger than that of our lake marine.

The development of railroad enterprise was equally well marked during the period that elapsed since the war. Only one new line, the Great Eastern—now the Pittsburgh, St. Louis, & Cincinnati—has been added to the list of those entering the city, but the traffic of all has steadily increased, while nearly all have been extended much farther; and in September, 1871, nearly half a dozen new railroad lines were knocking for admission into the busy hive that had swarmed around the southern end of Lake Michigan. The statistics of the produce movement given in the preceding pages, will give some idea of the growth of railroad traffic, because the business of Chicago is principally carried on by rail. But those figures scarcely indicate the full extent of the railroad augmentation, for the simple reason that each succeeding year brings a more strongly marked discrimination in favor of the railroad, as against transportation by canal or lake. The railroad has taken to itself more than two-thirds of the increase of commerce during the past five years.

Chicago is now intimately connected by rail with every part of the continent. Not less than four rival lines contend for the

Eastern traffic, while to the North, West, and South long lines run in every direction into the interior, stretching far away to the water that fixes the limits of the United States. Over all these roads a total of not less than 96 passenger, and 117 freight trains moved *each way* in the spring of 1871, making a total of 426 both ways, or an average of three in every ten minutes through the whole twenty-four hours of each day. The extent to which the building of new lines is progressing is shown in the following table of the work done in the North-western States in 1870, almost every mile of which is tributary to Chicago; the grading noted in the last column is in addition to that required on the lines already covered with the iron rails:

State.	Miles laid.	Miles graded.
Illinois,	1,371½	366
Iowa,	687½	190
Michigan,	623	110
Missouri,	497¾	357¼
Wisconsin,	192	108
Minnesota,	402	211
Nebraska,	365	77½
Kansas,	365	135
Colorado,	297	......
Total,	4,800¾	1,534¾

The total length of all the railroads in the world is only about 120,000 miles, and the total cost not far from ten billions of dollars.

XXIV. MANUFACTURES IN 1870.

CHICAGO had progressed even more rapidly in manufactures than in commerce, a greater proportion of her population being engaged in adding to the value of material by labor than by the mere process of transfer. The books of the Census Commissioner at Washington showed, for 1870:

Number of establishments,	1,149
Hands employed,	20,156
Wages paid,	$10,283,286
Capital employed,	27,948,501
Value of material,	35,973,531
Value of product,	62,736,228

These returns were doubtless accurate enough in many departments, but in others they fall far short. The following statistics of packing in Chicago in 1870 will show the difference between the statements in the census return and the truth:

	Returned.	Actual.
Number of packing establishments,	11	21
Hands employed,	578	2,500
Wages paid,	$204,711	$430,000
Capital,	1,501,000	6,000,000
Material,	5,550,154	9,000,000
Product,	6,475,802	13,000,000

The pork packing of the city for the winter of 1870–71, footed up a total of 918,000 head.

The writer of this prepared the following compilation for the *Chicago Tribune* Annual Review, at the close of 1870, following the census returns except where they were manifestly erroneous, and then made careful canvass for the result given:

Agricultural Implements,	$2,003,000	Lime, ...	$288,332
Baking Powder, . .	151,500	Lumber, ...	800,000
Boots and Shoes, . .	1,500,000	Maltsters, ...	347,320
Brooms, etc., . .	457,856	Nails, ...	245,744
Bridges, . . .	1,000,000	Oils	3,541,733
Breweries (262,035 bbls.),	2,620,350	Paints, ...	508,000
Bricks, ...	750,000	Planing Mills, etc., .	8,928,959
Boilers, ...	259,500	Picture Frames, etc., .	60,000
Books, Printing, etc., .	3,000,000	Patent Medicines, .	218,800
Buildings, . . .	12,000,000	Provisions (and curers),	13,500,000
Bakeries, ...	1,300,000	Paper Collars, . .	160,000
Cabinet-makers, etc., .	1,277,388	Refrigerators, . .	107,500
Carriages and Wagons, .	1,368,982	Rolling Mills and Forges,	2,229,221
Carpets, ...	1,300	Saws, ...	22,850
Car-wheels, and Fixtures,	529,573	Scales, ...	75,000
Cotton, ...	82,000	Shot, ...	210,000
Clothing, ...	1,000,000	Saddles, etc., and Trunks,	388,485
Cooperage, ...	450,000	Soap and Candles, .	334,400
Confectionary, . .	900,000	Ship Carpentry, .	216,000
Distillers and Rectifiers,	6,068,221	Steam Heaters, .	90,000
Flour and Grists, .	2,839,334	Stone Cutting, . .	1,265,375
Foundry and Machine Shops, ...	3,657,933	Telegraph Supplies, . .	6,000
Fire, etc. Safes, . .	110,000	Terra Cotta, . .	122,000
Gas, ...	2,200,000	Tin and Hardware, .	330,000
Gloves, etc., . .	6,000	Tobacco and Cigars, .	1,750,000
Honey, . . .	7,800	Type Foundries, .	25,000
Hats, Caps, etc., . .	400,000	Varnish, ...	445,000
Instruments, Musical, .	350,050	Vinegar, ...	209,100
Lanterns, ...	60,000	Wire Fabrics, . .	8,700
Lead Pipe, etc., . .	588,400	Total, .	$85,310,213
Leather, Tanning, &c., .	2,229,515	Add for Miscellaneous,	3,537,907
Lightning Rods, . .	8,000	Grand total . .	$88,848,120

So in 1868 there were in Cook County 1,034 establishments, turning out a manufactured product valued at $63,110,000.

The United States census report for 1860 gives the following for Cook County: 469 establishments, with a capital of

$5,571,025; employing 5,593 hands; paying $1,992,257 in wages, and turning out an annual product of $13,555,671.

The totals for the city in 1855 were, capital, $6,295,000; hands employed, 8,740; value of products, $11,031,491. The corresponding figures for 1854 were, capital, $4,220,000; hands, 5,000; value of products, $7,870,000.

The increase in the value of manufactures during the past decade is therefore as 100 to 653; or 553 per cent., while the increase of commerce is but 311 per cent., and of population 170 per cent. Even with this tremendous growth, we are justified in saying that the advantages presented by Chicago as a manufacturing point were but just beginning to be realized. Manufactories were springing up all around, promising large additions to the returns of 1870 on business already established, while several new ones were in process of formation—among these were a watch factory, and a cotton factory, both of which were being organized on a large scale. Chicago manufacturers had gained a wide celebrity, which warranted capitalists in expecting a remunerative return for their outlay. Before the Pacific Railroad was built, the Mormons preferred Chicago-made wagons to any other for travel across the mountains. Chicago clocks and watches, agricultural implements, files, boots and shoes, and clothing, have attained a reputation that made ready sales wherever they were offered.

The returned incomes of 1870 aggregated $21,766,837. We estimated the total incomes, acknowledged and unacknowledged, at not less than $74,000,000.

XXV. PROPERTY—REAL ESTATE.

WITH such rapid onward strides in population, commerce, and manufactures, it is no wonder that the value of property largely increased during this period. It could not be otherwise. The growing demands of business necessitated the keeping of larger stocks of goods and the purchase of new locations, while the ever advancing throng of people spread out in all directions, buying real estate for residence purposes, and covering it with buildings, well stocked with material wealth. Very much of the capital attracted thither from other points was invested in real estate, causing a steady demand for the article that kept the market on a continual advance, and enabled hundreds to grow rich by simply turning over the property. The growth of values in different portions of the city, is shown in the following table:

Year.	South.	West.	North.	Total.
1840,	———	———	———	$944,370
1850,	$4,633,726	$1,530,156	$1,056,367	7,222,999
1860,	20,648,083	10,513,887	5,891,542	37,053,512
1865,	40,926,874	14,359,573	9,422,730	64,709,177
1867,	113,773,535	52,073,935	29,179,374	195,026,844
1869,	141,272,926	84,956,000	39,795,969	266,024,880
1871,	148,682,370	96,485,350	43,391,280	288,559,000

Previous to 1866 the assessed valuations were usually made up at about one-fourth of the actual value. In 1866 the ratio was one-third; in 1867 it was supposed that the selling cash value of the property was represented by the assessor's figures. The assessors gradually fell behind, however, till 1871, when it was estimated that the real estate was rated at about sixty per cent. and the personal property at thirty per cent. of its true value. The following should, therefore, be the figures for September, 1871; the improvements are close approximations only:

	Assessed Value.	Cash Value.
South Division, Real,	$82,609,690	$137,683,000
" " Improvement,	28,055,500	46,759,000
" " Personal,	38,017,180	126,723,600
South Division, Total,	$148,682,370	$312,832,600
West Division, Real,	$65,964,930	$109,941,000
" " Improvement,	21,667,000	36,112,000
" " Personal,	8,853,420	29,511,400
West Division, Total,	$96,485,350	$175,564,400
North Division, Real,	$28,357,280	$47,262,000
" " Improvement,	10,234,000	17,057,000
" " Personal,	4,800,000	16,000,000
North Division, Total,	$43,391,280	$80,319,000
Total Land,	$176,931,900	$294,886,000
Total Improvements,	59,956,500	99,928,000
Total Personal,	51,670,600	172,235,000
Grand Total,	$288,559,000	$567,049,000
Add for churches, etc., and city property, not taxed,		$52,951,000
Grand Total Valuation in 1871, about,		$620,000,000

This is very nearly a duplication of values within five years—a result only possible under great activity in the real estate market. The sales of real estate in 1870 alone, footed up $42,000,000, or not far from one-tenth of all the property in the city.

Up to about 1868 the wholesale business of the city was concentrated between the river and Lake Streets. Wabash and Michigan Avenues were exclusively residence thoroughfares, except that the former avenue contained most of the churches in the South Division. Then the wholesale merchants invaded the avenues, amid numerous protests from the residents, and at the time of the fire some of the largest stocks in the city were burned up on the avenues, and on the three northern blocks on State Street. The same year Lasalle Street was improved, and became popular as the home of Insurance Companies and commission merchants, while the banks moved toward that and Washington Street, as the newspapers were gathering on and near Dearborn. Simultaneously with this came a lateral spread as the people found property in the heart of the city was becoming too valuable for residences, while it was also too much exposed to the noise and bustle of the city. Then arose a mania for suburban property, and the railroads were appealed to for more frequent accommodation trains to enable business men to live in the country and enter and leave the city speedily. Laterally, too, the manufacturing interests began to seek suburban locations, and many of them had moved out to the south and south-west portions of the city, near the limits. The great impetus to this spreading out of people and energy, was the grand park system, which was formally legalized by the Legislature in February, 1869, and provided for a series of parks and drives that would make Chicago superior, in this respect, to any other city in the world.

XXVI. THE PARKS.

A PORTION of the Fort Dearborn Addition had been set apart early in the history of the city, as a public park, and was improved by being surrounded with a railing, and provided with a few trees. Subsequently a tract of ground two miles west of the lake, between Lake and Madison Streets, was set off and called Union Park, but was not improved till after the close of the war. It contains seventeen acres, and an addition of more than two acres was in contemplation before the fire, but will not now probably be made, though the order had passed the Common Council. Union Park was brought into good condition by the winter of 1868, at a total cost of about $42,500; it has since been very much improved, and is now one of the finest parks in the country, extent being considered. The sum of $12,813.40 was expended upon it during the year ending April 1, 1871.

In 1866 a tract of eighty acres, lying just north of the old city cemetery, on the lake-shore, was taken hold of by the city, and about $60,000 expended on it to the close of 1868, in which year it was thrown open to the public. It has since then been wonderfully improved, no less than $38,971.61 having been expended on it in the year ending with March, 1871. It was extended by the act of February, 1869, to take in the old city cemetery, north from North Avenue, and to reach northwards a distance of one and a half miles, with a width, from the lake shore westward, of one-quarter of a mile, making a total area of 230 acres. Only the middle portion of this had been improved at the time of the fire; it contained a series of lakes, nearly three miles of fine drives, and a collection of wild animals and birds. The old cemetery had been practically vacated since 1866, but all of the bodies had not been removed, and the improvement of this tract was in progress in September, 1871.

Lake Park is a narrow strip of ground on the lake shore, extending from Randolph Street south to Park Row—about three-quarters of a mile. It was originally a basin of water separated from the lake by the breakwater built by the Illinois Central Company, on which their trains pass to and from the central depot at the foot of Lake Street. During the four years ending with March, 1871, about fourteen acres had been filled in with earth, at a total cost of $50,000, and $18,032.58 was expended in the latter year—a portion in grading. The process of filling in was much more rapid after the fire, an average of not less than 5000 cubic yards of rubbish being dumped in daily in the first month, the material being taken from the ruins left by the fire. It will contain about forty acres when filled.

The other parks in the city previous to 1869, were Washington Park, in the North Division, between Dearborn and Clark, and one mile north of the harbor; it contains two and three-tenths acres. Ellis park, of about three acres, near the Douglas Monument, just east of the site of the old Camp Douglas; Jefferson Park, of five and four-tenths acres, in the West Division, bounded by Monroe, Adams, Rucker, and Loomis Streets; Vernon Park of four acres, and the Wicker Park, of about five acres. The amounts expended by the city in improving these, within the last fiscal year, were; Ellis, $5,593.28; Vernon, $1,627.70; Jefferson, $2,086.63; Dearborn, $131.75; Washington, $14.30; Wicker, $15.75. We ought also to include the Dexter Park—a private enterprise, for racing pur poses, in the south-western part of the city, near the Union Stock Yards.

None of these, however, except Lincoln Park, formed a part of the grand park project authorized in 1869, by three separate Legislative acts, one for each division of the city. Those acts extended the limits to take in a portion of the town of Cicero to the westward, and provided that a part of the town of Jefferson should be included, if the inhabitants should consent—which they did not. This western extension included the West Parks; those of the South Division were to lie outside the city limits, in the towns of Hyde Park and Lake. These acts gave to the city an area of 36 square miles, or a little more than 23,000 acres.

The general features of the park scheme may be thus described: Beginning near the Water-works, on the lake-shore, five-eighths of a mile to the north of the harbor, a drive two hundred feet wide to the north end of Lincoln Park, of 230 acres, already noted; thence westward, a drive or boulevard three and a half miles long, to one mile west of Western Avenue, and meeting Milwaukee Avenue; thence south half a mile, east a quarter, and again southward three-quarters of a mile, the boulevard (called after Humboldt) extends to North Avenue, where it meets Humboldt Park of 193½ acres, lying one and a half miles north and three and a half miles west, from the Court-house. Then the Central Boulevard commences at the south side of Humboldt Park, runs south three-quarters of a mile, then westward three-quarters of a mile, and again southward one eighth of a mile, to Central Park, an irregular tract of land nearly a mile long from north to south, and containing 171$\frac{1}{10}$ acres, the middle line of which lies on Madison Street, 4½ miles from the Court-house. Thence the Douglas Boulevard runs south three-quarters of a mile, and eastward seven-eighths of a mile, to Douglas Park, containing $171\frac{15}{100}$ acres. From this, another boulevard runs south four and a half miles, and east four and a quarter miles (nearly touching the Dexter Park), to the northern of two parks in the South Division.

The whole of the West Division parks and boulevards, except the last named, were all laid out, and graded, and contracts let for the planting of about $30,000 worth of trees, at the date of the fire. Not less than four artesian wells have been sunk, with the most satisfactory results. One in Humboldt Boulevard has a flow of 350,000 gallons per day, from a depth of 730 feet; one in the Central Park flows 450,000 gallons daily, from a depth of 1220 feet; and one in Douglas Park had reached a depth of 780 feet. A considerable amount of draining had also been done. The boulevards are two hundred and fifty feet wide, and will form magnificent drives when completed. The one south of Douglas Park had not been specifically located at the date of the fire.

The South Park system comprises about one thousand and fifty-five acres, and is in a much more forward state than that of the West Division. The Northern or Western Park contains 372 acres, lying between Fifty-first and Sixtieth Streets. From the southern end of this park a broad avenue, some 850 feet wide, runs eastward for one mile, to the eastern division of the park which contains 593 acres, with a frontage of one and six-tenths miles on Lake Michigan. The length of the interior drives of these parks is 14 miles, and of walks 30 miles, besides the one mile of midway drive. A part of the plan is to run a pier out into the lake some 1100 feet, to protect a harbor on the south, which shall connect the lake with a series of meandering lakes in the interior. The whole of the South Park system had been graded and drained at the date of the fire, and much of the roadway made, giving first-class drives. From these parks several improved roads run east and west. A drive along the lake-shore to the old city limits has been graded and graveled, and two broad avenues run northward to the distance of more than a mile each, connecting with the wooden-block pavements of the city streets.

The general park system thus provides fully thirty-three miles of straightforward driving, without counting the length of the roadways round the parks, furnishing an attraction to equestrians and pleasure-seekers in carriages that is unequaled by any city in the world. As breathing places for the masses inside, these parks are probably too far distant to be extensively resorted to for some years to come, except those north and south, but as a real estate speculation on a mammoth scale they were a magnificent success. The prices of real estate in their neighborhood at once rose fully one hundred per cent., and great numbers of buildings were erected all along the lines of the principal boulevards, while numerous settlements, really suburban towns, sprang up in various directions from the central part of the city. The people of Hyde Park, the next township south of Chicago, judiciously coöperated in the work by entering on extensive plans for the improvement of their streets, and effected a radical change in the aspect of the place within three or four years.

These parks were untouched by the fire, except the cemetery portion of Lincoln Park, but their further improvement is necessarily suspended for awhile, except so far as contracts partially carried out at the time of the fire were completed. The park acts gave power to the commissioners to raise money by taxation, which can scarcely be enforced, while they also provided that the moneys arising from the sale of the lake front should also be applied to park purposes. That money will necessarily be placed at the disposal of the city, to aid in the work of rebuilding the public structures destroyed in the Great Conflagration.

XXVII. TAXATION.

THE above-noted enhancement in the values of real estate was accompanied by a marked increase in the amount of taxation. The city authorities had never levied a tax of so much as one per cent. for municipal purposes till 1856, when the rate was $1\frac{1}{10}$—and not until 1863 did it reach 2 per cent. It has never exceeded the latter figure, and was $1\frac{1}{2}$ per cent. in 1870. With this large increase in taxation, the city debt has also steadily augmented, till at the date of the fire it was nearly fourteen and a half millions. The following shows the amount raised for municipal purposes, by taxation, in each year since the war, with the bonded debt at the commencement of that year :

Year.	Taxation.	Bonded Debt.
1850,	$ 25,280	———
1860,	373,050	$ 2,336,000
1865,	1,294,183	3,701,000
1866,	1,719,065	4,369,000
1867,	2,518,472	4,757,500
1868,	3,223,458	6,484,500
1869,	3,990,373	7,882,500
1870,	4,139,798	11,362,726
1871,	Not known	14,103,000

In addition to this the city has paid each year an average of about 40 per cent. of the above in taxes, for State and County purposes, and a Government tax, which amounted to nearly $44,000,000 from the commencement of the war to the close of 1870. The Government taxes of the last year footed up $7,984,198; making a total taxation of thirteen and a half million dollars in 1870, besides assessments for local improvements The revenue collections of 1869 were $7,694,216.

The total amount of special assessments made for street improvements of various kinds, since the creation of the Board of Public Works in 1861, to April 1, 1871, was $10,648,463.44. Of this amount, not less than $2,359,836 was assessed in the last twelve months.

XXVIII. BUILDING AFTER THE WAR.

SUCH immense sums of money as those collected by the city government argue the carrying out of city improvements after the war, on a colossal scale. But the money raised by general taxation was really small in comparison with that raised by assessment on different parts of the city for grading, draining, and paving, and the cash expended in building.

We estimated that about 6,000 buildings were erected in 1864, at a total cost of $4,700,000; these included nine churches, two schools, and four halls and public buildings. In 1865 the number increased to fully 7,000 structures within the year, costing $6,950,000; these included nine churches, eight schools and colleges, and six public buildings and halls. The superior character of the architecture now introduced is apparent from the statement that one of these structures cost more than $300,000: two cost between $200,000 and $300,000; six cost $100,000 to $200,000 each; forty from $30,000 to $100,000 each, and seventy-two others more than $10,000 each.

Hitherto a great deal had been accomplished in the way of erecting fine structures, but little had been done with reference to a *tout ensemble* that should please the correct taste. The streets were heterogeneity in its most intense shape—the structures being as irregular in design and front line as the vertical sections of the sidewalks were a few years previously. But now the rule changed. Parties about to erect structures near each other, for business or residence purposes, began to consult with reference to something like uniformity, and the result was a much better order of things. Meanwhile several buildings were raised to grade, among which we may note the large iron-front block on the corner of Wells and South Water Streets, weighing some thirty thousand tons, that was lifted two and a half feet without disturbing even a spider's web inside.

In 1866 the aggregate number of buildings erected was about 5000—less than in 1865, but more costly, the total outlay being $8,500,000. The number would have been much greater but for the well-remembered strike for a day of eight hours among the building trades, which caused many to abandon their intentions to build. The list included seven churches.

An enumeration made in the spring of 1868 gave a total of 35,654 wooden buildings, and 3712 of brick and stone; total, 39,366. Of these 32,047 were dwelling-houses, 3980 were stores, 1696 saloons, and 1307 were workshops and factories. In this year the new structures numbered fully 7000, including 19 churches, erected at a cost of $14,000 000, which, minus those rebuilt, gave a total of 43,920 in the city at the close of the year. The operations of 1869 involved a total cost of $11,000,000, and those of 1870 about $12,000,000. The number of buildings in this city in September, 1871, was not far from 60,000, or an average of two to every eleven persons on the census roll. The official valuation of buildings and other improvements, gives an average of $1,000 to each building in the city. Our estimate of a 60 per cent. valuation gives $1,667 as the average value of each building in the city.

Among the new structures of this period, we note the Chamber of Commerce (1865) on the south-east corner of Washington and Lasalle, with two fronts of white stone, 93 feet on Washington and 180 feet on Lasalle Street. The Exchange room was 88 by 128 feet on the floor, and 45 feet in height. The cost was $250,000; it was built by a stock company, called the Chamber of Commerce Association, composed exclusively of members of the Board of Trade, to which organization it was rented for $20,000 per annum for ninety-nine years, in addition to which some thirty-six business firms paid rent for offices that netted a handsome profit.

Crosby's Opera-house was completed in the summer of 1865. It stood on the north side of Washington Street, on which was a front of four handsome stores, two on each side of the principal entrance. Behind this was the Opera-house, 90 feet by 150 feet, seating 2500 people. The entire space occupied was 140 feet by 153. The building was in the Italian style of architecture, and beautifully ornamented within and without; it cost $375,000. A fine brick block, 90 by 100 feet, was also built on State Street, at a cost of $75,000, to connect with the Opera-house proper. It contained a music-hall capable of seating 1800 people. The Opera-house was opened April

20, 1865, with a first-class opera company. On the 29th of the following December Mr. Crosby failed, and in the early part of the following year the famous lottery was drawn, by which the Opera-house became the property of a Mr. Lee, who deeded it back to Mr. Crosby on payment of $250,000.

About the same time that the Opera-house was built, McVickers Theater was remodeled throughout. It was afterward entirely rebuilt, in 1871, and formed one of the most superb places of amusement in the world. In 1871 the Opera-house was also remodeled. In 1865 Smith & Nixon's Hall was built just east of the Chamber of Commerce; it was used for amusement purposes, principally concerts, for about three years —then converted into a sale-room for musical instruments, about the same time that Bryan Hall was changed into a carpet store. In the winter of 1870–71 that carpet store gave place to the new and elegant structure known as Hooley's Opera-house. The Dearborn Street Theater was built in 1868.

A much greater number of fine churches was erected since the war than in any equal portion of time previously. Wabash Avenue in the South Division, and Washington Street in the West Division, seemed to have been set apart by tacit consent, some years previously, as church thoroughfares, and new places of worship appeared at almost every block along the more thickly settled portions, while in the North Division, church building was equally rapid, though not concentrated on a single street. And those now erected were all handsome stone structures, costing from $40,000 to $90,000 each, beautifully fitted up inside, and furnished with fine organs; indeed, in the latter respect Chicago was taking the lead of the seaboard cities—many of her church organs having no superiors on the continent.

This period was also known as one of magnificence in school buildings. The old Board of Education was legislated out of office in 1865, and a new Board of School Inspectors provided for, to be chosen by the Common Council—one from each ward in the city. On July 14th of that year there were 17 school districts, with 240 teachers, and an enrollment of 29,080 pupils, or only $76\frac{2}{3}$ per cent. of all the children of school age in the city. The necessity for more school accommodation was so palpable that in 1866 the Common Council placed $80,000 at the disposal of the Board of Education to be employed in the erection of new school-houses, and the State Legislature at its session of 1866–7 authorized the council to issue $500,000 in bonds for the same purpose. Before the close of the next school year the Board had purchased five additional school lots, and erected four frame buildings of eight rooms each, besides commencing the erection of a brick school on the remaining lot, and extending the accommodations of several of the older buildings. But even this large increase was found to be barely keeping pace with the growing requirements of the city, and the Board ordered the construction of additional buildings, most of which were of the costly order, and a great deal of fault was found with the Board for having expended so much money in bricks and stone, and costly heating apparatus, while so many little ones were left out in the cold. Among these were the Dore school, erected in 1867; and the Holden, Carpenter, Hays, and Clark, in 1868, at a cost of $58,000 to $74,000 each. After 1868 the Board was forced to secure less expensive buildings, but with all their efforts they were unable to keep pace with the growing demand for more room. In 1871 the school accommodations were barely equal to fifty per cent. of the number of children of school age in the city.

Educational institutions of a higher order were not forgotten. Prominent among these was the University of Chicago, situated in Cottage Grove, near the old site of Camp Douglas. One wing had previously been erected. In 1865 the main building was nearly completed, at a cost of $150,000; it covers 80 by 120 feet, and is built of rough hewn stone. Immediately to the west of this was erected the Dearborn Observatory (in 1864), at a cost of $30,000. It was supplied with what was then the largest and best refracting telescope in the world, the object glass having a clear aperture of 18½ inches, with a focal length of 23 feet. The big telescope is fitted with circles which enable the observer to measure accurately the position of a star or other object under examination, and is so mounted that it can be turned to any part of the visible heavens by the mere pressure of a finger; it is provided with clock work to carry it round at the same rate as the stars appear to move, so that when once pointed on an object, the observer can watch the same point for an hour together without the trouble of changing the position of the instrument. The Observatory was also furnished, in 1868, with a meridian circle, having a transit telescope of six French inches aperture. With this was undertaken the important work (by Prof. Safford), in conjunction with astronomers in a few other observatories, of recataloguing all the stars in the heavens down to the ninth magnitude inclusive.

In 1865 the Chicago Academy of Sciences (established in 1857) issued life memberships at $500 each, for the purpose of raising funds wherewith to erect a suitable building for their collections. Pending the completion of the new edifice, at No. 263 Wabash Avenue, near Van Buren Street, the collections of the Academy were removed to Metropolitan Block, which was burned in 1866, destroying over 18,000 specimens.

The new building, 55 by 50 feet, two stories high, was completed the next year at a cost of $46,000, and was thought to be perfectly *fire-proof*. The Chicago Historical Society erected another *fire-proof* building, in 1868, on the corner of Dearborn and Ontario Streets, at a cost of $35,000, as a part of a structure that should cost $200,000 when completed. In 1866, the old Metropolitan Block, on the corner of Randolph and Lasalle Streets, was remodeled for occupancy by the Young Men's Library Association.

Up to this time the buildings of the Academy of Sciences and of the Historical Society, were the only fire-proof structures in the city, except the Custom-house and Post-office—erected in 1859–60. Next in order was the *Tribune* building, on the corner of Madison and Dearborn Streets, and following that was the First National Bank building, on the corner of State and Washington Streets. Two or three others were subsequently erected, prominent among which was the Bryan Safe Depository building, on Randolph Street, just west of the Sherman House. Not one of these noble piles escaped, though money had been lavished in the attempt to make them secure from the visitations of the fire-fiend. In an ordinary conflagration they might have stood unharmed; but when the whole city was burning, the material of which they were composed fairly melted amid the intense heat of the surrounding structures.

A great number of hotels were erected during this period—so many that we can scarcely enumerate them. In the South Division the Palmer House, the Ogden Hotel, the Pacific Hotel, Michigan Avenue Hotel, the Bigelow, the Nevada, and several other minor ones, were all competing, or about to compete, with each other, and with the hotels already in existence at the close of the war; while in the North and West Divisions other structures were springing up, with the same intent, though not so prominent as those first mentioned. Indeed, the whole city was bristling with hotel structures, and not a few of them were unoccupied. Those in the West Division, that previous to the fire were void of tenants, have since been well filled, as the proprietors of the new Sherman and Briggs Houses can testify.

The principal building enterprises of the city during the after-war period, were the two tunnels under the river, the Water-works, the extension of the Court-house, and the new Bridewell.

As early as 1855 a company was formed, with W. B. Ogden as president, for the purpose of securing a system of tunnels under the river, but the financial depressions of succeeding years prevented the scheme from being carried out. Eleven years later it was found that though there was a bridge at an average interval of two blocks all along the river, in the more thickly settled portions of the city, with several others beyond, they were totally inadequate to meet the demand for travel, as the growth of the city was commensurate with a growth of its lake commerce which necessitated a more frequent opening of the bridges—not less than seven of which were built in 1868. Then it was decided to build a tunnel under the river at Washington Street, which was thrown open to the public for travel on the 1st of January, 1869. The tunnel cost about $400,000, and involved the excavation of 44,000 cubic yards of clay, and the laying of 10,000 cubic yards of stone masonry, besides 6000 yards of brick work, and 5000 yards of concrete. The roadway for carriages commences at Clinton and Franklin Streets, and is open for a distance of one block on each side of the river, the excavation being protected by iron railings set on heavy stone copings. From Market to Canal Streets the roadway is arched over for a distance of 983 feet, being divided into two passage ways, each 11 feet wide and 15 feet high. The underside of the crown of the arches is 2½ feet below the bed of the river, which has 14½ feet depth of water at that point, and is 200 feet wide. The total descent of the tunnel is about 26 feet. The total length of the tunnel is 536 yards. On the southern side of this tunnel is a separate passage for pedestrians, reached by a winding stairway on Market and Canal Streets. This tunnel proved so great a success that another was built in 1870 at Lasalle Street, to connect the North and South Divisions. It was opened but three months before the fire. The plan is somewhat similar to that of the first-named tunnel, but it contains many improvements. The cost is $549,000. The total length, including approaches, is 630 yards.

The Court-house square is the property of the County of Cook, and what was called the City Hall belonged to the city and county, the former owning eight parts in twenty-one of the building, which was erected in 1853, and enlarged in 1857. Ten years afterward a plan was agreed upon which provided for the erection of two fire-proof wings, each 80 feet wide and 130 feet long—three stories high. The west wing, owned by the city, contained the offices of the Mayor, Board of Police, Board of Public Works, Fire Marshal, fire alarm telegraph, and Council Chamber, etc. The east or county wing contained a jail in the basement, and above that the court rooms for the different judges of the county, the county records, the law library, etc. The original design was that the city wing should cost $250,000, and the county wing $200,000, but owing to insecure foundations, and buckling roof, and other etceteras of city contracting, the structures cost a great deal more than the sums above named. The cost of the city wing, to March 31, 1871, was $467,000. It was intended at some future time to take down the central portion and rebuild it 265 feet high, in harmony with the wings, with balconies outside to serve the needs of public speakers. But this part of the programme was not carried out. In the spring of 1871 a fine tower clock was placed in the dome, by the Astronomical Society, the funds having been raised by private subscription obtained by Mr. E. Colbert, principally from members of the Board of Trade. The correct time was furnished to the city, through this clock, from the Dearborn Observatory.

The new city Bridewell was opened in the early part of 1871. It is a fine brick structure, costing $304,637, located on the west bank of the south branch of the river, about half a mile west of Western Avenue. Only a portion of the building is finished, the remaining part being intended to be erected by prison labor. The plan includes a main building 448 feet long, the central portion 48 by 60 feet, and two stories high, surmounted by a tower 50 feet high. This serves as offices and rooms for the officers of the Bridewell, and their families. The right wing contains four tiers of stone cells for 288 male prisoners; the left wing is similar, divided into 200 cells for female prisoners. The portions to be subsequently constructed by the prisoners, were workshops, etc., running back at right angles from the main building, and inclosing two areas. Owing to a division of opinion between the Mayor and Common Council, the Bridewell commissioners were only appointed just before the fire, and no superintendent had been secured at the date of the conflagration.

The other important public building of this period, was the new water tower, the corner-stone of which was laid March 25, 1867. It is situated about half a block west of the old pumping works, on the east end of Chicago Avenue, and consists essentially of an iron column, three feet in internal diameter, and 130 feet high, up which the water is forced by powerful pumps, and thence flows by its own weight into the water-pipes and hydrants of the city. The column is surrounded by a spiral stairway, inside a stone tower, which stands on a fine stone base of twenty-four feet square. Adjacent to the water tower were erected buildings to contain the four pumping engines, with an aggregate pumping capacity of 71,000,000 gallons daily. The last engine was placed in 1871, and has a daily capacity of 36,000,000 gallons. These pumps are supplied from the celebrated lake tunnel, which is of sufficient importance to be briefly described in a separate chapter.

XXIX. THE LAKE TUNNEL.

THE tunnel under the lake, which has so often been cited as a proof of marvelous engineering skill, is a "great bore," which runs out from the lake-shore, starting about one mile north of the Court-house, and bears out under the lake a distance of two miles, in a direction of some two points to the north of east. At the shore end a shaft nine feet in diameter is sunk to a depth of about seventy-five feet. The shore being a shifting quicksand, to a depth of twenty-six feet, it was found necessary to sink a huge iron cylinder through it for that distance, within which the sand was scooped out till clay was reached, after which the regular excavation was made, and the whole bricked up from the bottom. The first ground was broken on the 17th of March, 1864, in the presence of the Mayor, the Board of Public Works, the projector of the tunnel —E. S. Chesborough, Esq., and numerous other city officials. Then the excavation for the tunnel was commenced, seventy feet below water level. Meanwhile a giant crib was being constructed to be sunk at the east end of the tunnel, and was towed out and sunk on the 25th of July, 1865, in the presence of Governor Oglesby and a large concourse of people.

The crib is forty and a half feet high, and built in pentagonal form, in a circumscribing circle of ninety-eight and a half feet in diameter. It is built of logs one foot square, and consists of three walls, at a distance of eleven feet from each other, leaving a central pentagonal space having an inscribed circle of twenty-five feet, within which is fixed the iron cylinder, nine feet in diameter, running from the water line to the tunnel, sixty-four feet below the surface, and thirty-one feet below the bed of the lake at that point. The crib is thoroughly braced in every direction. It contains 750,000 feet of lumber, board measure, and 150 tons iron bolts. It is filled with 4500 tons of stone, and weighs 5700 tons. The crib stands twelve feet above the water line, giving a maximum area of 1200 feet which can be exposed at one sweep to the action of the waves, reckoning the resistance as perpendicular. The outside was thoroughly caulked, equal to a first-class vessel, with three threads in each seam, the first and last being what is called "horsed." Over all these there is a layer of lagging to keep the caulking in place and protect the crib proper from the action of the waves. A covered platform or house was built over the crib, enabling the workmen to prosecute the work uninterrupted by rain or wind, and affording a protection for the earth brought up from the excavation, and permitting it to be carried away by scows, whose return cargoes were bricks for the lining of the tunnel. The top of the cylinder was subsequently covered with a grating to keep out floating logs, fish, etc. A sluice made in the side of the crib was opened to let in the water, and a light-house was intended to be built over all, serving the double purpose of guarding the crib from injury by vessels and of showing the way to the harbor of Chicago.

Down the iron cylinder, inside this crib, the workmen descended, and began the work of excavating toward the shore. They laid their first brick on the 22d of December, 1865, and in twelve months more the two sets of workmen met beneath the waves, the last brick (which was a stone) being laid by Mayor Rice on the 6th of December, 1866.

The inside width of the tunnel is five feet, and the inside height five feet and two inches, the top and bottom arches being semicircles. It is lined with brick masonry eight inches thick, in two rings or shells, the bricks being laid lengthwise of the tunnel, with toothing joints. The bottom of the inside surface of the bore at the east end is sixty-six feet below water level, or sixty-four feet below city datum, and has a gradual slope toward the shore of two feet per mile, falling four feet in the whole distance, to admit of it being thoroughly emptied in case of repairs, the water being shut off at the crib by means of a gate. The lower half of the bore is constructed in such a manner that the bricks lie against the clay, while in the upper half the bricks are wedged in between the brick and the clay, thus preventing any danger which might result from the tremendous pressure which, it was feared, might burst out the tunnel.

From this tunnel, water was first supplied to the hydrants of the city, March 25th, 1867, and from that time forward the people of Chicago had a bountiful supply of the best water in the world, always clear, as being taken from a point in the lake too far removed from the shore to admit of fouling from the city sewerage, or the washings of the land surface in a storm.

The tunnel will deliver under a head of two feet, 19,000,000 gallons of water daily; under a head of eight feet, 38,000,000 gallons daily, and under a head of eighteen feet, 57,000,000 gallons daily. The velocities for the above quantities will be one and four-tenths miles per hour, head being two feet; head being eight feet, the velocity will be two and three-tenths miles per hour; and the head being eighteen feet the velocity will be four and two-tenths miles per hour. By these means it will be competent to supply one million people with fifty-seven gallons each per day, with a head of eighteen feet.

Yet with this enormous capacity the full working limits of the tunnel bade fair to be occasionally reached in 1875. On one day in 1870 it supplied 28,750,000 gallons, the average for the year being about 22,000,000 gallons daily—added to this was the difficulty of forcing the water through the immense length of water pipe laid in the city. In 1870 it was decided to construct another tunnel of seven feet diameter, having double the capacity of the former one, and to carry it to some point in the south-western part of the city for an independent supply. Owing to a quarrel in the Council, relative to an alleged attempt to swindle the city in the purchase of a location for the new pumping works, the contract had not been signed at the date of the conflagration. The second tunnel will probably not be constructed for some years to come.

The total amount of water pipe laid during the twelve months ending with March 31, 1871, was:

North Division, ...	42,628 feet.
South "	56,656 "
West "	81,443 "
Total, ...	180,727 feet.

Or 34¼ miles, being 2½ miles more than laid in any previous year. This includes a large amount of two-feet pipe, which nearly completed a circuit of thirteen miles around the city, supplying the smaller mains.

The total amount of miles of water pipe in the city is 272½. The total in 1862 was 105 miles; at the close of 1868 it was 195 miles.

Of fire hydrants, there were erected during the year 63 in the North, 74 in the South, and 121 in the West Divisions. Total, 258; making a total of 1552 in the city to date. The number of water meters in use was 657.

The cost of the additions to water-works during the year was $602,491.20; total from the beginning $4,279,896.

The total length of water pipe laid in the city to date, in feet, was, 30 inch, 280; 28 inch, 160; 24 inch, 57,576; 16 inch, 31,340; 12 inch, 34,281; 10 inch, 7862; 8 inch, 161,489; 6 inch, 510,701; 4 inch, 607,048; 3 inch, 27,816. Total, 1,438,553 feet, or 272½ miles, of which 34.2 miles were laid in the past twelve months.

XXX. OTHER PUBLIC IMPROVEMENTS.

SINCE the war the city had rebuilt several of the bridges over the river, introducing important improvements in their construction. In September, 1871, there were not less than twenty-seven city bridges, erected at a cost of $20,000 to $48,000 each. In addition to these there were six railroad bridges. On the 31st of March, 1871, an account was taken of the travel over the city bridges. The reckoning aggregated 246,015 pedestrians and 45,306 vehicles on that day. The number passing through the Washington Street tunnel on the same day, was 7231 pedestrians and 1616 vehicles.

The sewerage system comprises 151½ miles of street sewers, besides drains to houses, etc., all laid since 1856. Of this about 15 miles were added in 1870–1. The number of private drains is 24,990; number of catch-basins, 4529. Total cost of construction to date (besides private drains), $2,872,488. There were only 75 miles of sewerage in 1865—the amount having been more than doubled since the war.

In 1865 the city had 2500 lamp-posts. On the 31st of March, 1871, the number had grown to 6555, of which 1468 were in the North Division, 1963 in the South, and 3124 in the West Division.

Previous to 1865, only about two and a half lineal miles of streets had been paved with wooden blocks. In the beginning of 1871, no less than fifty-seven miles had been paved with wooden blocks, of which nineteen and a half miles were laid the previous year. About three-fourths of the entire travel of the city was done on the improved streets. The following shows the number of lineal feet of each kind of pavement in each division, in April, 1871, with the total in miles for the whole city:

	North. Feet.	South. Feet.	West. Feet.	Total. Miles.
Wooden-block, ...	66,195	105,385	129,533	57.02
Boulders, ...	1,250	19,900	———	3.77
McAdam, ...	14,950	22,040	27,560	12.23
Gravel, ...	8,150	43,610	———	9.80
Cinders, ...	9,975	9,920	6,020	4.90
Curbing, ...	155,890	247,638	338,937	140.60
Total miles streets improved, ...				87.72
" " " unimproved, ...				446.27
Total streets in Chicago, miles, ...				534.

There were 561 miles of sidewalks in the city, mostly of pine planking. The quantity laid up to the spring of 1854, was 159 miles.

Next in importance to the lake tunnel, for the supply of pure water, was the work of deepening the Illinois and Michigan canal, undertaken by the city as a sanitary measure, that being the only feasible plan proposed for keeping the river pure. That bayou had gradually become so foul from the drainage of packing-houses, distilleries, gas-works, etc., with the general sewerage of the city, that it had become an annoyance to the people of Chicago, and a standing joke in other cities. The huge pumping works at Bridgeport, established for the purpose of feeding the upper level of the canal, had been used to clean out the river occasionally, but the remedy was only spasmodic, and the nuisance was soon worse than before. An act was passed February 16, 1865, by which it was provided that the city of Chicago might enter into an arrangement with the

Board of Canal Trustees with a view to complete the summit level of the canal on the original deep-cut plan, with such modifications in the line as would most effectually secure the cleansing of the river. The city received authority to issue bonds to the amount required, and it was provided that the cost of deepening should be a vested lien upon the canal and its revenues, provided the total cost did not exceed $2,500,000.

Under this guarantee the Common Council appointed a board of commissioners, and the money was raised. The work was begun in February, 1866, and finished July 15, 1870, at a total cost of about $3,251,621, the amount expended to April 1, 1871, exclusive of interest, being $2,982,437.

The length of the section of canal cut down during this work was twenty-six miles. The bottom of this section is now eight and a half feet below the ordinary water level of lake Michigan, and six feet lower than the city datum, which was fixed by the low-water mark of 1847. The bed of the canal has an inclination downward from Chicago of one-tenth of a foot per mile, which gives a current of about one mile per hour. The width of the bottom is forty-four to forty-eight feet, the slope of the banks is one and a half to one in the earth excavation, and one to one in the rock excavation, below the water line.

XXXI. COMMERCIAL IMPROVEMENTS.

THE needs of commerce demanded large extensions after the war. The harbor accommodations had long been too limited. The process of dredging and docking the river had gone forward rapidly, there being, in 1871, nearly fourteen miles of wharves, built at an average cost of $100,000 per mile; these included several slips, the largest being those of the South Chicago Dock Company, in the West Division, opposite Bridgeport. But much further extension in this direction was found to be impossible, as the number of vessels became so great that jams were frequent, and collisions unavoidable, in passing up and down the river. To obviate this it was proposed to form an outer harbor, inclosing large tracts of wharfage property on the lake-shore, north and south.

The first effort in this direction was made by the North Chicago Dock Company, of which Wm. B. Ogden was President. They commenced in 1863 to put down a line of piling north of the harbor, but it was swept away by the waves, and the work was abandoned till 1867, when it was again proceeded with, though slowly. The plan comprises a breakwater 500 feet long, built northward from the eastern extension of the north pier. From the northern extremity of this breakwater another will run eastward, a distance of 1500 feet, to the shore. An area extending 390 feet north from the pier, and west to the shore of the lake, will be filled in, and through the center of this made land will run a street from the main shore to the eastern channel. The block thus created will be divided into lots for dockage purposes. On the north side of this made land there will be a channel, 110 feet wide, penetrating Michigan Street as far as Sand Street. The water in the basin will be twenty-two feet, and the largest vessels will easily float in the canal. The two will give as much wharfage as is now afforded by both sides of the river, as far as the confluence of the two branches. It is believed that the extension, when completed, will obviate the difficulties heretofore caused by the exposure of the harbor mouth to the lake current, which now brings immense quantities of sand every year from the north-east, and has formed a bar through which a passage could only be kept open by constant dredging. The entrance to these docks will be through a gap in the pier near the light-house. When the north line of this work is filled up with sand, the breakwater will be extended still farther north, the enterprise contemplating the covering of the north shore as far as Chicago Avenue.

Another dock extension was begun in 1870, under the charge of Colonel D. C. Houston, United States Engineers. An appropriation of $100,000 had previously been made by Congress, most of which was expended in 1870. A breakwater, 900 feet long, is built eastwardly from the south pier, extending out into the lake as far as the north pier, leaving a passage of 500 feet between them for entrance to the harbor. From the eastern end of this breakwater another line of 2000 feet in length runs southward, which will be extended to 4000 feet, connecting with another line running 3400 feet westward to the present breakwater of the Illinois Central Railroad. This plan gives a basin of 275 acres, a portion of which is already twelve feet deep; it will be reached by an opening of 600 feet wide in the northern side. A further extension of these docks to the southward may be made by private or municipal enterprise almost to an indefinite extent, should the future commerce of the city require it.

Several other harbor improvements were in progress; prominent among which was the dock system, begun in 1871, by Hon. J. Y. Scammon, on the 1500 feet of lake front belonging to the Douglas estate, near Cottage Grove. He had purchased the right of the Douglas heirs to this property for $25,000, and had already built out several piers 120 feet long, into the lake, which had caught large quantities of sand from the north-east current.

Besides the docks outside the Chicago harbor, the greatest improvement was at the Calumet harbor, seven miles south of the city limits, and two and a half miles beyond the south park. Work was commenced there in September, 1870, under the charge of Colonel Houston, Congress having appropriated $50,000 for the construction of piers and the improvement of the channel of what is known as the Calumet River. Two piers are constructed; the north pier will be 1400 feet long, of which 730 feet are already completed; the south pier is built out to a distance of 430 feet. The bar at the mouth of the harbor has been dredged out to a depth of nine or ten feet. The total cost of the Government improvements projected is about $300,000, which it is believed will give a harbor fit to receive vessels of a heavy tonnage.

Outside the Government work, the Calumet and Chicago Canal and Dock Company had in hand a grand scheme of improvements in the summer of 1871. They own about 6000 acres of land in that vicinity, and had established coal and lumber works there, were building a hotel, and had begun the construction of some ten miles of dockage, of which one and a nalf miles was under way. Several factories are located there, and it is highly probable that Calumet will ere long be a prosperous city of itself, though the ambition of its founders be not realized. They shared in the belief, expressed by some people in farther distant places, that it will be possible to isolate Chicago from the commerce of the future.

Previous to 1865 the business of buying and selling live stock had been carried on simultaneously at several yards, at great disadvantage to both buyers and sellers. Very frequently it was the case, that the market for cattle or hogs was quite active at one yard, while at the others it was fearfully dull. Sometimes the receipts at one yard would almost equal the combined receipts of all the others, thus rendering trade brisk at the latter, and lifeless at the former; while the commercial reporters from the various papers had great difficulty from these causes in making up an accurate summary of the daily market. But the trade finally attained to such proportions that it was found necessary to consolidate it at one point, which could be reached by all the railroads running east and west. The issuing of the prospectus was followed by an almost immediate subscription of the stock of one million dollars, of which $925,000 was subscribed by nine railroad companies. On the 1st of June, 1865, ground was broken on the present site on Halstead Street, near the city limits south, and the work was rapidly pushed forward to completion, while the Hough House adjacent was erected as the head-quarters, and a bank was opened for the accommodation of those engaged in the trade.

The following is a summary of items: Opened for business, December 25, 1865; area of ground, 345 acres; number of acres in pens, 100; acres used for hotel and other buildings, 45; present capacity, 21,000 head of cattle, 75,000 hogs, 22,000 sheep, 200 horses; total, 118,200. There are in yards 31 miles of drainage, 7 miles of streets and alleys, 3 miles of water troughs, 10 miles of feed troughs, 2300 gates, 1500 open pens,

800 covered pens. 22,000,000 feet of lumber were used in the construction, at a total cost of $1,675,000. The water is supplied by an artesian well about 1100 feet deep.

XXXII. CHICAGO IN 1871.

WE have thus brought down the history of the city to the year 1871, just forty years after the organization of Cook County. It will be well to group briefly some of the leading facts of her condition just previous to the fire, that the reader may gain a clearer idea of the magnitude of the city that the fire fiend sought to destroy.

The following is a statement of the population, area, number of buildings, and value of property in the city, by divisions:

Divisions.	Population.	Area, acres.	Buildings.	Value property.
North,	77,758	2,533	13,800	$89,000,000
South,	91,417	5,363	16,300	340,000,000
West,	165,095	15,104	29,400	191,000,000
Total,	334,270	30,000	59,500	$620,000,000

The last column includes property not assessed for taxation.

The following were the numbers of the churches belonging to the different denominations:

Baptist—20 churches, 8 missions.

Christian—4 societies, 2 churches.

Congregationalist—13 churches, 2 missions.

Episcopal—15 churches, 4 missions.

Evangelical—17 churches.

Independent—1 church, 5 missions.

Jewish—5 synagogues.

Lutheran—6 churches, 1 mission.

Methodist Episcopal—21 churches.

Presbyterian—19 churches, 8 missions.

Roman Catholic—25 churches, 12 convents and schools.

Swedenborgian—2 churches, 2 missions.

Unitarian—3 churches and one other society.

Universalist—3 churches and a fourth society.

Friends—2 societies.

Miscellaneous—4 churches.

Total, 156 church structures, and 36 missions or societies not owning church structures; besides the 12 Catholic convents and schools.

The total attendance on these churches was 150,000 people; number of Sabbath-school scholars, 57,000. The value of the church property, including lands, was $10,350,000, or an average of $69.00 to each attendant.

The city owned forty school lots, having a total value of $1,086,735, on which 41 buildings were erected, and 11 buildings on lots not owned by the city; other buildings were rented. The total value of school buildings, including furniture and heating apparatus, was $1,199,906. Total of buildings and grounds, $2,286,641. Of these, one, the High School, was of stone; 27 of brick, and 22 of wood, most of the latter being branch schools. The contracts were also let, at the time of the fire, for 3 other brick buildings, each three stories in height. Of the above cited buildings, 34 were erected since 1860; and 8 in the school year ending June 30, 1871, giving 5639 additional seats.

The following are the principal educational statistics for the same year:

Schools (1 High; 23 Grammar; 15 Primary), ...	39
Teachers in High School (males 10, females 13), ...	23
Total Teachers in Schools (males 33, females 539), . .	572
Pupils enrolled in High School, ...	675
" other Schools (boys 20,395, girls 19,762),	40,832
School Census preceding year, ...	80,280
Average number belonging, ...	28,174
Average daily attendance, ...	27,023
Salaries of Teachers, ...	$444,635
Total expenditures of year, ...	596,388
Cost per Pupil for Tuition, on average attendance, . .	16.45
Total Cost per Scholar, " " " . .	25.54

Receipts from School-tax Fund, ...	$366,025
" " State Fund, ...	41,758
" " Rents and Interest, ...	69,299
Total received in year, ...	$477,082

The amount of tax *levied* in the year was really but $436,008.36 (1.58 mills), on a valuation of $275,986,550.

The real estate within the city limits, belonging to the School

Fund, was appraised at	$2,445,032
Do. outside city limits, ...	132,641
Money loaned, Principal of School Fund, .	128,940
Wharfing lot fund, ...	68,062
Total School Fund, ...	$2,774,675

The commercial status of the city, given statistically in preceding chapters, may be best understood by a glance at its railroad connections. Chicago is situated at the focus of a vast network of railroads, which have, to a large extent, supplanted the water routes of freight traffic for all but the bulkiest lines of goods. Building-stone and brick still enter the city by the Illinois and Michigan Canal, and a part of the lumber shipped to the interior has followed the same route, but the receipts of grain by canal in 1870 and 1871 were very small, while those per rail were limited only by the carrying capacities of the railroads; they averaged over 1200 car loads per day, or 12,000 tons, through a great portion of the summer of 1871. The lake held its own much better for the shipment of grain East, but the railroads leading to the seaboard were rapidly growing in favor as shipping lines for grain, especially in winter, and it was in contemplation to build a railroad through to New York, to be used exclusively for freight purposes—a project which was only kept back by the fact that the carriers on the lake were willing to guarantee weights of grain, which the railroads would not. The *receipts* by lake had dwindled down to a very small point, till the opening up of the Montreal route in the spring of 1871, by which large quantities of goods were imported direct from Europe.

The iron rail was the bond of union that connected Chicago with the world around. She lay on the great rail highway of travel around the globe, and the wealth of nations was poured into her lap by the long trains that followed the iron horse in his laborious puffings over the vast network of rail that owned Chicago as a center. We will make brief mention of the chief avenues of traffic with the world around her.

Hugging the lake-shore in its trend almost due north, is the Chicago & Milwaukee Railroad, connecting at the latter city with lines running into the interior of Wisconsin, and opening up valuable trade with its most important towns. The original North-western Railroad trends a little farther away to the west, striking directly into the heart of Wisconsin, and running direct to the Green Bay and Lake Superior regions, whose mineral wealth is only just beginning to be appreciated. Running almost due west is the Iowa Division of the North-western Road—formerly the Galena, the first to be constructed, and the first to make connection with the Great Pacific Railroad, by which this line connects with the mineral riches of the mountain territories, the vast Pacific slope, and the Asiatic continent beyond. Next in order is the Rock Island & Pacific Railroad, bearing away a little to the southward, crossing the Mississippi at Rock Island, and thence spanning the State of Iowa, through its most fertile portions to the "Mighty Missouri" at Council Bluffs, where it enters the Pacific trail as a competitor with the North-western. Bearing nearly south-west is the Burlington & Quincy, which crosses the Mississippi at two points, both of which are on the line of travel to the Pacific shore—the more southerly bearing across North Missouri to Kansas, where the Hannibal & St. Joseph is met by lines to Denver and those stretching out toward the rich Indian Territory and Texas. Still farther southward runs the line to St. Louis direct, connecting there with roads into the interior of Missouri, and the vast region beyond. And last in the line of feeders comes the mammoth Illinois Central, with its sixteen hundred miles of roadway and connections, bringing the city into intimate relations with the whole valley of the Mississippi, as far down as New Orleans, and the Gulf of Mexico, with the rich lands on the Southern Red River region. These lines, radiating from Chicago like the spokes of a wheel from its hub, were interlaced at short intervals by other lines, all of which formed rich feeders to those main arteries along which flowed the life blood that kept the pulse of Chicago beating healthfully, while two other roads were already organized, and several more talked of, to enter Chicago from the country westward of her meridian. All these formed the avenues of her western trade; along them was poured in a daily stream, of scarcely conceivable magnitude, the rich produce of the North-west into her lap, and the same trains carried back with them a return commerce that was of almost equally inconceivable proportions. Figures can hardly convey an idea of the extent of a trade to which that of Tyre in her palmiest days was a mere foreshadowing, any more than a statement of distance can enable the mind to grasp the distance that separates us from the fixed stars.

To the eastward there are four competing roads, the Pittsburgh, Cincinnati & St. Louis—first mentioned, though last in the order of time. Next, the Pittsburgh & Fort Wayne; then, running due east, the Lake-Shore route, formerly the Michigan Southern, and lastly, dipping a little to the north, the Michigan Central. Besides these, a fifth road, the Grand Trunk extension, is nearly finished, running through South Bend, Indiana, to Port Huron. These roads not only opened up a sea-board connection with the ports of Baltimore, Philadelphia, New York, Boston, Portland, and Quebec, and thence with Europe, but they furnished a means of reaching the Eastern States through numerous ramifications. How important to Chicago is the last named feature, may be judged from the fact that of the grain exports of the Garden City in 1870, not more than five per cent. of the corn, and not twenty per cent. of the wheat was sent across the Atlantic. The rest went to supply the needs of the dwellers on the Atlantic slope, and in return those roads brought back the products of the Eastern States, which, though laden with heavy protective duties, were still welcome to the people of Chicago and the wide expanse of country beyond.

The Board of Trade had a membership of 1224 in September, 1871; J. F. Preston, President, and Charles Randolph, Secretary.

The railroad system thus established the city as the commercial focus of the North-west. Her position at the head of the great chain of lakes attracted hither the commerce of the continent—East as well as West—as the neck of an hour-glass is the channel through which flows all the sand collected in the bulb above. The railroad was instituted as the competitor of the water route only when it was seen that the process would pay, and let it be remembered that this grand competition was instituted by outside capital. The city of Chicago never invested a dollar in railroad stocks, and the merchants did very little in that direction. Hence, the complaints of other cities, that Chicago was reaching round them in the matter of railroads, were unfounded. The capitalists of the East would have been just as willing to spend money in the construction of roads elsewhere if there had been an equally good prospect of profit. They united to build railroads running to Chicago from every direction, simply because they saw it would pay to do it, and the sagacity of the merchants of the Garden City has amply demonstrated the wisdom of their choice in the past, whatever it may do in the future.

And the proportion of home manufactures, in the immense annual aggregate of over four hundred million dollars worth of sales at first hand, was rapidly increasing. In 1871 it had attained to very nearly one-fourth part of the entire amount, and manufactories were springing up on every hand, in plentiful number, to change that fraction nearer and nearer toward unity.

With such an important position in the world at large, Chicago, in 1871, could not be other than a great and powerful city, her wealth filling capacious warehouses and stores, lining scores of miles of streets, her merchants and manufacturers princes in the land, residing in palaces that found few equals in the old world, and surrounded by every luxury that genius could invent or art supply. The following will give a general idea of the distribution of activity and population in the city:

A reference to the map shows that Chicago is divided by the river and its branches into three parts, designated the South, North, and West.

A strip of land all along the lake shore, from a quarter to three-eighths of a mile wide, and eleven miles long, included the more aristocratic residence portions of the city and its outlying suburbs—Lakeview and Hyde Park. Nearly the whole of this immense section was covered with the most costly buildings. That part of it in the North Division, which extends one mile from the harbor, was originally the most exclusive portion, being largely held by the oldest residents or their families. Then Michigan Avenue, lying near the lake-shore in the South Division, began to compete with it, and was soon filled up with princely structures of marble, that vied, both in architectural beauty and internal adornment, with the most ornate edifices of Europe. Then Wabash Avenue, next to the westward, with the cross-streets and "courts," was filled up by the wealthier classes, the line of improvements gradually spreading southward, and covering the avenues that run in to the east of Michigan as the lake recedes from that thoroughfare in the southern part of the city. For a distance of about a mile and a half south from the harbor, the lake is girt by the iron rails along which passed the traffic of three important lines to the great Central Depot at the foot of Lake Street.

The South Division, from the river south to Harrison Street, was pre-eminently the business portion of the city, and latterly the march of commerce had invaded the two principal avenues with tall piles of wholesale stores, and driving the inhabitants farther southward. In this section were situated all the banks of the city except two, all the principal hotels, and all the theaters, etc., except the sorry institution called the "Globe," as well as all the leading wholesale establishments in every branch of trade, and many large manufactories, principally of clothing and boots and shoes. The total value of the real estate, building improvements, and merchandise, in this tract of about three-quarters of a square mile in area, was not much less than one-third of the total value of real and personal property within the thirty-six square miles bounded by the city limits.

Along the river and its branches were ranged lumber-yards, containing some three hundred million feet of lumber, with proportionate quantities of lath and shingles; docks on which were piled one hundred and sixty tons of coal, and immense quantities of cord wood; seventeen elevators were dotted along the banks, containing six and a half million bushels of grain, being loaded to fully three-fourths of their working capacity at the time of the fire; immense depots filled with flour, pork, meats, and other produce, and several flouring mills at intervals along the wharf lines; to the northward, distilleries, slaughter-houses, and ship-yards; to the south, a host of packing-houses. These, with not a few factories, composed the chief elements on the bordering of the bayou, which only became a river, and then by inversion, in July, 1871. Outside of these lay the principal planing-mills and box factories.

West of the junction of the two branches, and spreading over an area of nearly half a mile square, was the great machine-shop district, where foundries were in full blast, and agricultural implements by the thousand were turned out annually, side by side with steam-engines, boilers, car-wheels, crushing-mills for the mines, burrs for flour-mills, pipes for conveying water, gas, or steam, wagons, carriages, etc. A similar district, but of less importance, existed in the North Division, in its south-west portion, bounded on two sides by the docks on the river. A grand exodus had begun in the spring of 1871, to the south and south-west, where several important workshops had previously existed. Some of the largest manufactories were in process of transference to these new quarters at the time of the fire, and new ones were springing up on every hand.

Outside of these limits the principal thoroughfares, in all directions, to a distance of fully two miles from the Court-house, were occupied exclusively for business purposes, except where the omnipresent saloon formed a break in the *cordon* of useful commerce. Beyond and around these were residences, churches, and schools; most of them of a superior order of architecture, the one great fault being that a large proportion of them were of wood. Near the middle of the southern limit of the city was the great Union Stock Yards, a town in itself; and the whole was surrounded by the magnificent system of parks and boulevards, which, when completed, would have made Chicago as much of a wonder in this respect as she had already become by virtue of her commercial importance.

Chicago was a healthy city. The previously low and marshy site had been raised sufficiently to permit of good drainage, but not high enough to allow any of the double-cellar style of life so common in New York, and the broad prairies furnished so much room for lateral expansion, that there was much less of crowding than in other large cities. The sickly tenement system was almost unknown, and it was very rare to see one residence at the back of another, on the same lot. Then the level character of the surrounding country permitted the winds to have free course in every direction, and the proximity to the lake was the cause of numerous gales that are not met with in the interior, while that lake supplied the people with an abundance of the very best water. The difference in these conditions, as affecting health, is remarkably shown in the fact that the death rate averaged 3.791 per cent. per annum, in the period from 1843 to 1856 inclusive, while from 1856 to 1870 it was only 2.397 per cent. per annum. The work of filling up and draining was commenced about the beginning of the last-named period. This rate of mortality is less than in any country in Europe, except Scotland, Sweden, and Norway, though the greater changes of temperature in the United States are usually supposed to operate unfavorably on human longevity. We may here note that the average annual rain-fall has increased about one and a quarter inches, and the annual range of temperature has been diminished several degrees, since the first meteorological observations were taken there by the government officials.

The statistics of churches and Sunday-schools given at the beginning of this chapter, show that the people of Chicago were preëminently a religious community, a fact attested by the large heartedness that has always accompanied their church work. Their houses of worship were noble structures, well attended, and so liberally supported that Chicago ministers were among the most talented of the land, and drew better salaries than the pastors of the majority of churches—East or West. The contributions of the churches to missionary work, to the erection and endowment of theological colleges, were always large; and the help they extended so continuously and lavishly to the boys in blue during the war for the suppression of the rebellion, covered them with lasting honor. We may not pass without note the Young Men's Christian Association, formed by the general church membership, which gave rise to the building and rebuilding of Farwell Hall, and has set an example of working in the Master's service that has been copied in the church work of many other cities.

As an educational point Chicago took high rank. Its school buildings were large, well lighted, heated, and ventilated, and supplied with good teachers, most of whom had been admirably trained in the normal department of the High School, on a plan which is acknowledged to be without a superior in the world. The one great fault was that the number of children grew more rapidly than school accommodations could be provided for them; and to this cause, rather than to any alleged superiority in teaching, is to be attributed the fact that not less than sixty-five private schools and colleges existed in the city, besides a few others in which a purely technical instruction was given, as in book-keeping or dentistry. The county had also a flourishing normal school at Englewood, near the southern limits of the city.

Of the higher institutions of learning the city had its full share. The Baptists, Presbyterians, and Congregationalists all had flourishing colleges—the Baptist institution having a well-attended law school, and an astronomical observatory, with one of the three largest refracting telescopes in the world; while the Methodists were represented in not less than three different institutes in Evanston, twelve miles north of the city, and had a connection with the Chicago Medical College. The Catholics had a training school for the priesthood, of a high grade. Of medical schools there were not less than six, one throwing its doors open to women.

In a purely scientific way, the city was represented by the Astronomical Society, in connection with the observatory above referred to, and the Academy of Sciences, which had a valuable collection of specimens, embracing the geology, flora, and fauna of the North-west, in its most extended sense. The votaries of pure science in the city were numerous. Among them we may name Colonel Foster, late President of the American Association for the Advancement of Science; Dr. Stimpson, Secretary of the Academy of Sciences; H. A. Johnson, M. D.; J. H. Rauch, M. D., the Sanitary Statistician; Professors Blaney and De la Fontaine, and Mr. Eberts, chemical investigators; Professor McChesney; Kennicott, the late eminent naturalist; Professor Safford, of the Observatory, who was known in early life as a mathematical prodigy; and Colbert, a voluminous writer on astronomy and its kindred sciences. Microscopic investigators were numerous; we can scarcely name S. A. Briggs and O. S. Westcott, without doing injustice by omitting others. The patrons of science were many; among them Hon. J. Y. Scammon deserves most honorable mention.

In its social aspects Chicago was probably not very different from other cities. There were, of course, many poor people within her borders, but pauperism on the European scale was a thing unknown. The rapid rise in the value of real estate had made many rich, while others had grown wealthy in trade; the number of well-to-do people forming a larger per centage of the population than is usual in great cities. A few had always prided themselves on being "First Families;" but it was not till about two years before the fire that a snobbish caterer found himself sustained in the attempt to form a directory of those who were admissible into first-class society. The distinctions which are kept in so closely in most other places found but few advocates, and there was really much more than the average of friendly feeling between rich and poor, though not much time was wasted in words. Indeed, the genuine Chicagoan, whatever his circumstances, had always some thing to do or to think of. A few loafers could be found, but they were importations—not indigenous to the soil.

That great numbers of the residents of Chicago were steeped in vice, and deeply tainted with crime, is too true; that she was especially wicked, as compared with other cities, we most emphatically deny. Chicago loose-livers were notoriously fast, and some of her rogues exhibited an audacity not always to be encountered elsewhere, outside of New York. This is admitted. But the police records show no larger proportion of crime there than in other cities, and there are few that have been governed by so small a per centage of police force. The true cause of the bad character of Chicago abroad is to be found in the fact that some of her newspapers were in the habit, for many years, of publishing to the world every little scandal that floated in society, whether true or not, which the press of other cities would have passed by in silence. The divorce business is easily explained. The dissatisfied ones of other places fled to Chicago, as to Indiana, in great numbers, because the courts had an expeditious way of dealing with such cases. That business has long been stopped, and the air of the courts is purified.

Chicago was celebrated for her high appreciation of art, and the liberal patronage she accorded to it. Painting and statuary flourished in her midst, and some of her artists had attained a world-wide fame. We need only mention Healy, as a master on canvas, and Volk, as the author of the statue of Douglas and the bust of Lincoln. Previous to 1860, there was little of the artistic element in the city. Since then large numbers of artists have been attracted thither, and the residences of many prominent citizens adorned with some of the best works of art—ancient and modern. The establishment of art galleries was fostered, and that in the Opera-house was moderately well supported, while many artists clustered around it. In 1870 an Academy of Design was established, in a building especially erected for the purpose on Adams Street, near the Custom-house, which was conducted under encouraging auspices in 1871.

Music and the drama nowhere found more enlightened or hearty encouragement. The Opera-house "made no sign" in 1871, beyond preparing, by a thorough overhauling, for the winter season. But it had previously been well patronized when first-class concert or operatic talent was on the boards; the place was too large for dramatic entertainments. Farwell Hall had recently received a first-class orchestra organ, and had recently become quite popular for concerts. Theodore Thomas there made his best hits. McVicker's Theater had been entirely rebuilt a few months before the fire, and was as attractive a place as could be found in the United States; it was generally run on the "Star" principle. Wood's Museum contained some half a million "hobjects hof hinterest," in addition to its stock company, which was one of the best, and its dramatic entertainments were uniformly well attended. The Dearborn Street Theater, erected in 1868, was occupied by the Wyndham Comedy Troupe in the summer of 1871, and was doing a rushing business. Hooley's Opera-house (formerly Bryan Hall) was doing a paying business under the management of Frank Aiken, formerly of the Museum. The Globe Theater, in the West Division, constructed on the barn principle, in 1870, was closed in 1871 (re-opened by Colonel Wood after the fire).

Besides these, there were several other minor places of amusement not necessary to be specified; and the German Theater, on North Wells Street, furnished dramatic entertainments in the Teutonic tongue.

As a musical center the city really stood forth prominently in the United States. Two organists, Creswold and Buck, who had only two other peers on this side of the Atlantic; Pease, as a pianist, and a hundred and fifty other professional musicians, without counting teachers, many of them ranking with the best performers of Europe, not to speak of vocal talent of no mean order—these flourished in the city where more than two thousand pianos were sold annually, with thousands of other instruments, and many tons of sheet music, much of which was written by home composers. It is no wonder that opera singers and concertists looked for the verdict of such a wide-spread musical culture with as much anxiety as for that of the seaboard cities.

The superior intelligence of the people was accurately reflected in its newspaper press, which was well supported, and occupied the front rank of journalism. The leading dailies of Chicago expended much more money than those of New York in the collection of news, and their columns were conducted with marked ability; while the corps of editors and writers were ample. The Chicago Press Club had about eighty-seven members, of whom seventy were workers on the following daily papers:

The *Tribune* (Republican), owned by a stock company, worth about $1,250,000, Horace White, editor-in-chief; the *Times* (Democratic), Wilbur F. Storey, editor and proprietor; the *Evening Journal* (Republican), E. L. Wilson, editor and proprietor; the *Evening Post* (Republican), D. H. Blakely, editor and principal proprietor; the *Republican* (Independent), J. B. McCullagh, editor and part proprietor; the *Evening Mail* (Republican), stock company, E. H. Talbot and H. R. Hobart, editors; the *Staats-Zeitung*, German (Republican), A. C. Hesing, proprietor, H. Raster, editor-in-chief; and the *Volks Zeitung*, German. These had an aggregate circulation of 78,500 copies daily, besides tri-weekly and weekly. The religious press was represented ably by the *Advance* (Congregationalist), the *Interior* (Presbyterian), the *N. W. Christian Advocate* (Methodist), and the *Standard* (Baptist). These were issued weekly, and had an aggregate circulation of 75,000 copies. The *Lakeside Monthly* was the leading magazine; the *Bureau* also having a good circulation as an organ of the Protectionists.

The total number of regular publications in the city, daily, weekly, and monthly, was about eighty. The list would be much extended if we included all claimants to the title.

In the matter of public libraries the city was deficient, but a united effort was being made, just before the fire, to establish a library on a comprehensive plan, which would probably have been successful but for the catastrophe. The collections of the Historical Society included some sixty thousand bound volumes, and over a hundred and fifty thousand pamphlets, besides full sets of the leading daily papers of the city, a great many valuable MSS., a fine collection of paintings, and numerous war relics. The Young Men's Association Library contained some twenty thousand volumes, including a full set of the English Patent Office Reports. Besides these there were the Catholic Library, Cobb's Library (seven thousand), the Young Men's Christian Association Library, and a smaller church library just in process of formation, on Michigan Avenue. The Law

Library, in the Court-house, was one of the largest and best in existence.

Private libraries were, however, numerous and valuable. Among the best we note those of E. B. McCagg (philological), J. Y. Scammon (Swedenborgian), I. N. Arnold, E. H. Sheldon, Obadiah Jackson, E. G. Asay, G. F. Rumsey, and H. H. Shufeldt. Besides these there were very many medical and law libraries, with good collections of scientific works, the property of individuals and small societies. The book business was a large one, the annual sales of the three leading houses aggregating over three millions of dollars; these included several valuable works by Chicago authors, besides no small amount of trashy matter of home production.

We close our sketch of Chicago in 1871, by a brief reference to the city government.

The Mayor, chosen every two years, was the nominal head, but had little beyond a veto power, with the privilege of making a few nominations, to be confirmed or rejected by the Council. Colonel R. B. Mason was Mayor at the time of the fire. Joseph Medill was elected to the office, November 7, 1871.

The Common Council consisted of forty aldermen, two from each ward, one of the two being elected each year for a two-year term. The presiding officer was chosen by the Council from among its own members. C. C. P. Holden was the President of the Council at the time of the fire.

The Board of Supervisors was a county organization, to which was elected one member from each ward, and two from each division of the city.

The Board of Fire and Police Commissioners consisted of three members: T. B. Brown, President, Fred. Gund, and Mark Sheridan. This body was organized in 1861, and had full authority over the two departments named, the only limitation being that the working expenses were paid by taxation, ordered by the Common Council. The members were elected by the people. The police force consisted of 425 men, including officers; W. W. Kennedy was Superintendent, and Wells Sherman Deputy Superintendent. The Fire Department, R. A. Williams, Fire Marshal, comprised about 200 men, working 17 steam fire-engines, besides trucks, horse-carts, fire-escapes, etc. The Fire Alarm Telegraph, E. B. Chandler, Superintendent, had 206 signal-boxes distributed over the city.

The Board of Public Works consisted of three members; J. McArthur, W. H. Carter, and Redmond Prendiville. They had full control of the street work, public buildings (except schools), bridges, etc., with power to make assessments on property benefited, subject to approval of the Council. The members were nominated by the Mayor, and confirmed by the Council. E. S. Chesborough was City Engineer.

The Board of Education consisted of one member from each of the twenty wards of the city, appointed by the Council. They had charge of school buildings, appointment of teachers, choice of text-books, and general school regulations. E. F. Runyan was President of the Board, and J. L. Pickard Superintendent of schools.

The Board of Health, organized in 1867, had charge of sanitary regulations, and the Sanitary Superintendent, J. H. Rauch, M. D., prepared the vital statistics, which are widely noted for their fullness and accuracy.

The three boards of Park Commissioners, and their functions, have been noted in the chapter on Public Parks.

Besides these, the principal corporation officers were a City Clerk, Corporation Counsel, City Attorney, and Tax Commissioner, with assistants. There were three Police Courts, one for each division of the city. The Courts of Record being United States, or State organizations, were not city institutions in the proper sense of the term, though the courts were held in Chicago. There were three Superior, four Circuit, and one County Court Judge.

Much has been written about the city government, and many charges of incompetency and corruption made. The greatest faults of the system have undoubtedly arisen from the fact that different individuals had been in the habit of visiting the State capital at every session of the Legislature, and there log-rolling special acts through to suit themselves or their friends. In conformity with their wishes new departments were created, or old ones changed, so as to give them ample powers independent of all the rest. Thus, the Board of Fire and Police Commissioners was almost independent of the Council, and entirely so of the Mayor. The same was true of the Board of Public Works, to a rather more limited extent. The Board of Health was independent of all these, except in the matter of salaries; the Board of Education acted at its own sweet will, and the Boards of Park Commissioners did not need even to say "by your leave" to any other city functionary, or department. The Common Council certainly contained several men who were not particularly wise, and, perhaps, a few whose ambition was to "make" out of the people. The Board of Supervisors was even nearer to a brilliant mediocrity than the Council. But we are not aware that the city authorities were dishonest, or its officials incompetent, though the city was so rich that there was a strong temptation to unscrupulous men to expend large sums of money in corrupting others, that they might Tammanyize a return of tenfold on the outlay. The Mayor was little more than a figure-head, his membership of the several Boards, and presidency of the Council, having been abolished by recent legislative acts.

It is really a wonder that the city authorities of Chicago should have accomplished so much, and worked together so harmoniously under such circumstances, especially when it is remembered that the rapid growth of the city, and the radical changes in aspect perpetually recurring, needed the wisdom of a Solon to frame ordinances that would meet the requirements of the case. There is not one of the departments of the city government that has not accomplished labors equally difficult with those of Hercules, and some of her city improvements are to-day ranked among the wonders of the world.

And this was Chicago in her prosperity. Great as she was then, she proved herself even greater in the day of an affliction so deep that it caused a throb of anguish throughout the whole civilized world.

SCIENCE OF THE FIRE.

THE CONFLAGRATIONS IN CHICAGO AND THE LUMBER REGIONS OF THE NORTH-WEST—A STARTLING CHAPTER IN THE WORLD'S HISTORY—METEOROLOGICAL AND CLIMATIC CHANGES INVOLVED—THE CAUSE—EXTRAORDINARY DROUGHT—SUN SPOTS.

CHICAGO was far from being alone as a subject for the dread visitation of fire. The first half of October, 1871, will long be remembered all over the United States as a time of wide-spread conflagration. The fires raged in the lumber districts of Minnesota, Wisconsin, and Michigan, in the woods of New York State, and in many of the cities of the Union from the Atlantic seaboard to San Francisco. We propose, in this chapter, to take a brief glance at the effects of the great conflagration upon the general conditions of the earth's surface; but the discussion must take in a wider field than that bounded by the limits of the Garden City. In the chemical and meteorological changes evolved, the Chicago fire really acted but a subordinate part—though immense in itself, it was but small in proportion to the whole.

It is yet too early to make an accurate estimate of the area traversed by the fire in the forests of the North-western States. That can only be done after the whole ground has been re-surveyed. But the very lowest estimate we can make places the amount of timbered land actually burned over at not less than 480,000 acres, of which 200,000 acres are in Michigan. This is equal to 750 square miles of territory, containing the material that would yield a product of 1,800,000,000 feet of lumber for the market, or nearly as much as Chicago has received during the past two years.

At least an equal extent of other than timbered land was burned over, including what are technically called "clearings," where the trees have been cut down, leaving vast quantities of combustible material; and many hundreds of farms, some of them a long way removed from the lumber regions. The total area of country burned over, wooded and open, can not be less than one thousand square miles, and is probably very much more than that amount.

And this vast tract of country was completely denuded. The ordinary fire in the woods only burns up the brush and the boughs of trees, leaving the trunks standing, with a mere char on the outside; they can still be utilized for lumber, provided they are cut down and thrown into the water before the well-known borer has a chance to attack them. But in the fires of October, 1871, a large proportion of the trees were burned through to the core, and fell to the ground, little better than attenuated sticks of charcoal. It was a *destroying* fire, that literally burned up "root and branch;" while the fences, hay, buildings, etc., on the farming lands, were so completely licked up that not even the ashes were left to indicate the places where they had formerly existed.

It is manifestly impossible to tell exactly the quantities of wood, hay, straw, and other combustibles burned up in those fires. Could we do so it would be easy to calculate the precise number of pounds of carbon set free in the process, because the science of chemistry enables us to say, to an ounce, how much of each of the elements enters into the composition of a ton of any named material. Thus, we know that straw and dry pine wood each contain thirty-eight per cent. of carbon, and hay nearly forty-one (40.73) per cent. But we can make a sufficiently close approximation to answer our present purpose. Taking the minima of estimated areas of country as a basis, the writer has made a careful calculation from averages of the quantities of material destroyed on those areas, and has made even a closer approximation for the city of Chicago, with the following conclusions:

As a chemical result of this immense combustion we have not less than 3,000,000 tons of carbon from the country, and 300,000 tons from the city, liberated from its union with other elements, and carried up into the air in combination with nearly nine million tons of oxygen, and adding twelve million tons to the quantity of carbonic acid gas already existing in the atmosphere. Knowing, as we do, how much the conditions of animal and vegetable existence depend upon the constitution of the aerial envelope of our globe, it becomes important to ascertain the extent of disturbance from the normal state, produced by this phenomenon.

The quantity of carbonic acid gas normal to the atmosphere at the present day is estimated to be about one part in two thousand, the weight will, therefore, be a little less than twenty thousand million tons; hence its proportion in the atmosphere has been increased by about one part in sixteen hundred. The total weight of atmospheric oxygen being a little over nine million million tons, its proportion has been decreased to the extent of nearly one part in a million. Accepting Liebig's estimate that the annual consumption of oxygen by the lower animals, and by combustion, is double the quantity consumed by human beings in breathing, we arrive at the astounding result that the oxygen taken up by the North-western fires was equal to the amount required to supply the consumption of ten months all over the globe.

So far as we are able to judge, the vegetable kingdom was intended by the Creator to act as an exact counterpoise to the animal world, the former returning to the atmosphere just as much oxygen as is taken up by the latter. This does not seem to be the case with carbon, the atmospheric portion of which appears to have slowly decreased, ever since the carboniferous era. At that time the quantity of carbonic acid gas in the atmosphere was probably three hundred times greater than now, holding in combination one-half of the oxygen, and forming fifteen to twenty per cent. of the total weight of the air. (Brogniart estimates seven or eight per cent.) The amount of free carbonic acid gas has diminished, approximately, at the rate of about one part in five thousand, each century since then. In this respect, therefore, the North-western fires have restored the atmospheric conditions of three hundred years ago.

A glance at the characteristics of the carboniferous era will enable us to appreciate the importance of this fact. We know that if we replace eight per cent. of the oxygen in the atmosphere of the present day with an equal volume of carbonic acid gas, the mixture is alike fatal to animal life and to combustion. Even the lower orders of animal life could only exist when the atmosphere had been partially cleared of its superabundant carbon. And this was accomplished by the vegetable kingdom, which then flourished with a luxuriance of which we can form but a faint conception, though the immense coal deposits, unearthed in the present century, tell the tale of primeval vegetable growth, proportionate in its exuberance to the abundant presence of the acid that formed its food. Farther along the stream of time, many scores of thousands of years nearer to the commencement of our written history, when these gigantic ferns had done their work, and fixed a large proportion of that carbon into the shape in which it is now utilized, animal existence became possible; and the same conditions that had previously ministered to immense vegetable forms, now made possible the elimination of a mammoth bony frame-work to support the muscular tissues of animals, giant-like even as compared with the elephant of our own day. There is no doubt that the human race appeared upon the earth just as soon as human respiration became possible; neither can there be any doubt that the "first families" lived in what was a genuine "Garden of Eden" when compared with the more sparse vegetation of the present epoch, or that the peculiar facility afforded to the formation of carbonate of lime justified the assertion of Holy Writ that "there were giants in those days."

The abstraction of carbonic acid gas from the atmosphere is still progressing, though not so rapidly as in the days of yore. This appropriation by the vitalized forms that exist upon the land surface is not a permanent loss, as all thus taken away from the general fund by the one is restored by the compensating activities of another, or yielded up in the disintegration that follows the death of organic forms. But it is not so with life in the sea. The immense quantities of carbonic acid taken up in the secretion of the bony coverings of shell-fish, mostly sink to the bottom of the ocean, where they lie forever undisturbed, except when upheaved by a hypothalassic volcano. At the immense depths to which they sink, there is no wind, no current, but eternal stillness reigns, and not even the play of organic affinities finds room to operate; it is even more than the stillness of death, for there no disintegration follows the departure of the vital principle from its material encasement. The lower coral formations are subject to but little more disturbance.

These fishy processes diminish the amount of carbonic acid in the atmosphere at the rate of about four million tons in each century. The process is, however, counteracted to some extent by the tremendous activity of manufacturing fires within the past few years. Indeed, it is not improbable that the last-named process will yet attain to such a magnitude as to form an effectual counter-balance to the secretory powers in the restoration of carbonic acid, though the compensation may not be effected without a decrease in the relative proportion of free oxygen in the atmosphere.

We see, then, that the North-western conflagrations have carried us back to nearly the same atmospheric conditions as those which existed three centuries ago, and this brings out another important thought. We see that, in the history of the past, the elimination of carbonic acid from the atmosphere has been accompanied by a gradual development of animal life, and an equally gradual retrocession of vegetable abundance. While the vegetable kingdom is less royal in its proportions than in the carboniferous era, the immense interval between then and now has witnessed the up-growth of all the animal orders above the reptilian, and the successive development of the higher order—man—from a state of savage ignorance to one of high intellectual culture and moral accountability. Knowing, as we do, the ultimate physiological connection of the mental with the physical, in man's nature, and the almost abject dependence of that physical nature upon its surrounding conditions—except those of temperature—we can scarcely resist the thought that the progress of the race toward the highest limit of perfection attainable by humanity, has been retarded not less than three centuries, while we estimate that the commercial status of the city of Chicago has been set back barely four years by the Great Conflagration.

Still another, and even more startling, idea suggests itself in this connection. What if these fires should be but one of a series of events, designed by the Great Ruler of the universe to prevent man from progressing too fast or too far, in his forward march toward the perfection of knowledge, and of that power which knowledge confers upon its possessors? Our study of the history of the past teaches us nothing more forcibly than this one fact, that all the nations whose records grace prominently the historical page, down to a few centuries ago, have reached an ultimus beyond which they could not pass, and have relapsed from that point into insignificance as powers, and barbarism as peoples. Whether it were the red hand of war, the plague-spot, a change in the beaten track of commerce, or the up-growth of a luxurious indolence that gnawed out the vitals of the nation, some cause has always operated to break down the power, and even the intelligence of peoples. And the records of history show that this grand reversal has occurred at least twice all over the civilized world; while the analogies of reasoning point to the same conclusion with geological deductions, that the world, as a whole, is not exempt from the providential visitation which sweeps out of existence the accumulated learning, as well as the treasures of the past, and leaves the race to begin again at the foot of the ladder up which it has toiled so painfully before. And so it is not impossible that, while the occurrence of the North-western fires has furnished to the atmosphere a superabundance of carbonic acid that will stimulate the vegetable world to increased activity to occupy the place of that destroyed, the animal creation will retrogress, and man may fall back into the mental conditions of the Reformation period, and reproduce the then exceptional intellectual splendors of Bacon and Shakespeare.

A recollection of the fact that large quantities of carbonic acid gas were generated by the fire, will enable us to understand how many individuals dropped down dead near the scenes of the conflagration, and were afterward found, without the least trace of fire upon the clothing or person. We have already stated that eight per cent. of this gas in the atmosphere is fatal to life. It would be generated in fully this proportion in the neighborhood of the flames, and would thence spread slowly through the air over the whole surface of the earth. The amount of carbonic acid gas evolved by these fires would suffice to saturate the air in the locality to the height of nearly fifty yards from the surface.

We may refer briefly to the more local, but still extensive effects of the fire, upon the meteorological conditions of the country devastated. It has long been regarded as axiomatic that the destruction of timber and the cultivation of soil, diminish the annual rain supply, and also produce changes in the temperature. This is not wholly true. The plowing of the ground undoubtedly lessens the amount of water that drains into the rivers, but it is only because the loosening of the soil permits a greater proportion of the rain-fall to sink in, instead of running off to feed the water courses. There is, however, the best of reason to believe that the presence or absence of trees has a great deal to do with the quantity of water that falls from the clouds, and so much, that we may expect the denudation of so much timber land to be marked by a diminution of not less than two inches, or seven per cent., of the annual rain-fall over a large section of the North-west, while the yearly range of temperature will be widened fully five degrees, the thermometer registering two or three degrees higher in summer, and lower in winter, than heretofore.

We have already referred to the probability that these fires were part of a section in the providential plan of earth government. While we can not accept the doctrine that they were sent either as a punishment to the people of one section, or as a benefit to those of another, we must recognize them as links in the great chain of events, each of which is an effect of some cause, and a producing cause of some subsequent effect. And the same philosophy teaches us that no effect can be greater than its cause, or combined causes. Hence it is absurd to look to the mere upsetting of a kerosene lamp in the city, or the emptying of burning tobacco from a laborer's pipe in the woods, as the efficient causes of these wide-spread disasters. These were the mere incitements—like the knocking of a chip from the shoulder of a man who is spoiling for a fight.

That Chicago was "favorably" situated and constructed for just such a fire, none will deny who remember that she presented a four-mile line of wooden buildings directly along the path of the south-west gale—so common in that region. But the forests, *per se*, presented no more unfavorable conditions than in years past. Yet they, too, were licked up by the devouring flames.

The proximate cause of the conflagrations was found in the fact that the country was unusually dry. One and a half inches of rain fell in Chicago on the 3d of July, but from that date to the time of the fire, on the 9th of October, only two and a half inches fell, whereas the average quantity for that time, as deduced from the observations of former years, should have been eight and three-quarter inches. The rain-fall of the summer season was only 28½ per cent. of the average in Chicago, while in the lumber districts it was fully twenty per cent. less than even this parsimonious allowance from the clouds. Meanwhile a hot summer's sun had dried out every particle of the "water of crystallization," as the chemists will perhaps pardon us for calling it, and left the whole as dry as so much tinder. All that it wanted was an *opportunity* to burn, and that want was soon supplied. Thenceforward the fire and the gale had free course, "with none to let or hinder."

But this was, evidently, only a proximate cause. There was some other cause, antecedent to this; we are long past the day when storms of wind or rain are regarded as mere accidents.

In the spring of 1870, Mr. Colbert wrote a series of articles in the Chicago *Tribune*, and then in the *Lakeside Monthly*, developing a meteorological theory which was very widely copied and commented on. He called attention to the fact that a large part of the sun's surface was then covered with black spots; they were fully as numerous in 1871 as at the time those articles were written. The theory has since been incorporated in his work entitled "Star Studies." The following were the effects which he stated would be produced by those spots:

First—A reduction of two degrees in the amount of heat supplied to the earth by the sun (to the whole globe of atmosphere, water, and land) corresponding to the lessened area of calorifying sun surface. Second—A diminution in the amount of water taken up by the sun, from ocean and land (principally from the sea), owing to the diminished evaporating power of the sun; and a decrease of fully four inches in the annual rain-fall. Third—Greater sensible heat at many points on the land surface, and a very irregular register of temperature; because a large proportion of the heat supplied by the sun is rendered latent by the evaporation of the water that falls as rain upon the earth's surface. Fourth—An increase in the amount of chemical activity, both in combination and decomposition, a greater display of electric and magnetic phenomena (hence unusual irregularities in temperature), a more rapid growth of vegetation (but) partial crop failures, etc.

That every one of the deductions then published, was accurately verified, is now matter of history. Of course local peculiarities of position, etc., caused many variations from the average; but, as applied to the whole globe, the theory has precisely agreed with the facts. There can be no doubt, therefore, that the very strongly marked deviations from the average rain-fall, both the general deficiency and the excessive floods in some localities, had their general cause in the fact that a greater portion of the sun's disc was obscured by black spots during 1870 and a part of 1871, than at any other time for a hundred years preceding.

The black patches on the face of the God of Day, too remote to be visible without the aid of a telescope, though sometimes covering several millions of square miles of his surface, have for some years been recognized by meteorologists as potential in the production of magnetic storms and auroral displays on the earth. It is but a step further in the same reasoning process to arrive at a point where we can look upon these as causes of greater change in the meteorological conditions of our earth, and as influencing materially those circumstances on which its inhabitants depend for the conservation of the order of things under which they live and move.

BUREAU OF ILLUSTRATION · BUFFALO

THE GREAT CONFLAGRATION.

BLACKENED and bleeding, helpless, panting, prone
On the charred fragments of her shattered throne
Lies she who stood but yesterday alone.

Queen of the West! by some enchanter taught
To lift the glory of Aladdin's court,
Then lose the spell that all that wonder wrought.

Like her own prairies by some chance seed sown,
Like her own prairies in one brief day grown,
Like her own prairies in one fierce night mown.

She lifts her voice, and in her pleading call
We hear the cry of Macedon to Paul—
The cry for help that makes her kin to all.

But haply with wan fingers may she feel
The silver cup hid in the proffered meal—
The gifts her kinship and our loves reveal.

Bret Harte.

CHAPTER I.

THE GREAT CONFLAGRATION.

The fire as a hero—It marches through four miles of solid buildings—It takes them all—A plain account of the operations of the "fiend."

IT was on the night of the 8th of October, 1871, and the forenoon following, that Chicago was wiped out. It is related, and piously believed by most readers of ancient history, that old Rome was once saved by the cackling of a goose. There is at least equal reason to believe that Chicago, which is no less noted, as a modern city, than Rome was as the olden capital of the world, was destroyed by the kicking of a cow. Leaving the details of the ancient example to take care of themselves, it may be explained that the great fire of the 9th October is attributed by the Fire Department of the city to the upsetting of a kerosene-lamp in a barn. If the woman who was milking the cow had not been late with her milking, the lamp would not have been needed. If she had plied the dugs of the animal with proper skill, the lamp would not have been kicked at all. There is no use foisting the blame upon the cow, for cows will kick when irritated, else they would not be true to their nature; nor to the oil in the lamp, for whatever hue and cry may be raised against coal-oil as an illuminating agency, it is unquestionably the material which nature has intended for such use, and one which only requires intelligent use to be as harmless as it is handy. The blame of setting the fire rests on the woman who milked, or else upon the lazy man who allowed her to milk. The name of this female we shall not hand down to posterity in these pages; for we have the familiar words of the poet to remind us that

> "The ambitious youth who fired the Ephesian dome,
> Outlives in fame the pious fool who reared it;"

And we have no desire to immortalize the author of the ruin of Chicago at the expense of the noble and indefatigable pioneers whose work in the building of Chicago has been recounted in the preceding pages.

So much for the origin of the fire of October. The causes which helped it to spread until it had devastated the city and laid three-fourths of its wealth in ashes, will be inquired into in a subsequent chapter. We shall leave the Fire Department out of the question at present, just as it seems to have been left out of the question by the destroying element on the fatal night of the 8th. It is necessary, however, for the reader to understand the following facts:

The city of Chicago is divided, by the river and its branches, as a glance at the map will show, into three principal divisions—North, South, and West. The North and South Branches unite at a point not quite a mile from the lake-shore (though the South Branch has previously approached it to within half a mile), and the united stream (if it may be called a stream) forms the boundary between the North and South Divisions. The West Division embraces all to the west of either branch. This division consists mainly of residences, with retail stores filling several long streets, and, lying along the bank of the river, a goodly number of factories, grain-elevators, railroad buildings, and a few merchandise warehouses. The "business quarter" proper, containing practically all the wholesale mercantile establishments, fine retail stores, public buildings and hotels, the newspaper offices, the two grand union railroad depots, and other institutions which usually occupy the central and select portion of the town, lies in the South Division, north of Harrison Street. Perhaps we can not illustrate the character of this quarter of the city more plainly than by stating that the valuation of the thirty-one miles of street front, excluding that of all buildings and other improvements, was not, on the morning before the fire, less than $1,000 per foot on the average, or $163,680,000; equal to the price of about *two thousand eight hundred and forty-two townships* of Government land in a new railroad town. To the south of this precious tract lie the residences of the wealthy and of the poor, divided by State Street, a thoroughfare of shops. The North Division is (or rather was) occupied, near the river and along Clark Street, by stores and factories, the rest mainly by residences. The homes of the humble lie mostly west of Lasalle Street; though toward the north, the residences of the more luxurious classes, which had formerly been confined to select tracts in the south-east quarter-section of this Division—the "old Chicago," substantial and elegant, and shaded with grand elms—had been of late seriously crowding the frugal Germans and improvident Irish out of their former haunts, and studding the country about Lincoln Park with mansions of the most elegant design and finish.

It should also be understood that a severe drought—the severest in many seasons—was prevalent at the time of the fire, not only at and about Chicago, but through the whole Northwest; and that, in addition to this, a gale of unusual violence was blowing steadily for several days and nights from the south-west. Had the gale been from the south-east instead, then the West Division would have been burned. Twice as many buildings would have been consumed and twice as many people rendered homeless; but the damage to Chicago would have been much less severe, because it would be much better for every clerk, artisan, and tradesman of Chicago to lose his home than to lose his business, the prop which sustains that home. As Shakespeare says truly, though he puts the words in the mouth of the despicable Shylock:

> "You take my house when you do take the prop
> That doth sustain my house; you take my life
> When you do take the means whereby I live."

What were the circumstances of this horrible event which eclipsed all similar catastrophes that the world knew; which burnt out a week from the teeming annals of the age?

There had been, on the previous evening (that of Saturday, the 7th October), an extensive conflagration, which the journals had recorded in many columns, devoting to it their most stunning head-lines, their most ponderous superlatives, and their most graphic powers of description. The location of this fire was in the West Division, between Clinton Street and the river, and running north from Van Buren Street, where it caught, to Adams Street, where, fortunately, it was checked, rather by the lack of combustible material than by any ability of the Fire Department to obtain the mastery over such powerful allies as the gale, the drought, and the fire, aided by the almost powder-like material which the devouring element found in the planing-mills, lumber-piles, and pine buildings of that region. The last structure attacked by the fire of Saturday night was the viaduct over the railroads at Adams Street, which, though of iron, contained sufficient wood-work to furnish food for the hungry flames. The damage by this fire was nearly a million dollars; and it formed undoubtedly the grandest spectacle thus far witnessed in Chicago, though not the most destructive conflagration, so far as values went. In the rapidity with which the flames progressed, consuming in their course one of the steam fire-engines which had been sent against them, and which had seemed but little more than boys' tiny squirt-guns in their effects upon the raging element, the people of Chicago saw, with a shudder, to what terrible danger they were subjected by the condition of the elements and the architectural faults of the city. But none of them dreamed—not even the most apprehensive among them—that another fire was to sweep over the city, even before the underwriters had begun to compute the damages by this, compared with which the conflagration of Saturday night should be but as the flicker of a farthing candle.

Yet so it was. A little while after nine o'clock on Sunday evening, the lamp was upset which was to kindle the funeral pyre of Chicago's pristine splendor. The little stable, with its contents of hay, was soon ablaze. By the time the alarm could be sounded, at the box several blocks away, two or three other little buildings—tinder-boxes—to the leeward had been ignited, and within five minutes the poor purlieu in the vicinity of De Koven and Jefferson Streets was blazing like a huge bonfire.

The spread of the fire, or, rather, the flight which it took along with the south-west gale, was very rapid. We suppose the Fire Department was on the ground, partly because it usually turns out at fires, and partly because one or two of its splendid engines were found burned up among the ruins the next day; but it might as well have been in Kamtschatka, for any thing which it was able to do toward arresting the progress of the flames. They marched on until they had devoured the thousand or more shanties, houses, planing-mills, in their path on the West Division. They heeded not the Marshal and his corps any more than the bull heeds the fly upon his horn. They heeded not even the broad river, but leaped it easily, after marching along northward until all between Jefferson Street and the river had been destroyed, up to the edge of the burned district of Saturday night.

The first vault across the river was made at midnight from Van Buren Street, lighting in a building of the South Division gas-works, on Adams Street. This germ of the main fire was not suppressed, and from that moment the doom of the commercial quarter was sealed, though no man could have foretold that the raging element would make such complete havoc of the proudest and strongest structures of that quarter. The axis of the column, as it had progressed from the starting-point in the south-western purlieus, had varied hardly a point from due north-east. Having gained a foothold upon the South Division, its march naturally lay through two or three blocks of pine rookeries, known as "Conley's Patch," and so on for a considerable space through the abodes of squalor and vice. Through these it set out at double-quick, the main column being flanked by another on each side, and nearly an hour to the rear. That at the right was generated by a separate brand from the western burning; that at the left was probably created by some of the eddies which were by this time whirling through the streets toward the flame below and from it above. The rookeries were quickly disposed of. They made a magnificent kindling material, and had never distinguished themselves half so well as habitations of man as they did as fuel for the fiend. Beyond them, however, along Lasalle Street, were a splendid double-row of "fire-proof" mercantile buildings, the superior of which did not exist in the land. Would these succumb to the shower of brands and the triple-heated furnace which had been thrown about them?

Alas, yes! One after another, they went as the column advanced. And the column was spreading fearfully—debauching to right and left, according as opportunities of conquest offered themselves. It was not long after one o'clock before the Chamber of Commerce was attacked, and fell a prey to the on-advancing force. Soon the Court-house was seized upon; but it did not surrender until near three o'clock, when the great bell went down, down, and pealed a farewell, dying groan as it went. The hundred and fifty prisoners in the basement-story were released to save their lives. They evinced their gratitude by pillaging a jewelry-store near by.

About the time the Court-house was attacked, the telegraph operators in the Merchants' Insurance building, opposite, in Lasalle Street, saw the propriety of falling back upon safer ground. The reporter of the Associated Press broke off in the middle of a word his account of the conflagration, and betook himself, in General Sheridan's carriage, to a suburban station.

From the Court-house the course of the main column seemed to tend eastward, and Hooley's Opera-house, the *Times* building, Crosby's magnificent Opera-house (to be re-opened that very night), fell rapidly before it. Pursuing its way more slowly onward, the fiery invader laid waste some buildings to the north-east, and, preparatory to attacking the magnificent wholesale stores at the foot of Randolph Street and the great Union Depot, joined forces with the other branch of the main column, which had lingered to demolish the Sherman House—a grand seven-story edifice of marble—the Tremont House, and the other fine buildings lying between Randolph and Lake Streets.

The left column had, meantime, diverged to pass down Lasalle Street and attack all buildings lying to the west of that noble avenue—the Oriental and Mercantile buildings, the Union Bank, the Merchants' Insurance building, where were General Sheridan's headquarters and the offices of the Western Union Telegraph, and in fact an unbroken row of the stone palaces of trade, which had already made Lasalle Street a monument of Chicago's business architecture, to which her citizens pointed with glowing pride, and of which admiring visitors wrote and published warm panegyrics in all quarters of the globe. The column of the left did its mission but too well, however, and by daylight scarcely a stone was left upon another in all that stately thoroughfare. But one building was left standing in this division of the city—a large brick structure, with iron shutters, known as Lind's Block. This was saved by its isolated location, being on the shore of the river, and separated by an exceptionally wide street from the seething furnace which consumed all else in its vicinity.

The right column started from a point near the intersection of Van Buren Street and the river, where some wooden buildings were ignited by brands from the west side, in despite of the efforts of the inhabitants of that quarter to save their homes by drenching their premises with water from their hydrants; and, we need hardly add, in despite of the desultory though desperate efforts of the Fire Department. The right column had also the advantage of a large area of wooden buildings on which to ration and arm itself for its march of destruction. Thus fed and equipped, it swept down upon the remaining portion of the best-built section of the town. It gutted the Michigan Southern Depot and the grand Pacific Hotel, and the tornado soon made them shapeless ruins. It spared not the unfinished building of the Lakeside Publishing Company, which had already put on a very sightly front, and which had scarcely any thing to burn but brick and stone. It licked up the fine new buildings on Dearborn Street, near the Post-office. Would it also master that solid edifice itself, isolated and fire-proof as it was?

The question was no sooner asked than the Post-office was seized upon and gutted like the rest, some two millions of treasure being destroyed in its vaults, which proved to have been shammily constructed. It swept down upon the new Bigelow House, a massive and elegant hotel which had never yet been occupied, and demolished that, together with the Honore Block, a magnificent new building, with massive walls adorned with hundreds of stately colonnades of marble. It reached out to the left and took McVicker's new theater in its grasp for a moment, with the usual fatal result. It assaulted the noble *Tribune* building, which the people had been declaring, even up to that terrible hour, would withstand all attacks, being furnished with all known safeguards against destruction by fire; but the enemy was wily as well as strong. It surrounded the fated structure, and ruined it too. It threw a red-hot brick wall upon the building's weaker side, a shower of brands upon the roof, a subterranean fire under the sidewalk and into the basement, and an atmosphere of furnace-heat all around. It conquered and destroyed the *Tribune* building at half-past seven in the evening. It marched on and laid waste Book-sellers' Row, the finest row of bookstores in the world. It fell upon Potter Palmer's store of Massachusetts marble, for which Field, Leiter & Co., dry goods importers, were paying the owner $52,000 a year rent. This splendid building, with such of its contents as had not been removed in wagons, went like all the rest. It deployed to the right, in spite of its ally, the wind, and destroyed the splendid churches and residences which adorn the lower or town end of Wabash and Michigan Avenues. Among these were the First and Second Presbyterian Churches, Trinity (Episcopal) Church, and the palatial row of residences known as "Terrace Row," in which dwelt, among others, Governor Bross, of the *Tribune*, Jonathan Y. Scammon, the banker and capitalist, and S. C. Griggs, the book-seller. Finally its course southward was stayed at Congress Street by the blowing up of a building. The southern line of the fire was for the most part, however, along Harrison Street, which is one square further to the south.

This is a brief sketch of the operations of the fire in the West and South Divisions. It effected a foothold in the North Division as early as half-past three in the morning; and it is remarkable that almost the first building to be attacked on the north side of the river was the engine-house of the Water-works; as if the terrible marauder had, with deadly strategy, thrown out a swifter brand than all others to cut off the only reliance of his victims, the water-supply. The Water-works are nearly a mile from the point where the burning brands must have crossed the river! The denizens of the North Division were standing in their doors and gazing at the blazing splendor of the Court-house dome, when they discovered to their horror that the fire was already raging behind them, and that the Water-works had gone. A general stampede to the sands of the lake-shore, or to the prairies west of the city, was the result.

Besides its foothold at the Water-works, from which the fire spread rapidly in every direction, it soon made a landing in two of the elevators near the river, and organized an advance which consumed every thing left by the scores of separate irruptions which the flames were constantly making in unexpected places. This was the system by which the North Division was wiped out: blazing brands and scorching heat sent ahead to kindle many scattering fires, and the grand general conflagration following up and finishing up. Within the limits marked upon the map nothing was spared; not any of the elegant residences of the patricians—not even those isolated by acres of pleasure-grounds; not even the "fire-proof" Historical Hall, with its thousand precious relics; not even the stone churches of Robert Collyer and the Rev. Mr. Chamberlain, protected by a park in front; not even the cemetery to the north, whither many people removed a few of their most necessary effects, only to see them consumed before their eyes; not even Lincoln Park, whose scattering oaks were burned to dismal pollards by the all-consuming flames; nothing but one lone house, the residence of Mahlon Ogden, which now stands as the sole survivor of the scourged district. The loss of life and the sufferings of those who managed to escape with life were severest in this quarter of the city. They will be considered in a separate chapter, the human element of the tragedy having been purposely omitted from this as far as practicable. Only at the lake and the northern limits of the city was the conflagration stayed—or, rather, spent—for lack of any thing to consume.

The sensations conveyed to the spectator of this unparalleled event, either through the eye, the ear, or other senses or sympathies, can not be adequately described, and any attempt to do it but shows the poverty of language. We have merely noted the general course of the devouring element, and shall add, in several subsequent chapters, some personal experiences, and a portion of the many thousand thrilling incidents accompanying the catastrophe. As a spectacle, it was beyond doubt the grandest as well as most appalling ever offered to mortal eyes. From any elevated standpoint, the appearance was that of a vast ocean of flame, sweeping in mile-long billows and breakers over the doomed city. A square of substantial buildings would be submerged by it like a child's tiny heap of sand on the beach of a lake; and when the flood receded, there was no more left of the stately block than of the tiny sand-heap. Anon the devouring element would present itself as if in a personal form, and seize upon a masterpiece of architecture as if it would say to the pale faces around and below: "See, now! Here is a pile of massive marble. You built it with great pains, and thought you had something substantial. Mark, now, what a bubble it is. *Piff!*" And the proud dome collapsed, and stately wall, and ornate capital,

"—— all, mingling, fell!"

nor left a vestige of their former splendor.

Added to the spectacular elements of the conflagration—the intense and lurid light, the sea of red and black, and the spires and pyramids of flame shooting into the heavens—was its constant and terrible roar, drowning even the voices of the shrieking multitude. And ever and anon—for awhile as often as every half-minute—resounded far and wide the rapid detonations of explosions, or of falling walls. The infirm crust of earth on which the city stands was shaken by each shock. At three o'clock in the morning the great gasometer exploded with a thundering sound. About the same hour the great bell of the Court-house fell. In short, all sights and sounds which terrify the weak and unnerve the strong abounded. But they were only the accompaniment which the orchestra of Nature was furnishing to the terrible tragedy then being enacted, in which the fate of every person of that surging throng was vitally involved.

CHAPTER II.

A NIGHT OF TERROR.

Fleeing for life—A city full of sleepers surprised and stampeded—Chased into the lake—The merciless elements—Ruffianism and rapine—A thousand dollars to a carter—Escape to the prairies.

IN the preceding chapter we have recorded the doings of the fire in an abstract way, leaving almost entirely out of the question the terrible concomitants of the conflagration and its results upon the human interests comprised in a vast city full of people, nearly half of whom (fully a hundred thousand) were driven by the raging element from their homes into the streets—from the streets into the lake or the open prairie; and all of whom were most deeply involved, either in regard to life, kindred, or property, in the direful event. This was a matter of sheer necessity; for we could not tell all at once; and it is clear that the priority of mention in describing a conflict like this belongs to the victorious party. In this case it was the fire which came off victor over all the devices of human ingenuity. The dread fiery Principle, which people might have called the Fire Fiend, had not the flippant use of that epithet on other occasions left it so lamentably inadequate to this—this elemental monster was the hero of the night, and all else was naught. Before his scorching, withering breath the proud city's populace scattered and squirmed like so many little ants disturbed in their hill by the mower's scythe. And yet among those powerless victims and terrified fugitives were senators, judges, generals, princes of commerce and queens of society and of letters--the wealthy and the great—very wealthy and truly great, except when scourged by such a manifestation of divine wrath—all brought low with the lowly themselves—all chastened and humbled together. And many were sacrificed; nor was the destroyer any respecter of persons in the choice of his victims. The rich banker perished in saving his gold or his accounts, as well as the poor laborer for lack of cunning, or his childing wife for lack of care.

The fire broke out in the densely-populated section of the city somewhat after midnight, as we have seen. The people of the quarter through which it first passed were of a class the most likely to be careless in the extreme. In that quarter were the low brothels of Griswold, Quincy, Jackson, and Wells Streets, as well as the more showy haunts of vice on more respectable streets, and the rooms of kept mistresses in the upper stories of business blocks. The rest of the population living in this quarter were people used to excitements and alarms, and not likely to be disturbed, especially on a Sunday night, by any fidgeting about fire. Among such the panic, when at length aroused by the close presence of danger, would naturally be the most intense. Awakened from their slumbers, or aroused from their orgies by the near approach of the flames, which traveled almost like lightning from house to house and from street to street, the denizens of that inflammable quarter had barely time to escape—half-clad, for the most part—and rush, pell-mell, through the streets—whither, they knew not. Nearly every body brought along something—a few articles of clothing—a pet bird or animal—perhaps a trunk—whatever their various impulses prompted them to seize upon in their hasty flight. A few were fortunate enough to secure a wagon or a carriage, at the fabulous prices charged for such accommodations. These filled and clogged the streets, and dashed down those on foot—for the sidewalks would by no means hold the crowds that surged, swearing, shouting, jostling, this way and that. The sidewalks, too, were occupied with men saving (that is, trying to save) and pillaging from the shops along the way. Stores were thrown open, and the people were told to help themselves to what they liked—it must all go. Saloons, too, were opened, and bottles and taps passed from mouth to mouth among the crowd. Many rough, transient fellows, who had nothing to save, or who came by thousands from distant parts of the city, attracted by curiosity or worse motives, drank deep potations and became wild and dangerous. Among these, to make the scene more revolting, were many boys.

The scene at this point of the conflagration's progress is thus graphically and for the most part correctly described by a local writer:

"The people were mad. Despite the police—indeed the police were powerless—they crowded upon frail coigns of vantage, as fences and high sidewalks propped on rotten piles, which fell beneath their weight, and hurled them, bruised and bleeding, into the dust. They stumbled over broken furniture and fell, and were trampled under foot. Seized with wild and causeless panics, they surged together backward and forward in the narrow streets, cursing, threatening, imploring, fighting to get free. Liquor flowed like water, for the saloons were broken open and despoiled, and men on all sides were to be seen frenzied with drink. Fourth Avenue and Griswold Street had emptied their denizens into the throng. Ill-omened and obscene birds of night were they. Villainous, haggard with debauch and pinched with misery, flitting through the crowd, collarless, ragged, dirty, unkempt, were negroes with stolid faces and white men who fatten on the wages of shame; gliding through the mass like vultures in search of prey. They smashed windows, reckless of the severe wounds inflicted on their naked hands, and with bloody fingers rifled impartially, till, shelf, and cellar, fighting viciously for the spoils of their forays. Women, hollow-eyed and brazen-faced, with foul drapery tied over their heads, their dresses half-torn from their skinny bosoms, and their feet thrust into trodden-down slippers, moved here and there, stealing, scolding shrilly, and laughing with one another at some particularly "splendid" gush of flame or "beautiful" falling-in of a roof. One woman on Adams Street was drawn out of a burning house three times, and rushed back wildly into the blazing ruin each time, insane for the moment. Every-where dust, smoke, flame, heat, thunder of falling walls, crackle of fire, hissing of water, panting of engines, shouts, braying of trumpets, roar of wind, tumult, confusion, and uproar.

"From the roof of a tall stable and warehouse, to which the writer clambered, the sight was one of unparalleled sublimity and terror. He was above almost the whole fire, for the buildings in the locality were all small wooden structures. The crowds directly under him could not be distinguished, because of the curling volumes of crimson smoke through which an occasional scarlet lift could be seen. He could feel the heat and smoke and hear the maddened Babel of sounds, and it required little imagination to believe one's self looking over the adamantine bulwarks of hell into the bottomless pit. On the left, where two tall buildings were in a blaze, the flame piled up high over our heads, making a lurid background, against which were limned in strong relief the people on the roofs between. Fire was a strong painter and dealt in weird effects, using only black and red, and laying them boldly on. We could note the very smallest actions of these figures—a branchman wiping the sweat from his brow with his cuff and resettling his helmet, a spectator shading his eyes with his hand to peer into the fiery sea. Another gesticulating wildly with clenched fist brought down on the palm of his hand, as he pointed toward some unseen thing. To the right the faces of the crowd in the street could be seen, but not their bodies. All were white and upturned, and every feature was as strongly marked as if it had been part of an alabaster mask. Far away, indeed for miles around, could be seen, ringed by a circle of red light, the sea of house-tops broken by spires and tall chimneys, and the black and angry lake on which were a few pale, white sails."

This writer evidently gets slightly "at sea" with his "pale, white sails," for no sail would be out in such a wind as blew that night—at least not with any canvas flying; but his scene is otherwise "drawn from the life."

The hotels—those immense caravansaries for which Chicago had become noted above all other cities—were filled with guests, who, having, up to two o'clock, no intimation that any danger threatened, were all soundly sleeping at that hour. There was the greatest danger—indeed one might say a certainty—that many of these would perish before they could be aroused and got out of the vast buildings in which they were imprisoned. It is now believed, however, that all the occupants of the hotels—the nine-story Palmer, the seven-story Sherman, with its mile of halls, the Tremont, Briggs, and the rest—all escaped in safety to the streets, whatever may have been their fate afterward. Undoubtedly many of them perished in trying to thread their way through the burning streets, unacquainted, as they were, with the geography of the city, and hindered by their attempts to save their luggage.

The lowest price at which a hack or cart could be obtained for this service was ten dollars; and from that figure it ranged upward, according to the ability of the owner or the degree of the hackman's devilishness. Mr. E. I. Tinkham, the cashier of one of the banks, actually paid an expressman one thousand dollars for taking a box to the railroad depot on the west side, a distance of a mile; but this was an unusual case, the box carried being full of treasure, amounting to $600,000, taken from the bank-vaults, and to be carried through walls of fire at the peril of the brave carter's life. This case is not to be reckoned among those of inhuman wretches of drivers who extorted all a poor man's means, or perhaps a helpless woman's, for taking on board a trunk containing a meager remnant of clothing, perhaps to be thrown off at the next corner, where the extorting process could be repeated upon another customer. It was in the North Division that the vulture-like qualities of the expressmen and other drivers culminated; for it was there that the distress was greatest, and the demand for vehicles most urgent. By the time the flames had reached the north side, all thought of checking its progress had long been abandoned, and the only hope of the most hopeful was to escape with their lives and a few of such valuables and clothing as they could lay hands upon in the haste of their flight. There were many carters about, but they wanted now fifty dollars for moving a load. Having found a victim, they would stop midway and assess him again, or if he refused to submit to their levies, or was unable to pay them, off went his goods into the street, to be ravaged by roughs, trampled upon by the crowd, or consumed by the flames. In more than one case, however, these unconscionable drivers were brought to a sense of their duty by a sudden declaration of martial law on the part of the owner, and the exhibition of a loaded revolver—a sort of *mandamus* fully excusable in such a strait.

The fugitives from the fire on the south side had fortunately had many avenues of egress, so that it was only those who too bravely or too rashly staid to save friends or treasures, or those who, by reason of the night's debauches, or other cause, slept too soundly in their isolated quarters, who fell a prey to the raging element. Others fled in the direction which their impulse or reason suggested. They had reason to thank the flat topography and square, open plan of the city for their delivery from being roasted by thousands in the flames. Without straight broad streets, plenty of bridges across the river and its branches, and an open country on three sides of the city, the slaughter must have been terrible; for the streets would have been irremediably choked with colliding vehicles and the people cornered up and consumed by the flames. As it was, those who, instead of flying straight to a point to the south or west beyond the reach of the monster, shrank to the nearest refuge—the lake-shore—or fled northward before the whelming wave, fared the worst of all. The narrow space of unoccupied lake-shore lying between Randolph and Congress Streets, and adjoining "the basin"—a section of the lake protected by a breakwater—was crowded during the night and early morning with forlorn creatures of all classes, and strewn with every description of goods snatched from burning homes. Each fugitive had brought along some article or other—whatever was most dearly prized or could be most hastily reached; but, by and by, as the rigors of the situation increased, they had abandoned these *impedimenta*, and strove only to save what was dearest of all, their lives. As the choking heat increased and the smoke blinded their eyes, and the sparks and brands fell in thicker showers, those poor creatures shrank further and further into the chilling water of the basin. The most of them were women, and their shrieks and moans enhanced the terrors of the scene. One of these—apparently quite delicate—came bringing an immensely heavy sewing-machine; and when her place of refuge became too hot to live in, she seized her ponderous burden and bore it on southward. Poor thing! she *must* sustain it, for it is now all that is left to sustain *her!* Another young woman clutches a small bundle—probably her clothing—so tenaciously as to excite the cupidity of a ruffian, who knocks her down, seizes her precious package and makes off with it. Here is another group—two daughters supporting an invalid mother, who faints repeatedly, each time as if dead. With such scenes as these the night wears away.

By and by all chance of escape to the southward, of which the braver ones have been availing themselves hitherto, is cut off, and the shrieking fugitives are now pent up between a fiery and a watery death—the terrors of which are increased by the suffering and ruffianism around them, and the wide-spread ruin beyond, the loss of home, property, and perhaps kindred, already accomplished, and the state of poverty into which they must now emerge, if emerge they should at all.

This was the situation through nearly twelve hours, from Sunday midnight to Monday noon, at which time the flames had been subdued at the south, and the immediate terrors of the situation removed. Those terrors were eclipsed by those suffered by the denizens of the ill-fated North Division. These were, for the most part, surprised at three o'clock in the morning, and woke to find themselves *surrounded by fire.* The manner in which the conflagration spread in this part of the city has been already described. Called from their beds to witness the fire upon the south side of the river, the people of the quiet and elegant residence-quarter east of Clark and south of Superior Streets were gazing at the magnificent spectacle and uttering their exclamations of pity for the unfortunate inhabitants across the river, when they discovered, to their horror, that the flames had already been communicated to their own quarter, and that the Water-works and other buildings to the rear of them were all ablaze! The appalling significance of this discovery was soon apparent to all. It meant that their own homes were doomed, and that, before they could save any of their goods—perhaps before they could escape with their lives—they would be walled in on either side by fire.

A terrible panic ensued. There was sudden screaming and dashing about of half-clad women, gathering up such valuables as could be suddenly snatched. There was frantic rushing into the streets and shouting for vehicles. There was anxious inquiry and anon distressed cries for absent protectors—a large portion of the men being on the far side of the river, and in many cases unable to reach their homes. Then there was a pell-mell rush through the streets, some of the wild faces pushing eagerly in this direction and others quite as eagerly in the opposite; and children screaming; and shouts resounding; and brands falling in showers; and truckmen running each other down; and half-drunken, wholly desperate ruffians peering into doors and seizing valuables, and insulting women; and oaths from lips unused to them, as hot as the flames which leaped and crackled near by; and prayers from manly breasts where they had slumbered since childhood; and every other sign of turmoil and terror.

Those who had sufficient warning endeavored to escape to the northward with their best effects. Mr. Eastman, the Postmaster of the city, whose house was on Erie Street, hauled out some trunks of clothing, and found a hackman whom he desired to take them on board, but the fee demanded exceeded his means, and he was obliged to drag his trunks along, with the help of a maid-servant, his wife carrying her infant in her arms. Four times they halted, exhausted, in what seemed a place of safety, and four times they were driven on by the insatiate flames.

The most natural resort of the people of the quarter mentioned, however, was the sandy beach of the lake, where there were but few houses, and those were shanties. This strip of shore, known as "the Sands," was famous, or, rather, infamous, in years agone, as the *locale* of numerous low brothels, to which "Long John" Wentworth, when Mayor of the city, gave the *coup de grace* by *allowing* them to burn up. Their place had never been fully occupied, and to the bleak, narrow area thus afforded, the terrified population shrank for refuge from the pursuing monster. Such an assemblage as there congregated, Chicago never witnessed before and probably never will witness again. It was the scene at the "basin" repeated, with more diversity. The extremes of wealth and squalor had been dwelling within a stone's throw of each other in this section of the city which had emptied itself upon this scant skirt of sand. These inequalities of societies were now leveled off as smooth as the beach itself. No, not leveled; for the landlord and aristocrat, whose many stores are burning on the other side, and his precious library and cabinet—the accumulation of a doting lifetime—has still a preferment over the boor who now jostles him;

he is allowed to lose more and to suffer more, and is required to lament less. But that is all; the two must for to-night share each other's bed—the damp sand—and to-morrow each other's fare—nothing but sights of horror.

Scarce a person among the thousands collected on the sands, and there pent up for thirty hours, but had lost some dear one in the confusion attending the escape from their burning houses. Whether these were alive or dead, none could know.

Here was the wife of a well-known musician, with her two children—one of them but three months old. When the flames came too close, she must retreat into the water, breast-deep, and bear them aloft. Her husband, after escaping with her from their house, had gone back to save some precious article from the fire, and had not returned to her.

Here was a distracted husband who had failed in his effort to reach his invalid wife—a cousin of the celebrated Madame Parepa Rosa, and a lady of rare gifts. (Poor woman! she died a few days afterward, a raving maniac, and one of the many victims of the conflagration.)

Here was a family of brothers and sisters, mourning a mother who had perished before their eyes. Here were sick ones, snatched from their beds, and dying of exposure.

Here was every imaginable scene of distress, and knotted threads of narrative, which, if followed, would fill this book many times over.

As the morning advanced, some of the sufferers, crawling along the shore and down upon a pier, were taken up by tugs and propellers and carried up the river or out to sea for safety. They embarked at the peril of their lives, for the docks were on fire, and more than one staunch steamer burned alongside.

Such of the north side people as did not resort to the lake

betook themselves toward Lincoln Park, where a day and night of imprisonment and exposure awaited them, or (which proved the wisest course) escaped to the west side, where they found shelter with friends, or, at least, safety upon the open prairie. Chicago Avenue was the main avenue of escape, and this becoming choked with vehicles and goods, many perished in the attempt to reach the next thoroughfare to the north. Bremer and Wesson Streets, in this vicinity, were found strewn with charred corpses when the smoke cleared away.

All Monday the fire raged through the ill-fated North Division; but its progress was noted with little interest, except by the luckless people whose abodes it seized upon as it advanced; for every body had given up the whole of that quarter as lost, and there was no longer any struggle, even of hope and fear. It seemed as if those emotions had run down, as a clock, neglected by its keeper, stops for lack of winding. The index had stopped at the figure of despair!

CHAPTER III.

PERSONAL EXPERIENCES.

The early stages of the fire—The purlieu which generated it—A scene for a fire-worshiper—A weird procession—Discussing the future by the light of the past.

ACCOUNTS of the experiences of eye-witnesses are like photographic views in conveying to the reader minute facts which can not be reached in a general sketch. Accordingly we give several statements—the most graphic, and at the same time strictly truthful, which we have anywhere seen. The first is that of Mr. J. E. Chamberlin, a young journalist, whose curiosity led him to follow up closely the conflagration of the 7th, as well as the Great Conflagration which followed on the 8th and 9th. He says:

"I was at the scene in a few minutes. The fire had already advanced a distance of about a single square through the frame buildings that covered the ground thickly north of De Koven Street and east of Jefferson Street—if those miserable alleys shall be dignified by being denominated streets. That neighborhood had always been a *terra incognita* to respectable Chicagoans, and during a residence of three years in the city I had never visited it. The land was thickly studded with one-story frame dwellings, cow-stables, pig-sties, corn-cribs, sheds innumerable; every wretched building within four feet of its neighbor, and every thing of wood—not a brick or a stone in the whole area. The fire was under full headway in this combustible mass before the engines arrived, and what could be done? Streams were thrown into the flame, and evaporated almost as soon as they struck it. A single fire-engine in the blazing forests of Wisconsin would have been as effective as were these machines in a forest of shanties thrice as combustible as the pine woods of the North. But still the firemen kept at work fighting the flames—stupidly and listlessly, for they had worked hard all of Saturday night and most of Sunday, and had been enervated by the whisky which is always copiously poured on such occasions. I stepped in among some sheds south of Ewing Street; a fence by my side began to blaze; I beat a hasty retreat, and in five minutes the place where I had stood was all ablaze. Nothing could stop that conflagration there. It must sweep on until it reached a broad street, and then, every body said, it would burn itself out.

"Ewing Street was quite a thoroughfare for that region. It is a mere alley, it is true, but is somewhat broader than the surrounding lanes. It has elevated board sidewalks, and is passable for teams in dry weather. On that night it was crowded with people pouring out of the thickly-settled locality between Jefferson Street and the river, and here the first panic began. The wretched female inhabitants were rushing out almost naked, imploring spectators to help them on with their burdens of bed-quilts, cane-bottomed chairs, iron kettles, etc. Drays were thundering along in the single procession which the narrowness of the street allowed, and all was confusion.

"When the fire had passed Ewing Street, I hurried on to Harrison, aware of the fact that the only hope for the staying of the conflagration was in the width of that street, and hoping that some more effective measures than squirting of water would be taken at that point. The same scene of hurry and confusion was repeated at Harrison on a larger scale than at Ewing; and that same scene kept on increasing in terror all night long, as the fire moved northward. The crowd anxiously watched the flames as they approached the street, and the universal remark was: 'If it passes this, nothing can stop it but last night's burned district.' At length the fire reached the street, and broke out almost simultaneously for a distance of two squares. The two fire-engines which stood in Harrison Street fled in terror. Brands of fire, driven on by the gale, struck the houses on the north side of the street. Though mostly of brick, they ignited like tinder, and the fire swept northward again.

"Again I passed into Jefferson Street, keeping on the flank of the fire. In a vacant square, filled with refugees from the fire and their rescued effects, I stopped a few minutes to watch the fiery ocean before me. The open lot was covered with people, and a strange sight was presented. The fire had reached a better section, and many people of the better class were among those who had gathered a few of their household goods on that open space. Half a dozen rescued pianos were watched by delicate ladies, while the crowd still surged in every direction. Two boys, themselves intoxicated, reeled about, each bearing a small cask of whisky, out of which he insisted upon treating every body he met. Soon more casks of whisky appeared, and scores of excited men drank deeply of their contents. The result was, of course, that an equal number of drunken men were soon impeding the flight of the fugitives.

"When I reached Van Buren Street, the southern limit of the Saturday night fire, I paused to see the end of the conflagration. A single engine stood on Van Buren Street, doing what seemed to me good service in preventing the fire from eating its way westward, against the wind, which it was apparently determined to do. Suddenly the horses were attached to the engine, and, as soon as the hose was reeled, it disappeared, whirling northward on Jefferson Street. What did it mean? I caught the words, 'Across the river,' uttered doubtingly by a bystander. The words passed from mouth to mouth, and there was universal incredulity, although the suggestion was communicated through the crowd with startling rapidity. There was a general movement northward and out of the smoke, with a view to discover whether it was really possible that the fire had been blown across the river, and had started afresh on the south side. I went with the rest, crossed the burnt ground of the night before, stood on the embankment that had been Canal Street, and perceived, through the clouds of smoke, a bright light across the river. I rushed to the Adams-street viaduct and across the bridge. The Armory, the Gas-works, 'Conley's Patch,' and Wells Street, as far north as Monroe, were all on fire. The wind had increased to a tempest, and hurled great blazing brands over our heads.

"At this point my duty called me to my home in the West Division; but within an hour I was back again to witness the doom of the blazing city, of which I then had a full presentiment. The streets on the west side were as light as broad noon. I looked at my watch and saw that it was just two o'clock. As I ran down Monroe Street, with the burning town before me, I contemplated the ruin that was working, and the tears rose to my eyes. I could have wept at that saddest of sights, but I choked down the tears, and they did not rise again that night.

"When I crossed the river, I made a desperate attempt to

reach my office on Madison Street, beyond Clark. I pressed through the crowd on Randolph Street as far as Lasalle, and stood in front of the burning Court-house. The cupola was in full blaze, and presented a scene of the sublimest as well as most melancholy beauty. Presently the great tower was undermined by the fire below, and fell to the bottom with a dull sound and a heavy shock that shook the earth. Somebody called out, 'Explosion!' and a panic ensued, in which every thing and every body was carried westward. Then I went to Lake Street, and found a torrent of sparks sweeping down that avenue. But I pulled my hat about my eyes, buttoned up my coat-collar, and rushed eastward, determined to reach my office. I turned down Dearborn, and leaped through a maelstrom of scorching sparks. The fiery storm at length drove me into an open store, from which the occupants had fled. I seized a large blanket which they had left on the floor, wrapped it around my head and body, and sallied forth again. I went as far as Washington Street, but any attempt at further progress would have been madness. I beat a hasty retreat to Lake Street, and came down Lasalle again to the immediate neighborhood of the fire.

"And now the scene of confusion had reached its height. Wagons were rushing through the streets, laden with stocks of goods, books, valuable papers, boxes of money, and every thing conceivable; scores of men were dragging trunks frantically along the sidewalks, knocking down women and children; fabulous sums of money were offered truckmen for conveyances. The scene was indescribable.

"But, as large as was the number of people who were flying from the fire, the number of passive spectators was still larger. Their eyes were all diverted from the skurrying mass of people around them to the spectacle of appalling grandeur before them. They stood transfixed, with a mingled feeling of horror and admiration, and while they often exclaimed at the beauty of the scene, they all devoutly prayed that they might never see such another. The noise of the conflagration was terrific. To the roar which the simple process of combustion always makes, magnified here to so grand an extent, was added the crash of falling buildings and the constant explosions of stores of oil and other like material. The noise of the crowd was nothing compared with this chaos of sound. All these things —the great, dazzling, mounting light, the crash and roar of the conflagration, and the desperate flight of the crowd—combined to make a scene of which no intelligent idea can be conveyed in words.

"When it became too hot in Randolph Street, I retired to the eastern approach of the bridge on that street. A knot of men had gathered there, from whom all signs of excitement had disappeared. It was then almost four o'clock, and whatever excitement we had felt during the night had passed away. Wearied with two nights of exertion, I sat upon the railing and looked down on the most appalling spectacle of the whole night. The Briggs House, the Metropolitan House, Peter Schultler's wagon manufactuory, Heath & Mulligan's oil establishment, stored five stories high with exceedingly inflammable material, the Nevada Hotel, and all the surrounding buildings, were in a simultaneous blaze. The flames, propelled by variable gusts of wind, seemed to pour down Randolph Street in a liquid torrent. Then the appearance was changed, and the fire was a mountain over our heads. The barrels of oil in Heath's store exploded with a sound like rattling musketry. The great north wall of the Nevada Hotel plunged inward with hardly a sound, so great was the din of the surrounding conflagration.

The Garden City House burned like a box of matches; the rapidity of its disappearance was remarked by every body. Toward the east and north-east we looked upon a surging ocean of flame.

"Meanwhile a strange scene was being enacted in the street before us. A torrent of humanity was pouring over the bridge. Madison-street bridge had long before become impassable, and Randolph was the only outlet for the entire region south of it. Drays, express-wagons, trucks, and conveyances of every conceivable species and size, crowded across in indiscriminate haste. Collisions happened almost every moment, and when one overloaded wagon broke down, there were enough men on hand to drag it and its contents over the bridge by main force. The same long line of men dragging trunks was there, many of them tugging over the ground with loads which a horse would strain at. Women were there, looking exactly like those I had seen all night, staggering under weights upon their backs. Whole establishments of ill-fame were there, their half-dozen inmates loaded into the bottoms of express-wagons, driven, of course, by their 'men.' Now and then a stray schooner, which, for want of a tug, had been unable to escape earlier from the south branch, came up, and the bridge must be opened. Then arose a howl of indignation along the line, which, being near, was audible above the tumult. A brig lay above us in the stream, and the captain was often warned by the crowd that he must make his exit at once, if he wished to save his craft—a suggestion the force of which he doubtless appreciated, as he stood upon the quarter-deck calling frantically to every tug that passed.

"I saw an undertaker rushing over the bridge with his mournful stock. He had taken a dray, but was unable to load all of his goods into the vehicle. So he employed half a dozen boys,

CHAMBER OF COMMERCE.

CHAMBER OF COMMERCE AFTER THE FIRE.

RUSH MEDICAL COLLEGE.

FIFTH NATIONAL BANK.

gave each of them a coffin, took a large one himself, and headed the weird procession. The sight of those coffins, upright, and bobbing along just above the heads of the crowd, without any apparent help from *any body* else, was somewhat startling, and the unavoidable suggestion was that they were escaping across the river to be ready for use when the *debris* of the conflagration should be cleared away. But just as men in the midst of a devastating plague carouse over each new corpse, and drink to the next who dies, so we laughed quite merrily at the ominous spectacle.

"At last it became too warm to be comfortable on the east side of the river. The fire was burning along Market Street, and many were the conjectures whether Lind's block would go. The buildings opposite burned with a furnace-heat, but Lind's block stands now, a monument to its own isolation.

"And then the question was every-where asked, 'Will Chicago ever recover from this blow?' Many suggestions were offered on this subject. The general opinion was that the city could never again obtain a foothold. Said one old gentleman, 'Our capital is wiped out of existence. You never can get what money is stored up out of those vaults. There is n't one that can stand this furnace-heat. Whatever the fire consumes to-night is utterly consumed. All loss is total; for there will not be an insurance company left to-morrow. The trade of the city *must* go to St. Louis, to Cincinnati, and to New York, and we never can get hold of it again. We could n't transact any business even if we had customers, for we have n't got anywhere to transact it. Yes, sir, this town is gone up, and we may as well get out of it at once.' Thus all seemed to talk, and there was none of that earnest, hopeful language of which I have heard so much since, and have been rejoiced to hear. But what else could I expect? Those men stood facing the burning city. They saw those great hotels and warehouses toppling, one after another, to the ground. Their spirits were elastic, as subsequent events have proved, but on that terrible night they were drawn to their utmost tension, and the cord came near breaking.

"Tired with my two nights' work and of the sad sight before me, I joined the crowd, crossed the river, went up Canal Street and lay down on a pile of lumber in Avery's yard. My position was at the confluence of the north and south branches, directly opposite the middle of the main river, and exactly on the dock. All solicitude for the remaining portion of the city, and all appreciation of the magnitude of the tragedy that was being acted across the river, had left me. I did not care whether the city stood or burned. I was dead, so far as my sensibilities were concerned. Half a dozen fellows—strangers—were with me on the lumber-pile, and were as listless as myself. The chief matter which seemed to interest them was the probable weight of one of their party—a fat fellow, whom they called Fred. I became quite interested in the subject, and joined in the guessing. Fred kept us bursting in ignorance awhile, and then, in a burst of confidence, told us he weighed 206, and begged us not to mention it. Meanwhile, Wells-street bridge took fire, and, as affording something novel, attracted our attention for a few minutes. The south end of the bridge caught alight, and then the north end. But the north end burned less rapidly than the south, and soon outbalanced the latter, when, of course, the whole structure tipped to the northward, and stood fixed, one end in the water, at an angle of about sixty degrees. Then the fire communicated with the whole framework, till the bridge looked like a skeleton with ribs of fire. But presently the support underneath burned away; then the skeleton turned a complete summersault and plunged into the river, as if, warmed into life, it had sought refuge from the flames which were consuming it."

[Our contributor here details his adventures upon the north side, which were not of particular moment.]

"When I had regained a footing in the favored West Division, it was seven o'clock. Then a curious-looking crimson ball came up out of the lake, which they said was the sun; but oh how sickly and insignificant it looked! I had watched that greatest of the world's conflagrations from its beginning to almost its end; and although the fire was still blazing all over the city with undiminished luster, I could not look at it. I was almost unable to walk with exhaustion and the effects of a long season of excitement, and sought my home for an hour's sleep. As I passed up West Madison Street, I met scores of working girls on their way 'down town,' as usual, bearing their lunch-baskets as if nothing had happened. They saw the fire and smoke before them, but could not believe that the city, with their means of livelihood, had been swept away during that night."

CHAPTER IV.

PERSONAL EXPERIENCES—CONTINUED.

Narrative of Alexander Frear—A fond mother's mishaps—Scenes on the Avenues—Rifling the dry goods palaces—How a pious soul prayed herself to death—Asking too much of Providence—Human diabolism—Cheapness of life.

MR. ALEXANDER FREAR, a New York alderman, seems to have seen as much of the fire and its concomitants as any other person in the city; and he tells his adventures in a plain and straightforward way which is at the same time very graphic. The beginning of his narrative, as we quote it, finds Mr. Frear upon the west side of the river, endeavoring to comfort his brother's wife (his brother being absent from the city) by assuring her (what proved to be the fact) that her house, on Ewing Street, would not be touched by the flames. Nevertheless, she would not be appeased until her goods and children had been sent over to the house of a friend on Wabash Avenue. Then, presently, the anxious mother had to follow in a coach, procured half a mile away, and with her satchel full of valuables in her hand. After a hard drive, through a roundabout route, they were stopped by the jam at the corner of Wabash Avenue and Washington Street. The narrative proceeds:

"In the confusion it was difficult to get any information; but I was told that the block in which the Kimballs lived (the refuge of Mrs. Frear's children) was burning, and that the people were all out. To add to my distress Mrs. Frear jumped out of the vehicle and started to run in the direction of the fire. Nothing, I am satisfied, saved her from being crushed to death in a mad attempt to find her children but the providential appearance of an acquaintance, who told her that the children were all safe at the St. James Hotel. . . . I found that Mrs. Frear's acquaintance had either intentionally or unintentionally deceived her. The children were not in the house. When I informed her of it she fainted. When she was being taken up stairs to the parlor I found she had lost her satchel. Whether it was left in the cab when she jumped out, or was stolen in the house, I can not say. It contained two gold watches, several pins and drops of value, a cameo presented to her by Mrs. Stephen A. Douglas, a medal of honor belonging to her husband (who was an officer in the First Wisconsin Volunteers during the war), and about $200 in bills and currency stamps, besides several trinkets of trifling value."

Leaving his charge in the care of some ladies, Mr. Frear proceeded in search of the children. He went to the Sherman House, where all was panic. "I looked out," he says, "of one of the south windows of the house, and shall never forget the terribly magnificent sight I saw. The Court-house Park was filled with people who appeared to be huddled together in a solid mass, helpless and astounded. The whole air was filled with the falling cinders, and it looked like a snow-storm lit by colored fire. The weird effect of the glare and the scintillating light upon this vast silent concourse was almost frightful. While in the corridor of the Sherman House I encountered my nephew, and he asked me if I wanted to see the fire, saying he had one of George Garrison's horses and only wanted a rubber blanket to throw over him to protect him from the sparks. I told him about Mrs. Frear, but he thought there was no reason to worry. He got a blanket somewhere, and we started off in a light wagon for Wabash Avenue, stopping at Wright's, under the Opera House, to get a drink of coffee, which I needed very much. There were several of the firemen of the Little Giant in there. One of the men was bathing his head with whisky from a flask. They declared that the entire department had given up, overworked, and that they could do nothing more. While we stood there an Irish girl was brought in with her dress nearly all burnt from her person. It had caught on the Court-house steps from a cinder. When we went out a man in his shirt-sleeves was unhitching the horse; and when we came up he sprung into the wagon, and would have driven off in spite of us if I had not caught the horse by the head. He then sprang out and struck my nephew in the face, and ran toward State Street.

"We drove as rapidly as we could into Wabash Avenue, the wind sweeping the embers after us in furious waves. We passed a broken-down steamer in the middle of the roadway. The avenue was a scene of desolation. The storm of falling fire seemed to increase every second, and it was as much as we could do to protect ourselves from the burning rain and guide the horse through the flying people and hurrying vehicles. Looking back through Washington Street, toward the Opera House, I saw the smoke and flames pouring out of State Street, from the very point we had just left, and the intervening space was filled with the whirling embers that beat against the houses and covered the roofs and window-sills. It seemed like a tornado of fire. To add to the terrors the animals, burnt and infuriated by the cinders, darted through the streets regardless of all human obstacles. Wabash Avenue was burning as far down as Adams Street. The flames from the houses on the west side reached in a diagonal arch quite across the street, and occasionally the wind would lift the great body of flame, detach it entirely from the burning buildings, and hurl it with terrific force far ahead. All the mansions were being emptied with the greatest disorder and the greatest excitement. Nobody endeavored to stay the flames now. A mob of men and women, all screaming and shouting, ran about wildly, crossing each other's paths, and intercepting each other as if deranged. We tried to force our way along the avenue, which was already littered with costly furniture, some of it burning in the streets under the falling sparks, but it was next to impossible. Twice we were accosted by gentlemen with pocket-books in their hands, and asked to carry away to a place of safety some valuable property. Much as we may have desired to assist them, it was out of our power. Women came and threw packages into the vehicle, and one man with a boy hanging to him caught the horse and tried to throw us out. I finally got out and endeavored to lead the animal out of the terrible scenes. When we had gone about a block I saw that the Court-house was on fire, and almost at the same moment some one said the St. James had caught on the roof. I was struck on the arm by a bird-cage flung from an upper window, and the moment I released the horse he shied and ran into a burning dray-load of furniture, smashing the wheel of the wagon and throwing my companion out on his shoulder. Fortunately he was only bruised. But the horse, already terrified, started immediately, and I saw him disappear with a leap like that of a panther.

"We then hurried on toward the St. James Hotel, passing through some of the strangest and saddest scenes it has ever been my misfortune to witness. I saw a woman kneeling in the street with a crucifix held up before her and the skirt of her dress burning while she prayed. We had barely passed her before a runaway truck dashed her to the ground. Loads of goods passed us repeatedly that were burning on the trucks, and my nephew says that he distinctly saw one man go up to a pile of costly furniture lying in front of an elegant residence and deliberately hold a piece of burning packing-box under it until the pile was lit. When we reached the wholesale stores north of Madison Street the confusion was even worse. These stores were packed full of the most costly merchandise, and to save it at the rate the fire was advancing was plainly impossible. There was no police, and no effort was made to keep off the rabble. A few of the porters and draymen employed by these stores were working manfully, but there were costermongers' wagons, dirt carts, and even coaches backed up and receiving the goods, and a villainous crowd of men and boys chaffing each other and tearing open parcels to discover the nature of their contents. I reached the St. James between two and three o'clock on Monday morning. It was reported to be on fire, but I did not see the flames then. Mrs. Frear had been moved in an insensible state to the house of a friend on the north side. I could learn no other particulars.

"The house was in a dreadful state of disorder. Women and children were screaming in every direction, and baggage being thrown about in the most reckless manner. I now concluded that Mrs. Frear's children had been lost. It was reported that hundreds of people had perished in the flames.

"There was a crowd of men and women at the hotel from one of the large boarding-houses in the neighborhood of State and Adams Streets, and they said they barely escaped with their

JACKSON STREET.

FIELD & LEITER'S STORE.

NEW HONORE BLOCK.

COR. LASALLE AND WASHINGTON STREETS.

lives, leaving every thing behind. At this time it seemed to me that the fire would leave nothing. People coming in said the Sherman House was going, and that the Opera-house had caught. Finally word was brought that the bridges were burning, and all escape was cut off to the north and west. Then ensued a scene which was beyond description. Men shouted the news, and added to the panic. Women, half-dressed, and many of them with screaming children, fled out of the building. There was a jam in the doorway, and they struck and clawed each other as if in self-defense. I lost sight of my nephew at this time. Getting out with the crowd, I started and ran round toward the Tremont House. Reaching Dearborn Street, the gust of fire was so strong that I could hardly keep my feet.

"I ran on down toward the Tremont. Here the same scene was being enacted with tenfold violence. The elevator had got jammed, and the screams of the women on the upper floors was heart-rending. I forced my way upstairs, seeing no fire, and looked into all the open rooms, calling aloud the names of Mrs. Frear's daughters. Women were swarming in the parlors; invalids, brought there for safety, were lying upon the floor. Others were running distracted about, calling upon their husbands. Men, pale and awe-struck and silent, looked on without any means of averting the mischief. All this time the upper part of the house was on fire. The street was choked with people, yelling and moaning with excitement and fright. I looked down upon them from an upper window a moment, and saw far up Dearborn Street the huge flames pouring in from the side-streets I had traversed but an hour ago, and it appeared to me that they were impelled with the force of a tremendous blow-pipe. Every thing that they touched melted. Presently the smoke began to roll down the stairways, and almost immediately after the men who had been at work on the roof came running down. They made no outcry, but hurried from the house as if for their lives. I went up to the fourth story, looking into every room, and kicking open those that were locked. There were several other men searching in the same manner, but I did not notice them. While up here I obtained a view of the conflagration. It was advancing steadily upon the hotel from two or three points. *There was very little smoke; it burned too rapidly*, or what there was must have been carried away on the wind. The whole was accompanied by a crackling noise as of an enormous bundle of dry twigs burning, and by explosions that followed each other in quick succession on all sides.

"From the street-entrance I could see up Dearborn Street as far as the Portland Block, and it was full of people all the distance, swaying and surging under the reign of fire. Around on Lake Street the tumult was worse. Here for the first time I beheld scenes of violence that made my blood boil. In front of Shay's magnificent dry goods store a man loaded a store-truck with silks in defiance of the employés of the place. When he had piled all he could upon the truck, some one with a revolver shouted to him not to drive away or he would fire at him, to which he replied, 'Fire, and be damned!' and the man put the pistol in his pocket again. Just east of this store there was at least a ton of fancy goods thrown into the street, over which the people and vehicles passed with utter indifference, until they took fire. I saw myself, a ragamuffin on the Clark-street bridge, who had been killed by a marble slab thrown from a window, with white kid gloves on his hands; and whose pockets were stuffed with gold-plated sleeve-buttons, and on that same bridge I saw an Irish woman leading a goat that was big with young, by one arm, while under the other she carried a piece of silk.

"Lake Street was rich with treasure, and hordes of thieves forced their way into the stores and flung out the merchandise to their fellows in the street, who received it without disguise, and fought over it openly. I went through the street to Wabash Avenue, and here the thoroughfare was utterly choked with all manner of goods and people. Every body who had been forced from the other end of the town by the advancing flames had brought some article with him, and, as further progress was delayed, if not completely stopped by the river—the bridges of which were also choked—most of them, in their panic, abandoned their burdens, so that the street and sidewalks presented the most astonishing wreck. Valuable oil-paintings, books, pet animals, musical instruments, toys, mirrors, and bedding, were trampled under foot. Added to this, the goods from the stores had been hauled out and had taken fire, and the crowd, breaking into a liquor establishment, were yelling with the fury of demons, as they brandished champagne and brandy bottles. The brutality and horror of the scene made it sickening. A fellow, standing on a piano, declared that the fire was the friend of the poor man. He wanted every body to help himself to the best liquor he could get, and continued to yell from the piano until some one, as drunk as himself, flung a bottle at him and knocked him off it. In this chaos were hundreds of children, wailing and crying for their parents. One little girl, in particular, I saw, whose golden hair was loose down her back and caught fire. She ran screaming past me, and somebody threw a glass of liquor upon her, which flared up and covered her with a blue flame. It was impossible to get through to the bridge, and I was forced to go back toward Randolph Street.

There was a strange and new fascination in the scenes that I could not resist.

"It was now daylight, and the fire was raging closely all about me. The Court-house, the Sherman House, the Tremont House, and the wholesale stores on Wabash Avenue, and the retail stores on Lake Street, were burning. The cries of the multitude on the latter streets had now risen into a terrible roar, for the flames were breaking into the river streets. I saw the stores of Messrs. Drake, Hamlin, and Farwell burn. *They ignited suddenly all over in a manner entirely new to me, just as I have seen paper do that is held to the fire until it is scorched and breaks out in a flame.* The crowds who were watching them greeted the combustion with terrible yells. In one of the stores—I think it was Hamlin's—there were a number of men at the time on the several floors passing out goods, and when the flames blown over against it enveloped the building, they were lost to sight entirely; nor did I see any effort whatever made to save them, for the heat was so intense that every body was driven as before a tornado from the vicinity of the buildings. I now found myself carried by the throng back to near Lake Street, and determined, if possible, to get over the river. I managed to accomplish this, after a severe struggle and at the risk of my life. The rail of the bridge was broken away, and a number of small boats loaded with goods were passing down the stream. How many people were pushed over the bridge into the water I can not tell. I myself saw one man stumble under a load of clothing and disappear; nor did the occupants of the boats pay the slightest attention to him nor to the crowd overhead, except to guard against any body falling into their vessels."

From the north side, Mr. Frear made his way to the west

side, where he fell down and slept in the hall of his brother's house; but was aroused in half an hour to join in another rescue of Mrs. Frear, whose refuge on the north side was about to be burned. This accomplished, just in time to save the lady from the flames, Mr. Frear and the friend who had told him of her whereabouts hauled her, shrieking with hysterics, in a baker's wagon, some four miles, over much debris, to the home where she ought to have staid in the first place. Her property, including the jewelry, money, and relics, were all gone; but the children were soon heard from. They were safe at the Riverside suburb.

CHAPTER V.

PERSONAL EXPERIENCES—CONTINUED.

Narrative of Horace White, Esq.—How the "bloated aristocrats" took it—A parrot equal to the emergency—Sheridan in the fray—The gunpowder cure.

AMONG the severest sufferers by the general calamity was Horace White, Esq., editor of the *Tribune*, who lost, besides other property, his elegant home on Michigan Avenue, containing a remarkably select and scholarly library, for which he would not have taken $25,000. Mr. White, on discovering that the fire was one of unusual magnitude, arose from his bed for the purpose of going to the *Tribune* office and writing an editorial paragraph—perhaps advising every body to build absolutely fire-proof edifices like the *Tribune* building. He thus describes the scene which met him as he passed out upon the street:

"Billows of fire were rolling over the business palaces of the city and swallowing up their contents. Walls were falling so fast that the quaking of the ground under our feet was scarcely noticed, so continuous was the reverberation. Sober men and women were hurrying through the streets, from the burning quarter, some with bundles of clothing on their shoulders, others dragging trunks along the sidewalks by means of strings and ropes fastened to the handles, children trudging by their sides or borne in their arms. Now and then a sick man or woman would be observed, half concealed in a mattress doubled up and borne by two men. Droves of horses were in the streets, moving under some sort of guidance to a place of safety. Vehicles of all descriptions were hurrying to and fro, some laden with trunks and bundles, and others seeking similar loads and immediately finding them, the drivers making more money in one hour than they were used to see in a week or a month. Every body in this quarter was hurrying toward the lake-shore. All the streets crossing that part of Michigan Avenue which fronts on the lake (on which my own residence stood) were crowded with fugitives, hastening toward the blessed water."

After a season at the office of the *Tribune*, during which the editorial was written (but never printed), Mr. White went home to breakfast, noticing as he went that the employés of Messrs. Field, Leiter & Co.'s immense dry goods store were showering that massive pile of pure marble and iron with water from their own pumping engines. He felt sure that that building, as well as the *Tribune*, First National Bank, and Illinois Central Railroad Depot, would, with every thing to the east of them, be reserved from the destruction of the flames. This was, perhaps, a good calculation, from his point of view; but he would not have made it if he could, from a balloon, or from a high vantage point to the south-west, have marked the general course and scanned the mighty plan (as it seemed) of the devastating monster. Mr. White's narrative continues:

"Thoro was still a mass of fire to the south-west, in the direction whence it originally came, but as the engines were all down there, and the buildings small and low, I felt sure that the firemen would manage it. As soon as I had swallowed a cup of coffee and communicated to my family the facts that I had gathered, I started out to see the end of the battle. Reaching State Street I glanced down to Field, Leiter & Co.'s store, and to my surprise noticed that the streams of water which had before been showering it as though it had been a great artificial fountain, had ceased to run. But I did not conjecture the awful reality, viz: that the great pumping engines had been disabled by a burning roof falling upon them. I thought that perhaps the firemen on the store had discontinued their efforts because the danger was over. But why were men carrying out goods from the lower story?

"This query was soon answered by a gentleman who asked me if I had heard that the water had stopped? The awful truth was here! The pumping engines were disabled, and though we had at our feet a basin sixty miles wide by three hundred and sixty long, and seven hundred feet deep, all full of clear green water, we could not lift enough to quench a cooking-stove. Still the direction of the wind was such that I thought the remaining fire would not cross State Street, nor reach the residences on Wabash and Michigan Avenues and the terrified people on the lake-shore. I determined to go down to the black cloud of smoke which was rising away to the southwest, the course of which could not be discovered on account of the hight of the intervening buildings, but thought it most prudent to go home again and tell my wife to get the family wearing apparel in readiness for moving. I found that she had already done so.

"I then hurried toward the black cloud, some ten squares distant, and there found the rows of wooden houses on Third and Fourth Avenues falling like ripe wheat before a reaper. At a glance I perceived that all was lost in our quarter of the city, and I conjectured that the *Tribune* Building was doomed too, for I had noticed with consternation that the fire-proof post-office had been completely gutted, notwithstanding it was detached from other buildings. The *Tribune* was fitted into a niche, one side of which consisted of a wholesale stationery store, and the other of McVicker's Theater. But there was now no time to think of property. Life was in danger. The lives of those most dear to me depended upon their getting out of our house, out of our street, through an infernal gorge of horses, wagons, men, women, children, trunks, and plunder.

"My brother was with me, and we seized the first empty wagon we could find, pinning the horse by the head. A hasty talk with the driver disclosed that we could have his establishment for one load for twenty dollars. I had not expected to get him for less than a hundred, unless we should take him by force, and this was a bad time for a fight. He approved himself a muscular as well as a faithful fellow, and I shall always be glad that I avoided a personal difficulty with him. One peculiarity of the situation was that nobody could get a team without ready money. I had not thought of this when I was revolving in my mind an offer of one hundred dollars, which was more greenbacks than our whole family could put up if our lives had depended on the issue. This driver had divined that as all the banks were burned, a check on the Commercial National would not carry him very far, even though it should carry me to a place of safety. All the drivers had divined the same. Every man who had any thing to sell had perceived the same. 'Pay as you go' had become the watchword of the hour. Never was there a community so hastily and completely emancipated from the evils of the credit system."

A quantity of trunks, etc., was thrown into the wagon, and Mr. White, taking in his hand a cage containing what he calls "a talented parrot"—the family pet—left his brother and wife to prepare the next load, and started off for a friend's house, half a mile to the southward. They were an hour or more on the way, owing to the jam, and were at one time deterred by a howling German, who declared that he had lost every thing, and others ought to do the same.

"Presently," Mr. White continues, "the jam began to move, and we got on perhaps twenty paces and stuck fast again. By accident we had edged over to the east side of the street, and nothing but a board fence separated us from Lake Park, a strip of made ground a little wider than the street itself. A benevolent laborer, on the park side of the fence, pulled a loose post out of the ground, and with this for a catapult, knocked off the boards and invited us to pass through. It was a hazardous undertaking, as we had to drive diagonally over a raised sidewalk, but we thought it was best to risk it. Our horse mounted, and gave us a jerk which nearly threw us off the seat, and sent the provision basket and one bundle of clothing whirling into the dirt. The eatables were irrecoverable. The bundle was rescued, with two or three pounds of butter plastered upon it. We started again, and here our parrot broke out, with great rapidity and sharpness of utterance, 'Get up, get up, get up, hurry up, hurry up, it's eight o'clock,' ending with a shrill whistle. These ejaculations frightened a pair of horses close to us, on the other side of the fence, but the jam was so tight that they could n't run.

"By getting into the park we succeeded in advancing two squares without impediment, and might have gone farther had we not come upon an excavation which the public authorities had recently made. This drove us back to the avenue, where another battering-ram made a gap for us, at the intersection of

Van Buren Street, the north end of Michigan Terrace. Here the gorge seemed impassable. We were half an hour in passing the terrace. From this imposing row of residences the millionaires were dragging their trunks and their bundles, and yet there was no panic, no frenzy, no boisterousness, but only the haste which the situation authorized. . . . Arriving at Eldridge Court, I turned into Wabash Avenue, where the crowd was thinner. Arriving at the house of a friend, who was on the windward side of the fire, I tumbled off my load and started back to get another. Half way down Michigan Avenue, which was now perceptibly easier to move in, I discovered my family on the sidewalk, with their arms full of light household effects. My wife told me that the house was already burned, that the flames burst out ready-made in the rear hall before she knew that the roof had been scorched, and that one of the servants, who had disobeyed orders in her eagerness to save some article, had got singed, though not burned, in coming out. My wife and mother and all the rest were begrimed with dirt and smoke, like blackamoors—every body was. The 'bloated aristocrats' all along the street, who supposed they had lost both home and fortune at one swoop, were a sorry but not despairing congregation. They had saved their lives at all events, and they knew that many of their fellow-creatures must have lost theirs. I saw a great many kindly acts done as we moved along. The poor helped the rich, and the rich helped the poor (if any body could be called rich at such a time) to get on with their loads.

. . . .

"Presently we heard loud detonations, and a rumor went around that buildings were being blown up with gunpowder. The depot of the Hazard Powder Company was situated at Brighton, seven or eight miles from the nearest point of the fire.

At what time the effort was first made to reach this magazine, and bring powder into the service, I have not learned, but I know that Colonel M. C. Stearns made heroic efforts with his great lime wagons to haul the explosive material to the proper point. This is no time to blame any body, but in truth there was no directing head on the ground. Every body was asking every body else to pull down buildings. There were no hooks, no ropes, no axes.

"I had met General Sheridan on the street in front of the post-office two hours before. He had been trying to save the army records, including his own invaluable papers relating to the war of the rebellion. He told me that they were all lost, and then added that the post-office did n't seem to make a good fire. This was when we supposed the row of fire-proof buildings, already spoken of, had stopped the flames in our quarter. Where was General Sheridan now? every body asked. Why did n't he do something when every body else had failed? Presently a rumor went around that Sheridan was handling the gunpowder; then every body felt relieved. The reverberations of the powder, whoever was handling it, gave us all heart again. Think of a people feeling encouraged by the fact that somebody was blowing up houses in the midst of the city, and that a shower of bricks was very likely to come down on their heads."

The experience of Mr. White and his family is perhaps the average one of the wealthier classes of the South Division. That of the same classes in the North Division (represented in the narrative of Mr. Arnold, contained in the next chapter) was much rougher, from which may be deduced an inference as to that of the fifty times more numerous poor families, who had no twenty dollars to give to an exceptionally liberal cartman, no sympathizing friends down the avenue to afford them shelter and other comforts, and generally no hour's or even a half hour's time in which to calculate upon the means of escape from the devouring element.

CHAPTER VI.

PERSONAL EXPERIENCES—CONTINUED.

Hon. Isaac N. Arnold defends his castle—A vain contest—Overpowered and routed—Running the fire blockade.

AMONG the many beautiful homes destroyed in the North Division of the city, few, if any, were at once more elegant and home-like than that of the Hon. Isaac N. Arnold, the friend and biographer of Lincoln. The house was a large, plain, brick mansion, occupying with its grounds the whole block bounded by Erie, Huron, Pine, and Rush Streets. The grounds were filled with the most beautiful shrubbery and trees, and entirely secluded by a very luxuriant lilac hedge. Perhaps the most noticeable feature was the vines of wild grape, Virginia creeper, and bitter-sweet, which hung in graceful festoons from the massive elms, and covered with their dense foliage piazzas and summer-houses. There was a simple but quaint fountain, playing in front, beneath a perfect bower of overhanging vines. A great rock, upon which had been rudely carved the features of an Indian chief, had been pierced, and through this a way had been made for the water, and over the head of the old chief the water of Lake Michigan was always throwing its spray. On one side of the entrance was a little greenhouse, always gay with flowers. Two vineries of choice varieties of foreign grapes, and a large greenhouse and barn, constituted the out-buildings. On the lawn was a sun-dial with the inscription:

"Horas non numero nisi serenas." *

Alas! the tablet vindicated its motto but too well. It was broken by the heat or in the melee which accompanied the fire, and the dark hours which have followed pass by without its reckoning.

But pleasant as was the outside, it was the interior wherein its great attractions lay; and the chief of these was the library. Here were the collections of the lifetime of a man of taste, wealth, and culture—a law library and a miscellaneous library of seven or eight thousand volumes. Many of the books were specialties, and the objects of pride and affection. Among them were the speeches of Burke, Sheridan, Fox, Pitt, Erskine, Curran, Brougham, Webster, Wirt, Seward, Sumner, etc., all superbly bound; a pretty full collection of English literature and history; the Abbotsford edition of Scott's novels, in full Russia binding; Pickering and Bacon, in tree calf; a full set of the British poets; all of Bohn's libraries, etc. In American literature and history the library was rich, including beautiful editions of the works of Cooper, Irving, Paulding, Willis, Bryant, Longfellow, Prescott, Holmes, the writings of Washington, Madison, Jefferson, Hamilton, Marshall, Story, Bancroft, and others.

Mr. Arnold had a very complete collection of the proceedings of Congress and the debates, from the organization of the Government down to the present day. In his library also was perhaps as full a collection of the books and pamphlets in relation to slavery, the rebellion, the war, and President Lincoln, as

* "I number none but sunny hours."

existed in any private hands. He had also ten large volumes of manuscript letters, written by distinguished military and civil characters during and since the war of the rebellion, including many from Lincoln, McClellan, Grant, Farragut, Sherman, Halleck, Seward, Sumner, Chase, Colfax, and others, of great personal and historic interest.

For the last ten years, Mr. Arnold had been collecting the speeches, writings, and letters of Lincoln for publication, and had many volumes of manuscripts and letters, the material for a strictly biographical work upon Abraham Lincoln, several chapters of which were ready for publication. These, with many rare and curious relics, prints, and engravings, have all perished.

The pictures were not numerous, but of very decided merit. There were landscapes by Kensett, Brown, and Mignot; family portraits by Healy; the original study of Webster's reply to Hayne, now in Faneuil Hall, Boston, in which were forty portraits of distinguished Americans, many of them from life; a portrait of Webster, by Chester Harding, etc.

The failure of Mr. Arnold to save any thing, was the result of a most determined effort to save every thing, and his too confident belief that he could succeed. Nor did this confidence seem to be unreasonable. His house, standing in the center of an open block, with a wide street and the Newberry block, with only one house, in front, and the Ogden block, with only one house, to the right, directly in the pathway of the flames, it is not surprising that he believed he could save his house. Besides, he had connections by hose with hydrants, both in front and rear of his house. Mrs. Arnold had placed what proved a better estimate upon the danger; and, calling up the family, and dressing little Alice, a child of eight years, she left the house and went to her daughter's (Mrs. Scudder), leaving Mr.

A. and the remainder of the family—consisting of an older daughter, a lad of thirteen, a school-girl of fifteen, and the servants—to fight the battle with the flames.

There was a sea of fire to the south and south-west; the wind blew a perfect gale, carrying smoke and sparks, shingles, pieces of lumber and roof, directly over the house. Every thing was parched and dry as tinder. The leaves from the trees and shrubbery covered the ground. Mr. A. turned on the water to the fountains, to wet the ground and grass, and attached the hose to the hydrants. He stationed the servants on each side of the house, and others on the piazzas, and for an hour and a half—perhaps two hours—was able, by the utmost vigilance and exertion, to extinguish the flames as often as they caught. During all this time the fire was falling in torrents. There was literally a rain of fire. It caught in the dry leaves; it caught in the grass, in the barn, in the piazzas, and as often as it caught it was extinguished before it got any headway. When the barn first caught, the horses and the cow were removed to the lawn. The fight was successfully maintained until three o'clock in the morning. Every moment flakes of fire, falling upon dry wood, would be kindled by the high wind into a rapid blaze, and the next instant they would be extinguished. Every moment the contest grew warmer and more desperate, until, by three o'clock, the defenders of the castle were becoming seriously exhausted. At the hour mentioned, young Arthur Arnold called to his father, "The barn and hay are on fire!" "The leaves are on fire on the east side!" said the gardener. "The front piazza is in a blaze!" cried another. "The front greenhouse is in flames!" "The roof is on fire!" "*The water has stopped!*" was the last appalling announcement. "Now, for the first time," said Mr. A., "I gave up all hope of saving my home, and considered whether we could save any of its contents. My pictures, papers, and books—could I save them?"

An effort was made to cut down some portraits—a landscape of Kensett–Otsego Lake, by Mignot—it was too late! Seizing a bundle of papers, Mr. Arnold gathered the children and servants together, and, leading the terrified animals, they went forth from their so dearly-cherished home. But whither? They were surrounded by fire on three sides; to the south, west, and north raged the flames, making a wall of fire and smoke from the ground to the sky. Their only escape was eastward to the lake-shore. Still leading the horses and cow, they went onward to the beach. Here were gathered thousands of fugitives, hemmed in and imprisoned by the raging element. The Sands, from the Government Pier north to Lill's Pier, a distance of three-quarters of a mile, were covered with men, women, and children—some half-clad, in every variety of dress, with the motley collection of effects which they sought to save. Some had silver, some valuable papers, some pictures, carpets, beds, etc. One little child had her doll tenderly pressed in her arms; an old Irish woman was cherishing a grunting pig; a fat woman had two large pillows, as portly as herself. There was a singular mixture of the awful, the ludicrous, and the pathetic.

Reaching the water's edge, Mr. A. says he paused to examine the situation and determine where was the least danger. South-west, toward the river, were millions of feet of lumber, many shanties and wooden structures yet unburned, but which must be consumed before there could be any abatement of the danger. The air was full of cinders and smoke; the wind blew the heated sand worse than any sirocco. Where was a place of refuge? W. B. Ogden had lately constructed a long pier north of and parallel with the old United States pier, which prolongs the left bank of the river out into the lake, and this had been filled with stone, but had not been planked over; hence it would not readily burn. It was a hard road to travel, but it seemed the safest place, and Mr. Arnold and his children worked their way far out upon this pier. With much difficulty the party crossed from the Ogden slip in a small row-boat and entered the light-house, where they, with Judge Goodrich, Mr. E. I. Tinkham, and others, were hospitably received.

The party remained prisoners in the light-house and on the pier on which it stood for several hours. The shipping in the river above was burning, the immense grain elevators of the Illinois Central and North-western Railroads were a mass of flames, and the pier itself, some distance up the river, was slowly burning toward the light-house. A large propeller, fastened to the dock a short distance up the river, took fire and burned. The danger was that as soon as the hawsers by which it was moored should be burned off, it would float down stream and set fire to the dock in the immediate vicinity of the light-house. Several propellers moved down near the mouth of the river, and took on board several hundred fugitives and steamed out into the lake. If the burning propeller should come down it would set fire to the pier, the light-house, and vast piles of lumber, which had escaped in consequence of being directly on shore and detached from the burning mass. A fire company was organized of those on the pier, and with water dipped in pails from the river, the fire was kept at bay. But all felt relieved when the propeller went to the bottom. The party were still prisoners on an angle of sand, and the fire running along the north shore of the river. The river and the fire prevented an escape to the south. West and north the flames were still raging with unabated fury. The party waited for hours, hoping the fire would subside. The day wore on—noon passed—one, two o'clock, and still it seemed impossible to escape to land. Mr. Arnold, scouting to the northward, found his gardener right where he had left him, sitting upon the horse, far out in the lake, and holding on faithfully to the pony by its halter, and to the cow by her horns. The escape to the north was pronounced impracticable for the ladies. And all the while they were in great danger and great anxiety concerning the fate of the missing mother and child.

Between three and four o'clock P. M., the tug "Clifford" steamed down the river, having escaped from the burning district, and tied up to the dock near the light-house. Could she return, taking the party up the river, through and beyond the fire to the west side? The captain thought he could. The bridges at Rush, State, Clark, and Wells Streets had all burned, and their fragments had fallen into the river. The great warehouses, stores, elevators, and docks along the river were still burning, but the fury of the fire had exhausted itself. The party determined to go through this narrow channel—to run the gauntlet of the fire to a point outside of the burnt district. This was the most dangerous experience of the day. The tug might take fire herself—her woodwork had been blistered by the heat as she came down. The engine might become unmanageable after she got inside the line of fire; or she might get entangled in the floating timbers and debris of the fallen bridges. However, the party determined to make the attempt. A full head of steam was gotten up, the hose was attached to the pumps, so that if the boat or the clothes of its passengers took fire they could be readily put out. The ladies and children were placed in the pilot-house, the windows shut, and the boat started—the men crouching close to the deck in the shelter of the bulwarks. At the State Street bridge the pilot had to pick his way very carefully through a mass of debris, and the situation began to look exceedingly hazardous. But it was too late to turn back, and so the voyagers pushed on, shooting as rapidly as possible past the hottest places, and slowing where the danger was from below. As they were passing State Street bridge the pumps gave out, and they now ran great risk from fire. Arthur's hat blew away, and his father covered his face and head with a handkerchief which he had dipped in the water. Finally they passed the Wells Street bridge, and were still unscathed.

"Is not the worst over?" asked Mr. Arnold of the captain.

"We are through, sir," was the answer.

"We are safe, thank God!" came from hearts and lips, as the boat emerged from the smoke into the clear, cool air outside the fire lines.

Search for the missing ones was immediately commenced. Mr. Arnold spent over twenty-four hours in driving and wandering in pursuit of his wife—now passing among the throng of refugees at Lincoln Park and peering into every grimy countenance—now getting a clue, whether true or false, and dashing off by a train into a suburb—now baffled entirely and compelled to commence the search entirely anew. Some time during the following afternoon his efforts were rewarded by learning that his wife and child were at the house of Judge Drummond, of the U. S. Circuit Court, at a suburb called Winfield; and there, during the evening of Tuesday, the family were reunited and joined in thanks to God for their mutual deliverance.

We have given this sketch of a single family's experience in this terrible ordeal, not because it is more thrilling than that of thousands of other families, but rather because it is a specimen of the whole, and because Mr. Arnold is well known in the West. There were many homes in the North Division which, like this one, were noted for their exclusive elegance—their aristocratic seclusion, one might say—and which gave the inhabitants of this quarter a just pride in their locality. The three residences mentioned in the present chapter—the Newberry, the Ogden (Wm. B.), and the Arnold places, with the famous McCagg place, on North Clark Street, and one or two others, occupied territory which alone was worth at least a quarter of a million to each place, and this gave the proprietors some such *prima facie* title to aristocracy as landed estates do to their owners in England. They indicated at once that the occupant must possess a mine of wealth in the form of stores over-town, in order to maintain such homesteads in the face of constant offers of hundreds of dollars per foot of their street front. But they are all gone now, stores and giant elms together! Mr. McCagg, who was away in Europe at the time, lost, besides his mansion and its contents, which included many precious paintings and a library of rare works, one of his greenhouses, the finest in the West. Mr. Perry H. Smith, the well known railroad manager and capitalist, lost a library valued at $50,000, and noted for the superb bindings of its volumes, many of which Mr. Smith had but just brought from Europe.

CHAPTER VII.

THE NIGHT AFTER THE FIRE.

Flood and flame—A hopeless sortie—A ghostly bivouac—Separation of families—Days and nights of suspense and anxiety—Nothing to eat.

THE fire raged all day in the North Division, and nightfall of Monday found the thousands of fugitives in the places of refuge which they had first sought—the open prairie to the north-west of the city, the cemetery and Lincoln Park at the north-east, and the beach and piers near the mouth of the river. Those in the last-named localities had suffered a great deal during the day from the advancing rigors and dangers of the heat. They were pent up in their uncomfortable prison by the wall of fire which still presented an impassable barrier. At times this approached so close as to drive the shrinking refugees far into the water, where they could keep their bodies submerged and their heads constantly drenched, as their only protection against the scorching air and shower of burning brands. This process was sometimes very dangerous, however, for if the panic on shore should become too great, the people farthest out in the lake—many of them mothers with babes in their arms—would be forced beyond their depth and drowned. On the piers, and on the shore of the basin, which is quite abrupt, this danger was very serious, especially at night; and it was reported that a number were drowned from this cause.

On the Sands, too, there were great numbers of animals, which had fled or been taken from their stables, and which constantly threatened to trample down the women and children, and greatly increased their terror.

Nor were the four-footed beasts the only brutes that congregated on that unhappy beach. There were many of the vilest inhabitants of the city swarming there among their vermin-haunted bedding, which they had tugged in, with great ado, and they were storming the sensibilities of the gentler victims by their mingled curses and carousals—for they had saved astonishing quantities of vile whisky, and many of them had become beastly drunk. Others were at the fighting stage, and made both night and day hideous with their howlings, and threatenings, and obscene utterances.

During the afternoon of Monday, the fire advancing into the collection of shanties which approaches the lake along the Sands, a sortie was organized by the men, with water in hats and all manner of improvised buckets, in the hope that the progress of the fiery wave might be stayed. As well attempt to beat back, with a puny broom, the breakers which sometimes come dashing in from the lake with almost earthquake force! The poor shanties were little and worthless enough, God knows; but the appetite of the flames was not yet appeased, and it demanded more. Therefore the shanties went into the monster's maw, along with all the noble blocks and magnificent homes that had gone before; and the men retreated, exhausted, to the brink of the lake.

Hunger had, by this time, added its terrors to those of exposure, fear of death, and anxiety for missing relatives and friends. None of the fugitives had tasted food since early on Sunday evening, and the most of them had to fast until some

time on Tuesday; so that the night of Monday, although less turbulent and exciting than that of Sunday, was one of greater suffering after all; suffering which the victims, exhausted by hunger, blistered with heat, and chilled by water, still in terrible suspense about missing ones, and deprived of the unusual stimulus of the sudden onset of the night before—indeed weakened by the reaction of that excitement, as well as by the other causes mentioned—were but poorly able to bear.

From all these horrors there was no avenue of escape, except for the few who were able to reach and board a tug or propeller, and find rest and refuge on the capacious bosom of the lake. The outlet to the west or north being shut off by fire, and that to the south by water, the prisoners had only to stand their ground, keep their vitality aglow as best they could, and trust to God "to deliver them from the fiery furnace."

At Lincoln Park and the old cemetery to the south of it, and along the Lake-shore Drive, the number of refugees was much greater and their sufferings much less. They were not imprisoned by the hostile elements; they were not threatened with death. They had merely lost all their property—even being compelled to see the household gods and valuables which they had moved into the cemetery or the park burn up before their eyes. They had only to lament the probable fate of a missing father or brother, or to hope against hope for his safe return. As to physical condition, they were simply blinded by smoke, weakened by hunger, and choking with thirst at every gland and pore—that was all. So these Lincoln Park and cemetery victims might be pronounced very comfortably off!

The scene in the cemetery was a very weird one, as may be imagined. It is an old burial-ground, from which many of the bodies had been removed, leaving some old headstones scattered about, and many, with their mounds, still standing among the thick undergrowth of grass and small oak trees. By nightfall on Monday there could not have been less than thirty thousand men, women, and children, huddled within this ghostly inclosure. Some had sat here all day, seeing the devilish flames advance from street to street, from mile to mile, and others now rushed in breathless, dragging a trunk, or carrying some bundle, piece of furniture, or household utensil. Almost all the new-comers ran rapidly about, crying for a brother, sister, child, or friend. As twilight became dusk, and dusk reddened into the mock daylight furnished by the conflagration, the assembled thousands, tired of searching for friends, disconsolately sought resting-places for the night among the grass-grown graves.

To quote the description of a writer in the *World:* "The eyes of all looked as if they suffered from ophthalmia—black and red with smoke and cinders till they were almost blind. There were piles of every sort of furniture that ever came to the city. There were pails, bureaus, chairs, tables, trunks, tubs, clocks, great plate mirrors leaning against the trees and flashing back the illumination, a few bedsteads in need of reconstruction, clothes in little piles, carpets, pictures, rolls of cloth here and there, new shoes on strings, and suspicious-looking boxes that had been 'saved' from jewelry stores by the wrong man. Here is a group of girls wailing in a poor, heart-broken way for their mother—their sick mother—whom they left in a burning bedroom. Here is a refined and handsome lady, all alone, with a bundle of dresses on her right arm, and a caster laid by her side on the ground. Here is a strong, able-bodied man, recognizable as a banker, sitting sadly on a grave, with his hat over his aching eyes, gazing thoughtfully into a frying-pan which he holds in his hand. Every-where are rushing crowds, exclamations, salutations of woe in every language under heaven, and weeping aloud by those who have lost their friends and will not be comforted. Here comes a young man who exhibits an ice-pitcher, and laughingly declares that it is all he possesses in the world. There are no strangers here. There are no ceremonies. The cement of a kindred sorrow has done its work. Every body speaks freely to any body, and even the churl finds his human side and turns it genially toward us.

"Meantime the roaring ocean of flame nears us. It bombards even this sacred necropolis with its hellish missiles. Every-where among the dead leaves fall the blazing embers. The torches alight head first upon the hollow graves. Groups dodge and run, and here and there a fire is kindled by the brands, and there is a struggle to stamp it out. The fire howls up to heaven, and bends and bows over the cemetery like an iris of doom. The park is lighted up as by a million fire-balloons, sailing over in endless succession. Now the dead-house is afire, and a shudder of horror runs through the multitude. It defies the extinguishers. It burns until it is consumed. But it was, happily, tenantless. At the head of the graves stands usually a cheap pine head-board, and these in many instances are burned up, and in a few cases the fire burrows down into the peaceful tenement beneath, for the drought has been so severe that the very soil is combustible. At last the raging sea sweeps by to the northward, following the line of houses, and the most reckless or courageous of these elfin junketers lie down upon the graves to sleep—the queerest camp that ever gathered under heaven. At two o'clock came the blessed rain, and the multitude shivered with chill while they welcomed it. It was a dreadful night in the cemetery. A muffled moan of discomfort went through it from night to morning, and hundreds doubtless contracted fatal diseases in the exposure. It was a night not to forget in this world or the next—a night in which the demon of fire invaded the realm of the quiet angel of death."

The scene on the prairie to the westward of the city, whither the fugitives had been thronging all through Sunday night and Monday, was much the same, minus some of the weird features. There was the same contrast of classes—Mr. McCormick, the millionaire of the reaper trade, and other north-side nabobs, herding promiscuously with the humblest laborer, the lowest vagabond, and the meanest harlot. There was the same community of suffering, which brought them all to the level of weak mortals, humbled before a power whose superiority, however they might have ignored it heretofore, they must now acknowledge. There was the same terrible suspense about absent ones, whose fate, through many, many hours, was unknown to those who held them most dear.

This general separation of families may at first seem extraordinary; but it will be recollected that the onset of the fire was very rapid, and that it soon had the city divided in twain by an impassable stream or wave of flame; that, in the attempt to save property, which the instincts of all prompted, the weaker ones would be consigned to some place of supposed safety, while the stronger went back to wrestle with the rapacious monster for some of the precious possessions on which he had fixed his levy; and that in this attempt—so rapidly did the foe advance—separation was almost inevitable. It is also to be noted that the flight, on this occasion, was in all directions—the thoroughfares being glutted not only with the stream of north-side fugitives, but with the vast throng which, until the bridges were burned, came pouring over from the south side, and also with the thousands who rushed in from the west, either as idle spectators or to help in the rescue of friends whom they hoped to reach. Under these circumstances, it is not to be wondered at that hundreds perished in the flames; that almost every family became separated, and that each straying member was racked with the tortures of a terrible anxiety concerning the fate of the missing ones.

Thus passed the long and weary hours of Monday night over a hundred thousand houseless heads.

CHAPTER VIII.

THE DEATH ROLL.

Fatalities of the fire—How brave men met their death—A fatal leap—A neighborhood swallowed up by flames—Scene at the Morgue.

THE loss of life in this conflagration was less than would have been predicted in view of the extent and rapidity of the burning. The exact number will never be ascertained. The destruction was in many districts so complete that no vestige of a human body or skeleton would be discernible among the debris of consumed buildings; and in other cases the excavation and rebuilding went on in such a hurry that no report would be made, if indeed notice was taken by the workmen, of bones found. Perhaps twenty or thirty persons were known to have perished, and were reported in the first issue of the newspapers. The coroner found, during the fortnight following the fire, the remains of one hundred and seven persons, only a very few of which were identified.

The fire in the West Division resulted, so far as is known, in the death of but two persons, Jacob Wolf, an old man, who was overtaken in his house on Harrison Street, near Jefferson, and Mary Dealm, who perished on Jackson Street, near Clinton. In the south section of the city it was reported that a group of six men, stationed on the roof of a Madison Street store to fight fire, were carried down with the building and swallowed up by the flames; also that five men in a cart, passing by one of the tall dry goods stores, were killed by falling walls; but we can find no confirmation of these statements in the coroner's records. Several deaths in this quarter of the city are, however, well authenticated. One of the victims was John McDevitt, the noted billiard champion, who was wandering about, intoxicated, in the neighborhood of the post-office, and who perished, a victim to his dissolute habits. Samuel Shawcross, a merchant tailor who did business on Washington Street, and who kept a bachelor's room, was wakened only when surrounded by flames. He rushed, half dressed, toward his shop, and while passing through the alley by Field & Leiter's immense store, was crushed by the falling walls of that building. Another victim was Henry J. Ullmann, a banker, who rushed into his office to save a large quantity of coin and currency, and who never came out alive; though some of his friends feel sure that he did escape and was struck down upon the street by a ruffian, who escaped with his booty. There were four other dead bodies recognized in the South Division of the city—two of them of notorious cracksmen who were trying to rifle a store on South Water Street. Another was that of H. P. Dewey, an insurance agent, who perished in an attempt to escape from a fourth story window, at No. 125 Dearborn Street. The scene was witnessed by hundreds of people, including one of the editors of the *Tribune*,* who thus describes it:

"While Madison Street, west of Dearborn, and the west side of Dearborn were all ablaze, the spectators saw a lurid light appear in the rear windows of Speed's Block. Presently a man, who had apparently taken time to dress himself leisurely, ap-

* Mr. Sydney Howard Gay.

peared on the extension built up to the second story of two of the stores. He coolly looked down the thirty feet between him and the ground, while the excited crowd first cried jump! and then some of them more considerately looked for a ladder. A long plank was presently found, and answered the same as a ladder, and was placed at once against the building, down which the man soon after slid. But while those preparations were going on there suddenly appeared another man at a fourth story window of the building below, which had no projection, but was flush from the top to the ground—four stories and a basement. His escape by the stairway was evidently cut off, and he looked despairingly down the fifty feet between him and the ground. The crowd grew almost frantic at the sight, for it was only a choice of death before him—by fire or by being crushed to death by the fall. Senseless cries of jump! jump! went up from the crowd—senseless but full of sympathy, for the sight was absolutely agonizing. Then for a minute or two he disappeared; perhaps even less, but it seemed so long a time that the supposition was that he had fallen, suffocated with the smoke and heat. But no; he appears again. First he throws out a bed; then some bed-clothes, apparently; why, probably even he does not know. Again he looks down the dead, sheer wall of fifty feet below him. He hesitates, and well he may, as he turns again and looks behind him. Then he mounts to the window-sill. His whole form appears, naked to the shirt, and his white limbs gleam against the dark wall in the bright light as he swings himself below the window. Somehow—how none can tell—he drops and catches upon the top of the windows below him, of the third story. He stoops and drops again, and seizes the frame with his hands, and his gleaming body once more straightens and hangs prone downward, and then drops instantly and accurately upon the window-sill of the third story. A shout more of joy than applause goes up from the breathless crowd, and those who had turned away their heads, not bearing to look upon him as he seemed about to drop to sudden and certain death, glanced up at him once more, with a ray of hope, at this daring and skillful feat. Into this window he crept to look, probably, for a stairway, but appeared again presently, for here only was the only avenue of escape, desperate and hopeless as it was. Once more he dropped, his body hanging by his hands. The crowed screamed, and waved to him to swing himself over the projection from which the other man had just been rescued. He tried to do this, and vibrated like a pendulum from side to side, but could not reach far enough to throw himself upon its roof. Then he hung by one hand and looked down; raising the other hand he took a fresh hold and swung from side to side once more to reach the roof. In vain; again he hung motionless by one hand, and slowly turned his head over his shoulder and gazed into the abyss below him. Then, gathering himself up, he let go his hold, and for a second a gleam of white shot down full forty feet to the foundation of the basement. Of course it killed him. He was taken to a drug store close by, and died in ten minutes."

It was in the North Division, however, that the fatalities were the most numerous and shocking. There, especially in the quarter adjoining the river and north of Chicago Avenue, which was thickly covered with the cottages of the poor, the flames ran along as fast as a man could walk, and, what was worse, was constantly leaping to new points, both due forward and laterally, and propagating itself faster than its victims could possibly flee before it, even if they had not attempted to save any of their goods. It was in this way that the monster devoured hundreds with his fiery breath. Between Townsend Street and Wesson, and within three blocks of Chicago Avenue, on an area of not more than forty acres, there were found the bodies of forty-five poor creatures, none of which were recognizable, but which were undoubtedly the German and Scandinavian people inhabiting that quarter. The rapidity of the flames alone, however, would not have caused the destruction of so many lives, but for the combination of other circumstances which worked fatally. There was a general hegira across all the bridges leading to the west side, and Chicago Avenue was the best of the thoroughfares tending in this direction—through this the people poured like the mountain torrent through its too narrow gorge. All at once, when the fiercest blasts of the monster furnace had begun to sweep through this section with heat which threatened death to thousands, it was discovered that the bridge was for the time impassable. The people were rushing, tumbling, crowding, storming toward it in terribly irresistible numbers. Those who were nearest the burning bridge could not turn back because of the pressure of the frantic multitude. They attempted to make a stand, by passing along the word to beat back the on-surging mass of men, and women, and horses, and wagons. But the task was simply impossible, as at the rearmost of the crowd were now fairly lashed by the flames and could not stop. Whether the foremost hundreds would or not, they were forced to turn to the northward and attempt to escape through the burning streets to North Avenue, half a mile further north, where was another bridge. Into the vortex of flame they plunge—may Heaven send them guidance through it! Out from that vortex of flame some two-score of them never emerge. May Heaven send sweet mercy to their souls! Alas! They knew not that those streets, or lanes, had no outlet for some three hundred yards or more.

This exceptional case of great mortality, caused by people being pent up in "no thoroughfares," serves to illustrate how lives were saved in other cases by the fact that nearly every street in Chicago is a thoroughfare; that they are straight and level; and that bridges occur at frequent intervals. Had it been otherwise and the fire stretched, as it did, over three miles, as the streets run, in barely six hours, the poor citizens would have been mown down by thousands.

One noble fellow, Johnny Beart, perished at Lill's Brewery while attempting to rescue the horses which he had been wont to drive. Mrs. Inness, a Scotch lady, mother of two Lake Street merchants, who, and a sister, made up the family, was killed by a falling wall, at Indiana and Erie Streets, after becoming separated from her family and lost in the smoke. One Andrew Monahan, an old constable, died on North Market Street, from suffocation. Other poor wretches, who had evidently been sick or intoxicated, died on the very door-step, or the sidewalk, while trying to crawl into the open air. Others, who found themselves stifled with the hot breath of the flames, insanely sought refuge in confined places. One such was found dead in a water pipe lying on the ground near the water-works. In one house on Bremer Street, eight bodies were found; evidently a whole family had died together. Something remarkable was the devotion to property of ten blacksmiths who assembed at the shop at which they worked, on Chicago Avenue, broke in the door, rushed in for their tools, and were all crushed by falling walls. Others died—but not many, as was at first reported and widely believed—on the prairie to the westward, from the effects of the exposure which they had undergone in the fire. Maria Burgess, a woman of the town, died two days afterward from exposure. Indeed, the cases of death resulting from exposure, as well as those of death produced indirectly by the fire, like that of W. E. Longworth, a carpenter, who committed suicide on account of the ruin of his property, are numerous, but are not capable of being collated.

The total number of deaths caused by the fire is estimated by Coroner Stephens and Dr. Ben. C. Miller, county physician, at near three hundred. This does not include still-born children. The amount of illness, and the seeds of disease, permanent or temporary, traceable to the fire and the exposure, excitement, etc., incident to it, can not, of course, be computed; but it is worthy of remark that some half dozen cases of insanity, growing out of the dreadful event, have come under the notice of the county physician.

The dead bodies were gathered up as soon as possible by the coroner and given interment at the county burying-ground. That officer brought in, on the second day after the fire, some seventy bodies, or fragments of bodies, which were placed in an extemporized morgue and exposed to the view of such of the public as chose to see the horrid sight. Over three thousand persons availed themselves of the privilege, on that day, all in the hope, or rather the dread, of being able to recognize the remains of some missing friend. The sight of the charred and shapeless fragments was as loathsome as that of the anxious, wretched throng was heart-rending. A few, and only a few, of the fragments were recognized; and so the mourners of missing ones went back to their places of temporary shelter, to hope against hope, and to continue the search for that which, all the while, they dreaded most bitterly to find.

CHAPTER IX.

THE DESOLATION COMPLETED.

The day after the fire—A glimpse at the feeling in the country—A view at daybreak—Chicago's ghost.

MONDAY was not a day of blank dismay only. There was a prompt manifestation of vitality in the city government, which showed itself in several practical ways. First, the Mayor telegraphed to neighboring cities for aid; for fire-engines to help stay the ravages of the fire, and for bread to feed the many thousand hungry and destitute. He also got together a council of the city officers, consisting of himself, the Comptroller, and the President of the Police Commissioners, who jointly signed a proclamation for the purpose of restoring confidence, and organizing measures for relief and protection. The head-quarters of the city government were fixed at a church, nearly two miles to the west of the ruined City Hall, and the authorities immediately commenced to act as the emergency required.

Business men were acting, too, on their own individual responsibility. Some of them had engaged new quarters before the roofs of their old establishments had fallen in. It will not do to say that many of them ordered goods by telegraph on that day, for, in the first place, the telegraph wires and machinery mostly went with the rest so that people were besieging the out-of-town offices all day in vain to transmit news of their own safety to distant friends; and, in the next place, the direful consequences of the conflagration upon the business credit of the city were at first overestimated, at home as well as at the East. Hence the most that could be done in the way of business on that day was for some heads of houses to dash into the surviving district—the west side or the extreme south—and engage, at a smart bonus, such quarters as they could find for the continuation of their business.

It was impossible to make visits to the ruins on Monday, on account of the great heat and the still tumbling walls. All travel between the east and west sides of the river was done through Twelfth Street, which thus became gorged with vehicles and pedestrians. All railroad trains on the south side stopped at Twenty-second Street, two miles south of their usual terminus. There was no gathering together of the people on this day, for there was nowhere to gather. Even the loafing power of the city was staggered for the time. There was no running of the street-railroad cars, or other of the signs of life which usually are visible, even on Sabbaths and holidays. In short, the day seemed a *dies non*—a day burnt out of the history of the city.

This was the aspect of the case in the South Division of the city. That in the north, where the flames were still raging with fury, has already been described. At night, all who had beds to lie in or roofs to shelter them, lay down and slept heavily, as was necessary to recuperate them from the exhausting experiences of the past twenty hours, and to prepare them for the duties of the morrow—the raising of the new Chicago out of the chaos in which all was now enwrapped.

A citizen of Chicago, who was so unfortunate as to miss seeing the terribly grand spectacle of the fire, thus describes for us his impressions on reëntering the city on Tuesday morning, after the fatal Monday:

"I was spending a few days at Burlington, Wisconsin, to recruit my health. This occupation was of course superseded by the news of Monday morning; for with Chicago burned, no Chicago man could afford to be on the sick list any longer. The village mentioned is off on a cross-road, having very poor connections with Chicago; yet it did not take fifteen minutes to inflame the people with the most intense excitement over the great disaster. The panic set in about eleven o'clock in the forenoon, and during the rest of the day the post-office and especially the telegraph office were thronged with persons eager to communicate with relatives in the city, and utterly unable to do so. I could not get a train to Chicago that day, so I went to Milwaukee, where communication with the center of interest would be easier. At Racine, boarding the train from Chicago, I found it doubled in length, and filled with refugees from the doomed city—at least a thousand of them—plunged in all degrees of despondency, and manifesting all degrees of hardship and privation. From some of these I learned particulars of the conflagration. At Milwaukee we were met at the depot by what seemed to be the entire population of the town—come to hear the latest news, or tender their hospitality to any friends who might be on board the train. They told me there had been no business transacted in the city since the news of the fire came in the forenoon. Every body was carrying water to his house-top, and watching for the extras which the newspaper offices were issuing nervously every half-hour.

"Taking a night train, I reached Chicago at daybreak. Drawing aside the curtain of my berth in the sleeping-car, I gazed upon the scene as we passed along by the remains of the North Division. I will confess it, I was at that moment in a mood for sight-seeing. But it was soon subdued, I assure you, by the scenes upon which I gazed. For half a mile along the north branch, there was little visible but the flames and smoke of objects still burning. The way in which the devouring element was left to revel at will in factories, warehouses, and stores of fuel, even along the river's bank, told but too plainly how complete had been its victory over every capability of resistance. There had been copious showers during the night, and the gale had died away; yet the fire seemed superior to all these, as well as all human obstacles, and continued its work unconcerned. But it burned languidly, and tossed off racks and sprays of flame in a wanton way, as if the monster had glutted himself on human blood and human handiwork, and was now dawdling with the relics of his feast, like a sated and stupefied glutton. And the ribs of the burning buildings showed against the red flame like the naked bones of the monster's victims.

"Alighting from the car, I took my way, in the gray dawn, through the damp and deserted streets. The rain was over, but the leaden clouds added a gloom to the already gloomy scene. To relieve this gloom there was, if I chose to accept it, the bright glow of a mile of burning coal—a mountain-range of flame along the river—containing fuel enough to have made cheerful ten thousand households through all the long, cold winter. Alas! the waste and the want! It seemed to me at that moment as if I should never enjoy again the ruddy glow of an evening fire. I passed down Canal Street—a forlorn sort of thoroughfare, at best—a relic of the old Chicago, upon which we had all come to look with contempt. To the left was the worthless wreck of the new Chicago—of all which had begotten this pride, and this contempt for the 'day of small things.' Its black, bleak desolation, its skeleton streets, its shapeless masses of brick and mortar, its gaunt and jagged spires, only remnants of walls but yesterday so proud and stately, stared at me from every point.

"The turbid river was encumbered with masses of charred wood, with black hulks of vessels, and skeletons of fallen bridges. One or two propellers were hugging the hither shore, like white doves frightened from their nests, and shrinking toward what semblance of cover offered itself, if, perchance, it might shelter them from the fell pursuer.

"The hour was early, and so exhausted—exhausted or paralyzed—had the people apparently become by their excitement and suffering, that the streets were almost utterly deserted. I was thus left alone with these pitiful ruins; and the intensity of the emotion which they excited was doubtless greatly enhanced by the circumstance. There had been a few men at a saloon on the way, evidently firemen and watchmen, who had availed themselves of the approach of daylight to refresh themselves with a dismal sort of carouse; but I had left these behind, and was alone with the ruins.

"ALONE WITH THE GHOST OF CHICAGO!

"It stared at me till I was fain to hide it from my eyes, and to rush on more rapidly. My bosom was heaving with an unwonted emotion; my eyes were filling, and my throat beginning to tingle with a feeling to which I have been of late years a stranger.

"Coming upon Adams Street, where the ruins of an iron viaduct were still standing, I resolved to look the situation in the face. The structure, though tottering, bore my weight, and I pushed on to its further end. The ruins of the river bridge lay

24

in the stream beneath me. The town, or what had been the town, lay prostrate beyond. It was with the greatest difficulty that I could trace any semblance by which the various landmarks of Chicago could be identified. But for the still erect walls of the Court-house, Post-office, and *Tribune* building, this would have been utterly impossible. The Chamber of Commerce, the Sherman House, the elegant stores of State Street, the Palmer House, the Opera-house, the new palaces of marble to the south of the Post-office—all were leveled in the dust, or shattered into unrecognizable fragments. The grand Pacific Hotel, which I had been accustomed to gaze on with pride each morning from this precise point of view, was a jagged and crumbling ruin—beautiful still, but a hopeless ruin—nothing more. My idols—and I now realized to what an unwise extent I had made them my idols—were now shattered and scattered at my feet. My interests were in some, but I had loved them all, and now I mourned them all equally.

"The scene of Sunday night must have been terrible, but it could not, with all its horrors, have been so affecting to the tender emotions as this. Then there were flames roaring and devouring, men cursing and striving, noble hearts risking themselves to save others, brutes of men plundering and extorting, women and children fleeing and screaming, and every thing to excite the mind and stimulate the nerves. Here every thing tended to subdue and overcome one. Here I saw—not a few bodies threatened with sudden destruction; I saw the coined product of the mind, the muscle, the flesh and bones, the hopes and ambitions of a hundred thousand fellow-beings, expended through twenty years, all swept into oblivion. There was more life represented in those miles of streets, now prostrated, than in all that surging, shrieking throng of Sunday night; and here it was—all—all—confronting me, like a fleshless, lifeless ghost, and holding up to me, in token of distress—to me alone—its spectral hands; for such seemed the gaunt obelisks which the demon had left as monuments of his rage, along with the yellow and mephitic flames which flickered from the coal-heaps among the ruins, as if they were traces of the sulphurous domain from which the destroyer had come.

"The mute appeal, the solitude, the hour, all together so overcame my feelings, that I leaned against a column of the bridge, and gave way to tears—wept as I had not supposed I could do, by whatsoever moved.

"From this condition of feeling I was aroused by the approach of a young man, who, though of rather fine mien in most respects, bore that unkempt, unshaven, unwashed appearance which I afterward found to characterize the whole population of the city for the week following the fire. He came with a small flask to procure water from the river. He was a stranger to me, but somehow he seemed like a brother, so close did the great ordeal bring men together. We talked considerably of the details of the conflagration. I remarked upon the fearful danger to the remainder of the city, resulting from a total failure of the water supply.

"'Oh,' he said, cheerfully, 'we'll have water again in a few days. We'll be all right again soon.'

"'Yes,' I echoed, though mechanically, 'we'll be all right again soon.'

"And the sun shone out at that moment from a rift in the clouds, at the point where the cloudy arch dipped into Lake Michigan, diffusing a rosy light and warmth, as if in confirmation of our cheerful prophesyings. His brightness seemed to foreshadow the future glory of Chicago quite as plainly as the paling lamps behind us had suggested the faded luster of her past. And with this my Chicago buoyancy came back, and I regained such a flow of spirits that it was not for any mere purpose of keeping my courage up that I whistled all the way past a huge stock of coffins, which some enterprising undertaker had saved from the ruins in a capacious wain and left to embellish the street which led to my home."

CHAPTER X.

THE LOSSES BY THE FIRE.

Property destroyed—Can land burn up?—Values of business blocks, hotels, and other prominent buildings—Produce and merchandise destroyed—Real estate as affected by the fire—Uninsurable losses—Commerce and manufactures—The effect on business—The grand total.

AMID such a general wreck, the attempt to gather correct statistics of the losses entailed by the great conflagration, may well seem a hopeless one. So many records were destroyed; so many people driven from the city, who could alone give accurate information on some essential point; such a universal scattering and destruction among those who remained, that it is practically impossible to cover every item in the immense aggregate of loss.

We essay the task with diffidence, notwithstanding the fact that we have taken all possible pains in the investigation of loss. The following statements are probably very near the truth in the aggregate—made up of details obtained by personal inquiry from many hundreds of the parties most interested in the sad exhibit.

The limiting lines of the area swept by the flames have been already indicated, and the position of the burnt district will be easily understood by a glance at the accompanying map.

In the West Division about 194 acres were burned over,

including 16 acres swept by the fire of the previous evening. This district contained several lumber-yards and planing-mills, the Union Depot of the St. Louis and Pittsburg & Fort Wayne Railroads, with a few minor hotels and factories, several boarding-houses, and a host of saloons. The buildings burned—about 500 in number—were nearly all frame structures, and not of much value, but were closely packed together. About 2250 persons were rendered homeless in this division.

In the South Division the burned area comprised about 460 acres. The southern boundary line was a diagonal, running, from the corner of Michigan Avenue and Congress Street, west-south-west to the intersection of Fifth Avenue (Wells) and Polk Street. On the other three sides the bounding lines were the lake and the river—only one block (the Lind) being left in all that area. This district contained the great majority of the most expensive structures in the city, all the wholesale stores, all the newspaper offices, all the principal banks, and insurance and làw offices, many coal-yards, nearly all the hotels, and many factories, the Court-house, Custom-house, Chamber of Commerce, etc.—as stated more at length in our chapter descriptive of Chicago in 1871. The number of buildings destroyed in this division was about 3650, which included 1600 stores, 28 hotels, and 60 manufacturing establishments. About 21,800 persons were rendered homeless, very many of whom were residents in the upper stories of the palatial structures devoted, below, to commerce. There were, however, many poor families, and a great many human rats, resident in the western part of this territory.

In the North Division the devastation was the most widespread, fully 1470 acres being burned over, out of the 2533½ acres in that division. And even this statement fails to convey an idea of the wholesale destruction wrought there, because the territory unburned was unoccupied. Had there been any except widely-scattered structures in the unburned portion, they, too, would have been destroyed, as the fire licked up all in its path, and paused only when there was no more food whereon to whet its insatiable appetite. Of the 13,800 buildings in that division, not more than 500 were left standing, leaving 13,300 in ruins, and rendering 74,450 persons homeless. The buildings burned included more than 600 stores and 100 manufacturing establishments, the latter being principally grouped in the south-western part of this division. That part next the lake, as far north as Chicago Avenue, was occupied by first-class residences, of which only one was left standing—that of Mahlon D. Ogden. Next north of these was the Water-works, and this was the initial point of a line of breweries that stretched out almost to the cemetery. The river banks were piled high with lumber and coal, which was all destroyed, except a portion near the bend of the river, at Kinzie Street. The space between the burned district and the river, to the westward, contained but little improved property. Lincoln Park lay to the northward, on the lake-shore. The fire burned up the southern part of this park—the old City Cemetery—but left the improved part untouched, except a portion of the fencing. One of the saddest among the many sad scenes that met the eye after the conflagration had done its work, was that in the old cemetery—the flames had even made havoc among the dead, burning down the wooden monuments, and shattering stone vaults to fragments, leaving exposed many scores of the remnants of mortality that had smoldered for years in oblivion.

The total area burned over in the city, including streets, was 2124 acres, or very nearly 3⅓ square miles. The number of buildings destroyed was 17,450; of persons rendered homeless,

98,500. Of the latter, more than 250 paid the last debt of nature amid the carnage—fell victims to the Moloch of our modern civilization.

To give a statement of individual losses would be to publish a directory, which no one would read. Instead of this we propose to give a synopsis of the principal losses, in buildings, produce, merchandise, other personal property, on churches and schools, public improvements, etc., with the effects of the catastrophe on the pecuniary values of the property untouched by the fire. Before tabulating, we may premise that the depreciation in the price of the real estate in the city is estimated by the most careful judges to average fully thirty per cent. Several sales in the burned district in the South Division were made immediately after the fire, at a reduction of about eighteen per cent. from previous prices. Since then a reaction has set in, and real estate in that district has sold at nearly previous prices. Property situated directly south and west of that area has slightly increased in selling value, owing to the enhanced demand for business purposes. But in the North Division, and in the boulevard regions of the West Division, prices have fallen not less than fifty per cent., and not far from thirty per cent. on the south side, in the suburban districts.

The following are approximate estimates of the values of seventy-nine principal business blocks, exclusive of their contents. In the preparation of this table we have reeeived valuable assistance from C. N. Holden, Esq., City Tax Commissioner, and Assessor W. B. H. Gray. Of course the value of the land is not included:

Arcade, Clark, near Madison,	$75,000
Berlin, Monroe and State,	15,000
Boone's, Lasalle, near Washington,	15,000

Bowen's, etc., Randolph, near Michigan Avenue,	$200,000
Bryan, Lasalle and Monroe,	250,000
Burch's, Lake, near Wabash,	120,000
Calhoun, Clark, near Madison,	30,000
Chicago Mutual Life Ins., Fifth Avenue, near Washington,	30,000
Cobb's, Lake and Michigan,	180,000
Commercial, Lasalle and Lake	50,000
Commercial Ins. Co., Washington, near Lasalle,	40,000
Crosby's, State, near Washington,	75,000
De Haven, Dearborn, near Quincy,	35,000
Depository, Randolph, near Lasalle,	80,000
Dickey's, Dearborn and Lake,	50,000
Dole's, South Water and Clark,	30,000
Drake & Farwell, Wabash and Washington,	400,000
Ewing, Clark, near Kinzie,	75,000
Exchange Bank, Lake and Clark,	80,000
Fullerton, Washington and Dearborn,	60,000
Garrett, Randolph and State,	25,000
Honore, Dearborn, near Monroe (2),	500,000
Keep's, Clark, near Madison,	65,000
Kent's, Monroe, near Lasalle,	55,000
King's, Washington and Dearborn,	30,000
Larmon, Clark and Washington,	25,000
Lincoln, Lake and Franklin,	30,000
Link's, Lake and Lasalle,	60,000
Lloyd's, Randolph and Wells,	100,000
Lombard, Monroe and Custom-house Place,	200,000
Loomis, Clark and South Water,	30,000
McCormick's, Lake and Michigan Avenue,	180,000
McCormick's, Randolph and Dearborn,	100,000
McCormick's Reaper Factory, near Rush Street bridge,	800,000
Magie's, Lasalle and Randolph,	50,000
Major's, Madison and Lasalle,	150,000
Marine Bank, Lake and Lasalle,	75,000
Masonic, Dearborn, near Washington,	50,000
Mechanic's, Washington, near Lasalle,	50,000

Mercantile, Lasalle, near Washington,	$100,000
Merchants' Ins. Co., Washington and Lasalle,	200,000
Monroe, Clark and Monroe,	60,000
Morrison, Clark, near Monroe,	100,000
Morrison, Clark, near Washington,	40,000
Newberry, Wells and Kinzie,	50,000
Norton, South Water, near Fifth Avenue,	25,000
Newhouse, South Water, near Fifth Avenue,	60,000
Oriental, Lasalle, near Washington,	140,000
Otis, Madison and Lasalle,	100,000
Otis, State and Madison,	15,000
Phœnix, Lasalle, near Randolph,	40,000
Pomeroy's, South Water, near Lasalle,	30,000
Pope's, Madison, near Clark (2),	160,000
Portland, Dearborn and Washington,	100,000
Purple's, Clark and Ontario,	100,000
Raymond's, State and Madison,	100,000
Republic Life Ins., Lasalle and Arcade Court,	350,000
Reynolds', Dearborn and Madison,	150,000
Rice's, Dearborn, near Randolph,	100,000
Scammon, Randolph and Michigan Avenue,	130,000
Shepard's, Dearborn, near Monroe,	80,000
Smith & Nixon's, Washington and Clark,	200,000
Speed's, Dearborn, near Madison,	50,000
Steele's, Lasalle and South Water,	60,000
Stone's, Madison, near Lasalle,	30,000
Turner's, State and Kinzie,	50,000
Tyler's, Lasalle, near South Water,	55,000
Uhlich's, Clark, near Kinzie,	55,000
Union, Lasalle and Washington,	120,000
Volk's, Washington, near Franklin,	15,000
Walker's, Dearborn, near Couch Place,	60,000
Wicker's, State and South Water,	60,000
Wright's, State and Kinzie,	30,000
Lill's Brewery,	150,000
Sand's Ale Brewing Co's. Establishment,	100,000

Illinois State Savings, ...	$75,0000
First National Bank, ...	160,0000
City National Bank, ...	50,000
Total of 79 blocks, without contents, ...	$8,015,000

Public Buildings, etc.—Custom-house and Post-office, $650,-000 (money in do., $2,130,000); Court-house, $1,100,000; Chamber of Commerce (2), $284,000; Armory, $25,000; Huron Street Police Station, $14,000; Larrabee Street Police Station, $22,000; Gas-works, $50,000; Water-works (partially), $200,000; Long John Engine-house, $14,000; J. B. Rice do., $7,000; A. C. Coventry do., $7,000; A. D. Titsworth do., $8,000; Fred. Gund do., $14,000; Hook and Ladder buildings, $10,800; machinery of Fire Department, $26,550; battery of artillery, $10,000; 800 muskets, $10,-400; eight bridges, $200,000; lamp-posts, $20,000; damage to river tunnels, $6,000; telegraphic apparatus, including 50 miles of wire, and 60 alarm-boxes, $50,000. The lineal feet of sidewalk burned was 486,029 in the North Division; 132,-662 in the South, and 24,130 in the West; total, 642,841 feet, or 121$\frac{3}{4}$ miles. The half of this would give 60$\frac{7}{8}$ as the number of miles of street-line burned over; but the street crossings make fully one-sixth of the whole; allowing for this we have 73 miles of streets in the area of the conflagration. This included not far from one-half of all the wooden-block pavement in the city, much of which was partially ruined. The destruction of streets foots up $500,000, and of sidewalks $940,000, involving a loss of about $1,440,000. Total loss on public buildings, bridges, and streets, $6,298,750.

Central Railroad depots and dockage, $775,000; Rock Island & Lake-Shore Depot, $450,000; Galena depots, $525,-000; West Side Union Depot (damaged), $10,000. Total on railroad buildings, and rolling stock, without contents, $1,-760,000.

Newspapers, buildings, and newspaper stock—*Tribune*, $325,-000; *Times*, $100,000; *Journal*, $100,000; *Republican* (stock $61,000), $186,000; *Staats Zeitung*, and *Post*, $160,000; *Mail* and *Union* (stock alone), $12,000; *Volks-Zeitung* (stock), $5,000. Total, nine dailies, $888,000.

Hotels—Palmer, $250,000; Sherman, $360,000; Tremont, $360,000; Briggs, $200,000; Bigelow, $300,000; Metropolitan, $100,000; Adams, $125,000; Massasoit, $75,000; Matteson, $75,000; City, $60,000; St. James, $120,000; Revere, $150,-000; Nevada, $80,000; Hatch, $60,000; Anderson's, $40,000; Burke's, $60,000; Central, $40,000; Clifton, $150,000; Eagle, $10,000; European (Rohrback's), $40,000; Everett, $30,000; Garden City, $50,000; Girard, $10,000; Hess, $20,000; Hotel Garni, $50,000; Howard, $10,000; Hutchinson's, $20,000; New York, $25,000; Orient, $50,000; Schall's, $40,000; Washington, $20,000; Wright's, $10,000. Total loss on enumerated hotels, $2,890,000, without including furniture.

Theaters, Halls, etc—Opera-house, $250,000; McVicker's, $75,000; Farwell Hall, $150,000; Hooley's, $35,000; Dearborn; $50,000; Museum, $100,000; Metropolitan, $100,000; Turner Hall, $25,000; Academy of Design, $30,000; Olympic, $50,000. Total on public halls, $865,000, without including furnishing of numerous offices in those buildings.

Public Schools—Jones, $13,170; Kinzie and branches, $21,390; Franklin and branch, $77,195; Ogden, $39,-675; Pearson Street, $16,750; Elm Street, $16,950; Lasalle Street, $32,650; North Branch, $32,000. Total, including furniture and heating apparatus, $249,780.

The following was the loss on churches and church property:

Baptist—North, $15,000; Second German and Swedish Churches, $7,000; North Star, $20,000; Lincoln Park Mission, $3,500; Publication Society, $10,000; "Standard," $25,000. Total, $80,500.

Congregational—New England, $70,000; Lincoln Park, $2,000; other losses, $3,000. Total, $75,000.

Episcopal—Ascension, $20,000; St. Ansgarius, $17,500; St. James, $200,000; Trinity, $100,000. Total, $337,500.

Jewish—North Side, Sinai, and Kehilath Benai Sholom, $30,000; hospital, $25,000. Total, $55,000.

Methodist Episcopal—First (business block), $130,000; Grace, $85,000; Van Buren Street (German), $10,000; Clybourne Avenue (German), $10,000; First Scandinavian, $10,000; Bethel (colored), $10,000; Quinn's (colored), $15,000; Garret Biblical Institute (property in Chicago), $85,000. Total, $355,000.

Scandinavian Lutheran—First Norwegian, and Swedish. Loss, $25,000.

Presbyterian—First Church and mission, Second, Fourth, Bremer Street Mission, Erie Street Mission, Clybourne Avenue Mission; total, $465,000. The University was saved, also the Fullerton Avenue Church.

Roman Catholic—Holy Name, $250,000; St. Mary's, $40,000; Immaculate Conception, $30,000; St. Michael's, $200,000; St. Joseph's, $120,000; St. Louis, $25,000; St. Paul's, $25,000; these losses include pastors' residences and schools. *Convents*—Sisters Mercy, $100,000; Good Shepherd, $90,000; also, St. Joseph's Orphan Asylum, $40,000; Christian Brothers' College, $80,000; Alexian Hospital, $60,000; Bishops' residence, $40,000; other losses, $250,000. Total, $1,350,000.

Swedenborgian—Temple, $36,000; North Mission, $5,000. Total, $41,000.

Unity Church (Rev. Robert Collyer), $175,000; Illinois Street Mission, $25,000; Mariners' Bethel, $5,000.

Grand total of Church loss (some only estimated), $3,-000,000.

Leading Book Stores—Western News Co., S. C. Griggs & Co., and Keen, Cooke & Co., books, $600,000; buildings, $500,000; others 265,000.

Law Libraries,	$200,000
Young Men's Library (20,000),	30,000
Historical (60,000 books, 145,000 pamphlets),	200,000
Academy of Science (5000), books.	20,000
Young Men's Christian (10,000),	12,000
Union Catholic (5000),	7,000
Franklin (3000),	4,000
Other public libraries, (10,000)	16,000

The loss on private libraries can scarcely be estimated; Mr. McCagg's was worth fully $40,000; other private libraries would foot up a total of over $500,000. Total books, with three stores, $2,354,000.

Grain Elevators—Central A, $150,000; National, $80,000; Galena, Hiram Wheeler's, and Munger & Co.'s, average, $125,000 each. Contents, 1,642,000 bushels of grain, worth $1,210,000. Several small warehouses near them, where grain was stored on private terms, swell the aggregate to $2,100,000.

Provisions, 8000 bbls. pork, 6000 tierces lard, 1,000,000 lbs. meats; total, $340,000. Flour, 15,000 barrels, worth $97,500.

Lumber, 65,000,000 feet in yards, with 2,500,000 feet more

n planing-mills, and 2,000,000 each of shingles and lath. Total, $1,040,000.

Coal burned (80,000 tons), $600,000.

National Banks—(All burned but one.) Clearing-house, City, Commercial, Cook County, Corn Exchange, Fifth, First, Fourth, German, Manufacturers, Mechanics, Merchants, National Bank of Commerce, Loan and Trust Co., North-western, Second, Third, Traders, Union.

Other Banks—Germania; Hibernian (Savings); Marine; Real Estate, Loan & Trust Co.; Union Insurance & Trust Co.; Chicago (Savings); Commercial Loan Co.; German (Savings); Merchants, Farmers, & Mechanics (Savings); Merchants (Savings); National Loan & Trust Co.; Normal Co.; Illinois State Savings Institution, and twenty-one other banking firms.

The loss on personal property of banks, exclusive of buildings, could not be obtained. It was probably about $1,000,000. This includes money burned up, but does not include evidences of indebtedness in one form or another, as if any of those accounts were lost to the banks, it was simply so much less to be paid by the debtors.

Dry Goods, Wholesale—O. L. American & Co.; Bowen, Hunt & Winslow; Day, Tilden & Co.; J. V. Farwell & Co.; Richards, Crumbaugh & Shaw; Stetthauers & Wineman; Field, Leiter & Co.; D. W. & A. Keith & Co.; Rosenfeld, Munzer & Co.; Carson, Pirie & Co.; C. Gossage & Co.; Hamlin, Hale & Co.; J. B. Shay & Co.; Simpson, Norwell & Co.; Price, Rosenblatt & Co.; Stine, Kramer & Co. Total loss, $10,000,000, of which about forty per cent. will be paid by the Insurance Companies, three-quarters of the stocks being insured. Also, thirty-five retail firms; loss, $3,500,000. Total loss, wholesale and retail, $13,500,000.

Drugs, Wholesale—(Fuller & Fuller escaped.) Burnham & Son; Cory, Barrett & Co.; Hurlbut & Edsall; Lord, Smith & Co.; Rockwood & Blocki; Tolman & King; Van Schaack, Stevenson & Co. Total loss, $750,000; and 45 retail dealers, $250,000. Total loss on drugs, $1,000,000.

Boots and Shoes, Wholesale—W. S. Crowley; Phelps, Dodge & Palmer; Doggett, Bassett & Hills; C. H. Fargo & Co.; Farnum, Flagg & Co.; T. B. Weber & Co.; C. M. Henderson & Co.; C. B. Sawyer & Co.; M. D. Wells & Co.; Whitney Bros. & Yundt. All the above were manufacturers. Goldman Bros.; McAuley, Yeo & Co.; J. F. Morrill & Co.; Cummings & Co.; North Bennington Co.; Geo. P. Gore & Co.; C. O. Thompson & Co.; Wiswall, Nazro & Thompson; Weage, Kirtland & Ordway; Greenfelder, Rosenthal & Co.; and 63 retail dealers. The total losses of boots and shoes alone, amounted to $2,500,000 among the wholesale dealers; and about $1,000,000 among the retailers, some $75,000 worth of the stock held by the latter being saved.

The loss in leather and stock, among hide dealers, etc., aggregated $1,750,000 more; the stock of French skins was much less than stated by the *Shoe and Leather Reporter*. Eighteen dealers in hides and leather were burned out, besides the sole and upper-leather houses who tanned their own stock.

Grocers, Wholesale—Beckwith & Sons; Barbour & Son; Bliss, Moore & Co.; Burton & Pierce; Church & Co.; G. C. Cook & Co.; F. D. Cossett & Co.; Day, Allen & Co.; J. W. Doane & Co.; Downer & Co.; Durand Bros. & Powers, and Durand, Powers & Mead; C. E. Durand & Co.; Farringdon, Brewster & Co.; Forsyth & Co.; Gould, Briggs & Co.; J. A. & H. F. Griswold

& Co.; Grannis & Farwell; Gray Bros.; Hibben & Co.; Harmon, Messer & Co.; Hoyt & Co.; Ingraham, Corbin & May; Kellogg & Covell; Knowles, Cloyes & Co.; Kussell Bros.; China Tea Co.; F. Macveagh; McKindley, Gilchrist & Co.; Mead & Higgins; W. F. McLaughlin; Knowles, Burdsall & Bacon; Quan & Co.; Reid, Murdock & Fisher; Sayres, Gilmore & Co.; Sibley & Endicott; Smith Bros. & Co.; H. C. Smith & Co.; Sprague, Warner & Co.; J. W. Stearns & Sons; Stewart, Aldrich & Co.; Taylor & Wright; Wells & Faulkner; Willard & Co.; N. Sherwood & Co.; Bennett, Fuller & Co.; Bittinger & Bro.; M. Graff & Co. Total loss, $3,750,000; and 218 retailers, aggregating $450,000, making a total loss on groceries, etc., of $4,120,000.

Clothing, Wholesale—Clement, Morton & Co.; Morse, Loomis & Co.; H. W. King & Co.; C. P. Kellogg & Co.; Tuttle, Thompson & Wetmore; H. A. Kohn & Bros.; A. & H. Kohn; Leopold, Kuh & Co.; Cahn, Wampold & Co.; Clayburgh, Ernstein & Co.; Meyer, Strauss & Co. Total loss, $3,400,000; besides $250,000 worth of furnishing goods. Whole loss on clothing, etc., at wholesale, $3,650,000.

Hardware, etc., Wholesale—E. Hunt & Sons; Larrabee & North; Hall, Kimbark & Co.; Miller, Bros. & Keep; H. W. Austin; William Blair & Co.; J. K. Botsford & Son; Brintnall, Terry & Belden; Greenbaum Sons; Haywood, Cartledge & Honore; Hibbard & Spencer; J. Leibenstein; Markley, Alling & Co.; E. A. Mears; Sieberger & Breakey; J. L. Wayne & Son; Western H. Manufacturing Co.; Hurlburd, Herrick & Co.; Kellogg & Johnson; T. B. & H. M. Seavey; J. A. & T. S. Sexton; S. J. Surdam & Co. Total loss, $4,030,000; and 33 retailers lost $480,000. Total loss on hardware and metals, $4,510,000.

Millinery, Wholesale—D. B. Fisk & Co.; Keith Bros.; Gage Bros.; Webster Bros.; Mayhon, Daly & Co.; Walsh & Hutchinson, H. W. & J. M. Wetherell, and several smaller firms. Loss, $1,500,000. Also, 55 retail dealers lost $110,000. Total loss, $1,610,000.

Hats, Caps, and Furs, Wholesale—Keith Bros.; Fitch, Williams & Co.; Hotchkiss, Eddy & Co.; Carhart, Lewis & Co.; David P. Brown; Gimbel & Lowenstein; Innes Bros.; King Bros. & Co.; Sweet, Dempster & Co. Loss, $940,000. Also, 38 retail dealers lost $120,000. Total loss, $1,060,000.

Paper Stock, Wholesale—Bradner, Smith & Co.; J. W. Butler & Co.; G. H. & L. Laflin; Cleveland Paper Co.; Oglesby, Barnits & Co. Loss, $700,000.

Musical Instruments and Books—Root & Cady; Lyon & Healy; Smith & Nixon; A. Reed & Sons; W. W. Kimball; Julius Bauer & Co.; J. H. Foote; Molter & Wurlitzer; and several others. Loss, $900,000.

These, which include the leading lines of wholesale business in the city, will give an idea of the proportionate losses in other departments. We need not extend the list.

The following is a summary of losses on buildings. Where the contents of the building are included, the fact is indicated by a star. The footings do not in all cases correspond to those above given. For instance, the Chamber of Commerce is noted above as a public building, but it is taxable property; we therefore include it below in our footings of warehouses, depots, etc., which *were* subject to taxation. National, county, city, church, and public school property was not taxed:

Eighty business blocks (3 book-stores),	$8,515,000
Railroad depots, warehouses, and Chamber of Commerce,	2,700,000
Hotels (some not enumerated),	3,100,000
Theaters, etc.,	865,000

Newspaper offices (daily),*	$888,000
One hundred other business buildings,	1,008,420
Other taxable buildings (16,000, average $1,800),	28,300,000
Churches,*	2,989,000
Public schools,*	249,780
Other public buildings not taxed,	2,121,800
Other public property,	1,763,000
Total buildings,	$53,000,000

Our estimate of $1,800 each for the 16,000 buildings not enumerated is very low; many of them cost from $10,000 to $20,000 each. Outside of these, the great majority of the lower classes of dwellings were worth $1,000 to $1,200 each. Were the data attainable in each case, the loss on buildings would probably foot up to more than fifty-five millions. Where absolute accuracy is not possible, it is best to follow the lead of the insurance adjusters, and cut down rather than pile up the figures.

The losses on produce, etc., may be thus stated:

Flour, 15,000 barrels,	$97,500
Grain ($35,000 worth in private store),	1,245,000
Provisions (4,400,000 pounds),	340,000
Salt,	100,000
Wool,	100,000
Lumber (65,000,000 feet in yards),	1,040,000
Coal (80,000 tons),	600,000
Wood,	400,000
Other produce in store and warehouse,	1,340,000
Total produce, etc.,	$5,262,500

Not less than 350 produce commission offices were burned out.

The following were losses on stock and fixtures in business:

Dry goods,	$13,500,000
Drugs,	1,000,000
Boots and shoes, etc., and leather,	5,175,000
Hardware and iron,	4,510,000
Groceries and teas,	4,120,000
Wholesale clothing,	3,650,000
Jewelry, etc.,	1,300,000
Musical instruments and musical books,	900,000
Books on sale,	1,145,000
Millinery,	1,610,000
Hats, caps, and furs,	1,060,000
Wholesale paper stock,	700,000
Auction goods,	350,000
Shipping and dredges,	800,000
Banks (not including buildings),	1,000,000
Furniture of business offices (including safes),	2,250,000
Manufactories (stock, machinery, and product),	13,255,000
Other stocks,	22,000,000
Other publications than daily newspapers,	375,000
Total business (stocks and fixtures),	$78,700,000

The following are losses on personal effects:

Household property,	$41,000,000
Manuscript work (records, etc.),	10,000,000
Libraries, public and private,	2,010,000
Money lost (Custom-house, $2,130,000),	5,700,000
Total personal effects,	$58,710,000

The following is, therefore, our summary of losses by the fire:

Improvements (buildings), ...	$53,000,000
Produce, etc., ...	5,262,500
Manufactures, ...	13,255,000
Other business property, ...	65,445,000
Personal effects, ...	58,710,000
Miscellaneous, ...	328,000
Grand total, ...	$196,000,000

A few items included by us in improvements in the preceding pages, should be credited to personal property, as daily newspapers for instance. This would make business property foot up to about $66,000,000, and buildings $52,000,000, but this change would not affect the grand total of loss.

This estimate of $196,000,000 loss is much lower than some that have been made by prominent parties; we believe it is as near the truth as is possible to be arrived at under the circumstances. It should, however, be remembered that in this aggregate we have not included mere evidences of indebtedness, for the reason given above, even though property be lost in consequence. Neither do we add the enormous sums paid for removing personal effects, etc., during the fire, nor the extra prices paid for labor and material in rebuilding the city. It is evident that what is a loss to one man, in such cases, is a gain to another; the result is simply to change the distribution of property among holders. The question we have endeavored to answer in this chapter is, "How much property was *destroyed* in the fire?" In doing so we could not take cognizance of mementoes, etc.; that class of property, however valuable to the owner, like human life, can not be priced.

Allowing four million dollars as the salvage on foundations of prominent blocks, and on bricks that are available for rebuilding, we shall have ONE HUNDRED AND NINETY-TWO MILLIONS OF DOLLARS as the value of the property actually destroyed by the fire.

To this total we must, however, add $88,000,000 for the depreciation of 30 per cent. on real estate, making the total of pecuniary loss by the fire equal to $280,000,000, or 45 per cent. on the total property value of $620,000,000 in the city before the fire.

A still further addition must be made for the loss to commerce and manufactures. We estimate that the fire has kept back some $50,000,000 worth of receipts, which has interrupted business to the extent of about $125,000,000 worth of trading, wholesale and retail. At eight per cent. of profit—a moderate estimate—this would entail a further loss of $10,000,000, making the total loss $290,000,000, or 46⅘ per cent. on the entire property value of the city. We may remark that this sum total of loss is a little greater than the whole valuation of property, real and personal, made by the assessors in 1871, for the purposes of city taxation.

The number of books destroyed in the fire is estimated at nearly two millions.

The Academy of Design, though recently instituted, had become a prominent art center, and its destruction was a great blow to art in the West. Rothermel's Battle of Gettysburg, on exhibition there, was literally "saved as by fire." Of the other art treasures there consumed, Mr. Alvah Bradish writes as follows, to an Eastern paper: "There were Drury's large and precious collection; Ford's beautiful Ohio wood scenes; Deihl's careful studies and designs; Jenks' conscientious labors; Elkin's world of Rocky Mountain studies; Bradish's popular 'Leather Stocking,' his full length portrait of the late Douglass

Houghton, and numerous smaller works; Pine's attractive group of children; James Gookin's charming 'Fairy Wedding,' a gift to the academy. Cogswell's studio contained some of his best portraits. Reed & Son's studio was crowded with pictures and studies. Pebble's studio contained numerous works of high promise. Other young artists, or students, occupied rooms and pursued their studies in the building." The collection in the academy will not soon be replaced.

CHAPTER XI.

INSURANCE.

The fire underwriters—Better than expected—The adjusters—Statement of assets and losses of companies doing business in Chicago—Insolvent companies—What is essential to real protection against loss by fire.

THE question of insurance on the fire is not one of absolute, but of relative loss. So much property was destroyed; the point at issue between insurers and insured was simply who should bear the loss, or in what proportion the loss should be distributed. If the insurance companies had failed to pay one cent, the loss to the community would have been just the same as if they had paid every dollar claimed.

But these two supposable cases would have involved widely different conditions to the great mass of those insured; to them it was a question of utter ruin, or a chance to begin the world anew. Yet there were many, even among this class, who had comparatively little interest in the matter. They were among the largest property holders, and that property was insured, but they were also large stockholders in the insurance companies, and to them the result, either way, could be little else than the making of one liability to offset the other, with no avails in any event. These were really the most to be pitied of all those whose possessions were swept away by the flames.

The first general thought which succeeded that involved in

the effort to find a place of safety, was that all fire insurance was utterly worthless. Scarcely any one thought that any company would pay ten per cent. on its liabilities. It was apparent at a glance that the Chicago companies were bankrupt, and few dared to hope that the others would not repudiate.

But within two or three days a change was noticeable. First one telegram, and then several, came over the wires from the seaboard bearing the welcome intelligence that this and that company was prepared to pay all losses in full. Some of these professions have since proven to be only buncombe, but there was a good deal of truth, though some of it needed to be taken with a few grains of allowance. Then followed great uncertainty as to the amounts of loss and liability. Some companies understated their losses, in the hope of inspiring confidence and securing large accessions of new business, while others overstated theirs in the hope of inducing the sufferers to compromise for a small per centage of their claims. Meanwhile, the field was taken by a whole army of "adjusters," some of whom acted fairly enough, while the great majority seemed to have but the one aim in view of pressing the poor as closely to the wall as they could, under cover of the law. At the date of this writing (November 13, 1871), it is not possible to make an exact statement of the situation.

The following tables show the net assets of each company having risks in the burned district, the figures being taken from the sworn statements made by each company at the close of 1870, with the real losses as nearly as can be ascertained, and the per centage of insurance upon those losses which the companies will be able to pay. This may be called the collectable per centage.

We give the *net* assets, because the gross assets of a company are not always available in payment of losses, though it is true that the difference between the two is made up of items, some of which are arbitrarily established, and sometimes unfairly counted as deductions from the company's ability to pay

The figures here given as representing the total losses by the fire do not correspond, except in a few cases, with the losses admitted by the companies after the fire. This column has been carefully prepared for us by Dan. M. Bowmar, a well-known Chicago underwriter, from the latest data available at the time. It is only approximate, and may be found wide of the truth in some instances, but we believe it gives a much nearer approximation to the aggregate than any statement compiled from the exhibits of the insurance companies themselves.

In the list of companies continuing business, we have placed none whose net assets are not nearly equal to the losses incurred. Such companies will undoubtedly pay one hundred cents on the dollar, because they can not continue without doing so; and the required amounts will be made up by assessment upon the stockholders, and by the large gains accruing from receipts at the present enormous rates of insurance.

Of course the column of per centage is not intended to show a basis on which insurers should settle with the companies for their losses. We may have unintentionally overrated or underrated the ability of some companies to pay. The best way for the policy-holders to do is to act in concert, in the way indicated at the meetings now being held in the city, and ascertain the full extent of the losses and resources of each company that refuses to pay in full. These facts may not be ascertained accurately for some months after our book goes to press.

Illinois Companies in Liquidation.

	Net Assets, Jan. 1, 1871.	Actual Losses.	Per Cent.
Aurora, of Aurora, ...	$ 187,966	$ 600,000	.30
Chicago Fire, Chicago, . . .	117,387	1,500,000	.07
Chicago Firemen, Chicago, . .	240,742	6,000,000	.04
Commercial, Chicago. . . .	302,877	4,000,000	.07
Equitable, Chicago, ...	198,203	3,500,000	.05
Germania, Chicago, ...	223,967	3,000,000	.07
Home, Chicago, ...	223,419	2,500,000	.08
Illinois Mutual, Alton, . . .	286,097	2,000,000	.12
Merchants, Chicago, ...	746,183	5,000,000	.12
Mutual Security, Chicago, . . .	303,055	1,600,000	.18

Illinois Companies which Continue.

	Net Assets, Jan. 1, 1871.	Actual Losses.	Per Cent.
Great Western, ...	$ 235,556	$ 200,000	100
Republic, ...	953,771	3,000,000	100

The Republic has made an assessment upon its stockholders to meet the loss.

New York Companies in Liquidation.

	Net Assets, Jan. 1, 1871.	Actual Losses, Estimated.	Per Cent.
Ætna, ...	$ 334,570	$650,000	.55
Astor, ...	206,755	350,000	.75
Atlantic, ...	361,659	600,000	.55
Beeckman, ...	230,635	400,000	.50
Excelsior, ...	239,090	475,000	.45
Fulton, ...	216,964	800,000	.30
Irving, ...	251,938	450,000	.55
Lamar, ...	469,792	500,000	.80
Lorillard, ...	1,395,063	1,500,000	.80
Manhattan, ...	987,350	2,000,000	.48
Market, ...	473,949	1,000,000	.45

	Net Assets, Jan. 1, 1871.	Actual Losses, Estimated.	Per Cent.
North America,	$545,975	$600,000	.80
Security,	1,000,396*	2,000,000	.50
Washington,	403,863	750,000	.50
Albany City,	165,393	600,000	.25
Capital City,	266,676	500,000	.50
Buffalo City,	251,469	800,000	.30
Buffalo, F. & M.	326,452	600,000	.50
Western,	364,679	1,000,000	.35
Yonkers & New York,	588,651	1,000,000	.55

New York Companies which Continue.

	Net Assets, Jan. 1, 1871.	Actual Losses.	Per Cent.
Adriatic,	$206,754	$5,000	100
American,	361,659	30,000	100
American Exchange,	230,635	50,000	100
Buffalo German,	222,104	5,000	100
Citizens,	399,283	40,000	100
Columbia,	386,306	3,000	100
Commerce (Albany),	514,652	500,000	100
Commerce (New York).	225,384	26,000	100
Commercial,	259,384	5,000	100
Continental,	1,870,297	1,800,000	100
Corn Exchange,	283,861	800,000	100
Exchange,	150,604	5,000	100
Firemen's Fund,	127,498	25,000	100
Firemen's Trust,	187,951	5,000	100
Germania,	704,517	230,000	100
Glen's Falls,	242,225	10,000	100
Guardian,	230,411	40,000	100
Hanover,	404,541	200,000	100
Hoffmann,	200,337	30,000	100
Home,	3,011,455	5,000,000	100

* It is believed that a large amount of assets reported by this company are unavailable.

	Net Assets, Jan. 1, 1871.	Actual Losses.	Per Cent.
Howard,	$702,762	$500,000	100
Humboldt,	211,623	20,000	100
Importers' and Traders',	271,082	22,500	100
International,	860,250	450,000	100
Jefferson,	360,739	42,500	100
Kings County,	222,032	30,000	100
Lafayette,	160,770	8,000	100
Lenox,	214,271	30,000	100
Long Island,	347,763	——	100
Mechanics',	175,438	22,500	100
Mechanics' and Traders',	369,926	41,500	100
Mercantile,	235,208	100,000	100
Merchants',	332,031	15,000	100
Nassau,	346,812	——	100
National,	254,000	36,000	100
New Amsterdam,	364,852	500,000	100
New York Fire,	328,611	15,000	100
Niagara,	1,020,598	250,000	100
Pacific,	367,835	13,500	100
Phœnix,	1,372,946	600,000	100
Relief,	249,560	40,000	100
Republic,	436,457	250,000	100
Resolute,	204,265	75,000	100
Sterling,	213,199	7,500	100
Tradesman's,	311,226	25,000	100
Williamsburgh City,	389,871	60,000	100

Other States—Companies in Liquidation.

	Net Assets, Jan. 1, 1871.	Losses.	Per cent.
Atlantic, Providence, R. I.,	$249,109	$285,000	.75
American, "	321,012	400,000	.75
Allemannia, Cleveland, O.,	269,732	600,000	.40
City, Hartford, Conn.,	319,164	1,000,000	.30
Cleveland, Cleveland, O.,	417,714	800,000	.50

	Net Assets, Jan. 1, 1871.	Losses.	Per cent.
Connecticut, Hartford, Conn., . .	$314,229	$600,000	.50
Detroit Fire and Marine, Detroit, Mich.,	204,969	400,000	.50
Enterprise, Philadelphia, . . .	222,505	500,000	.40
German, Cleveland, O., . . .	222,660	500,000	.40
Hibernia, " . . .	200,000	450,000	.40
Hide and Leather, Boston, Mass., .	300,402	900,000	.30
Hope, Providence, R. I., . . .	158,568	150,000	100
Independent, Boston, Mass., . .	314,749	1,000,000	.30
Merchants' & Mechanics', Baltimore, Md.,	274,962	300,000	.85
Merchants', Hartford, Conn., . .	337,295	800,000	.40
North American, Hartford, Conn., .	275,711	800,000	.35
N. E. Mut. Marine, Boston, Mass., .	376,063	2,000,000	.18
National, Boston, Mass., . . .	513,252	700,000	.70
Norwich, Norwich, Conn., . .	259,864	650,000	.50
Occidental, San Francisco, . .	316,993	500,000	.60
Pacific, " . .	1,303,831	1,900,000	.63
Putnam, Hartford, Conn., . .	403,053	750,000	.50
Providence Washington, Providence, R. I.,	315,646	550,000	.55
Roger Williams, Providence, R. I., .	183,228	300,000	.60
Sun, Cleveland, O., ...	230,259	225,000	100
Teutonia, "	190,000	400,000	.45

OTHER STATES—COMPANIES CONTINUING.

	Net Assets, Jan. 1, 1871.	Losses.	Per cent.
Bay State, Worcester, Mass., . .	$196,275	$5,000	100
Boylston, Boston, Mass., . . .	933,256	13,000	100
Commercial Mutual, Cleveland, O., .	282,882	200,000	100
City, Boston, Mass., . . .	399,427	15,000	100
Elliott, " . . .	594,700	12,500	100
Fireman's, " . . .	1,038,330	35,000	100
Franklin, " . . .	541,908	50,000	100
Howard, " . . .	311,334	27,500	100
Laurence, " . . .	262,502	12,500	100
Manuf'ctur'rs, " . . .	950,578	150,000	100
Merchants', " . . .	813,887	10,000	100
Neptune, " . . .	600,000	60,000	100

	Net Assets, Jan. 1, 1871.	Losses.	Per cent.
North American, Boston, Mass., .	$500,000	$10,000	100
People's, Worcester, Mass., . .	603,798	500,000	100
Shoe and Leather, Boston, Mass., .	464,513	25,000	100
Suffolk, " .	283,288	23,000	100
Tremont, " .	294,543	70,000	100
Washington, " .	759,390	25,000	100
Fireman's Fund, San Francisco, .	618,242	300,000	100
Union, " .	873,124	500,000	100
Merchants', Providence, . . .	248,974	13,000	100
Narragansetts, " . . .	523,719	30,000	100
Franklin, Philadelphia, Penn., . .	1,476,833	500,000	100
Ins. Co. N. A. " . .	1,796,085	1,200,000	100
Lycoming, " . .	516,896	1,000,000	100
Alps, Erie, Penn., ...	265,524	200,000	100
American Central, St. Louis, Mo., .	216,836	300,000	100
Anchor, " .	121,974	27,000	100
Boatman's, " .	51,786	20,000	100
Citizen's, " .	271,373	25,000	100
Maryland, Baltimore, Md., . .	276,642	18,000	100
National, " . .	219,856	35,000	100
Peabody, " . .	193,888	10,000	100
People's, " . .	105,825	17,000	100
Potomac, " . .	157,986	10,000	100
Union, " . .	173,418	25,000	100
Ætna, Hartford, ...	3,757,006	3,250,000	100
Fairfield Co., Norwalk, Conn., . .	216,358	38,000	100
Hartford, Hartford, Conn., . .	1,553,188	1,500,000	100
Phœnix, " . .	936,591	1,000,000	100
National, Bangor, Me., . . .	208,354	27,500	100
Union, " . . .	255,905	5,000	100
American, Cincinnati, O., . . .	98,000	10,000	100
Andes, " . . .	1,076,402	1,000,000	100
Burnet, " . . .	75,369	4,000	100
Cincinnati, " . . .	176,302	40,000	100
Citizen's, " . . .	41,495	20,000	100

	Net Assets, Jan. 1, 1871.	Losses.	Per cent.
Commercial, Cincinnati, O., . . .	$140,062	$14,000	100
Farmer's, " . . .	14,596	5,000	100
Fireman's " . . .	182,651	30,000	100
Franklin, " . . .	118,745	50,000	100
Globe, " . . .	111,573	40,000	100
Home, Columbus, O., . . .	545,193	300,000	100
Merchant's and Manufacturer's, Cin., O.,	221,380	15,000	100
Miami Valley, Cincinnati, O., . .	115,111	30,000	100
Ohio Valley, " . . .	51,541	5,000	100
People's, " . . .	22,969	50,000	100
Union, " . . .	111,448	25,000	100
Washington, " . . .	132,918	21,000	100
Western, " . . .	143,346	28,000	100
Brewer's, Milwaukee, . . .	183,681	250,000	100
N. W. National, ...	191,202	100,000	100
St. Paul F. & M., ...	280,593	100,000	100
Aurora, Covington, Ky., . . .	163,543	35,000	100

FOREIGN COMPANIES—ALL CONTINUING.

	Net Assets, Jan. 1, 1871.	Losses.	Per cent.
Liverpool and London and Globe, .	$20,136,420	$5,000,000	100
North British and Mercantile, .	4,104,598	2,000,000	100
Imperial, ...	5,438,665	150,000	100
Royal, ...	9,274,776	98,000	100
Commercial Union, ...	4,000,000	65,000	100

The Home, of New York, claimed to have reinsured $750,000 of its Chicago risks; we have not recognized this claim in these tables.

Of the enormous assets of the Liverpool, London, and Globe, a large portion is credited to the Life Insurance department.

The losses tabulated above (only approximate in some cases), with a few others not noted, foot up a total of fully $100,000,000 worth of insured loss. On this some $40,000,000 is collectable, but many of the companies claiming to pay in full are "shaving" heavily. We estimate that not more than $35,000,000 will be paid, of which nearly $30,000,000 was adjusted by the end of November. The insurance companies will pay about eighteen per cent. of the total value of all the property destroyed, whether insured or not.

The *Spectator*, of New York, gives the following as the aggregate losses of the companies by States, the number of companies in each State, and the number suspended:

State.	No. of Companies.	Aggregate capital.	Total gross assets.	Total losses.	No. suspended.
New York,	103	$30,161,231	$54,675,359	$21,637,500	20
Ohio,	50	5,896,753	7,988,076	4,818,627	5
Massachusetts,	34	8,051,800	13,880,763	4,483,500	3
Pennsylvania,	34	5,025,800	13,582,644	2,082,000	1
Missouri,	25	2,783,254	3,088,034	575,000	1
Illinois,	20	4,314,951	5,788,917	33,878,000	14
Maryland,	18	2,837,651	4,133,003	397,165	1
Connecticut,	11	6,700,000	13,829,884	9,325,000	7
Kentucky,	11	2,000,000	2,224,543	6,800	—
Rhode Island,	9	1,900,000	3,116,836	2,072,500	6
California,	7	3,753,600	5,730,630	2,950,000	—
Michigan,	3	400,000	690,463	175,000	—
Maine,	3	550,000	900,161	30,000	—
Wisconsin,	2	314,175	374,883	290,000	—
Minnesota,	1	120,000	280,593	100,000	—
New Hampshire,	1	100,000	134,586	——	—
Total of U. S.,	335	$74,939,216	$135,420,426	$82,821,122	—
Foreign,	6	——	10,459,095	5,813,000	—
Grand total	341	——	$145,879,521	$88,634,122	57

The managers of the insolvent insurance companies have been severely blamed, and not without reason. It was their business to provide against just such a contingency as that presented by the Chicago fire, though not to anticipate it as likely to occur. Insurance is good for nothing unless it be an absolute protection to the insured, and those companies which have proven themselves equal to the test will assuredly have no reason in the future to regret the outlay. We do not claim, as some have done, that no company should be permitted to assume a greater aggregate of risks than the amount of its assets, but some measures ought to be taken to prevent the swinging of lines of insurance in any one place so enormously disproportionate to its capital as is presented in the returns of some companies.

Another lesson taught by the Chicago fire is the folly of local action, the aim of which is to drive out companies organized in other States. The object of insurance is to scatter a loss as widely as possible, so that the effects will not be disastrous to any one man or class of men, and this end can best be attained in fire underwriting by placing the insurance of any city in companies whose capital is not likely to be destroyed by the very same fire on which it is called to meet the loss. Any thing like a tax on foreign companies in the future, will be as odious as the wild-cat plan of insurance itself, which is only intended to bring in dividends, and not to meet losses.

CHAPTER XII.

WHAT WAS LEFT.

The city not ruined—Mistaken advice—A statement of profit and loss—Comparison of 1868 with 1871—The disaster equivalent to a destruction of three years' growth.

WHEN the news went forth that Chicago had been swept almost from one side to the other by the devouring flames, there were a few who accepted the statement as a highly colored exaggeration. But this view quickly gave place to the other extreme. It seemed to be generally accepted as a fact that Chicago was blotted out from the number of cities, nothing remaining but the location and the name. It was conceded that the wondrous energy of the people was adequate to the task of rebuilding, but it was thought that the work must be re-begun, *ab initio*. The outside impression was that not only the buildings, but even the streets, were obliterated, and the city razed as effectually as if it had been taken in hand by one of the old-time conquerors—its site plowed up, and the land sown with salt.

And so the good-natured, and really well-meaning, advisers, who lived and wrote at a distance, filled hundreds of newspaper columns with advice that was entirely inappropriate to the occasion. The people of Chicago were recommended to lay out entirely new street lines, on an improved plan, and then to build. The truth is, however, that the streets remain almost intact in the burned districts, the damage to the wooden-block pavement scarcely exceeding half a million of dollars, while the immense systems of sewers, and water pipes, and gas mains beneath, are scarcely disturbed. But beyond all this, the largest part of the city was unvisited by the conflagration, though the burned part was valuable, almost beyond comparison with what remained, in a commercial aspect. To remodel street lines in the burned district would have involved changes elsewhere, and entailed a heavy additional expense upon an already impoverished people. However, that is not the subject of the present chapter. Our present object is to tell what remained besides life and energy, and hope, on that terrible night, when the fire had well-nigh spent its fury in the search after fresh victims, and settled back to the work of feeding upon the ruins, till every atom of combustible matter should be resolved into the original elements.

The destruction was practically complete in the North Division, not more than 500 houses being left out of nearly 14,000; while even a less proportion of the residents were left with homes. The houses unburned were generally of the smaller class, and capable of accommodating but a very few persons in each one.

In the South Division the devastation was complete over but a comparatively small area, and what remained was enough to form a fine city in itself. South of the southern limit of the fire, as far as the eye can reach, the streets were lined with buildings, all, without exception, of a superior class; the poorest one within two miles of Harrison and east of State scarcely cost less than eight to ten thousand dollars. Westward of State Street a poorer class of residences prevailed, but the streets were generally in good order, and the docks along the river were crowded with merchandise and factories.

In the West Division the proportion of loss was even less. The burned district was the poorest in that section, in regard to the character of its buildings, though rich in the products of labor and the means of providing more wealth. But behind this district was an imposing array of fine streets, thickly lined with substantial buildings, containing many thousands of the well-to-do classes of citizens.

The city contained a population of 334,270 souls. Of these, 98,500 were rendered homeless; leaving 235,770, or seventy per cent., unharmed. About 50,000 left the city within a few weeks, but many of these returned subsequently, and many hundreds of workers came in from other places to aid in rebuilding the city. In December, 1871, Chicago contained a population of not much less than 300,000.

The number of buildings burned was 17,450; remaining 42,000, or seventy per cent. The value of the buildings burned was not less than fifty per cent. of the whole—saved, fifty per cent.

Of lumber and grain the proportion destroyed was about twenty-six per cent., of fuel fifty per cent. Of grain there was saved 5,000,000 bushels; of lumber 240,000,000 feet; of coal 79,000 tons.

On mercantile stocks, manufactures, and personal effects, the loss averaged seventy per cent. of the whole, the saved, thirty per cent.

All the land remains, substantially, as before the fire, and the street improvements were but little disturbed, except in the matter of sidewalks.

A comparison of these facts, with the statistics given in preceding chapters of this book, leads to startling conclusions, and no less cheering than startling. The population of Chicago in November, 1871, one month after the fire, was fully equal to that of the spring of 1869. Aggregating the losses on property, even after making due allowances for a depreciation in the selling price of real estate (much of which can be but temporary), and adding in to the sum the amounts received and to be received by the sufferers, from insurance companies, the stocks of which are not held by Chicago men, we have a grand total of nearly four hundred millions of dollars, which is considerably greater than the aggregate of actual values of real and personal property in the summer of 1868. Equating these two comparisons, we find that:

The Great Conflagration set back the city of Chicago not more than three years in her career of progress. A week after the fire she was fully as "well to do," in a pecuniary sense, as three years previously. In that triennial period—less than one-tenth of an ordinary generation, she had gained all that she lost on that eventful day, the 9th of October, 1871.

If we mistake not, the commerce and domestic manufactures of Chicago, in the twelve months next succeeding the fire, will be found to exceed those of three years previously, the gold dollar being taken as the standard for the comparison of money values.

CHAPTER XIII.

THE BUSINESS OUTLOOK.

The first two days after the fire—Preparing to resume—Extraordinary calmness under suffering—Working with a will—The newspapers—Meeting of bankers and business men—Cheering news from insurance companies.

IN our statement of what was left after the fire, we omitted mention of the one great possession which the flames could not destroy. The genius that had built up Chicago could not be reduced to ashes; that remained—stimulated to renewed activity by the calamity that had befallen the scene of so much effort in the past. The kind of material of which Chicago men were made was well typified in the motto on a shingle stuck up amid the ruins long before they had cooled, "All gone but wife, children, and energy."

Indeed, if one could but have ignored the presence of the smoldering ruins, and drawn a veil over the memory of the scene of a few hours previously, it would have been impossible to tell by looking in the faces of the people, or noting the tone of voice, that any serious loss had occurred. Not only was there no tearing of hair, or wild raving about lost fortunes, but absolutely no reference to the event, on the part of any business man, except as one might speak of a business failure in which the individual had no immediate interest. The business portion of the community seemed to think it beneath them to utter a word of complaint. Several of the telegrams sent East for more goods actually contained no word of reference to the disaster that had swept away the accumulations of many years; and we heard of one who sent word that he would be unable to remit for a day or two, his affairs being somewhat deranged by a hasty removal. Every body acted as if there was neither time nor occasion for grieving.

The first impulse of those not actually burned out of house and home was to care for the real sufferers. This assured, the second thought was about growing again. Within two days from the date of the fire, a large proportion of the business men had secured localities outside the limits of the burned district, or had given orders for temporary structures to be erected on the old site, while many had contracted for a rebuilding of their property substantially as before. The Board of Trade had established itself in west-side quarters, and organized a committee of one hundred to aid in distributing the supplies of food and clothing; the leading hotel proprietors had secured new locations; no one even waiting to see what was saved before resolving to go ahead again. Scarcely one, out of the entire host, gave up in despair. And it should be remembered that this steady preparation for new business was proceeded with, for several days, amid the greatest uncertainty with regard to the grand result. Scarcely any man was able to define his position; for even those who had not been burned out of home, as well as office, knew not whither they might drift in the general "sea of troubles." It was scarcely expected that any policy of insurance would be worth a rush. None knew how much the banks might be crippled; as not only their resources but their records were believed to have been destroyed, in that intense furnace-heat which scarcely ever met with a parallel except in the infernal regions. Ninety per cent. of the mercantile accounts were believed to have been burned up. And, worse than all, the destruction of the Court-house had reduced to ashes the only recognized evidence of title to property that constituted the sole means of support to thousands. Not only stocks and building improvements had vanished into smoke and thence into thin air, but the record of the one, and the title to the site of the other, had departed in like manner. It really seemed as if the wail of *La Somnambula* must be repeated in chorus by every one of the residents of the city, "All is lost now!"

In this respect all was chaos. But there was one point on which all were clear. The universal sentiment was, "We will square up old business, if possible; if not, we will commence anew, and trust to Providence to the end." They had even more confidence in the result than had the old lady whose faith held out till the breeching broke, and then collapsed.

The suspense was but short. The first reassurance was given by the expressions of *practical* sympathy that flashed along the wires by the hundred, from places far and near, telling how much (in dollars) they felt for the sufferers. Perhaps the second was the statement that several of the insurance companies would pay in full. Then a meeting of bankers was held—on the third day—at which it was resolved to "go ahead." Then the lumbermen met, and resolved that they would not take advantage of the situation to advance the price of lumber. And simultaneously the wholesale dealers wheeled into line, while the Board of Trade unanimously voted down the proposition to repudiate contracts outstanding at the time of the fire. All this within one week. Seven days had scarcely elapsed before general confidence was restored, and business was on its feet again.

Though crippled for the nonce, it was healthy; and business men had resolved to make the best of the situation.

All day on Monday the fire was raging, and none knew during the succeeding night that it would not sweep the entire city. But on Tuesday morning it was evident that that conflagration had done its worst. Then business men began to work. Early that morning the *Tribune* and *Journal* found a location on Canal Street, west of the river, and began work, the *Journal* issuing that evening, and the *Tribune* on Wednesday morning. All the other dailies were equally enterprising, except the *Times*, the proprietor of which preferred to wait for a couple of weeks and start again in "ship-shape." On that Tuesday morning the officers of the Board of Trade secured a large room at No. 53 South Canal Street, and threw it open for business, while many of the commission merchants secured offices near that point, and called in all the carpenters, gas-fitters, etc., that could be found, to put their places in order. The same enterprise was exhibited by the wholesale dealers, most of whom had secured temporary quarters before nightfall, either in the West or South Divisions, within a few blocks of the still burning ruins. The prominent hotel keepers were also on the alert, the Sherman and Briggs Houses being re-opened on Madison Street, a little west of the bridge.

On Wednesday the principal bankers held a meeting, W. F. Coolbaugh presiding, at which it was tacitly resolved to continue business, though no formal action was taken. Before nightfall not less than twelve of the banks had been temporarily located, and announced their intention to recommence just as soon as the places chosen could be set in order. It was not known exactly how much they would be able to do, but their behavior inspired confidence, which was further strengthened by the report that the Bank of Montreal, the richest on this continent, had determined to open an agency in Chicago. Then came in the telegrams from the insurance companies, full of cheer. The Liverpool, London and Globe telegraphed that they could and would pay at least three million dollars immediately on adjustment, provided they were liable for so much. The Union Insurance Company of San Francisco telegraphed to their agent to pay every dollar of the half million lost by them, and immediately called an assessment upon their stockholders to keep good their $750,000 in gold capital, and $400,000 surplus. The North British and Mercantile, and two or three other companies whose names do not now occur to us, made similar announcements.

The effect was electrical. The Board had been on the point of wiping off all contracts pending at the time of the fire, but now a majority of the members were in favor of honoring all their engagements, as far as could be ascertained amid the general destruction of accounts; the decision to this effect was not, however, formally made until the following Saturday. On this day (Wednesday) the Directors of the Chamber of Commerce decided to rebuild on the old site as quickly as possible, and several of the leading merchants obtained permits from the Board of Public Works to erect temporary wooden buildings, so that they could resume at an early date. Several meetings were held by prominent citizens, the object being to prepare for the resumption of business; and the head-quarters of the city government were temporarily held in the Congregational Church, on the corner of Ann and Washington Streets. A telegram was also received from Governer Palmer, stating that a special meeting of the Legislature had been called for the next day to render such aid as could be given by the State to Chicago in her dire affliction.

All this within forty-eight hours after the fire had passed into history, long before the smoke had cleared away or the cellars stopped burning—nearly a week before the great coal heaps ceased to light up the evening sky with a lurid glare that made night hideous. All this, too, in addition to the work of providing shelter for, and distributing food and clothing to, nearly a hundred thousand homeless ones. Talk about energy! Why, the people of Chicago themselves never understood till then the extent of their own resources, the amount of energy, still less their almost superhuman self-possession. There was none of the hurry that impedes progress, none of the grumbling that interferes with action—nay, not even the boasting in which some are tempted to indulge when troubled, to hide their fears. In those two days scores of thousands of people had lived half a century, and the hair of many men had grown precociously gray (a sober fact), but there was no despondency in the countenance; not even the sternness that some suppose to be necessary to a successful struggle with misfortune.

CHAPTER XIV.

AID FROM THE STATE.

Much sympathy and great expectations—The Governor's message—The canal lien assumed by the State—The new Custom-house and Post-office—The old land-marks to be renewed.

THE Legislature of the State of Illinois met on the 13th of October, the fourth day after the fire, the object of the session being to provide for the relief of the sufferers, as far as it could be done in a constitutional way. Governor Palmer delivered a message in which he strongly recommended that the State should relieve the county of Cook and city of Chicago of the care of their poor, insane, and criminals, and release the lien on the canal which the city held for the improvement of that water route. There was, however, no money in the treasury with which to carry out these measures; and to the recommendation of the Governor that the money be raised by direct taxation of the State, it was replied that the Constitution prohibited the creation of any State debt beyond $250,000, except for the purpose of repelling invasion, suppressing insurrection, or defending the State in time of war. The Governor really discussed these objections in his message, arguing that the spirit of the Constitution was that that sum might be exceeded in any great emergency, like the destruction of Chicago. His arguments were cogent, but the Legislature granted no relief except that couched in the assumption of the canal debt, in pursuance of a contract entered into between the State and the city long before the adoption of the new Constitution. That contract was to the effect that the State might at any time assume the debt incurred by the city in deepening the Illinois and Michigan Canal. The cost of that work, with interest, amounted to $2,955,340. It was ordered that six per cent. bonds, payable in ten years, be issued for this amount; that not less than one-fifth, nor more than one-third of the money so paid should be applied by the city in constructing the bridges, and the other public buildings and structures, upon the original sites thereof, and that the remainder should be applied to the payment of interest on the bonded debt of the city, and to the maintenance of the fire and police departments thereof.

One other measure was passed for the relief of commerce, changing the wording of the warehouse bill, which prohibited the proprietors of grain elevators from delivering up grain without the due surrender of the warehouse receipts issued for such grain. Many such receipts had been burned up in the fire, and could not be so surrendered. But this measure did not involve any pecuniary outlay. Expressions of sympathy fell thick and fast from the lips and pens of members of the Legislature and Senate, but the wordy discussions in which they indulged on the subject lasted till the ardor had cooled down, and the Legislature adjourned without action, to meet again in the middle of November.

At the time of this writing the Legislature has met, but accomplished nothing in regard to the Chicago disaster, looking toward relief from the State. It is thought that the State and county taxes will probably be remitted on the burnt district for a year or two—nothing more. The proposition to assume the expense of conducting the Reform School and the county Poor-house will probably be negatived.

The gravest duty to be performed by the Legislature is in regard to the question of titles to property—not only in the burned district, but all over the county. Not less than one million distinct titles were jeopardized, more or less, by the destruction of the records in the Court-house. The difficulty was all the greater as many owners of real estate wished to sell, or mortgage, in order to raise money wherewith to build, or resume business, but found that the question of proof of title stood in the way. For some weeks the newspapers were liberally supplied with articles on the subject, and the best legal talent in the city was exercised in framing bills that would remove the difficulty. It was found that the books of three abstract firms had been saved, and it was proposed to make one or all of these legal proof of ownership, unless in cases where they were defective, or other overwhelming evidence proved facts not quoted by them. It was proposed by one eminent lawyer to throw the whole thing into Chancery, making it necessary to prove title at an expense of several hundred dollars on each piece of property. But this proposal was received with such universal disfavor that it was essentially modified by the author.

The latest probability was that all claimants to ownership, where such claim was not disputed within a reasonable time, should be determined to be the real owners, without separate legal process, and that the burden of disproof should lie with any one who might afterward dispute that title. It was furthermore announced that deeds issued in the place of those destroyed by fire, do not need to be stamped according to value, if the former deed were properly stamped, and the fact of such reissue were recited in the instrument.

No inconsiderable stimulus was given to the hopes of the people by the announcement that the Government of the United States would immediately reconstruct its buildings in Chicago —the Custom-house and Post-office—on a grand scale, involving the expenditure of four to five millions of dollars in the city within the next three years. The supervising architect, Mr. Mullet, arrived in Chicago in the early part of November, and announced that the work would be speedily proceeded with, and that the building would be erected on the old site, though some additional ground might be required for the purpose.

This, and the provision made by the Legislature, that the public buildings of city and county should be rebuilt where they had stood before the fire, settled matters. A few men, more zealous than wise, had advocated the removal of the business center of the city to other points, forgetting that the attempt to do this would raise a war of contending interests that would have made Chicago almost equally odious, in the eyes of the outside world, with Paris after the surrender to the German armies. Mr. Mullet's answer to some of these pleaders was that the Government had determined to put the buildings back where they stood formerly, and if the location were not the best, the blame would rest with those who had made the original choice. It is probable that no better place could be found for the Post-office, and the United States Courts, with other offices, except the Custom-house—that institution ought to be located on or near the bank of the river, and as near to the mouth of the harbor as possible. It is probable that a separate building will yet be erected in that vicinity, for use by the Custom-house authorities.

CHURCH OF THE HOLY NAME.

ST. JAMES' CHURCH.

FIRST PRESBYTERIAN CHURCH—SOUTH SIDE.

SECOND PRESBYTERIAN CHURCH.

CHAPTER XV.

THE RESURRECTION.

Business on its feet again—The course pursued by the banks—A plethora of money—The Board of Trade, and produce movement—Mercantile indebtedness—Action of Eastern creditors—Strength of Chicago's business men—Retail dealers in council.

OF course little was done in the way of business during the remainder of the first week, beyond the retail supply of the wants of the people. Chicago was cut off from connection with the outside world, for awhile, in a business way. The railroads were disarranged by the burning of depots and rolling stock, and the personal distresses of their employés, while their crippled facilities were taxed to bring on the clothing and provisions contributed abroad, and to carry away those who wished to flee the city. A great many goods were left untouched by the fire, outside the limits of the conflagration, but few of the merchants were prepared to receive them, and all the vehicles at command were employed in hauling fuel or provisions for those who had been burned out, or in transporting lumber to the places where it would be used to rebuild. The Board of Trade could not very well resume till the banks were again in running order.

On Thursday the banks came to the conclusion that they would begin at once to pay out fifteen per cent. to depositors, and this action was made public in the papers of Friday morning. They had little doubt of their ability to pay more at the outset, but preferred to set this limit as a protection, in the event of a run. The Savings Banks also decided to pay out twenty dollars to all having that sum or more on deposit, and to pay in full those depositors having twenty dollars or less on the books. The action of the banks was excepted to by many as too close, but it was afterward conceded that their policy was a judicious one. They were all sound, but a considerable proportion of their assets was in the shape of commercial paper, which it would have been cruel to press for collection, and they wished also to keep at command a sufficient amount of money to keep the wheels of trade in motion by aiding the shipment of produce eastward.

The greater number of the banks resumed on the following Tuesday (October 17th), and experienced no trouble in coping with the situation. On the contrary, they found that the money offered on deposit amounted to more than that withdrawn. This was the case even with the Savings Banks. The fact showed the utter absence of a panic in Chicago, as other facts had already shown that the city, not only had the sympathy but, retained the confidence of the capitalists of other cities. This was markedly instanced by the establishment, on the 15th of November, of a branch of the Bank of Montreal in the city, the principal object of which was to forward the mercantile movement by granting credits on the East and on Europe and China. The status of the Chicago banks had been inquired into on the 16th of October by Comptroller Hurlburd, who reported them as satisfactory. Indeed, from that time to the date of this writing (November 15th), the banks have had more money than before the fire. Large quantities of capital were sent on from other cities, to be invested in real estate at the reduction which it was anticipated would ensue. A great deal of money was forwarded by insurance companies to pay on losses, and the immense relief-fund itself was necessarily deposited in banks till such times as the money should be wanted to meet the hardships of winter. All these things, operating together, produced a perfect flush of bank funds in November, though large quantities of money were sent East in payment of mercantile accounts. The banks could have loaned at least twice as much money as they did, had the right kind of paper been offered. Of course they had many applications for loans which they were obliged to refuse, the security tendered being hazardous.

We have stated that the Board of Trade did no business during that first week, but it is not true that there was nothing doing in produce. On the contrary, the grain received during that week aggregated not less than 1635 car loads, or 649,000 bushels, and the shipments amounted to 220,460 bushels, to move which required the outlay of fully $165,000. Most of these funds were brought direct from New York, but a portion of the money was obtained from Milwaukee.

The Board of Trade formally resumed business on Monday, one week after the fire, and thenceforward the trading in produce was almost equal in volume to what it had been before the fire, while it actually exceeded that of a year preceding. The following table of receipts and shipments of breadstuffs for the weeks ending as dated, is interesting and instructive:

RECEIPTS.

	Nov. 11, '71.	Nov. 4, '71.	Nov. 12, '70.
Flour, barrels, ...	35,272	33,016	36,053
Wheat, bushels, . . .	390,538	285,502	334,840
Corn, bushels, ...	817,904	638,907	205,956
Oats, bushels, ...	270,367	369,856	109,995
Rye, bushels, ...	26,474	36,883	17,445
Barley, bushels, . . .	87,530	91,120	45,350

SHIPMENTS.

	Nov. 11, '71.	Nov. 4, '71.	Nov. 12, '70.
Flour, barrels, ...	10,156	19,597	45,519
Wheat, bushels, . . .	413,909	326,451	511,289
Corn, bushels, ...	547,834	764,614	402,328
Oats, bushels, ...	449,825	529,505	250,504
Rye, bushels, ...	32,999	116,126	34,474
Barley, bushels, . . .	107,329	71,611	104,838

These figures are a sufficient answer to the statement that the produce business of Chicago was ruined by the fire. And this has been the result, notwithstanding the fact that one-quarter of the storage-room, and receiving and shipping facilities, was burned up. The immense packing interest was scarcely touched. A few small packing-houses were destroyed in the North Division, but the great bulk of this business is carried on at the Stock Yards, or on the south branch, far outside the burned district.

Except that the Board of Trade occupied more dingy quarters than six weeks previously, there was little difference at the above dates between the volume of business then and before the fire. An effort had been made a week after the event to cause a division on the question of locality, a portion of the members meeting in Standard Hall, on the corner of Michigan Avenue and Thirteenth Streets, but the difficulty was soon settled by the agreement to remove back to the old site as soon as the edifice could be rebuilt, and the acceptance of an offer made by Judge Farwell to meet meanwhile in his new building on the east end of Washington Street tunnel, which would be ready for occupancy in the early part of December.

The mercantile community was equally successful in getting on its feet again. It was really touching to read some of the telegrams sent by Eastern houses to some of the leading merchants, in the early days of their distress, before any one knew the extent to which the calamity would affect them. They took it for granted that the Chicago sufferers would commence anew, and had full confidence in their ability. The tenor of the dispatches sent was generally about as follows: "We suppose you are burned out; order what goods you require, and pay when you can; WE WANT YOUR TRADE." Of course there was much of worldly wisdom in this, but it was cheering nevertheless to those who had so lately seen the accumulations of years go up in smoke. Soon there came from the East a number of men to *investigate*—not as Sheriff's officers, but to learn the full extent of the disaster. The result of their inquiries was better than they had dared to hope. The great majority of the wholesale dealers showed themselves able to pay their bills in full, though many asked a short extension of time. A very small per centage wanted to compromise at less than a hundred cents on the dollar; they wanted to pay up.

The heaviest losses were sustained by the dry goods interest; they had very large stocks on hand, not less than ten million dollars worth, at wholesale, and those stocks were turned over much less readily than those in many other lines of trade, involving longer credits at the seaboard. These facts give especial significance to the following in the New York Daily *Bulletin* of November 2, 1871:

"There are about twenty firms, representing by far the greater part of the indebtedness, who pay in full at maturity. Another firm, having probably the largest indebtedness of any one house there, meets its paper in full, but at an average extension of a year and three quarters, and at six per cent. interest. One or two other firms, with a comparatively limited indebtedness, get extensions averaging from nine months to a year, and propose to pay in full, but without interest. Four of the leading firms, representing aggregate liabilities to the amount of $1,500,000, compromise at an average of sixty cents, payable at periods ranging from three to twelve months, without interest. This showing comprises all of the wholesale and larger retail Chicago houses that have suffered, and here we have an actual loss not exceeding $600,000. Making liberal allowances for the possible losses that some of our jobbing houses may sustain through the small retailers, therefore we think that it may be safely estimated that $1,000,000 will pay all the actual losses sustained by our dry goods merchants; and this estimate is entertained by our most intelligent merchants. That this is far below what dealers expected may be inferred from the fact that on the day after the fire one of our largest jobbing firms estimated their losses at about $1,000,000, reckoning among the creditors with whom they would have to make liberal compromises several houses who have since announced their ability to meet their liabilities in full and promptly at maturity. The favorable settlements have had the effect of restoring confidence among merchants; and even those most given to croaking fail to see how the disaster is likely to bring panic upon the dry goods interest through their direct losses. The clothing trade was largely represented in Chicago, but out of the eight or ten large houses there not one, we believe, has asked for an extension over any great length of time. The result shows the Chicago dry goods merchants to have been more solid, financially, than they had been supposed to be by merchants generally, although the fact that most of them purchased their goods on very short time always made them favorite customers in this market. Those who held encumbered real estate are pinched the most by their losses; but even those are likely to be able to weather the storm without sacrificing their property at its present depreciated value, by the aid of the liberal extensions which their creditors have readily accepted."

And this exhibit of loss was great, in comparison with that of any other line of trade, or even of all combined, so far as Eastern debts were concerned.

The situation was the most embarrassing for the smaller business men and women—those who had been engaged in the smaller retail trade, with a capital of five thousand dollars or less, upon which they had traded successfully, without credit, in what we may call the pre-igneous period. All that they had was swallowed up. With no bank account, no credit, no location, they were in sorry plight, and knew not which way to turn for relief. In this extremity many of them held two or three meetings in the Court-house Square, and resolved that a portion of the relief fund should be placed at their service, but the utter impossibility of such a thing was too palpable, and the movement died out quietly. Some of this class obtained help from friends to start again in an humble way, but the majority had not been able to re-commence as we go to press. Many of these were genuine objects of pity. They wanted to earn a legitimate livelihood, but were unable to do so, while those higher and lower than they, in the business scale, found little trouble in starting again. As a class, these were the last to resume business, and on them the calamity laid its heaviest hand.

CHAPTER XVI.

RECONSTRUCTION.

Business on the lake-front—Wooden and brick structures—Loss of time—Old customers and new friends—Railroad earnings—Price of lumber—The fire limits—How shall the city be rebuilt?

CONFIDENCE once restored, business men proceeded with renewed energy in the work of reconstruction. A drive through the burned district in the middle of November showed very many of the edifices partially rebuilt, while from the sites of many more the rubbish had been cleared away and workmen were busy in re-arranging foundation lines, and preparing to raise other piles more durable, if less imposing, than those which had so recently succumbed to the fiery element. On several sites temporary wooden structures had been thrown up, and "shingles" announced that the occupants were ready to do business. These were, however, of the irregular order. The general current of endeavor evidently was in the direction of getting back permanently to the old place as quickly as possible. Hence, those who could not obtain quarters westward and southward of the burned district, had constructed temporary wooden buildings on the lake-shore, on what was known as Lake Park, on the base-ball grounds to the northward of that tract, and on Dearborn Park. The whole of this area was covered with frame structures, placed

FIRST NATIONAL BANK BEFORE THE FIRE.

CROSBYS' OPERA HOUSE.

POST-OFFICE AND CUSTOM-HOUSE.

WHERE THE FIRE BEGAN.

there by permission of the Board of Public Works, the altitude being limited to twenty feet, and the tenure to one year. Most of these places were already open, and there the wholesale dry goods, and groceries, and boots and shoes, and iron and hardware merchants displayed their goods, as close to the old theater of operations as possible, yet not so close as to interfere with the work of reconstruction. The work of rebuilding was proceeding with almost equal rapidity in the North Division.

With all this, there were a great many indications of radical changes in the direction of business. It seemed probable that while the heavier wholesale houses would return to the old quarters, large numbers of the lesser dealers, the banks, etc., particularly those handling the lighter classes of goods, would become permanently located much farther south than heretofore, while much of the commission business would remain in the West Division, instead of re-concentrating in the neighborhood of South Water Street. The indication was that the center of the business portion of the city would be removed at once some five or six blocks farther southward by the fire; it was already spreading slowly in that direction previous to the date of the great conflagration.

One noticeable feature of the situation was the time lost in traveling among business men. Some had settled down in the South Division, and others in the West, and the journey between the two sections was a long one, while it was not of the most pleasant, as the streets were filled with heavily laden vehicles, and deep in mud with every shower. Then there was considerable inequality in prices, a fact that was not materially remedied by the establishment of several branch offices, by bankers and others, in that division in which the main office was not located. The effect of this scatteration was shown in the middle of November, by the sale of New York exchange between banks, on the same day—in one place it sold at par, in another at a premium of three-quarters of one per cent.

But there was one cheering fact amid all this; and that was that the merchants were all busy, the orders pouring in upon them from all quarters to such an extent as to tax all their powers to supply the demand. Many of them were actually bare of stock, though large consignments had been sent from the East, but the delivery of a considerable proportion of these goods was delayed by the fact that the railroads, too, were taxed to the utmost, and one or two lines were fairly glutted with merchandise. It was remarked by many of the leading merchants that none of their old customers in the country had forsaken them to try the advantages proffered by a thousand and one other places, each of which endeavored to seize the "opportunity" to make itself great by catching a few of the crumbs that had fallen from the table of Chicago. More than this: not a few remarked that buyers who had previously hovered between Chicago and other points, purchasing a little here, and a little there, now sent *all* their orders to the men who had suffered so much, and borne it so bravely.

The following statement of the October earnings of a number of prominent Western railroads shows the effect of the fire in Chicago:

	1871.	1870.
Chicago & Alton,	$ 459,577	$ 475,628
Central Pacific,	1,005,475	828,447
Illinois Central,	761,965	903,225
Kansas Pacific,	392,500	355,899
Lake Shore & Michigan Southern,	1,395.041	1,287,778
Milwaukee & St. Paul,	841,150	908,313
Toledo, Wabash & Western,	600,204	451,291
Union Pacific,	800,000	719,523
Michigan Central,	532,802	511,477

The character of many of the structures erected was necessarily temporary. So much lumber was used that the price of common descriptions had advanced more than thirty per cent. within a month—from $15 to $20 per thousand feet—though a part of the advance was credited to the destruction of the forests by the fires that raged so extensively in the lumber regions of Wisconsin and Michigan about the time of the Chicago disaster. So many wooden buildings had been run up that a universal protest went out against the erection of any more, in those districts where other buildings would be imperiled by their contiguity. Then ensued a lengthy newspaper discussion of the case, and the general expression of sentiment that no more wooden buildings should be permitted to be erected within the boundaries of the city of Chicago. The fire limits were extended by the Common Council after the fire. They will probably be still further extended to include the whole city.

That a stringent fire ordinance is wanted in Chicago, none can doubt. Brick buildings are not indestructible by fire, but they do not feed the flames like wooden ones; and are not only safer, but cheaper when the ultimate cost is taken into the account. No other city of the size of Chicago permits the safety of the whole to be jeopardized by frame structures; and, with an inexhaustible supply of good clay for brick-making, and first-class building stone in her immediate neighborhood, there is no necessity for permitting this suicidal policy in the future. With a raised grade, which permits better drainage, and proper regulations concerning the erection of buildings, the future Chicago may prove that she has learned a valuable lesson from adversity, and show that she had the good sense to profit by it.

CHAPTER XVII.

THE LOSSES AGAIN.

Particular cases—Noted buildings destroyed—The Germans—How the millionaires came out—Not a vestige of a law library left—Art and literary treasures despoiled—Who lost and who gained by the fire.

THE most noteworthy buildings lying within the burnt district, and consequently falling a prey to the flames, are comprised in the following list:

Churches.—Trinity (Episcopal), First Presbyterian, New Jerusalem Temple (Swedenborg), North Presbyterian, St. James's (Episcopal), New England (Congregational), Unity (Unitarian), Grace (Methodist), Cathedral of the Holy Name (Roman Catholic), St. Joseph's (Roman Catholic), St. Mary's (Roman Catholic), Synagogue (Hebrew), St. Paul's (Universalist), Sisters of Mercy (Convent), Illinois Street (Union), St. Joseph's Priory.

Public Buildings.—Court-house and City Hall, Post-office, Water-works, Historical Hall, Chamber of Commerce, United States Warehouses, South Side Gas-works, North Side Gas-works, Armory (police station), Elm Street Hospital, Franklin School, Mosely School, Lincoln School, and many smaller schools.

Theaters, etc.—Crosby's Opera-house, Hooley's Opera-house, McVicker's Theater, Dearborn Theater, Farwell Hall, Metropolitan Hall, Crosby's Music Hall, German House, Turner Hall, Academy of Design, Wood's Museum, Olympic Theater.

Hotels (first class).—Sherman, Pacific, Tremont, Bigelow, Palmer, Briggs, St. James, Matteson, Revere, Metropolitan, Nevada, Clifton, Adams.

Railway Buildings.—Great Central Depot, Michigan Southern Depot, Galena Depot, Illinois Central Freight Depot, Michigan Central Freight Depot, Galena Freight Depot, Galena Elevator, Wheeler's Elevator, Illinois Central Elevator "A," Munger & Armour's Elevator, National Elevator, Pullman's Palace Car Building.

Principal Business Blocks.—Bookseller's Row, Field & Leiter's Store, *Tribune* Building, Merchants' Insurance Building, First National Bank, Union National Bank, Drake-Farwell Block, Sturges' Building, Honore Block, McCormick's Reaper Works.

Among the heaviest individual losers were Messrs. Wm. B. Ogden, Cyrus H. McCormick, and Potter Palmer; though Mr. Ogden's losses would scarcely have been felt by that large capitalist, had it not been for the nearly simultaneous destruction of immense interests in the Wisconsin pineries, in which he was an owner to the extent of two million dollars or more. In Chicago his principal losses were in railroad buildings, insurance stock, and north-side real estate, which Mr. Ogden made a specialty, and which was greatly depreciated in value by the conflagration. Mr. McCormick's losses also mounted into the millions, as did those of his brother, L. J. McCormick. Each of the McCormicks owned many stores and houses, and among their joint property was their extensive reaper works, which contained at the time two thousand finished reapers and a large store of unfinished machines and materials. Potter Palmer has long been reputed to own a mile of front upon State Street, the principal thoroughfare from the river to the south end of the city. Upon this avenue he had already erected stores and hotels to the value of over three-quarters of a million of dollars, and the Grand Hotel, which would swell the amount to two millions, was already well upward with its massive walls. Mr. Palmer also owned large interests in two or three mercantile establishments, and was popularly understood to have mortgaged all his real estate for carrying on his speculations. On the day following the fire it was currently reported and generally believed (so prepared was the popular mind for any thing wonderful) that Mr. Palmer had gone crazy over his losses, and shot himself in a paroxysm of insanity. Nor was this impression dispelled until, from a town in New York, whither Mr. Palmer had gone to attend the dying bed of a parent, came his clarion note: *"I will rebuild my buildings at once. Put on an extra force, and hurry up the hotel."*

And within a few days the New York merchants received his telegram announcing, "The mercantile firms with which I am connected, either as special or general partner, will pay *in full* at maturity."

Another severe sufferer was John B. Drake, proprietor of the Tremont Hotel. His furniture, silver, etc., were very rich, and his largest building (part of the Drake-Farwell Block) had but just been re-occupied, after its fatal destruction of one year ago. But Drake was buoyant, like the rest, and was soon ensconced in the biggest hotel the flames had left for him to hire, and had his workmen overhauling the warm bricks of the twice-consumed store.

It is useless, however, to attempt any enumeration of the brilliant ruins which this unparalleled disaster worked. In the first place, they are like the goods in the auctioneer's catalogue, "too numerous to mention," and in the next place, they will not stay ruined long enough to be caught and impaled in the cabinet of the historian.

There were, however, many cases of complete ruin—or, at least, of such sweeping disaster that it will take years, and in some cases more years than the victim has left in him, to recover any thing like his former foothold. The merchants, as a rule, fared as hard as any equally numerous class. Messrs. Field, Leiter & Co., the heaviest dry goods dealers, saw $2,300,000 worth of their goods dissolve before their eyes, with no hope, at the moment, that they would be indemnified for any considerable fraction of its value. Messrs. J. V. Farwell and C. B. Farwell (M. C.), members of the dry goods firm which bears the former's name, saw $1,900,000 of their stock go the way a similar amount had gone just a year before. A score of other merchants could count up losses scarcely less than these. But large dealers have great credits and great facilities of other kinds for resuming business. It is the smaller dealers who have suffered, proportionately, the worst.

Professional men suffered severely too—even those whose homes were spared them. Many of the physicians and all of the lawyers had their offices within the burnt district of the South Division, and therein were their libraries, apparatus, and all their professional outfit. The legal gentlemen of Chicago—six hundred and fifty in number—lost over half a million dollars worth of law books alone—all the law books, in fact, that there were in the city.

Operators in the great characteristic staples of Chicago trade—grain, provisions, etc.—the "commission men," or "Board of Trade men," did not suffer so severely. Of many of these the stock in trade is of an altogether too unsubstantial sort to suffer much by fire. These gentlemen, many of them, deal in actual commodities, but a small proportion of which, fortunately, was destroyed in this wreck. Many others deal so exclusively in "options," "puts," and "calls," that a smart shower in the country during the summer will make or unmake them much more completely than ever so terrible a fire in Chicago. Besides this advantage, the most of your Board of Trade men have become so accustomed to the vicissitudes of business that they bear the buffetings' of fortune as well as the prize fighter bears the bruises which prostrate another. So they can count themselves rich on Wednesdays and Saturdays, they are content to be "ruined" on Thursdays and Mondays, and "come up smiling" every time.

A class who suffered very severely are the musicians. A majority of them lived in the ill-fated North Division, and lost their homes. Others lost the churches or the theaters where they principally earned their livelihood. Others lost very valuable collections of books, music, and instruments; while those who escaped with these, had their *public* burned away from them—that is, forced upon such a course of economy as should very seriously interfere with the revenues of music teachers and all such. Among the prominent musicians who fled before the fiery monster were Dudley Buck, the celebrated organist, who has gone to Boston; Hans Balatka, the conductor, gone to Milwaukee; A. J. Creswold, organist, gone to St. Louis; Alfred H. Pease, pianist, gone to Buffalo.

Akin to this subject is that of art and letters generally. Chicago had accumulated a much greater wealth of art treasures than the world generally knew of; much greater than any other city of its age ever amassed. Besides the galleries of the Academy of Design, and the Opera-house, there were the private collections of Albert Crosby, which must have been worth $75,000; those of E. B. McCagg, S. M. Nickerson, and R. E. Moore, at least $50,000 each; and those of E. H. Sheldon, Perry H. Smith, and others, which approximated these values. The gallery of Mr. McCagg contained, among its most valuable works, Powers' statue of Pocahontas, and Healy's great painting of the Conference at Hampton Roads, both of which were lost. Of public libraries, the city had none worth mourning after very bitterly. Cincinnati and St. Louis both eclipsed her in this respect. The collection of the Historical Society—books, pamphlets, papers, and paintings—was totally destroyed. It contained 17,500 bound volumes, 175,000 pamphlets, and complete sets of files of the Chicago newspapers. This collection embraced a complete record of the history of Chicago from its earliest days to the present. In addition to the library, the society owned the original draft of the Emancipation Proclamation by President Lincoln, a complete set of the Chicago battle flags, the Healy Gallery of three hundred paintings, Diehl's Hamlet, Couture's Prodigal Son, and Volk's bust of Mr. Lincoln, the only one for which Mr. Lincoln ever gave a sitting, and the most perfect likeness of the departed statesman then extant. We take this memorandum chiefly from a pamphlet recently published by the society which therein felicitates itself upon the "splendid fire-proof building" in which its precious archives are stored!

Reckoned by nationalities, our German fellow-citizens suffered the worst. They dwelt mostly upon the north side of the river, which the satirists were wont to call *Nordseit*, in their honor. They loved their homes, and invested upon them their savings; storing them with household treasures, and investing them with the home comforts and luxuries in which the German, more than any other European, delights. Through these the billows of flame came sweeping on that fatal morning, a hundred times more ruthlessly and ruinously than the warlike Frenchman would have swept through other German homes had the tide of battle turned otherwise than it did at Worth and Saarbruck. And a most bloody invader, and a most pitiless foreigner, the fire-fiend proved to be!

The old saw that "it's an ill wind that blows nobody any good" did not miscarry in this memorable case. There are several classes who have profited materially by the general calamity. We have already seen how the cartmen profited, temporarily, during the horrible night and day of the fire; nor did their profits soon cease; for there was a vast deal of hauling and shifting of personal effects following the general upheaval of locations. The Relief Society had a world of carting to do, too, and the drays and express wagons never had so busy a month before. Teams and heavy wagons were also in feverish demand all winter, and the streets were so full of them as to be dangerous to light craft and pedestrians. Builders and their employés, especially brick masons, profited by the catastrophe, as might be expected; also brick-makers, from Omaha to Philadelphia, who sold out their stocks at once at several dollars per thousand advance. Insurance agents reaped a harvest also, whatever may have been the hardships of their principals in settling for losses; for every body wanted new insurance after the experience of the 8th and 9th. Lawyers will get plenty of business at adjusting insurance, managing land-title cases, and other litigation growing out of the commercial earthquake caused by the event. The county records having been destroyed with the Court-house, and all legal titles to real estate having thus been seriously impaired, the lawyers will have plenty of jobs at nursing into life the faint glimmers of titles now remaining, and to be found chiefly in the abstract books of two or three firms devoted to that business. These archives were, fortunately, saved from the general wreck, and containing, as they do, complete chains of title, from the original Government patent down to the time of the latest transfer, are expected to yield not only much benefit to the public, but comfortable fortunes to their owners.

Indeed, it is impossible to enumerate the classes who will be pecuniary gainers by the great fire; but it is sufficient to say that, with the classes already mentioned, the retail news men, some of whom made thousands of dollars during the first fortnight after the fire, the shop-keepers of the West Division, the holders of leases who sold out at large bonuses, and the dealers in safes (each of whom had "the *only* strictly fire-proof" after the fire), and all others similarly favored, there are not less than 75,000 persons, out of the 300,000 remaining in Chicago after the fire, who will be better off next spring than if the city had not burned. These did not, except in a very few isolated instances, willfully extort profit out of the misfortunes of their fellows, but merely gained, incidentally, by having something to sell, labor or property, the demand for which was enhanced by the crisis. The opposite rule of course prevailed much more extensively; and in general it may be remarked that the severest losers by the fire were those who had most, or had ventured most; those whose property was in the form of buildings, or stocks of goods, or investments in the future of Chicago; and those whose trade or industry depended upon the patronage of the luxurious classes.

CHAPTER XVIII.

INCIDENTS AND CURIOSITIES.

Oases in the desert—A dwelling saved with cider—Thrilling scene in the tunnel—How the heat burnt up iron columns and left butter unmelted—The man at the crib—Human nature—Good and bad phases—Drawing the long bow.

HUNDREDS of incidents of the Great Conflagration might be related, in addition to the hundreds which have already been told in the narratives of eye-witnesses. Indeed, there is no limit to the stories, either thrilling or curious, which are truthfully told, illustrating the wonderfully rapid progress and terrible fury of the flames, or the peculiarities of human nature under the influence of extreme excitement. Unfortunately there is a limit to our space, which can not be devoted exclusively to these incidents at the expense of the more important events accompanying or following the conflagration.

One of the most curious features of the fire was the escape of two houses in the midst of the burnt district of the North Division. One of these was the residence of Mahlon D. Ogden, brother of Wm. B. Ogden, and himself an extensive property holder. His house faces Washington Park; but so does Robert Collyer's Church, and so did other buildings now no more, which had the park to the windward, and had also the benefit of stone walls, whereas the Ogden mansion is of wood, with an elaborate

French roof and several combustible out-buildings. The park in front, a mere square, had been devoted to the city by Mr. Ogden, many years ago; and it proved a valuable breastwork against the fire on this occasion, as if in acknowledgment of the wisdom and generosity of the gift, and as a hint to other landlords to do likewise. It was not, however, without a severe struggle that the falling brands were extinguished, and the mansion, with its valuable contents, saved from destruction. As another curiosity, one of the elegant conservatories of Mr. E. B. McCagg, directly west of Mr. Ogden's house, and close upon Lasalle Street, went through the fire without the cracking of a glass or the withering of a leaf, while the other green-house to the leeward, and the mansion, in the center of the spacious grounds—both seemingly more protected than the other—were consumed.

The other house mentioned is that of a policeman named Bellinger, which had apparently little advantage of isolation, but was saved by dint of much exertion on the part of its occupant, aided by a favorable freak of the flames. Bellinger was fortunate enough to have a small quantity of water on hand when the supply from the Water-works gave out. He tore up a section of sidewalk, and determined to shed the last drop—not of his blood, but of his water, which, in such a crisis, was still more precious—in defense of his castle. This he did to the best advantage, that is, reserving it until a spark alighted on the shingles. He stood his ground manfully until the red demon approached threateningly near, and then he redoubled his vigilance. Of this there was need, for now the sparks and brands fell thicker and faster, and his scant ladlefuls of water hissed and went up in puffs of steam as they struck the blistering shingles. By and by the last ladleful was gone, and the flames had not yet ceased to rage around him. If he only had a little more water—a bucketful merely—he thought he could save a home for his wife and little ones; the home which he had been struggling so long to build for them. The wish did him honor, and the divine source of it sent him a thought which proved the wish's realization. In the cellar was a barrel of cider, which he had lately got in to drink with the winter's nuts and apples. He rightly judged that the red guest who now threatened his house with a visit wanted that cider worse than he did. To speak in plainer and more policeman-like terms, he knew that cider would quench fire as well as water, and that his cider was what was wanted on the roof at that time. He called to the family to draw and bring to him all the contents of the cask. It was done. The libation was poured out (in the right spots), and the home was saved.

There was a thrilling scene in the Washington Street tunnel. About three o'clock in the morning of Monday, while the tunnel was filled with people rushing wildly in both directions, the gas-works blew up, stopping immediately the supply of gas, and causing total darkness throughout the long and narrow passage. The situation was a terrible one. The sudden darkness, the great excitement under which all the persons were laboring, and the fact that many were bearing articles of furniture, etc., with which it would be dangerous to collide, all served to increase the danger of a panic such as should inevitably result in the crushing and killing of many persons—perhaps in detaining them until all should be suffocated by a blast of flame and smoke. But some one with a quick judgment and stentorian voice cried out, "Keep to the right!" and so every one did, the word "to the right!" being passed along from mouth to mouth. But there was not much more going through the tunnel to the eastward that night.

The fact that building stone was every-where baked and blistered into mere chips, even where it was used only for sidewalks or foundations, attests to the fearful heat which prevailed every-where. But in the interior of buildings the fervor was unprecedented; as witness the melting of the great Court-house bell, the burning up of many safes, so that they could be punctured with a single touch of the crowbar, and the fusion of metals generally. In the stores of Messrs. Heath & Milligan, on Randolph Street, filled with paints and oils, the temperature was above 3000 degrees, as shown by the melting of white lead and other stores requiring that degree of heat to fuse them. How much hotter it became, there was no index to determine; but this is known: that large masses of iron, such as iron columns, and the framework of a large elevator, were literally burned up, so that no trace of them could be found; but (what will strike some unthinking ones as curious) the little wire ropes which were used to work the elevator were not seriously injured. Iron wire is, owing to the peculiar process by which it is spun, one of the least fusible or combustible of substances.

The contents of hundreds of safes were utterly consumed. Indeed, this was the rule with all safes not in vaults; while all fairly built brick vaults brought every thing intrusted to them out safely. A box of matches and linen coat came out of the *Tribune* vault as good as new, and a jar of butter preserved its integrity completely through three or four days of fire in the vault of the Fidelity Deposit Company, without once lapsing into the *melting mood.* This fire has shown that brick is the most fireproof of building materials; that brick and air are the only trustworthy non-conductors of heat, and that iron is, by reason of its tendency to swell and warp, a bad material to use for floors, girders or lintels, in the erection of large buildings.

The "Man at the Crib" is a character dear to public esteem in Chicago, though not one in ten thousand of the citizens has ever seen him. They all know that he is always there in his wave-washed prison, two miles out into the lake, watching the mouth of the tunnel from New Year to New Year. On this night his vigils were directed toward the atmosphere above instead of the water below, for even there his view of the burning city, which would otherwise have been splendid, was shut out first by black smoke and then by the driving shower of fire brands and livid coals which were falling about him, *three miles* from their place of starting. The man had one advantage over the inhabitants of the city on that dread night. There was no danger of his water supply giving out; and he used it freely, to subdue the flames from which even his lonely, isolated perch was not exempt. If the house had burned down, even to the water's edge, the accident would not have affected the water supply; but it would have been uncomfortable for the "Man at the Crib," unless he could have got his boat out betimes.

As already remarked, one of the most interesting features of the conflagration was the suddenly clear insight which it afforded of the innermost recesses of men's hearts. If a man was a coward, or a selfish knave, he could not conceal it from the gaze of his fellow-men on that dread night; while if he was a hero (as many and many proved to be, let it be said to the credit of humanity!) his sterling metal shone clear and bright in the glare and heat of the all-assaying flames. Nor did the gentility or social standing of the man always afford the true clue to the result. The Rev. Robert Collyer told in the hearing of the writer, that during the small hours of Monday morning, while all was panic and terror, and women and children and invalids were in danger, and heroes were developing out of simple souls who had never suspected themselves of heroism before, he saw "the biggest man in the city" scampering away at his best pace and exclaiming, "It's all going to burn up, and I'm going to get out of this as soon as I can." "And so saying," added Mr. Collyer, "he kept on running toward the north, and for aught I know he is running yet."

The opposite kind of cases are more pleasant to contemplate. One of the city journals puts such a one on record in this language:

"On Monday evening, a knot of men, from 35 to 40 years of age, stood on Michigan Avenue, watching the fire as it fought its way southward in the teeth of the wind. They were looking grimy and dejected enough, until another, a broad-shouldered man of middle height, with a face that might have belonged to one of the Cheeryble brothers shining through the over-spreading dust and soot, approached them, and clapping one of their number on the shoulder, exclaimed cheerfully: 'Well, James, we are all gone together. Last night I was worth a hundred thousand, and so were you. Now where are we?' 'Gone,' returned James. Then followed an interchange, from which it appeared that the members of the group were young merchants, worth from $50,000 to $150,000. After this, said the first speaker, 'Well, Jim, I have a home left, and my family are safe; I have a barrel of flour, some bushels of potatoes and other provisions laid in for the winter; and now, Jim, I'm going to fill my house to-night with these poor fellows,' turning to the sidewalks crowded with fleeing poor, 'chuck full from cellar to garret!' The blaze of the conflagration revealed

30

something worth seeing in that man's breast. Possibly the road to his heart may have been choked with rubbish before. If so, the fire had burned it clear, till it shone like one of the streets of burnished gold which he will one day walk."

A few items are worthy of noting down for their personal interest merely. Col. John Hay writes to the New York *Tribune* concerning Mr. Robert Lincoln, son of the late President: "He entered his law office about daylight on Monday morning, after the flames had attacked the building, opened the vault, and piled upon a table cloth the most valuable papers, then slung the pack over his shoulder, and escaped amid a shower of falling firebrands. He walked up Michigan Avenue with his load on his back, and stopped at the mansion of John Young Scammon, where they breakfasted with a feeling of perfect security. Lincoln went home with his papers, and before noon the house of Scammon was in ruins, the last which was sacrificed by the lake side." Mr. Scammon's house, it may be mentioned, was in the famous Terrace Row, spoken of in Mr. White's sketch (Chap. V.), as were also the residences of Ex-Lieutenant-Governor Pross, of the *Tribune*, and S. C. Griggs, of the book trade. It was a row of Illinois-marble fronts, five lofty stories in height, and eclipsing Rockingham Palace in elegance, according to the Rev. Newman Hall, of London.

Among those who fled from the fire was Hon. Lyman Trumbull of the United States Senate, who escaped, with a trunk full of clothing only, from the Clifton House, where he was boarding. There were many theatrical and musical exhibitors at the hotels when the fire came along and settled their bills for them. Theodore Thomas and his famous orchestra were at the St. James Hotel, and escaped with their instruments only. Mrs. Lander, the *tragedienne*, was also among the fugitives. Mrs. Abby Sage (McFarland) Richardson, whose griefs and grievances have made her name familiar to the country, was sojourning in the city at the time, and intending to become a permanent resident; but the fire altered her determination in this regard, and she fled to New York.

Many celebrated persons own property in Chicago, and lost more or less, according to its location; for instance, General Buckner and Ex-Governor Magoffin, of Kentucky, among noted Southerners, and Madame Parepa Rosa, Mlle. Nilsson, Mr. Joseph Jefferson, and Mr. Ole Bull, among musical and dramatic celebrities. The two ladies named, nevertheless, contributed liberally to the relief of those made destitute by the fire.

So far as wonderful and startling incidents go, it would have been better (at least more thrilling to the reader), if this account could have been made out on the week of the fire; for then a thousand blood-curdling stories were passing current, which have since been proved to be without foundation. Here is one of them:

"A wealthy railroad man, on the north side, was holding a party at his residence when the conflagration commenced. When his house became endangered by the fire drawing near, he dispatched his wife and children to a place of safety, and then commenced—with a select few—a bacchanalian revel. When the fire became unbearable, the party moved to the front steps of the mansion with their bottles and glasses. There they continued the horrible carnival, their demoniac yells and wild laughter becoming louder and more boisterous as the fire became more threatening. On the south side, the distilleries were running their liquors from the buildings. The gutters were full of the raw spirits, while men were flocking to them with every conceivable manner of vessels, some even wallowing in the liquor. In some places the fire communicated with the alcohol, and the street became instantly a burning sheet of flame. In some cases the men drank freely and immoderately, sunk into a drunken torpor, and only awoke from their insensibility to find themselves irretrievably enveloped in flames."

The writer of the above has been dubbed the champion liar by some of the newspapers; yet he is altogether excelled by a writer in an Illinois newspaper, who requires his readers to swallow (and in all probability they did) the following yarn:

"The scene now manifested beggars all description. Nothing like it since the burning of Moscow. The only elevator standing is burning underneath its pier. The fire is still burning and spreading west. Eight hundred persons were smothered to death in Washington Street tunnel. Thirteen hundred prisoners in the Bridewell were left to suffocate: not one escaped! Seventeen men were shot who were caught firing buildings. The whole has been the act of an incendiary clique. People are dying for want of water; nothing but the lake remains with which they can quench their thirst, and that is covered with dead bodies, oil, filth, etc. Fifteen thousand people to-night lay outdoors without blankets to shelter them. The *Journal*, *Tribune*, and *Times* establishments are among the ruins. There is not a newspaper left in the city. Potter Palmer's loss is over four millions of dollars. Every Insurance Company in the United States is ruined, and will not be called on to pay the losses. What the people want is something to keep them from starving. The towns along the Illinois Central Railroad are doing nobly. Can not you get up a car-load and send them to-day. Any thing will do that can be eaten. There is not one hundred buildings left within three miles of the Court-house in any direction. The loss of lives is now estimated at between 9000 and 10,000."

We can perhaps excuse this writer's enthusiasm in killing off thirteen hundred persons in the Bridewell (two miles to windward of Chicago), and eight hundred more in the tunnel, as his object was obviously to excite sympathy, bring in the provisions, and (incidentally) to furnish something relishable for the patrons of his paper; but he ought, in the interest of the public health, to have forborne to strew the surface of the lake with "dead bodies, oil, etc.," thereby injuring greatly the quality of the only obtainable water supply!

In the art of drawing the long bow, the clergymen were scarcely behind the newspaper writers. The Rev. Mr. Eddy went from Chicago to Indianapolis, whence he spread a fearfully exaggerated story of the situation in Chicago; and in Baltimore he stood up in the pulpit and told his hearers (before asking them to contribute their money) how he "*saw* the blackened corpses of robbers and incendiaries hanging to gibbets," whereas no such hanging took place, except in the imagination of the Rev. Mr. Eddy and other persons of excitable imaginations. One of the several "histories" of the conflagration, written by a Chicago clergyman of great piety, treats the hangings as actual facts, and solemnly asserts that *five hundred* children were born on the streets and prairies during the night of Monday. This last statement is not so bad an exaggeration as the others; for it is a matter of fact, or at least founded upon a very intelligent estimate, that more than one hundred women were brought to labor by the excitement and exertions of those fearful nights. Doctor Paul, who himself had six cases (another physician having eight), estimates the whole number at one hundred and fifty.

CHAPTER XIX.

INCIDENTS AND CURIOSITIES—CONTINUED.

Remarkable revelation—Scripture for the occasion—Married in the smoke of the flames—How Robert Collyer and his people fought for their church—Grandmother's rocking-chair—How a coal-dealer saved his pile—Fire as a curative agency—More about the degree of heat—The divorce business, etc.

AS a curiosity, this incident, which is strictly authentic, is worth recording: Among the ruins of the Western News Company's establishment, where an immense stock of periodicals and books was reduced to ashes, there was found a single leaf of a quarto Bible, charred around the edges. It contained the first chapter of the Lamentations of Jeremiah, which opens with the following words: "How doth the city sit solitary that was full of people! how is she become as a widow! she that was great among the nations and princess among the provinces, how is she become tributary! She weepeth sore in the night, and her tears are on her cheeks: among all her lovers she hath none to comfort her." And that was the only fragment of literature saved from the News Company's great depot.

In elaboration of this idea, the Chicago *Times* commenced its first issue after the fire with this scriptural quotation, which many will say was written with a prescience of Chicago's calamity:

. . . The merchants of the earth are waxed rich through the abundance of her delicacies.

How much she has glorified herself, and lived deliciously, so much sorrow and torment give her; for she saith in her heart, I sit a queen and am no widow, and shall see no sorrow.

. . . She shall be utterly burned with fire. . . .

And the kings of the earth . . . shall bewail her, and lament for her when they shall see the smoke of her burning,

Standing afar off for fear of her torment, and saying, Alas, alas, that great city, that mighty city! for in one hour is thy judgment come.

And the merchants of the earth shall weep, and mourn over her, for no man buyeth their merchandise any more:

The merchandise of gold, and silver, and precious stones, and of pearls, and fine linen, and purple, and silk, and scarlet, and all thyne wood, and all manner vessels of ivory, and all manner vessels of most precious wood, and of brass, and iron, and marble:

And cinnamons, and odors, and ointments, and frankincense, and wine, and oil, and fine flour, and wheat, and beasts, and sheep, and horses, and chariots, and slaves, and souls of men;

. . . The merchants of these things, which were made rich by her, shall stand afar off . . . weeping and wailing,

And saying, Alas, alas, that great city, that was clothed in fine linen, and purple, and scarlet, and decked with gold, and precious stones, and pearls!

For in one hour so great riches is come to naught. And every shipmaster, and all the company in ship, and sailors, and as many as trade by sea, stood afar off,

And cried when they saw the smoke of her burning, saying, What city is like unto this great city!

And they cast dust on their heads, and cried, weeping and wailing, saying, Alas, alas, that great city wherein were made rich all that had ships in the sea by reason of her costliness! for in one hour is she made desolate.

It may be added, as another incident for the curious, that while the great disaster increased greatly the number of births and deaths, it seriously diminished the number of marriages during the week. Indeed, it might be supposed that at such a time of general distress, there would be neither marrying nor giving in marriage; yet such was not entirely the case. The books of the County Clerk show that twenty licenses were issued during the week commencing with the 8th—the usual number per week being between ninety and a hundred. The reader can readily see that one effect of a common misfortune would be to bring all its victims closer together in feeling, as well as in fact; and that the natural tendency among betrothed pairs would be to become united at once. It seems that this tendency prevailed over the drawback of reduced means in the proportion of cases named. Among the twenty grooms was the son of Chicago's most widely-known divine; and it is no disparagement of the bride to record that, her bridal *trousseau* having been seized by the flames, along with other more valuable, but perhaps not more valued possessions, she "stood up" in a calico frock, and depended upon friends who were not among the "burnt out" for other articles of feminine wear essential to the nuptial occasion.

There were great quantities of movables lost during the flight of the people from the pursuing element, which were not ultimately consumed. Some of this property was carried off by thieves or by treacherous carters, with intent to appropriate it to their own uses; some of it left—somewhere, the flustered and flurried owners knew not where; some of it was taken care of by kindly-disposed persons, who saved the property, but lost all trace of its owner. Of all such property there was a depot soon established at the Central Police Station, where were collected a great store of goods wanting owners; some of them brought in voluntarily, and others (and much the greater part) ferreted out by the police. Within three weeks nearly a million dollars' worth of movable property was thus accumulated and ultimately restored to its owners. Of course this Bureau of Missing Property was diligently visited by all who had reason to hope for any good out of it; and some of the scenes, as the seekers for that which was lost came upon the object of their search, were very interesting. Every article had become trebly valuable now; for, in the first place, hard times had come on, and possessions of any sort were none too plenty; and, in the next place, each article recovered was a tie which bound its owner to the dear old home, the dear old times, and the dear old Chicago.

A single incident will illustrate this. Two ladies enter the rooms, one of them being in quest of certain lost trunks of wearing apparel, etc. They pass through the several rooms in a tedious quest, relieved only by feminine satisfaction in inspecting other people's property. Of this there was an endless variety. There were oil paintings, trunks, bedsteads, bureaus, carpets, gamblers' tools, chairs, sewing-machines, clocks, clothing, silverware, boots and shoes, books, sofas, *etageres*, billiard-balls, guns, and almost every thing conceivable. The place resembled a magnified pawn-shop, or a demoralized bazaar. At length the lady finds that for which she was searching, and goes to the office to sign the necessary papers and receive her certificate. Meanwhile the other lady continues her stroll through the building. Suddenly a glad cry sounds in the furniture-room, "Great heavens! that 's grandma's rocking-chair!" is heard from the lady, and in the next instant she had picked up the chair and hugged it in her arms. It was an ordinary-looking chair, with rockers, the paint worn off in many places, with here and there a bit of iron to brace the joints together; but it had been in the family over seventy years.

"Streaks of good luck" seemed to be rare on this bitter occasion when all fell together; yet they were not altogether wanting, as for instance: A few weeks before the Great Conflagration, there appeared in the morning papers the report of an incipient fire in Mr. Holbrook's coal-yard. The loss was but nominal, but the mere fact of a fire in a coal-yard led to an investigation, and the result was that Mr. Holbrook and several other dealers were satisfied the fire was the result of spontaneous combustion. One of the dealers present, a Mr. Pratt, having thought the matter over, determined, after consultation, to take out policies for insurance in the sum of $45,000. Coal-dealers very seldom insure their stock; but Mr. Pratt argued that if Holbrook's yard caught fire from spontaneous combustion, Pratt's yard was liable to the same calamity; hence the insurance. Then came the great fire, and Mr. Pratt's was one of the first coal-yards consumed. He now finds himself the holder of policies in Eastern and foreign companies, and will undoubtedly receive fully $30,000 in payment of his losses. Very singularly, he was the only dealer in the city who was insured.

Per contra, there were numerous narrow escapes from good luck, if the expression be allowable. There was, for instance, the heaviest firm in the diamond and jewelry line. They had always insured in Eastern companies, especially the Ætna, to the exclusion of Western. Quite lately, however, the head of the firm had been persuaded to relinquish his staunch adherence to Eastern insurance, and patronize home institutions. Then the fire came on, and his insurance was burned up with his other effects. The safes in which the silver and jewels were placed, proved to be no more protection than as if they had been pasteboard. The elaborately carved ornaments of gold were reduced to poor little nuggets, and the many trays full of costly diamonds were found to have their "life burnt out of them," as the jewelers say; that is, their brilliancy was gone, and they were as worthless as glass. The diamond is pure carbon, and quite susceptible to heat, though impervious to most other destructive influences.

A paragraph was given, in the preceding chapter, to the illustration of the terrible heat which prevailed every-where within the range of the fire. One fact, which perhaps shows more forcibly than any other what a fiery furnace was the whole atmosphere, is this: that the contents of some safes which were taken into the open street were badly singed. It is also remarkable, that the massive stone work of the Lasalle Street tunnel, standing in the middle of a broad street, was much chipped and charred by the heat clear into the arched passage; while the iron railing around the unenclosed portion of that thoroughfare was so twisted and torn as to show that it must have been at a white heat during the worst of the fire. All this heat must have been derived by radiation from the buildings thirty feet away.

Mr. Fred. Law Olmsted, a well-known architect of New York, writing on this subject, remarks: "Besides the extent of the ruins, what is most remarkable is the completeness with which the fire did its work, as shown by the prostration of the ruins and the extraordinary absence of smoke stains, brands, and all debris, except stone, brick, and iron, bleached to an ashy pallor. The distinguishing smell of the ruins is that of charred earth. In not more than a dozen cases have the four walls of any of the great blocks, or of any buildings, been left standing together. It is the exception to find even a single corner or chimney holding together to a height of more than twenty feet. It has been possible, from the top of an omnibus, to see men standing on the ground *three miles away*, across what was the densest, loftiest, and most substantial part of the city. Generally, the walls seem to have crumbled in from top to bottom, nothing remaining but a broad low heap of rubbish in the cellar—so low as to be overlooked from the pavement. Granite, all sandstones, and all limestones, whenever fully exposed to the south-west, are generally flaked and scaled, and blocks, sometimes two and three feet thick, are cracked through and through."

The fatal effects of the conflagration on human life, and its influence in inducing disease, have already been referred to. It is also noticeable that many permanent cures were effected by the excitement attendant upon the fire—aided perhaps, in some cases, by the greater necessity for *work* after the fire. A friend of the writer of this chapter bears personal testimony to this. He was suffering from a painful local inflammation, which had refused for several weeks to yield to medical treatment. The fire came on, and the disease was among the things missing when the debris was cleared away. Having seen similar instances in the army, when even such diseases as incipient fever have been cured by a battle, we were not surprised at this. The physicians report numerous cases of chronic debility, whether local or general, cured by the extraordinary stimulus of the occasion. As a bad effect of the same stimulus, many went crazy over the event. Of this, two notable instances are those of an architect and engineer, and of a safe-dealer, named Harris. The latter rushed to the telegraph office, ordered an appalling number of safes from the manufactory, and hired the ruins of an immense church to exhibit them in, before his lunacy was discovered.

The divorce business, for which Chicago has become somewhat famed, was revived the moment the Equity Courts resumed their sessions; but the credit for this promptitude is due rather to the enterprise of the divorce shysters than to the activity of married pairs in promoting this branch of industry, for, although the lawyers were promptly out with their advertisements, announcing "divorces legally obtained without publicity," and "no fee unless decree is obtained," the people did not seem to respond with any enthusiasm, and it it is worthy of note that even after five or six weeks had elapsed, the applications for divorces did not reach more than one-fifth the number before the fire. Perhaps this paragraph properly belongs in the chapter of benefits derived from the disaster.

CHAPTER XX.

WHY SHE WAS DESTROYED.

Origin of the fire—Why it spread so fast and far—Was there incendiarism?—The Communist story—Chicago architecture—Chicago administration—Operations of the Fire Department.

IN the first chapter of this history of the Conflagration, we attributed the origin of the fire to the upsetting of a lamp in a cow-barn. No investigation made since that chapter was written has disproved the theory therein set forth; nor has any revelation of any achievements or exploits of the Fire Department on the night of the great fire demonstrated the propriety of altering any thing which we have written or implied concerning that force. On the contrary, a statement of the Marshal of the Fire Department, taken with a view to setting him and his aids right in this history, has but confirmed the opinion that the efforts of the department on the night in question were tardy in being got on foot, and of the most weak and desultory character thereafter.

It is a sufficient commentary upon the energy and force of the Police and Fire Commission of Chicago to mention that at the date of furnishing this chapter to the press—some five weeks after the Conflagration—no investigation has been made, or ordered, into the conduct of the Fire and Police Departments on that occasion; no recommendations submitted; nobody removed for cowardice or incompetency; nobody promoted for bravery or efficiency.

The causes which contributed to the rapid spread and fearful extent of the Chicago Conflagration have already been hinted at in various places in this volume. They may be summarized thus:

1. The city was carelessly, and, with the exception of a single square mile, very badly built.

2. The weather at the time was remarkably dry.

3. The wind blew a steady gale, in the most fatal direction, during the whole prevalence of the fire.

4. The Fire Department, though well equipped, is not well officered.

5. The Fire Department was particularly demoralized on the night of the fire.

These are, it will be seen, reasons enough to insure the destruction of the city; and one had but to know them, and to supply the initiatory outbreak of flame in the De Koven-street quarter, to predict the precise programme of the occasion. There was no need to kindle an incendiary fire, for scarcely a day elapsed without, at the least, three or four outbreaks, and some of them were almost certain to happen in the fatal spot. The only points lacking to enable one to predict the fire beforehand as well as we have all been doing it since, were those hinging on the question, how great a degree of heat could be produced by so many burning buildings, with such a monstrous blow-pipe to furnish the oxygen and such a mighty bellows to waft the brands onward? The data for answering these questions had never been furnished by any previous conflagration. They will be lacking no longer.

As to (1), the architecture of Chicago, it may be remarked,

that while it had been of late years noted for its airy elegance and its appearance of massiveness, it had been open to serious objection, which the city press had not neglected to make public, on account of the profuse use of flimsy ornamentation about the cornices and windows, and the inflammable character of much of the roofing. It is also a fact that many of the most showy and massive-looking front walls were nothing but thin brick ones, veneered with the Chicago marble. This marble (a limestone which barely misses being marble) is, like other limestones, more pervious to heat than brick, sandstone, or granite. But when the storm of fire had blown over, and the completeness of the ruin was ascertained, even including all the buildings which had dispensed with show for the sake of strength and the fire-proof quality, it was difficult to say that *any* kind of buildings would have stayed the flames after they had gained such terrible impetus in traversing the mile lying between the historical cow-stable and the well-built portion of the city.

At all events, the fault which tempted Chicago's fate, lies more with the Chicago public than with Chicago architects. The temptation in Chicago to build of lumber was very great; and such was the hurry of every body to get under cover and commence producing revenue; and such the desire of every citizen to see the city grow, and productive enterprise to build up, that these tinder-boxes were allowed to be placed wherever it happened—even in the most dangerous places. As the writer of this had the opportunity of saying in one of the daily journals, a few days after the fire: "We have been too good-natured toward those who have, to save a few hundred dollars of their expenses, persistently kept in jeopardy the safety of the whole community, by maintaining in the heart of the city great numbers of the most inflammable structures. It was the thousand or so of dry pine shanties and rookeries between the lake and the river, and south of Monroe Street, which did the business for Chicago on that terrible night. With these huddled around them, and emitting vast clouds of burning brands, which the hurricane forced into every cranny and through every window, the fine stone rows of the avenues and of the principal streets could no more resist the raging element than the chaff can resist the whirlwind. There may have been, and doubtless were, occasional weaknesses in the construction of the later-built stores and public edifices—a too fragile cornice, or windows too much exposed—but the fact that buildings for which every thing possible to architecture had been done to make them fire-proof went with the rest, tells plainly that the only fault —the grand fault to which the general destructiveness is traceable—was in allowing the fire so much material on which to feed until it became too great for human power to resist. We had spent hundreds of thousands of dollars in spasmodic efforts to exorcise the fire fiend from our limits, and yet we were all the while furnishing him with the material and the space with which to organize for his deadly work. We had been industriously feeding him on the only rations whereon he could thrive." So far as the question of building is concerned, it may be added that the fire at De Koven Street needed only to have been started a mile further to the south and west, among the rookeries which there abound, to have swept away nearly all the West Division, as well as the North and South.

The wind and the drought were the dispensations of Providence, and were sent in accordance with the All-wise plan and the good and beneficient laws of nature. It rested with the people to fortify themselves against any such disastrous consequences of these laws—not as defying God, but as using diligently the intelligence which He has given them to protect themselves against such disaster. If Chicago had been destroyed by an earthquake or a volcano, or any other convulsion of the elements which could not be foreseen or provided against, it might then have been called a special judgment of Heaven, whether of obvious or occult purport; but, coming as it did, in a way which made the only wonder why it had not come before, it can not be construed otherwise than as a timely reminder of the power of God, working through the elements, and as a hint to fear Him, love our fellow-men, subdue our pride, and make our walls of brick, eschewing wooden roofs. A fire-proof building is perhaps as proper a monument to the superiority of the Divine power as any we can raise.

As to (4) and (5) the Fire Department: The principal officers of this body are appointed to their places through political influence, which is perhaps saying enough to indicate the degree and direction of their talents. They are the creatures of one of those independent boards for which Chicago is distinguished, and it would not be practicable for any Mayor or Council, however faithful, to ferret out and dismiss from the roster any officer not actually guilty of a misdemeanor. It was said, after the fire, that the Chief Marshal of the department was under the influence of liquor on the night of the fire; but careful inquiry has convinced us that this charge is untrue. It is a fact that many were the worse for their potations at the time the alarm sounded; it being the habit with many to celebrate all great fires, like that of the previous evening, by a good thorough drunk. As a consequence of this and the fatigue from the night's work (which should have been slept off during Sunday), the men were not in condition to do good service on Sunday night—brave and willing though they were on most occasions.

After the steamers arrived on the ground and got, at length, a stream or two on the fire, there was nothing done but to "fire and fall back" as the flames advanced. The Marshal, Williams, was in front of the enemy with a part of his force, while his first assistant, Shanks, was in the rear. The latter was, of course, powerless to do any good in that position. Neither of these men saw or communicated with the other during the whole progress of the fire. The Marshal and his force kept falling back, losing a section of hose here and an engine there. It was a running fight, like the retreat of Pope from the Rappahannock. Nothing was done toward heading off a conflagration on the east side of the river, until the buildings near the Armory (Adams Street) were actually seen to be in flames. Then the Marshal pulled up and hastened, by a roundabout route, across the river, where the same story was repeated, viz: Lead on a stream here, to be driven out presently by the heat, then try it yonder for a few minutes, give it up, then dash off and play away, as if at random, upon some building further on. It was somewhere near the Sherman House that the contest was given up, except that efforts were made, during the day, to check the flames as they ate their way back toward the wind, in the vicinity of the broad avenues, at Congress Street. A house was blown up here, but no one will say, from looking at the situation, the place, and the time, that much was gained by the operation.

The Water-works went before four in the morning of Monday. It was a sin of some one's that a wooden roof covered that precious ark of the city's safety; yet it is doubtful whether, at or after the hour named, much could have been done toward checking the progress of the flames, or preserving any particular buildings, which was omitted by reason of a lack of water at the hydrants. The district burned subsequent to that hour was near enough to the river or to the lake to have been saved by water from these sources, if engines could have been brought to bear, or if any thing could have saved what lay in the track of the then irresistible, insatiate flames. But, at least, the panic and privation which ensued among the people of the city would have been spared, but for the loss of the Water-works.

Various theories were set up, chiefly by persons anxious to produce a sensation or to fill up a column, concerning the reason for the unprecedentedly wide spread of the devastation. One of these was invented by a morning paper in Chicago, which purported to be the confession of a member of the International Society—a Communist of Paris, and one of a gang deputed to burn Chicago. The motive for such a deed did not appear to be sufficient, nor was the story free from marks which betrayed its origin in the brain of a professional newspaper writer. Another theory, equally ridiculous, was that the stone used in Chicago buildings was impregnated with petroleum. This theory was founded upon certain Munchausenish stories of New York reporters, and upon a statement by Prof. Silliman, that a certain stone near Chicago, used to some extent in building, contains large quantities of petroleum. But it so happens that the only edifice built of the "oil-burning" stone (the Second Presbyterian Church) is the best-preserved ruin anywhere in the vicinity, while Potter Palmer's immense store, of Vermont marble and iron, which stood near by, had scarcely one stone upon another on the second day after the fire.

That there may have been cases of incendiarism which helped on the conflagration is not improbable. If so, they were the result of the excitement and demoralization produced by the terrible event, rather than of any preconcerted plan. It is not impossible that the building near the Water-works, from which the roof of the engine-house caught, was set on fire by an incendiary, or by accident, independent of the general conflagration. Some circumstances would seem to indicate this; yet the people who went through the fire and witnessed its awful phenomena believe, almost without exception, that this fire also was not by a brand from the main conflagration.

Some of the grounds for anticipating disastrous conflagrations, and for providing against them by all available means, may be found from the following table of fires occurring in Chicago during the eight years preceding 1871:

Year.	Fires.	Losses.	Insurance.
1863, ...	186	$355,660	$272,500
1864, ...	193	651,798	485,300
1865, ...	243	1,216,466	941,692
1866, ...	315	2,487,973	1,646,445
1867, ...	515	4,215,332	3,427,288
1868, ...	468	3,138,617	1,956,851
1869, ...	490	1,241,151	841,392
1870, ...	700	2,305,595	2,052,971
Total, ...	3,110	$15,612,592	$11,624,439

This enormous total of losses includes only those sustained by the insurance companies of New York and Hartford, leaving out of the reckoning the home companies, the Cincinnati, Cleveland, Buffalo, Albany, and Boston concerns, and the few foreign companies which have consented to take risks in Chicago. The city has the worst fire record of any large city in America.

CHAPTER XXI.

THE NEWSPAPERS AND THE FIRE.

What they said on Sunday morning, October 8—Prophecies suddenly fulfilled—"Old and tried" insurance companies tried too much—The episode in the Tribune office—A "red hot" newspaper—Cheery counsel in trouble—How the journals rose from their ashes—Curiosities of advertising.

IT is not amiss to devote a chaper to the record of the newspapers of Chicago, in connection with the Great Conflagration. They are such powerful, and altogether noteworthy establishments, and represent so truly the ambition, the energy, and the progressiveness for which the people of Chicago are distinguished, that they bear to the aggregate of the city's constituencies at least the proportions which a chapter of this book bears to the whole. Nowhere in the world does the growing power of the newspaper press, and the growing disposition to use that power independently for good ends, find better illustration than in Chicago; and when the fire came and tried the stuff of which all of us were made, the newspapers went through the crucible with the rest; and not only did they prove pure metal, but they evinced the qualities of the true philosopher's stone, transmuting into gold that which seemed to be but ashes; or what is more to the point, they acted like quicksilver in resolving out from the dross, with which it had become incrusted, the pure gold of many a faltering citizen's heart.

On the morning of the eighth of October—the day of Chicago's doom—the *Tribune* (by common consent the acknowledged chief of these salient journals) contained (as illustrating its own enterprise) three columns—equivalent to eighteen pages of this book—of description of a fire which had broken out after midnight on the night of the seventh. It contained also over one thousand advertisements, all devoted to Chicago business, or the "Wants" of Chicago people. It contained sixty long columns of matter in all—equal to four hundred pages of this book, or nearly two complete numbers of any of our first-class monthly magazines. Its real-estate article, on that morning, commenced with this epitome of the condition of affairs in Chicago:

"There has scarcely been a time for ten years past when there seemed to be so many schemes of one kind or another on foot, and which, if carried out, will affect the value of real estate in nearly all parts of the city and its suburbs. To use the expression of one who has been warily watching the growth of the various projects for new railroads and new suburban quarters, for both residences and manufactories—'Every body seems to be swelled up with big schemes.'"

Further on we read:

"The new manufacturing enterprises, of which not less than six or seven will have been started within the next nine months, thus furnishing employment for from fifteen hundred to two thousand more mechanics than are at work here now; these, together with the new railroad projects, and the rapid increase of population and business from other causes, have stimulated the speculative feeling until it has even infected some of the coolest and most conservative people who have always held aloof from speculation. It is in this that lies the only danger of the present situation, and it would be well to remember that when prospects look the most flattering, is the very time when it is necessary to exercise the greatest caution."

This was not prophetic, though it almost seems so now; it was merely the good advice which had been doled out in moderate doses to the fortune-chasing Chicagoans, at intervals for years, and in spite of which they had gone on and made fortunes. But this good advice vindicated itself at last.

In the same day's issue of the *Times* the real-estate article commenced thus:

"There never was a time when there was more going on in Chicago in the way of construction than now. New buildings are looming up in every direction above the surrounding structures, while probably not a day passes without the construction of new buildings, even though the season is so far advanced. The city's growth this year has been unparalleled."

The *Tribune*, in the article referred to, went on to describe the routes by which three of the five great new lines of railroad contemplating an entrance into the city were going to effect that entrance. Thus the newspapers of October 8th, the last day of the old Chicago, placed on record the fact that the people of the city were never so active, never so prosperous, never so ambitious, never so sanguine of the future as on the morning of that fatal day. These cheering announcements read now like a mockery of the cruel fate that followed so close upon their heels. Not so the hint thrown out in this paragraph from the introduction to the account of the Saturday night fire:

"For days past, alarm has followed alarm, but the comparatively trifling losses have familiarized us to the pealing of the Court-house bell, and we had forgotten that the absence of rain for three weeks had left every thing in so dry and inflammable a condition that a *spark might start a fire which would sweep from end to end of the city.*" Within twenty-four hours that prophecy was verified; the fire *was* kindled, and the conflagration *did* "sweep from end to end of the city." But it would seem as if corporations had not the gift of prophecy, for we find in the same issue of the *Tribune* a paragraph headed "The Great Fire," and remarking with regard to that fire and the Mutual Security Insurance Company, that "the agents will be ready to commence the work of adjusting early on Monday morning," that "happily for the stockholders of this sterling old company, their ample surplus far exceeds the loss, and leaves their handsome capital unimpaired," and that "the result is a lesson to property-owners to insure in none but old and tried companies." This "old and tried company" which had been so brave through the "Great Fire," and which had dispatched an agent, post-haste after midnight, to insert a flaming advertisement and an editorial puff in the morning papers, could not find assets enough, twenty-four hours afterward, to pay five cents on each dollar of its losses.

The journals of that morning announced for the week and for the winter an unprecedentedly rich season of stage amusements—opera, with the world's best prima donnas and the finest accessions ever known in America, the opening on the morrow of the finest temple of music and the drama to be found on this continent, and all manner of feasts for the senses of the luxurious and the taste of the refined. Chicago had become almost another Pompeii in luxury, if not in licentiousness; she has become almost another Pompeii in the suddenness of her fate!

The storm struck; the offices of the journals referred to were busy hives on that awful night, nothing like it had ever been known in the city. The city editor and his reporters rose to the emergency. Supernumerary reporters were called in and given their orders in quick, nervous tones. They sped away and reaped a harvest of horrors much more quickly than they could bind them for the garnering of the editor. That garnering never happened at the office of the *Times*, for the force was driven away by the flames before work upon the grand report had commenced. At the *Tribune* it was otherwise. That paper rejoiced in a building which was "absolutely fire-proof," and Medill, the city editor, was determined to have a seven-column description of the grand fire in the morning, whether there was any town left to read it or not. So he mapped out his *magnum opus* of the year. One after another the reporters came in, without the usual jocularity, took their places in the "local" room, in the top story of the *Tribune* Building, and commenced desperately at their task. One or two were set to watch, from the roof, the progress of the devastation. Others were writing out what they had already seen. Johnny English, the regular night reporter, whose chief glory was in a fire of the first magnitude, came in declaring that he had matter enough to keep him writing for a week. To work they all went and resolutely wrestled with their task—a greater one than mortal will ever yet achieve, adequately, to describe the sublime event. Walls were toppling around them, flames mounting above them, the ground shaking like an earthquake beneath them, the red foe glaring in at the windows and crackling, hissing, and roaring in their ears, but still they wrote on. The buildings at the north, across the street, were all mown down like grass—and still they wrote on. The "fire-proof" post-office went—and still they wrote on. The Reynolds' Block, opposite, was invested by the flames, the large plate-glass panes of the *Tribune* windows began to snap under the intense heat—and still they wrote on. The limit was reached at last—of time, not of matter—and the brave compositors had placed the record in type by the light of the incandescent atmosphere; for the gas jets had already ceased to flow. In that lurid light, and in the two-fold heat of the fire without the building, and the fire within their own breasts, these artisans completed their work—emptied their last "take," and consigned the "turtles" to the pressmen far below. These fellows alone proved unequal to the emergency; and pleading a lack of water for steam to run their engines (which may have been true), they fled, leaving the forms upon the huge press, and the candles, suddenly obtained, glimmering uselessly about the tables.

Others had been busy attempting to save the files of the paper—a very valuable series, embracing some forty volumes; but they were obliged to drop these on the way out and run for their lives. The building did not succumb until nearly ten o'clock, after every thing in the vicinity had gone down before the united force of the fire and the tornado. It was a remarkably strong building, its walls being of Athens marble, and at least two feet thick. Its castings were of corrugated iron, arched, between heavy wrought iron "I" beams. These were imbedded in cement, over which laid the floors of ash and walnut. All partition walls were of brick, and all staircases of stone or iron, those leading to the second floor having been laid up from the ground, in the solidest manner, before ever the walls rose. But every Achilles has his vulnerable heel, and the *Tribune* Building proved weak in two places—at least not strong enough to keep out the waves of the lake of fire which had surged around it for seven hours. The basement caught first, from under the sidewalk; then the falling of McVicker's Theater let in the flames through a window on an alley, whose iron shutters the men had been unable to close. Then the fine stronghold in which, not only its proprietors, but all the people had proudly confided, fell, and they said "there's no use hoping any longer. Every thing must go."

This was a little after ten o'clock on Monday morning. At three o'cock, when the business part of the town was all gone, and every Chicago newspaper with it, and fifteen thousand buildings were burning simultaneously throughout eight wards of the city, and the terror-stricken population were all shrinking along the margin of the lake or the suburban prairies, the *Evening Journal*, true to the spirit of Chicago journalism, came out with a small extra, containing a clear and comprehensive account of the conflagration. Some printers of the *Evening Post* establishment rallied at a small job printing shop, on the west side of the river, and got out a *Post* for the emergency. The *Tribune* Building had not ceased to blaze, or rather to melt, for there was not much about it to make a blaze of, before Joseph Medill, one of its chief stockholders (since elected mayor of the city), had sought out a job-office on Canal Street —a locality where nobody had dreamed there was any thing of the sort—and bought it out, type, presses, and lease of three spacious floors; so that on the morrow the force of the *Tribune* was at work producing a broadside sheet for Wednesday morning. That issue sounded out like a tocsin which called every man in Chicago to his duty. It gave a twelve column account of the great calamity. It was headed "Chicago destroyed;" but this was merely a rhetorical flourish of the younger Medill, for the editorial columns abounded in ringing, cheering utterances. We can not forbear quoting the principal of these:

"CHEER UP."

"In the midst of a calamity without parallel in the world's history, looking upon the ashes of thirty years' accumulations, the people of this once beautiful city have resolved that CHICAGO SHALL RISE AGAIN!

"With woe on every hand, with death in many strange places, with two or three hundred millions of our hard-earned property swept away in a few hours, the hearts of our men and women are still brave, and they look into the future with undaunted hearts. As there has never been such a calamity, so has there never been such cheerful fortitude in the face of desolation and ruin.

"Thanks to the blessed charity of the good people of the United States, we shall not suffer from hunger or nakedness in this trying time. Hundreds of train-loads of provisions are coming forward to us with all speed from every quarter, from Maine to Omaha. Some have already arrived—more will reach us before these words are printed. Three-fourths of our inhabited area is still saved. The water supply will be speedily renewed. Steam fire engines from a dozen neighboring cities have already arrived, and more are on their way. It seems impossible that any further progress should be made by the flames, or that any new fire should break out that would not be instantly extinguished.

"Already contracts have been made for rebuilding some of the burned blocks, and the clearing away of the debris will commence to-day, if the heat is so far subdued that the charred material can be handled. Field, Leiter & Co. and John V. Farwell & Co. will recommence business to-day. The money and securities in all the banks are safe. The railroads are working with all their energies to bring us out of our affliction. The three hundred millions of capital invested in these roads is bound to see us through. They have been built with special reference to a great commercial mart of this place, and they can not fail to sustain us. CHICAGO MUST RISE AGAIN.

"We do not belittle the calamity that has befallen us. The world has probably never seen the like of it—certainly not since Moscow burned. But the forces of nature, no less than the forces of reason require that the exchanges of a great region should be conducted here. Ten, twenty years may be required to reconstruct our fair city, but the capital to rebuild it fire-proof will be forthcoming. The losses we have suffered must be borne; but the place, the time, and the men are here, to commence at the bottom and work up again; not at the bottom neither, for we have credit in every land, and the experience of one upbuilding of Chicago to help us. Let us all cheer up, save what is yet left, and we shall come out right. The Christian world is coming to our relief. The worst is already over. In a few days more all the dangers will be past, and we can resume the battle of life with Christian faith and western grit. Let us all cheer up!"

This bugle-call had an electrical effect upon the spirits of the people. Perhaps it only echoed the sentiment which they were already uttering to each other, as the "soul of a young man speaks to another," in Longfellow's Psalm of Life; and the refrain of it was the same as that which the poet has made a household word:

"Let us then be up and doing,
With a heart for any fate;
Still achieving, still pursuing,
Learn to labor and to wait."

But Chicago would not consent to wait any such period as their *Tribune* had set for them; and to-day one can hear no longer period than five years appointed among Chicagoans for the complete rebuilding of their city.

The *Journal* and *Post*, at the same time, joined in the strain with manful utterances. The latter said, on Wednesday: "There is now only one way to look—ahead. Chicago has a future as certainly as it has a past. Upon all the blackened walls and tottering towers, upon clinging cornice and ruined pavement, is written broadly the cheery word RESURGAM. There is manliness enough left here to reconstruct the city even in this terrible calamity and this deep desolation. There is waste, but there is not despair. The brave hearts of our citizens, even more than the sympathy of other cities, stands to us as a pledge of victory. The land is left, the grand position is left, and the men are left who reared the recent magnificent city from the prairie mud. They can do it again, and they will do it again. The consequences of the most disastrous fire the world has ever suffered, will be conquered and forgotten by the most intrepid spirit of determination the world has ever reared." At the same time the *Post* had coolness enough to interpose a timely word in deprecation of panics, and warning against acts of violence, in the name of the law, such as were liable to result from the excited condition of the public mind at that time.

There were but three or four presses large enough to print a newspaper of respectable size in the city; and these were single cylinders, and not in first-rate condition, so that the working of the editions was very slow. The *Tribune* had been accustomed to two eight-cylinder Hoes, either working 10,000 sheets per hour, and the other papers had had a four-cylinder each; so that but a small portion, even of the city editions of either newspaper could be printed. None were mailed, or even sent to city subscribers by carriers, for several days. The price of a newspaper for the first few days was twenty-five cents, invariably, except the *Tribune,* which on the first day sold readily for half a dollar, and even a dollar. To obtain them for sale upon the street, the boys (and such men as desired) had to "fall in," form a queue and wait, perhaps an hour or two for a chance to buy. The price at the counting-room was never raised above the regular five cents, nor was the price of advertising raised. Displayed advertisements were refused by the *Tribune,* as more was received than could have been printed in the paper, leaving out all other matter. There was never such a rush of advertising in Chicago as during the few weeks following the fire. The lists of missing persons were advertised constantly without charge, and on some days filled two columns of space. The *Republican* resumed publication on the 12th, and the *Evening Mail* on the same day. The German papers were slower; while the *Times,* after announcing an intention to suspend for a month rather than issue an inferior sheet, resumed on the 18th in good style.

On the 15th, the *Tribune* said:

"When, on last Wednesday, we called upon the people of Chicago to cheer up, we did not appreciate or estimate the force of character that was in them. Our citizens have displayed a noble heroism, worthy of the abounding charity that has been showered upon them. They have shown capacity to help themselves, and that alone is worth every thing in the way of re-establishing their credit and procuring the necessary capital to build up again. Let them go on as they have begun, not calling on Congress or the gods for donations, or stay laws, and they will come out of the fire right side up, and presently we shall have our Chicago again, nobler and more beautiful than before. . . . With tears for the dead and dying, with sorrow and tender care for the maimed and sick, with faith in God, and stout hearts in our breasts, we now begin to clear away the ruins."

The newspapers were, indeed, during the terrible week following the conflagration, among the most necessary articles, ranking along with food, water, and fire-engines. Besides furnishing the facts about the calamity which still hung like a spent thunder-cloud in the horizon, and disproving many harassing falsehoods which were circulating about, and which thronged like vermin in all the out-of-Chicago papers, they served the very necessary purpose of enabling thousands of persons to announce their whereabouts, and advertise for those who were missing; also for announcing the new location of men of business—a class of announcements which soon became very numerous. The *Tribune* of the 22d of October—the thirteenth day after the fire—contained 1536 advertisements, chiefly of business and professional men announcing their change of location. The manner of this announcement was as cool as could be. It was usually to the effect that "Messrs. A. & B. have removed their store to No. — C. Street." No reference to any fire or other indication that the removal was not entirely a commonplace affair.

The advertisements of those days will be found valuable mementoes of the time whenever in future days the few existing files of Chicago papers for October, 1871, shall be overhauled. Some of them indicated the new lines of business which had been created by the fire. Thus several scientific men announced their readiness to restore charred papers to legibility; printers and stationers announced blank "proofs of loss" as their main stock in trade; and all the lawyers in town were found to have been transformed into "Adjusters." The sign-painting interest also looked up wonderfully. The "Personal" advertisements of doubtful morality, asking "the beautiful blonde with the blue parasol who noticed gentleman in McVicker's Theater" to "communicate," etc., etc., had all disappeared—given place to appeals of this sort:

If the gray-whiskered man who was seen removing trunks marked M. E. W. & T. C. Welsh, from the open space opposite Lincoln Park, at junction of North Wells and Clark Streets, will deliver them at 91 South Peoria Street, he will be liberally rewarded, and no questions asked.

PERSONAL—The party that took contents of large trunk, carried away small canvas covered trunk, and oil painting, left in carriage on lake-shore, foot of Erie Street, last Monday, will be paid more for return of same to subscriber, and no questions asked, than they will sell for. Address J. D. HARVEY, 36 South Canal Street.

PERSONAL—If A. W. Morgan can furnish information regarding Rillie Snow's trunks, or if he has them, and will forward to Rillie Snow, Council Bluffs, Iowa, he will be liberally rewarded.

Some advertisers showed their disposition to smile through it all. One firm, dealing in stoves, announced that "the warm climate at the old stand, 168 Lake Street, being rather unfavorable to the stove business," the business would henceforward be carried on at such a place. A firm of jolly sign-painters announced their removal in this choice poetic fashion:

SINCE the great k-
  Lamity to our pat-
Rons we would say
  That we are not quite flat

Broke, but conclu-
  Ded to move our ENTIRE
STOCK into our new
  Shop (away from the fire).

111 Desplaines, corner Monroe,
SIGNS painted at prices
Remarkably LOW,
For MORE information see
MOOERS & GOE.

A list of the newspapers published in Chicago on the 7th of October, 1871, was given in an earlier chapter of this book. On the forenoon of the 9th, but one of them, and that an inferior weekly, could boast an office of publication, or an ounce of type.

CHAPTER XXII.

A WEEK WITHOUT WATER.

A day of chaos—The exodus from the city—No water—Nights of terror—Fear of incendiarism—The citizen patrol—Stories of summary vengeance—Military law—Halt!—The relic business—Restoration of water and confidence.

TUESDAY, the 10th of October, may be called a day of transition from chaos to order; though it looked upon the surface like chaos merely. The Mayor and city government were busy providing for the re-establishment of quiet and confidence, and the Board of Trade and other authorities in business were organizing for the resurrection of Chicago; but little of this was apparent to the general observer. The visitor to Chicago (that is the unburnt part of it), Tuesday morning, saw, perhaps, first of all, an occasional puff of smoke, curling upward from chimney-tops of houses, and yet not many; for the Mayor's order of the previous night had prohibited all kitchen fires, and only the very reckless or the very hungry made bold to construe the shower of the previous night as a contravention of the order. He saw an occasional face show itself on the street, haggard and red-eyed, from the effects of the previous twenty-four hours' experience. He saw water-carts moving through the streets and being surrounded, every time they halted, by men in dressing-gowns and women in their meanest wear, bearing buckets and pitchers, to buy, at a shilling a pailful, the fluid which had suddenly become so precious. He saw wagons drive up to church doors, carrying sick or wounded or burnt victims of the flames, now first furnished with a shelter. He saw fire engines, probably from abroad, getting into position to play upon the blazing coal heaps along the river; their occasional sharp whistle was almost the only sound to break the solemn stillness of the morning. By and by, however, the people began to stir, and then suddenly all became a Babel of confusion. Wagons of every description, and in numbers which no one thought the city could boast, were plying hither and thither with reckless speed. The whole male population, apparently, was soon on the street—some hastening to the places of general congregating, as if to escape from the state of apprehension in which the night had been passed—some seeking for tidings of friends whom they knew to have been burned out—some on the hunt for a new place of business—some bound for the burnt district on a tour of curiosity, if for no other motive.

The streets through the burnt district were found—some of them—to be passable for carriages, though there were such accumulations of fallen bricks and stones, fragments of tin roofs, telegraph wires, and rails of street railways, warped so as to stand like huge pot-bails all along the street, that this method of locomotion was by no means easy. Only one bridge between the east and west sides of the river was passable without going far south—that at Randolph Street. Across the North Branch there was also but one—that at Kinzie Street; while there was for several days no communication at all across the main river, the bridges being all destroyed and the Lasalle Street tunnel obstructed. The streets having been, in grading, raised from five to twelve feet above the original level of the town, stood up like causeways, and conveyed to the senses a gloomy impression, like the skinny bones of a wasted invalid, whom we had known only as a rotund person. Over these cadaverous causeways the population poured, stopping occasionally to gaze at the ruins of known buildings, or to accost each other with the new salutatiou, "How did you come out of it?" instead of "How do you do?"

The appearance of the most conspicuous ruins on this and the few following days is correctly portrayed by the cuts which are contained in this work; but the sight which confronted the people of Chicago the most painfully on that day can not be reproduced by the artist. It was the *completeness* of the wreck; the total desolation which met the eye on every hand; the utter blankness of what had a few hours before been so full of life, of associations, of aspirations, of all things which kept the mind of a Chicagoan so constantly crowded, and his nerves and muscles so constantly driven. Even the distances seemed to have been burned up with all things else, and any of the few landmarks left would suddenly come up and confront one, like an apparition, when he thought it far away. These landmarks were so few, however, that, even in the most frequented quarters of the city, which one had never missed sight of for a day, one found himself frequently puzzled, and inquiring, "Where are we now? What building was this?"

The nearest street, outside of the burnt district, at all adapted to the purposes of commerce, was Canal Street, running along the west side of the river. At right angles with this were Randolph and Madison Streets, constituting the main thoroughfare to the western city limits; and these streets, as well as State Street, and Wabash Avenue, upon the south side, were thronged, during Tuesday and Wednesday, with people in search of stores and offices. These jostled each other desperately upon the rough sidewalks of this quarter, as did the carts and wagons flying over the pavements, with trunks and household goods from the lake-shore and prairies. This rush has kept up ever since; but the character of the traffic has been changed—the wagons being now laden with merchandise and building materials, and the grimy, smoky, excited crowd of citizens having given away, in part, to a current of sight-seers from abroad.

These began to arrive in large numbers on the very day following the fire; so that the trains which came into town were greatly overloaded; but those which went out were much more so. An exodus set in on the 9th, and was followed up so well that by the 16th some 60,000 people had left the city; but of these nearly a half came back within the next two or three weeks.

The destruction of the day gave way, as night approached, to a dread of further fires, founded upon stories of incendiarism, which were rife. Every hour brought new accounts of attempted arson and of summary justice upon the perpetrator of the heinous act. The police reported numerous cases of men, women, and children hung to lamp-posts, beaten to death or shot down for acts of incendiarism. These were all religiously believed, even by those not constitutionally credulous. The general belief was that not only was the town beset by incendiaries who burned to plunder, but that a mania for arson had overtaken the more desperate and ignorant classes of the community. The consequence was a fearful state of panic on Tuesday and the following nights. Fifteen hundred special policemen were sworn in on the west side and five hundred on the east side, and, armed with pistols, muskets, and such other weapons as they could produce, patroled every square in the city, challenging every person seen after nine o'clock in the evening. There were but few out, however, since there was no longer any business, any shows, or any carousing—all saloons being closed at eight o'clock by the Mayor's order. It will be readily imagined that few citizens slept soundly through these nights of panic and alarm. With a remnant of the city far more inflammable than the part which burned, with incendiaries prowling about to kindle fires, with plenty of wind prevailing to spread them, with no water to check them, and with the bright glare of the burning coal piles to deceive the watcher ever and anon into the belief that the dreaded conflagration had actually set in, it is no wonder that the people of the West Division were kept in a miserable state for the few days and nights succeeding the fire, before the military came to their relief, and some water from the river was got into the mains, and the stories of incendiarism were, for the most part, exploded.

On the 10th, it was found that the bakers and provision dealers were, as might have been expected, putting up the price of food. The supply of provisions, it was supposed, had been seriously affected by the conflagration; the wholesale meat markets, located on Kinzie Street, were all destroyed; but the sharks found Chicago a bad town in which to get up a "corner" on provisions, for the supply was not interfered with for a day; and even had not the Mayor come out with a stringent proclamation against extortion,* it is not likely that any rise in prices of eatables could have been maintained. Not a single article of food, or fuel, or wear was, to our knowledge, enhanced in price on account of the fire. On the contrary, meats became

* See Appendix "B," I.

cheaper than ever on the week succeeding the conflagration, and so continued. Perhaps there is not another city in the world where such quantities of provisions could have been destroyed, with such a result.

Meantime, what were the constituted authorities of the city doing toward restoring order and confidence to the citizens? The Mayor (R. B. Mason) had convoked his staff on Monday forenoon, and issued a proclamation suited to the exigency, pledging the faith of the city for the expenses of relieving the suffering, warning all lawless persons against the consequences of their acts, and assuring the citizens that the fire had spent its force, and that "all would soon be well." The headquarters of the city government were fixed in the church on Washington Street, a mile west of the river. Other proclamations followed in quick succession; one, which appeared on the 10th, giving orders relative to police organization, and investing "the military" with full police power. Unfortunately, however, "the military" of Chicago was a very limited army—the only force capable of mustering and arming was two companies of Norwegian militia, who were put on duty on Tuesday.

Militia companies from other Illinois cities began to come in on Tuesday also—six companies in all, from Bloomington, Springfield, Champaign, and other towns, having arrived by Wednesday, under the charge of Adjutant General Dilger, who was sent by Governor Palmer for the purpose. Up to this time the panic had been increasing. But little confidence was felt in the police force, although that body numbered near 400 regulars, and any number of "specials." The people were in such a state that they welcomed the sight of muskets and the signs of martial law as heartily as the citizens of this free country are generally supposed to abominate such demonstrations of force. Especially did they hail with acclamation the announcement—made in a proclamation on the 11th—that the preservation of good order in the city was entrusted to Lieutenant-general Sheridan.*

This gallant officer immediately, by virtue of his authority, as commander of the Military Division of the Missouri, ordered hither six companies of regular U. S. troops—two from Omaha, three from Fort Leavenworth, and one from Fort Scott. He was also furnished by General Halleck with four companies from Kentucky; so that he had soon a full regiment of troops at his command, exclusive of the State militia. The regulars were stationed through the Burnt District of the South Division, which being destitute of street lamps and strewn with valuable safes—two or three score to every block—was extremely liable to the depredations of thieves. It was currently reported that a thousand of these had left New York on the evening of the 9th for Chicago. Doubtless there were many such who started hither, but the preparations, and the announcement that Sheridan was at the helm, doubtless demoralized their calculations, for few of them were heard from through their works. The militia troops were set to patrolling the unburnt division of the city, in which duty they were superseded, before Saturday night, by a battalion raised under Colonel Frank T. Sherman, ex-postmaster, and sworn in for twenty days' service.

For several days Chicago might be said to bristle with bayonets. Military rule seemed to be the form of government best adapted to the emergency in which the community found itself and was unanimously approved by the hearts of the citizens, whatever constitutional lawyers and jealous police commis-

* See Appendix "B," I.

sioners may have thought of it. Under the shadow of the American Eagle's protecting wing, the people went and came with equanimity about their business, and at night they lay down and slept soundly, lulled by the tread of the vigilant sentry. The abnormal susceptibility to excitement about fire continued, however, and whenever there was an alarm sounded, you might see a sudden rush of the whole population in that vicinity, and a very sudden stamping out of the incipient conflagration. Millionaires (those who *had been* such) would rush out to two-penny fires and come back, much blown, with full particulars. The Fire Department seemed to have been mustered out of service, and the old-fashioned era of axes and water-buckets to have returned. A gentleman's barn took fire on Wabash Avenue, and before an engine could arrive, the citizens had formed a line from the lake to the barn, and extinguished the fire by passing buckets of water.

Meantime, however, the engines of the Water-works were still disabled, though a hundred men were working on them constantly, night and day. A way had been found, however, to fill many of the mains by pumping water from the river into them. Locomotives—all sorts of engines—were rigged to pump, and set to work with all their might; and with such success that, in a week after the fire, about a third of the people of the inhabited portions of the city had water—such as it was—in their basements. By this time, however, it was found out that the stories about the catching and hanging of incendiaries were all false, and the popular mind was quite easy about fires; especially as copious showers of rain had fallen on the sixteenth.

The privation resulting from a lack of water for drinking and culinary purposes was still seriously felt, however. The people were obliged to supply themselves from the artesian wells at the western extremity of the city, or from the lake; and the progress of the work at the Water-works was anxiously watched. The engineer, Mr. Cregier, could not give any positive assurance whether the engine at which he was working, with his three hundred machinists, would not prove to be so swollen or warped by the fire that its delicate pistons and cylinders would refuse to play. In that case it was not simply a week, but a *winter* without water! On the evening of the 17th, just eight days after the fall of the insane roof of shingles, the thousand pieces of the great engine were all put in place, and the crucial experiment made on which so much comfort or privation, health or sickness, soberness or intemperance, depended. The fires were lighted under the boilers, and a head of steam was put on in order to thoroughly test the engine before setting it to work. The engineer, and the whole corps of tireless men who had toiled to complete the work, stood around. It was an anxious moment, and the faces of those present betokened the intensity of the strain. The word was given, and at 8:27 o'clock the machine was set in motion, the giant wheel slowly revolved, and once more the iron heart throbbed on Chicago Avenue, forcing the precious fluid from the lake at each pulsation through the monster arteries away to the city limits. And then, once more, the city breathed freely; and not only breathed, but drank freely, not considering that the pipes had become foul from the deposits of the muddy stream from the river. The consequence was much sickness for about two weeks, especially among children.

On the 24th the city was visited by dense clouds of smoke, which rendered the atmosphere almost utterly opaque—as much so as the thickest fog of an autumn morning. It did not come from the coal heaps, several of which were burning, for the whole country for a radius of a hundred and fifty miles around Chicago was visited by the same phenomenon. The smoke was doubtless from the burning woods of Michigan, and was brought across the lake by a strong easter; but that it should visit so large an area at once, and only for a single day, while no similar effect came from the great Chicago fire, nor from the vast burnings then going on in Wisconsin, was somewhat remarkable.

The relic business came to be a notable feature of the situation about these days. This was carried on by boys, who gathered relics of the conflagration from the cellars of ruined stores—melted crockery and steel ware being the staples—and peddled them at ridiculously low prices to visitors and citizens. "Relics of the fire," their regular cry, became a sort of byword; so that people, advertising for board, in the newspapers, would jocularly describe themselves as "relics of the late fire." Fragments of the Court-house bell were the relics most sought after, and are highly prized by those fortunate enough to secure them. The Italians, ever on the lookout for odd branches of trade, went into the relic business more elaborately than the *gamins*. Passing along Randolph Street, a week or more after the fire, the writer came upon one of these compatriots of Garibaldi, whose countenance, indeed, bore a striking resemblance to that reputed hero, except that it had taken on a hard Yankee look which almost disguised its nationality until the speech of the man betrayed it. He had pre-empted, miner fashion, a "claim" consisting of the basement of a crockery store, and had excavated a few dozen pieces of demoralized table-ware. Surrounded by these and by two large heaps of rubbish, and covered from head to foot with a thick sprinkling of ashes, he harangued his audience: "Step up, dzentlemen, buy relics of the fire. Here's beayoutefool china soocher bool (displaying a badly smoked and misshapen article); you haf him for only twanety-five cents. Here's beayoutefool set cups—eight of 'em all froze together—do for walking-stick;" and he found customers pretty readily. Himself undoubtedly a victim of the conflagration, he was a true specimen of the Chicago business man—ready to do business on no capital if none is at hand, and prompt to organize victory out of defeat; to "mount," as the poet says, "on stepping stones of our dead selves."

The period of military rule came to an end on the 23d of October. It was doubtless by a melancholy occurrence which served to elicit some serious animadversions on the policy of employing military usages to the extent which characterized this period. Thomas Grosvenor, Esq., prosecuting attorney for the city in the police-courts, was shot fatally, on the morning of the 21st, by a young man named Treat, belonging to Colonel Sherman's "home-guard," and acting as sentinel near the Douglas University, of which he is a student. Mr. Grosvenor, going home after midnight, was challenged by the sentinel, and refused to halt. Treat told him he should fire upon him if he did not obey. The reply was "Fire, and be d——d." The sentinel, true to his word, drew up and fired, shooting Grosvenor through the lungs. He was soon after arrested and held for the action of the grand jury. The popular voice generally sustained the boy, and blamed the victim for his rashness; but a gloom was spread over the community by the event, not only because the deceased was a popular man, but because the situation had really become such as not to require military aid any longer. Accordingly, on the 23d, Mayor Mason, after some sharp correspondence with the Board of Police Commissioners, who had been piqued from the first at the temporary diminution of their consequence, relieved General Sheridan of the duty which he had asked him to accept, twelve days before. And thus ended the period of dearth, of panic, and of military law.*

* Unless we are to make a note of a blustering correspondence inaugurated by Governor Palmer, who considered his prerogatives invaded by the "invasion" of his territory by United States troops, and proposed to indite General Sheridan for the murder of Grosvenor, this is a phase of the affair not by any means completed at the time of putting this work to press. Nor is it of interest, except as a matter of constitutional law, the fact being that the people of Chicago, whose welfare was mainly concerned, were well satisfied with the action of Mayor Mason in taking the responsibility at a time when the safety of the people (the "supreme law") seemed to demand such action. The main question which the courts, when called on, will have to decide is, apparently, the legal right of the mayor to put the keeping of the city's peace out of the hands of the police authorities, even with their consent, which he claims was obtained.

CHAPTER XXIII.

THE CHURCHES AFTER THE FIRE.

The next Sunday—Assembling under the ruined walls—Robert Collyer's adventures—Trying to save Unity—Lessons of hope and courage.

IT was a sad day, the Sabbath after the fire, when the stimulus of work was off, and quiet meditation was in order. The solemnity and suggestiveness of the day were, moreover, greatly heightened by the meetings which the worshipers of the ruined churches held under the walls of their beloved sanctuaries. Chicago had come to be noted for the beauty of her church architecture, and the large number of her stately churches, built as they were, for the most part, of rough ashlars of Illinois gray limestone. A score or more of the best churches destroyed in this Conflagration were nearly new, and had been built only after great effort. The congregations of the most of them gathered on Sunday morning, and were addressed in the open air by their pastors. As a specimen of these exercises, we will describe those at the church of the Rev. Robert Collyer, whose name is the best known of any Chicago clergyman's. Mr. Collyer had labored during five or six years very zealously to build up his congregation, and rake together funds enough to erect their splendid church, which, with its organ, cost $135,000. An account of how they tried to save it, Mr. Collyer has written out for us, along with some other of his adventures on the night of the fire, in the subjoined sketch:

"You want me to tell you how we lost Unity Church. I was roused from a heavy sleep, at half-past one on Monday morning, by my wife, who said the fire was increasing on the south side, a storm of fire flakes, sweeping over northward and eastward, and we must get the children up and dress them —it was not safe to delay another minute.

"I was broad awake in an instant, did just as I was bidden, and then, when we were all ready, we roused some of the neighbors, who dressed their children too, and the policeman on our beat told us he had roused up all the people in his district. We did not think then there was very much danger the north side would take fire, except from these flying embers, and they were drifting eastward, toward the lake, more than they were northward toward our street. So when the children begged me to go with them over the bridge to see the fire, I went. We crossed at Wells Street, because that was almost entirely free from the falling flakes; the Court-house was afire at that time, the dome standing almost white with the intense heat, and buildings were catching to the eastward rapidly. We wanted to cross back by Clark or State Streets, but by that time the shower of fire was so heavy on Water Street, eastward of Wells, that I durst not take the children down in that direction, so we went back as we had come, reaching Clark Street by Michigan. By that time the north side seemed to be thoroughly alarmed; there were lights in all the houses, swift moving figures could be seen in the rooms, and the people were getting their belongings into the streets. When we got home I sat down a little while, and then went to the corner of State Street and Chicago Avenue, to see how the fire seemed across the bridge. As I stood there the great unfinished spire on the Church of the Holy Name began to lurch eastward in the terrible tornado, and, as I watched it, went down with a great crash on the roof of the church northward. This must have been an hour before the fire swept up as far as that corner. John Wentworth came along just then with a boy and two bags, which he said were full of papers; I invited him to come in and sit down, as my house was near; but he said he should go on, because the whole city was going to be burnt up. I did not believe him, and walked home; but presently my little son ran in and said: 'Papa, the fire has crossed at State Street.' I ran down and found it was so. Then there was a light a little south of Lill's Brewery—the neighbors said it was a cooper's shop. My wife had already begun to pack. I took a load on my shoulders and started for the church. As I turned the corner a poor woman said 'Oh! Mr. Collyer, that is not what you meant, is it?' 'Yes,' I said, 'Chicago Avenue is going, but I think we can save the church; you had better all come there and bring your things.' By daylight the north side of the church was heaped up with the poor belongings of many German families, while they sheltered with their children inside. Our own people came also and piled many precious things in the lecture-room, and in my study. Indeed, we hindered nobody; all came in who would, and brought what they had. The fire then was sweeping up eastward, and a little more slowly westward. Ogden School caught from Chicago Avenue, then Chestnut Street from Ogden School, and then the New England Church. By this time we had begun to break down the fences, and hammer away at the sidewalks with our hands and feet, for we had no tools, except, I think, one hatchet and a shovel. A number of young men belonging to the church, and some others I did not know, worked with all their might. Mr. N. E. Sheldon, who lived near, came up and said: 'Mr. Collyer, I think we can save your church—the fire will catch in the basement first, where the coal and wood is; let us go down there.' So some staid outside to fight off the fire, and I went down with Mr. Sheldon, and three or four more, to take care of the inside. We pulled back the kindling-wood, got water out of the waste-pipe, wet the windows, and Mahlon D. Ogden generously let us have as much more water as we asked for out of his cistern, though he knew it was all he had to save his own home, for by that time the Water-works had gone. I was very jealous all the while lest the fiend should come on us some other way, and take us by surprise. There was deadly danger I knew, and a little host of men and boys were carrying my library out of the study and tumbling it into the park for fear of the worst. When we felt pretty sure that the fire was fought off from the lower windows and doors, I went with an armful of books myself, possibly several, I do not clearly remember; but I know that as I came back out of the park I saw a little puff of black smoke, intensely black, rising above the roof on the north side of the church, near the tower. It rose up presently into a great cloud; then I knew we were beaten, shouted to the men to come out of the cellar, told what women were left to get away with their children as fast as they could, for the church would presently be in a blaze, and either then, or a little sooner, I think, I went up stairs into my pulpit, where I had stood the night before and talked to my people about poor, burnt Paris, as I saw it in July, took one great, mighty look at it, as you look at a dear friend you know you will never see again, then I took the Bible, came down stairs, locked my study-door, put the key in my pocket, and came away. I have the key still, and when we get another Unity Church, I shall have a lock made for that key, and the lock put on to my study-door. Very truly, yours,

"ROBERT COLLYER.

"P. S.—As I read this over, I find I must make a stronger mark than I have made against Mr. Sheldon's name. He was not a member of my church, I only knew him by sight, but when he came among us it was like a captain with an unflinching heart coming into a regiment that has half a mind to give up the fight. We had fought a hard battle; he put fresh courage and pluck into us all, and worked like a hero to save our precious pile. If there was a special Providence over Mahlon Ogden's house to save it, I think its cool wings must have come down and about the place while his kinsman (Sheldon) was doing such a grand, unselfish work to save our church. R. C."

When the next Sunday came, Mr. Collyer, as well as the pastors of the New England Church and St. James's Episcopal Church, not far off, gathered his hearers under the walls of the sanctuary and addressed them. The preacher stood upon a carved stone which had fallen from the arch above, with his people gathered about him in a half circle. The scene is described by a spectator as calling to mind the meetings of the early saints in caves and subterranean tombs. Plain hymns were sung, and prayers put up, after which the pastor said:

"I wanted to get you to come together this morning, my friends, as many as could, who were left of our congregation, in order that I might say a word or two to you out from my own heart, and then we might go home and think it over, and realize something of our altered, and yet unalterable, relations. I could not before trust myself to speak to you in regard to the great thought nearest to the heart of each; I could not trust you to listen. The calamity was too near, and we all broke down in the effort; that is a subject that we must approach no more.

"Some men of a stronger heart are, perhaps, able to thank God for this great affliction. I, myself, have tried to find some altitude of soul, some height of moral sentiment, from which I might look down and thank God for overshadowing us with this great sorrow. To such an elevation I may climb at last, but I have not yet attained it. Perhaps I may say, with the psalmist, at length: 'It is well that I was afflicted; before I was afflicted I went astray, but now I keep Thy law.' I might, in such an event, find the elements of grace for this life and that which is to come, which could not have been found except in such a calamity.

"But I can not get up to it this morning. I see, as yet, too vividly your homes burning, and you all, my poor, dear friends, fleeing in mortal terror for your lives, and I wanting to help you, and myself powerless to act. Well, well! It is too near. [A pause, and audible sobs in the congregation.] We will thank God as soon as we can. These great walls of hinderance are about you now. One day, doubtless, we shall be big enough in soul, and good enough, to get into this atmosphere of praise and thanksgiving for this great sorrow."

He then told his hearers how well they could get along without the property which they had lost; how they had once been even poorer than they were now; and how Lot's wife had been turned into a pillar of salt (which he said meant a bitter woman) for turning back and mourning over a burning Sodom. Further on he said, with much feeling:

"The relations between us as pastor and people, dear friends, has been of the deepest and truest love ever known. I have always felt that it was so, and you have felt it too. Now we have received a shock in this relation such as we never expected, such as we never could have expected. For two or three days after it came I was stunned and did not know what to do. I could tell nothing about the future. I think I must have been personally injured by my long fight with the fire. It was a day or two before I began to look about and think with myself what I could say to these, my children. At last it came to me in one word—and this is what I have to say about it. If you will stay by me I will stay with you; if you will work with me, I will work with you, and we will make the best fight we can against this adverse situation. I am not going to be a burden to you. You can not find a cheaper man anywhere than I will be. I preached seven years for seventy-five cents a year. I won't take any more than that if you can't spare any more. I don't mean to task Unity Church, but I mean to stick by you if you will stick by me. Never fear for me, I can get along well enough. People will give me more for a lecture than they will give some folks, and if the worst comes to the worst, I can make as good horse-shoes and nails as any man in Chicago."

It did not become necessary, however, for Collyer to resume his hammer and anvil, for gifts poured in upon him and his church from all quarters. He himself received as many as a hundred and seventeen packages by express in a single day, and his church was at once made the care of many wealthy societies at the East, which furnished money enough to rebuild it. Mr. Collyer went East after a little; and while in Boston received many gifts, including an order from a wealthy Unitarian to draw on him quarterly for a salary of $5,000 a year, in addition to the $3,000 which his parish had already voted him.

CHAPTER XXIV.

SYMPATHY AND RELIEF.

How the world was shocked by the event—The excitement in America—Nothing like it since the war—Showers of money and avalanches of goods for the sufferers—Scenes and deeds in New York, Boston, Cincinnati, St. Louis, London, and other cities.

WE can not tell the story of the Relief of Chicago. We can not adequately describe the acts in which all Christendom leant over Chicago and poured the precious balm of sympathy into her wounds, and bathed with the wine of relief her parched and blistered lips. In the first place, to give a full account of the measures in aid of the sufferers by the Chicago fire, would be to write the history of the civilized world for a very eventful week; for the whole civilized world was mainly absorbed, during that week, in getting news from and sending succor to Chicago. Besides, if we had all the facts gathered in some series of volumes more bulky than any library now left in Chicago, they could not be justly epitomized here. Those facts which are at hand are so numerous that we can hardly do aught more than to let out a few at random, though each presses itself upon us as richly worthy of mention.

If the spread of the flames through the streets of Chicago was swift as the wind, the spread of the news of it, and of the sympathy which it awakened, was infinitely more so. A speaker, addressing one of the ten thousand relief-meetings which sprung up in every city and hamlet in America, described this phenomenon well when he said there was no acre of the United States but that some cinder from Chicago had lighted on it and kindled the fire of sympathy. And yet that figure does not express the suddenness and directness of the passage of the feeling. Chicago was connected with the world more intimately than perhaps any other city. In the first place, nearly every county, district, and department in the Northern United States, in Great Britain, Ireland, and continental Europe, is represented in Chicago by persons who have immigrated hither, and left kindred and acquaintances at home. In the next place, the rapid growth of the city, and the remarkably active, enterprising, ambitious, audacious class of citizens which has accumulated with that growth, have attracted to Chicago the attention of the world, and brought hither travelers from all climes. Indeed, the press and the telegraph, which make all men travelers, in a sense, had been for the past few years so full of Chicago, as a theme, that every body in Christendom knew Chicago, or thought he did. The average emotion toward Chicago was that of admiration; which, at least, was not sufficiently offset by any other feeling to prevent the most hearty and unalloyed sentiment of regret and practical sympathy when the news of her misfortune came flashing along the wires. To say nothing now about the veins and arteries of commerce, which permeated the whole civilized world, and makes the blood ebb away at New York or London whenever Chicago bleeds, there is a nervous system, of wires and printers' types, which connects all together, and which places Chicago in close *rapport* with all parts of the world, especially Anglo-Saxondom and the greater Germany. The world never knew how complete and perfect this system is, until the shock at Chicago thrilled through all lands, and made the farthest extremities smart with pain or tingle with anxiety. The community of language, the community of interests, but revealed the community of human nature and human sympathy, one touch of which can "make the whole world kin." The proud cities of the earth then wept on each other's breast, and found that they were rivals no more, but loving sisters. Blessed is that affection which reveals such precious things!

The desolation of Chicago was fully known to all her citizens at daylight on the morning of the 9th October. Within three or four hours it was known in fully ten thousand cities and villages of the United States, and ten millions of people were bestirring themselves, and asking each other anxiously for tidings from the stricken city. Almost the first thought which suggested itself was of the destitution which must prevail, where a hundred thousand people had been so suddenly made homeless, and (as was supposed) their whole stock of provisions, clothing—in fact, all the accumulated wealth of the city—destroyed, as it were, in a breath. The heart of every man told him what to do at once.

The West had, fortunately, great stores of provision and of comfortable clothing; and these were sped on their way so promptly that, by the morning of the 10th, within thirty-two hours of the first kindling of the flames in Chicago, fifty carloads of provisions had arrived, to the relief of the destitute, some of them coming from towns three hundred miles away; and hundreds of thousands of dollars had been contributed, by means of the same beneficent telegraph whose agency had both communicated the news of distress and quickened to sensitiveness the hearts of its recipients.

To mention a few instances of generosity:

At Milwaukee the news of the conflagration was published in the morning papers, and by nine o'clock the whole population was on the street discussing the event excitedly, and waiting for the extras which appeared at short intervals throughout the day from the newspaper offices. Three fire-engines were dispatched by a special train, which did excellent service in Chicago, saving, it is believed, a considerable portion of the West Division from destruction. Milwaukee itself was greatly threatened, by reason of the drought and neighboring prairie-fires, and the Mayor issued a proclamation directing the citizens how to proceed as a precaution against fire. The Chamber of Commerce took action at noon, which resulted in the filling of two cars with cooked provisions. These went by the evening passenger-train, and arrived in Chicago at half-past seven, in charge of Messrs. Larkin and Ilsley, who immediately proceeded to distribute the food to the hungry victims of the fire. Further contributions of money, food, and other necessaries followed.

St. Louis proved herself a most generous neighbor. Mayor Mason, of Chicago, appealed to her during Monday for aid, and Mayor Brown, of St. Louis, addressed himself most bravely to the duty of supplying it. He called meetings, dispatched fire-engines, and proved himself a host in the emergency. Two immense meetings were held, at which the Mayor presided, and at the first one (at noon) $70,000 were subscribed, and committees appointed to canvass every trade, interest, and profession in the city for subscriptions. By five o'clock a relief train was on the track, ready to move, and at the evening meeting it was announced that eighty tons more of provisions were ready to go. Large quantities of bedding and other articles were also made up and dispatched, with the provisions, during the night.

With the first train a committee was sent, of which Hon. Henry T. Blow, late Minister to Brazil, was the moving spirit. This committee reported at Chicago at daylight on Tuesday morning, and became the nucleus of several such committees, which staid in Chicago a week, and rendered valuable assistance, especially during the few days before the authorities of the smitten and shattered city had fully organized the work of relief. The St. Louis Common Council appropriated $50,000 to the relief-fund, the County Court a like sum, and contributions from other bodies and private citizens swelled the sum to over $500,000, or about $1.70 from each man, woman, and child in the city!

Nor was Cincinnati less prompt and generous. Even as early as two o'clock on Monday morning, before even the wave of fire had passed the Chicago Court-house, and the half of the destruction had not been accomplished—much less told in Cincinnati—the editor of the *Commercial* was penning this paragraph, which went out as a double-leaded leader in the morning's issue:

"A Terrible Calamity.—The news from Chicago is most distressing. The most awful fire in the history of the city, and one of the most destructive that ever took place in the country, is, as we write, raging, and our dispatches indicate a degree of alarm almost amounting to despair. It is impossible to conjecture the extent of the calamity. Certainly it is appalling. Action should be taken here without a day's delay to express our profound sympathy, *and to render substantial assistance to the multitude of houseless people.* The latest intelligence is absolutely portentious. It seems possible that the whole city may be laid desolate."

This fell upon the popular mind like good seed timely sown. Of the scenes enacted and deeds done in Cincinnati during that and the following days, Mr. Edward Betty, of the *Commercial*, furnishes for these pages the following account:

"The reception of the news of the great conflagration in this city produced the most profound sensation. The effect upon the public mind was such as the news of defeat produced during the war for the Union. Business was suspended by common consent, and the citizens flocked to the newspaper offices in crowds that completely blockaded the sidewalks, and required the interference of the police to render pedestrianism possible. The suspension of telegraphic communication only served to heighten the excitement and make more unendurable the terrible suspense, for such was the public sense of the calamity that every individual felt that in some manner he was a sufferer.

"This was the condition all of Monday and Monday night, October the 9th, but in the midst of the wild whirl, sadness, and depression, the sympathies of humanity found expression, and during the earlier hours of the day the Chamber of Commerce became the theater for such a spontaneous action, for the relief of the burning city, as never was witnessed before in Cincinnati.

"Governor Hayes arrived by the earliest train from Columbus, and took an active part in putting in motion the sympathetic movement. The Chamber subscribed five thousand dollars, and adopted a resolution requesting the City Council to appropriate a hundred thousand.

"The Mayor called for private subscriptions, and these commenced to tumble in by the thousand, five, three, and two hundred dollars, with the money paid down rapidly as the secretary could record the names. Before the close of the day the private subscriptions amounted to *sixty thousand dollars*.

"In the meantime a special meeting of the City Council was convened by the Mayor. Nearly every member of the body was in his seat, and a well-worded resolution was adopted, appropriating $100,000 for the relief of Chicago. The Mayor announced that he had already dispatched by special train three first-class steam fire-engines, and four thousand feet of hose. Church societies under the direction of noble Christian women, were also called into action, and provisions and clothing were prepared in immense quantities. Before the day closed a committee with a commissary train, loaded with provisions and blankets, was sent off on the wings of steam to succor the houseless people of the smitten city, which in the hour of her calamity forgot to call upon her bounteous sister on the banks of 'the beautiful river,' but left her to proffer the helping hand, and thereby merit the love of Him who 'loveth the cheerful giver.'

"But the aid movement did not cease here. It was renewed next day. By the first trains of Tuesday the 10th October, more provisions, blankets, and clothing were forwarded, and one of them conveyed an outfit of type sent to the Chicago *Tribune*, by M. Halstead, Esq., editor of the Cincinnati *Commercial*, in a spirit of noble liberality, characteristic of the man. The Masonic and Odd Fellows bodies, the Medical Colleges, and eleemosynary institutions of the city, all proffered substantial aid, and made suitable provision for the sufferers who should seek a temporary asylum among them. And, indeed, throughout the remainder of the week, the movement was kept up. On Sunday the entire Protestant pulpit called aloud upon the people for the exercise of the most liberal beneficence, and in one week from the day the terrible misfortune fell upon Chicago, the relief fund had reached two hundred and ten thousand dollars. Besides this there were liberal donations of furniture, hollow-ware, bedding, clothing, and dry goods for domestic use. The list of these is interminable. In brief, every hand gave, from the millionaire to the little child in the lowest grade of the common schools. Every body seemed to realize the blessedness of giving, nor is the stream yet dry. Some of the benevolent institutions are making daily provision for the unfortunates that may come this way, and it is quite safe to say that the call of a Chicago sufferer will meet with a generous response for many a day to come.

"EDWARD BETTY.

"CINCINNATI, *Nov.* 3, 1871."

Mr. Betty's description of the general scene—the eagerness for news, the thronging together in the streets, the pall of sadness over the countenances in the crowds, and the spontaneous outpourings of material aid—were all repeated in hundreds of cities and thousands of villages and hamlets throughout this broad land.

At New York, where, owing to the more eastern longitude of the place, the news did not arrive in season to work its full effect through the morning journals, measures of relief were not organized until Tuesday noon. A great excitement set in, however, early on Monday, taking effect most violently in that place where New York is most sensitive—her Stock Exchange. In that institution a panic and fever prevailed, rivaling that of the memorable Black Friday. Stocks tumbled under the influence of the news, and fortunes melted away as if in the full blaze of the fire which was raging a thousand miles away. Many refused to believe the accounts of the disaster. The city was fairly crazy for news, and nothing else was talked of that day but the Chicago calamity.

New York was more vitally interested than any other city in the fate of Chicago. Her merchants had all given extensive credits there, and had apparently lost not only their accounts but their future custom. Her capitalists all had money invested there. Her insurance companies all had heavy risks there, and twenty of them were made insolvent by the event. Indeed, the loss, so far as dollars and cents go, fell quite as heavily upon New York as upon Chicago. Yet was New York the most liberal of all in her good Samaritan labors. At the Chamber of Commerce the next day the work was organized, and a committee, headed by Mr. A. A. Low, submitted an eloquent and practical appeal for contributions. These were received at the Chamber, at the Gold Exchange, at the Stock Exchange, at the *Herald* office, and by committees who passed around among the merchants. Within thirty hours' time nearly half a million dollars had been raised, and within a fortnight the aggregate had exceeded two millions of dollars, or more than two dollars for each inhabitant of the city. A. T. Stewart gave $50,000, and Robert Bonner, of the *Ledger*, $10,000.

In Philadelphia, a hundred thousand dollars was raised by the citizens within an hour, and subscriptions were immediately set on foot which realized an aggregate of about half a million dollars within ten days.

Boston rallied in force on Tuesday evening at her glorious old Faneuil Hall, "Cradle of Liberty," which now proved a cradle of charity as well. Senators Sumner and Wilson, the Rev. Edward Everett Hale, and other distinguished orators, made eloquent speeches, and the old "cradle" resounded with the applause of the multitude whenever the speakers touched with emphasis upon the future greatness of Chicago, or the importance of prompt aid. The Rev. Mr. Hale himself sketches the scene at Faneuil Hall thus, in a letter to the Chicago *Tribune:* "Few men have seen more remarkable public meetings in Faneuil Hall than I have, as a school-boy, as a reporter for the press, and as a citizen generally. I have, therefore, the right to say that, within this generation, there has been no public meeting which could so speak for the best life of Boston as the assembly which met almost at a moment's warning, in the midst of our agony at our first news from you. It was at noon Tuesday. There was none of the false grandeur of a packed platform; nobody had been invited, except, perhaps, one or two of the speakers; and the only call for the meeting had been the published request that every one would come to Faneuil Hall. That is our Boston way in a crisis. We fall back on the instincts of its pure democracy. Well, I think I have never seen such an assembly of men together. The floor was crowded from floor to ceiling—crowded, you remember, by people standing; for the characteristic of a true Faneuil-hall meeting is, that no one sits down. It means work. I say no one. But the reporters were sitting, and I was sitting among them. As I looked down upon that 'sea of upturned faces'—to repeat the words I heard Mr. Webster use in that place long ago—the four men I recognized first in the dense throng before me were, Franklin Haven, President of the largest bank in Boston; Judge Thomas, late of our Supreme Bench, whom we count our first jurist; Henry Wilson, of the United States Senate, and your old friend, William B. Wright, the minister of the largest Protestant church in Boston. Afterward, of course, I recognized hundreds of other men whom I knew; but when, at the moment of my arrival, I saw these four representative men standing in the dense throng in front of the platform, I could not but think that little picture was in itself an illustration of the true town-meeting." The depth of the interest felt in Boston concerning the calamity of Chicago may be inferred from the fact that we find in the *Transcript*, of the 17th, 276 items of intelligence bearing upon the subject. It is also worth while to add that fully a third of them are false, like many others of the statements published in the out-of-Chicago press right after the fire. In Boston the work of securing aid for the sufferers was carefully divided up, and more than half a million dollars were obtained within a fortnight.

Pittsburgh and Louisville made noble contributions, each about $150,000 in cash, and many car-loads of clothing and other articles. In Pittsburgh, on 'Change, the members and citizens pulled off their own coats and threw them into the boxes, so enthusiastic was the feeling for giving. Detroit raised $35,000 at a public meeting on Monday. Cleveland, four hundred miles east of us, sent on twenty-three car-loads of food and clothing within twenty-four hours after receiving the news of our disaster. Cairo, nearly as far to the southward, had two car-loads of provisions started toward Chicago at eleven o'clock on Monday morning. Indianapolis raised $8,000 at once, and sent it, with two well-manned steam fire-engines by an extra train, and on Monday evening her Council appropriated $20,000. Those gifts were followed up for days by others from the less impulsive citizens. By Wednesday evening, the second day after the fire, Brooklyn had subscribed $112,000 for the relief of the sufferers; Buffalo, $100,000; Rochester, $70,500; Baltimore, $35,000; Providence, $21,000; Portland (mindful of Chicago's generosity toward her in her own hour of need), $11,000; Salem and Linn, $50,000 each; Utica, $20,000; and other American cities an aggregate of about $2,000,000 in cash; besides which, and the contributions of goods already referred to, must be mentioned the forces of policemen and militia, and some twenty-five steam fire-engines, sent from New York, Cincinnati, Pittsburgh, Detroit, St. Louis, Indianapolis, Dayton, Milwaukee, and Racine, and coming like "friends in need, friends indeed."

The societies and orders—Masons, Odd Fellows, Knights of Pythias, etc., and the various trades unions—contributed to their own brethren, through their own channels, and relieved much distress which probably would not have been reached through the more public methods.

Excepting for the maintenance of the integrity of the Union, the people of America have never voluntarily taxed themselves so heavily in any behalf, nor given so cheerfully and spontaneously what they did give. And never, since the thrilling events which crowded the last two weeks of the war for the Union, have the American people been so agitated and absorbed by any event, of whatever nature.

Nor was the excitement, nor were the blessed benefactions confined to this continent. The news of the disaster shocked Europe as well, and formed the only topic in the clubs and the exchanges of London, Hamburg, Paris, Berlin, and all European capitals. At London meetings of private citizens, especially of Americans there sojourning, were held at once, and subscriptions opened for the relief of the destitute. The Lord Mayor of London went so far as to summon his Aldermen together without their customary period of notice—something which had not, probably, been done in years—for the purpose of inaugurating officially a movement for relief. At the meeting of the Council sympathetic speeches were made and a thousand guineas voted; after which books were kept open at the Mansion House of the Lord Mayor, and something over $200,000 subscribed. Similar movements were inaugurated at Liverpool, at Manchester, at Birmingham, at Bradford, at Dublin, at Wolverhampton, at Southampton, at Edinburgh, at Newcastle, and a hundred other towns of the United Kingdom, and at Vienna, Berlin, Hamburg, Paris, and other continental cities. The Queen of England and Empress of Germany joined heartily in the cause; and it was announced as an item of importance (as it doubtless is in England) that Queen Victoria reads every line which appears in the newspapers on the subject. If so, she had plenty of reading, for the London journals had telegraphed to them from Queenstown, where the vessels from America were boarded, whole broadsides of American papers having a bearing upon the all-important topic.

Thus all the civilized world united in one grand work of generous good-will. Thus the sweet exhalations from a hundred million true souls came down in a blessed rain of charity, to soften the stern soil of our adversity, and swell the bud of hope and gratitude. Thus civilization proved that its beauty was not of the surface merely, but deep and constant as the Divine love from whence it springs!

CHAPTER XXV.

ADMINISTRATION OF RELIEF.

Gathering in the homeless—Scenes in the churches—Caring for the sick—The "Relief and Aid Society"—Plan of its work—History of its operations—Board and lodging for 60,000—11,000 houses built and furnished for $110 each in two months.

HOW was the world's munificence applied? How was all this relief administered? Did human nature, which had approved itself so nobly in giving, also stand the strain, both of honesty and of tact, and dole out the precious trust to the best advantage?

The fate of the city was known at daylight on Monday morning, the 9th; but at that hour, and indeed until past noon of that day, the conflagration was still raging, and threatening, we may say, all the remaining portion of the city, including the most valuable residence portion on the avenues near the lake, which it was approaching by a lateral movement nearly at right angles with the wind. The Mayor, who had been on duty at the Court-house until that edifice began to tumble about his ears, was fighting the fire near his own premises, on Wabash Avenue. About noon Mr. Mason was importuned by Alderman Holden, President of the Common Council, and a resident of the West Division, to come over and do something in his official capacity toward reassuring the community and securing shelter for the houseless victims of the fire.

In compliance with this request, the Mayor repaired, at about two o'clock, to the First Congregational Church, on West Washington Street, of which Mr. Holden had taken possession as the headquarters of the City Government. Mr. Holden had summoned also Commissioner Brown of the Board of Police, and one or two Aldermen, the City Clerk, Mr. Hotchkiss, and one or two prominent citizens. Together they drew up a proclamation of assurance, as recorded in a previous chapter, and formed a relief committee, consisting of Orrin E. Moore, *Prest.*, C. C. P. Holden, *Treas.*, C. T. Hotchkiss, *Secy.*, John Buchler, Ald. Devine, John Herting, Ald. McAvoy, and N. K. Fairbanks. This Committee, in anticipation of any funds, secured teams, which commenced to gather in the sick and wounded. For the accommodation of these, and of such others as came in, the churches were all thrown open, some of their own motion, some by order of the Relief Committee. Orders were given to all the bakers left in the city to run their ovens to their full capacity in making bread for the hungry. That night one carload of food came in from Milwaukee and was distributed to such as called for it. There was also much food carried out upon the prairies and given to the refugees there by the benevolent ladies of the West Division. But water was the greatest desideratum in this day, and all, housed and unhoused, suffered alike for lack of facilities for procuring it.

The vigorous work of relief did not fairly commence until Tuesday morning. Early on that morning the committees from abroad began to come in, bearing their offerings—among them the committee from St. Louis, headed by Mr. Blow; the committee from Cincinnati, headed by Mr. Goshorn; and a committee from Louisville, headed by Wm. M. Morris, came later in the day. There was now plenty of food (probably some fifty carloads had arrived on Tuesday morning), and supplies of clothing were coming in rapidly. The task was to reach the sufferers with it, or to bring them to points where aid could be conveniently distributed. For this purpose, teams were sent out to bring the weak and infirm into the city, and gather them into the churches. To give them beds, the seats were stripped of their cushions, and mattresses were brought in from the houses of the citizens. Five hundred cots sent from the Planters' House, St. Louis, and a quantity of blankets from the army stores, were found of great value now.

The women of the city came nobly to the rescue. Their first impulse, on learning of the state of suffering of thousands on the prairie, was to snatch up all the food they had, and all the clothing, except immediate wear, and hurry with them to the sufferers. Stories of starvation were rife, and were generally credited—the hearers forgetting, in their warm impulse to succor, that people could not starve in twenty-four hour's time, and would not, when provisions were so near at hand. There was really less suffering from exposure and hunger than the world was left to suppose from the news which went out during the first few days after the fire. One of the angels of mercy already referred to, a lady of the West Divison, tells an amusing story of her hopeless attempt to find some one who was really suffering for food or clothing on the Tuesday mentioned. She drove among all the fugitives, offering food and clothing. The former was a drug in the market, and for the latter she could not find suitable customers until she came upon an elderly Irish woman, nearly naked, and fairly howling with distress.

Delighted at the opportunity of relieving such acute suffering, the lady hastened to "rig out" the poor creature with a complete set of apparel—clothing which was by no means of the "cast-off" variety. She was rewarded by copious tears and invocations of blessings from the "Holy Mother," and on returning that way a few minutes later, she had the satisfaction of seeing her beneficiary stripped again and in the same state of howling misery as before, the good clothing having been spirited away and stored up, or perphaps sold for whisky!

Such cases of imposition as this were, however, the exceptions, and the fact that respectable people were obliged to consort with such mendicants and imposters as these, and be subjected to the same questioning as they, before receiving aid, only illustrates one of the most painful phases of the calamity.

The work of administering succor was systematized as rapidly as possible, and by Wednesday shelter had been provided for all who were houseless, and immense depots for the distribution of food and clothing were in operation at nearly all the churches. The cooking and serving was all done by lady volunteers, and the draft was a very severe one upon the women of the city, who not only served as the almoners of the bounty from abroad, but carried plentiful stores of delicacies from their own larders, in order that the victims of the fire might feel their privation as little as possible. The building of commodious barracks for housing the homeless was commenced at once in all the eligible vacant places in the city, and many of these were already occupied by Friday night.

By this time the work of relief had grown so in magnitude that it began to suffer seriously for want of organization. A responsible head was wanted to receive and account for the munificent offerings of the outside world, and a skillful executive

BIGELOW HOUSE.

PACIFIC HOTEL.

NORTH-EAST CORNER CLARK AND RANDOLPH STREETS.

TREMONT HOUSE.

agency for the just distribution of the benefits, so that no real suffering should go unrelieved, and, if possible, no bounty be wasted upon the undeserving. Fortunately, there was already existing in Chicago, a Relief and Aid Society which had, for several years, made the succor of the needy its care, and had accomplished a vast amount of good in the relief of special cases of misfortune. It was an incorporated institution, its directory and officers consisted of men of the very best character, and it had a system of seeking out cases of need and administering relief, which adapted it happily to the work now before it. Its principal officers are, Henry W. King, President; George M. Pullman, Treasurer; Wirt Dexter, Chairman of the Executive Committee; and O. C. Gibbs, Superintendent. The President is mainly a figure-head, the others are active; and Mr. Gibbs is the only professional philanthropist among the officers—that is, who receives a regular salary for his services in this line. Mr. Pullman is the inventor of the famous palace-cars, and has become a millionaire through the revenues of his car system. Mr. Dexter is a business lawyer of extensive practice and large means.

To this Society the work of relief was intrusted by the Mayor on the Friday following the fire. The contributions of cash were to be received by David A. Gage, Esq., the City Treasurer, and turned over by him, without delay, to the fund of the Relief Society, taking the Treasurer's voucher therefor. Other contributions were to be receipted for and reported to the Mayor.

Under these conditions, the Relief Society strengthened a weak spot or two in its officering or organization, expanded somewhat its plan of operations, and addressed itself to the mighty task before it, of relieving a hundred thousand destitute persons, many of whom were too sensitive, or, as their neighbors would say, "too high toned" to apply for aid; to keep out many thousand undeserving applicants who would fain avail themselves of an opportunity to feed, lodge, and dress at the public expense through the winter; and to satisfy a million or more of generous donors, who, knowing the corruption to which nearly all administrations in large cities have become subject, could not but be jealous upon the matter of the distribution of their bounty. The *plan* upon which this was to be accomplished was briefly this: A treasurer to receive funds and account for them (necessitating, of course, a very complete set of books, and some "red tape"); an executive committee, to pass upon all questions concerning the general policy of the Society, and upon all bills brought against the Society; a superintendent to portion out the work in the field, and supervise the labors of the district superintendents; seven committees beside the executive committee, viz: (1) On receiving, storing, and issuing supplies; (2) on shelter; (3) on employment; (4) on transportation; (5) on reception and correspondence; (6) on distribution of food, clothing, and fuel; and (7) on sick, sanitary, and hospital measures. The plan further embraced a series of districts, each with a local superintendent, a main depot, sub-districts and sub-depots for the distribution of supplies; also a complete system of house-to-house visitation, by which each district superintendent, or certain of his aids, should know each recipient of bounty by his or her place of abode, as well as face. The method of distribution was somewhat similar to that of the quartermaster's department in the army, being by rations, and upon requisitions; but there was, of course, as there should be, much less "red tape," and much more elasticity of operation. A fuller statement of the plan will be found in Appendix "D," where we print the report of Major-General Meade and others, a committee sent hither by the Philadelphia contributors to examine into the workings of the relief business, and ascertain whether their bounty was being faithfully and wisely administered. It will be perceived that these gentlemen are very positive and unqualified in their praise of the arrangements for relief; a verdict, which, with perhaps advantages for observation superior to those of the Philadelphia committee, we can conscientiously confirm.

As a matter of course, the temptations to exercise favoritism in the distribution of benefits is very great in a community where almost every person can rightfully put forward *some* excuse for receiving gratuities, and where a general prevalence of hard times takes away in many cases the barrier of pride which would otherwise deter persons from accepting relief from a public source. To guard against this, very close supervision and very trustworthy officers and employés are necessary; and, though the theory of the system requires that two undeserving applicants shall be served rather than one deserving person be neglected, the superintendent found himself compelled, in order to carry all his pensioners through the winter upon the funds in hand, to exercise great precautions against imposition, and against fostering habits of dependence and indolence. Accordingly, Mr. Gibbs found it necessary to issue, on the 24th of October, a circular to the employés of the Society under his command, of which the following is the body:

"I am fully justified in saying that, in taking into account the amount of relief funds and stores received or reported to date, and those likely to be received hereafter, without the most rigid economy in their disbursement, mid-winter is likely to find us with our treasury bare, with outdoor labor to a large extent necessarily suspended, and with a city full of poor looking to us for food and fuel. You will, therefore, see the pressing necessity that not a single dollar be appropriated for persons able to provide for themselves, no matter how strongly their claims may be urged by themselves or others. Every carpenter or mason can now earn from three to four dollars per day, every laborer two dollars, every half-grown boy one dollar, every woman capable of doing household work from two to three dollars per week and her board, either in the city or country. Clerks and persons unaccustomed to outdoor labor, if they can not find such employment as they have been accustomed to, must take such as is offered, or leave the city. Any man, single woman, or boy, able to work and unemployed at this time, is so from choice, and not from necessity. You will, therefore, at once commence the work of re-examination of the cases of all persons who have been visited and recorded upon your books, and will give no aid to any families who are capable of earning their own support if fully employed, except it be to supply some needed articles of clothing, bedding, or furniture, which their earnings will not enable them to procure and at the same time meet their ordinary expenses of food and fuel.

"No aid should be rendered to persons possessed of property, either personal or real, from which they might by reasonable exertion procure the means to supply their wants, nor to those who have friends able to relieve them.

"Our aid must be held sacred for the aged, infirm, widows, and orphans, and to supply to families those actual necessaries of life, which, with the best exertions on their part, they are unable to procure by their labor. You will entrust this work of re-examination to your most judicious and intelligent visitors, who will act conscientiously and fearlessly in the discharge of their duties.

"This circular is issued with the full approval of the Executive Committee, and any failure on the part of any employé of the Society to conform to the instructions above given will be regarded as sufficient cause for his instant dismissal."

On the same day the treasurer submitted to the public the following report, which we give as showing not only the magnitude of the work, but the proportions of the expenditures for different objects:

Total amount cash received in direct remittances,	$ 599,276 12
Total amount for which drafts have been made and sent forward for collection,	726,752 16
Total amount for which drafts have been drawn, and are to be forwarded to-morrow,	160,957 78
Aggregate receipts,	$1,486,986 06
Disbursements to date,	34,449 80
Balance on hand,	$1,452,836 26
Of this amount there is on deposits in banks of this city,	649,208 10
In banks of New York,	419,657 17
In banks of Boston,	128,462 84
In banks of Montreal,	2,500 00
Total,	$1,199,828 11
Drafts to be sent on for collection,	160,957 78
Cash on hand, principally checks,	92,050 37
Total,	$1,452,836 26

The estimated requisitions for the next thirty days are as follows:

For houses and barracks, including those already completed,	$ 850,000 00
For stoves and furniture,	150,000 00
For bedding,	80,000 00
For fuel,	100,000 00
For food,	750,000 00
For labor and teams,	45,000 00
Total,	$1,975,000 00

The stock of clothing on hand and advised of as being on the way, is supposed to be sufficient to supply the demand for the next thirty days.

In the last days of October some scandal was raised concerning the disposition of certain funds during the provisional administration of the so-called Relief Committee—a self-constituted body, composed, for the most part, of unquestionably honest men, but still having no responsible or tangible or practicable organization. One of the members of that committee, Mr. Holden, was a candidate for the mayoralty, and the newspapers, all of which were arrayed against him, came out in articles impugning the honesty and disinterestedness of his administration as custodian of the relief fund; so that, although he disproved their main allegations, and though he was then entirely disconnected from the relief business, the stench raised over the subject served undoubtedly to deter a few contributions which had been raised from coming to Chicago; but the friends of the sufferers can have the consolation of knowing that the subscriptions were nearly all in at that time, and that comparatively little was lost in this way. On the 28th of October Mr. Dexter sent out telegrams to "our friends throughout the civilized world," asking complete duplicate reports of all their gratuities, with the obvious purpose of tracing up any miscarriages or misappropriations, if there should be such; but without any unpleasant discoveries so far.

On the 7th of November, six weeks after the fire, and five weeks after the Society had fairly commenced business, the executive committee had received 5859 applications for houses, and had granted 4299 of these. On that day the committee reported further:

"We are now able to give the amount received to this date, and the probable amount of the entire subscriptions, with approximate accuracy. We have actually received $2,051,023.55. Arrangements have been made by which the Society draws 5 per cent. on all balances in bank. So far as our present information goes, and we think we have advices of all sums subscribed, the entire fund will vary but little from $3,500,000. This includes the funds in the hands of the New York Chamber of Commerce, amounting to about $600,000, and the balance of the Boston fund, about $240,000, both amounting to about $840,000, not yet placed to the credit of this Society, but which may undoubtedly be relied upon to meet the needs of the future. As to our disbursements, we can only say that we are at present aiding 60,000 people at our regular distributing points. Some of this vast number we relieve in part only, but the greater portion to the extent of their entire support. This is in addition to the work of the special relief committee for people who ought not to be sent to the general distributing points, and which is largely increasing upon our hands. It is also in addition to the expenditures of the committee on existing charitable institutions.

"The great matter pressing upon the committee is shelter for the coming winter. We may feed people during the mild weather, but where and how they are to be housed—permanently housed—we regard as a serious question. To this end we have been aiding those burned out to replace small but comfortable houses upon their own or upon leased lots, where they can live, not only this winter, but next summer, and be ready to work in rebuilding the city. Of these houses—which are really very comfortable, being 16 by 25 feet, with two rooms, one 12 by 16 feet, and one 8 by 16 feet, with a planed and matched floor, panel doors, and good windows—we have already furnished over 4000, making permanent houses, allowing five to a family, for 20,000 people, and with the 7000 houses which we expect to build, shall have rooms for 35,000 people. These houses and some barracks, in both of which is a moderate outfit of furniture, such as stoves, mattresses, and a little crockery, will consume, say $1,250,000, leaving $2,250,000 with which to meet all the demands for food, fuel, clothing and general expenses, from the 13th of October last—when we took the work—until the completion of the same, which can not possibly end with the present winter.

"The committee need hardly say, that if the demand should continue as great as the present, the fund would be exhausted by mid-winter, but we hope to cut this down very largely as soon as we can get people into houses, so that they can leave their families and find work. Indeed, this is being done already. Within a few days we shall arrive at the exact daily expense of food and fuel rations; but the demand, as might be expected, is a fluctuating one. If the weather is good and men can work, it falls off; if cold and stormy, it at once increases at a fearful rate."

In addition to the labors of the Relief Society, much was done toward succoring the distressed by benevolent and co-operative societies, and by individual munificence; and among the most wholesome of the agencies called into operation was the Ladies Industrial Aid Society, formed for the purpose of furnishing remunerative labor to those women and girls whose self-respect prompted them to earn a livelihood, but who found themselves deprived of opportunities by the general contraction of business; also the Ladies Christian Union, which labored for the same praiseworthy end.

It is hardly necessary for us to observe, in leaving this subject, that there were necessarily many cases of distress, or of privation bordering on physical distress, and including a great deal of mental distress, which it was impossible to relieve. A special bureau, organized for the purpose as a branch of the Relief Society, did much in this direction; but it could not do all—that was simply impossible. Indeed, for those many cases of misery which resulted from lost station, or fallen pride, or blighted ambition, or bereavement of kindred, it was impossible, even if the constituted authorities had the whole wealth of London at their command, to administer relief.

This is, of course, a matter of grave regret; but it must be added that a good deal of mawkish sentiment was wasted on the cases of those who were "too proud to beg," and yet not too proud to accept bounty if it was offered them. Such, it was argued, must be sought out and pressed to take little delicacies and choice tidbits of charity, and furnished with enough of

LASALLE STREET TUNNEL.

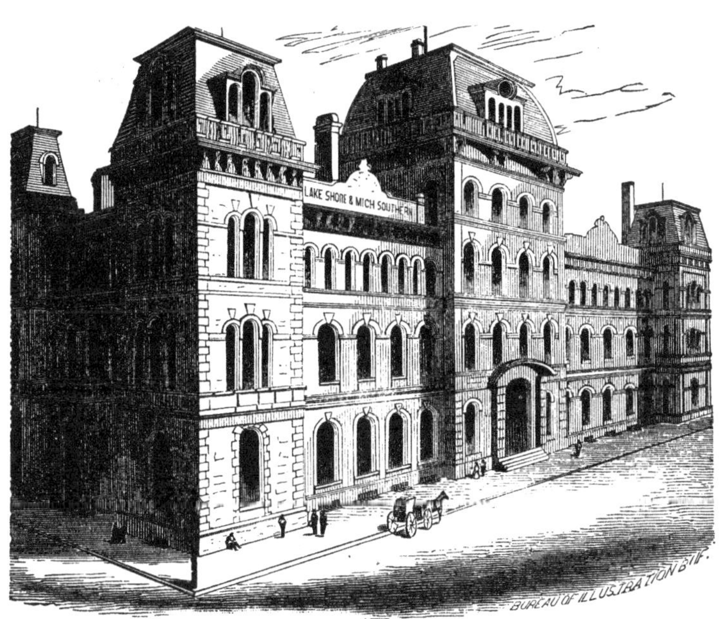

MICHIGAN SOUTHERN RAILROAD DEPOT.

INSURANCE BLOCK.

CORNER CLARK AND RANDOLPH STREETS.

filthy lucre to keep them through the winter in at least a shabby genteel manner, as if they were the heirs of the world and were kept on a rather stingy allowance until they should come into their inheritance. Now pride is a quality, or faculty, or habit, quite as simple to regulate as any other faculty—for instance, physical appetite; to indulge it costs money, or ought to. If a person values his pride highly enough to do without money, or food, he can indulge it at that expense and rejoice in the act. If his appetite for food or for gain is stronger than his pride, he sacrifices the latter, and rejoices in his bargain all the same. Pride is a luxury, and should be paid for like all other luxuries. The man who can keep his pride through adversity has reason to felicitate himself upon it; but he has no right to demand that his pride be kept up for him at the public expense. Receiving charity and at the same time affecting to despise it, is the meanest kind of hypocrisy, and is moreover as foolish as the scheme of the child who thought that he could eat his cake and have it too. We have no sincerer tears than those which flow for the ambitious young Chicagoans who found themselves smitten at once in their purse, pride, and prospects, and who therefore had a mental and moral blight added to the physical privation which the fire brought on; but such was the fate of many who bore it heroically; and the man who came out of the fire poor, and yet never asked *nor received* gratuities during all the trying period that followed, has the best title of all to be proud henceforth.

CHAPTER XXVI.

HUMORS OF THE FIRE.

Enjoying a bonfire of one's valuables—How a lap-dog was saved—Burning up the freedom of the Negroes—"Billy, propose a resolution"—The first conundrum of the new era—The calamitous cow—No confidence in Chicago as a ruin—The pathetic ballad of Eva Boston, etc.

THOSE who think there were no comical or humorous elements about so vast an affair as the Chicago fire, labor under a great mistake. There were many such, and, far from the people being overwhelmed by the shocking events of the catastrophe, the reaction of the mind from the state into which it would be thrown by that scene and its consequences, rather heightened the appreciation of the ridiculous. This is not a phenomenon—it is a simple and very natural fact, which the reader has doubtless had occasion to observe before now, that the extremely pathetic and the ludicrous often blend with one another. Such was the case with a gentleman in the North Division, who tells us, between his convulsions of laughter, excited by the recollection, how, on the night of the principal fire, having found his own house on the verge of destruction, and loaded some of his most prized keepsakes, such as an heirloom easy chair, etc., upon a wagon which his man drove, and following after with a small load in his buggy, he was thrown into a violent fit of laughter at seeing the goods upon the front wagon blazing up in the streets before his eyes, and behind the back of the unsuspecting driver. The gentleman is unable to this day to tell what there was funny in the sight, but knows that it affected him ludicrously, just as the recollection of it has ever since.

The selections, which people made in their flight, of articles to save, was almost invariably ludicrous, or at least remarkable. Women for the most part took pets, as canary birds, lap-dogs, etc., while men tried to save valuables, but were often greatly confounded to find, on escaping from immediate danger, that they had brought away an empty cigar-box, or some such rubbish, instead of their title deeds or private ledger. One gentleman, to our knowledge, rushed up stairs, seized a box of paper collars and bore it away, leaving a valuable paid-up life-insurance policy in the same drawer; and it is credibly related that an exquisite young man was seen emerging from a boarding house on Wabash Avenue, very fastidiously dressed, and bearing solemnly in his hand an article of chamber furniture with which, to say the least, he would not have been seen thus in his cooler moments. Equally ludicrous was the sight of two young women--one a mother, evidently, escaping in a basket carriage to the west side. They were fashionably dressed, and were lashing their horse to the top of his speed. One of them held, clear from the ground with great difficulty, a baby carriage, while the other plied the whip. A gentleman meeting them, ejaculates, "Your dog, ma'am," but they dash on, unheeding. The object of the gentleman's solicitude—a poodle of diminutive size—was attached to the axle of the carriage and bobbing about like a foot-ball. He had been fastened with the tenderest care, with plenty of padding about his neck, but none, unfortunately, around his head, which was beaten nearly to a jelly, the dog being *very* dead. But the ladies were happy in the fallacy that they had saved their precious pet.

A curious fact (at least the Southern papers tell it for a fact), was the notion of the simpler negroes at the South, that since the original draft of the Emancipation Proclamation of President Lincoln was burned up in the fire, they must all be remanded to slavery! The New Orleans *Picayune* tells of a lady in that city who was reading to her servants an account of the Chicago fire. The incident of the burning of the Emancipation Proclamation arrested the attention of one old colored woman, a slave all her life, who viewed the proclamation much as the Israelites did the Ark of the Covenant. "What dat!" she said, "burned up?" "Yes, aunty, burned up." "Den what gwine come of us again?" "I don 't know; may be you 'll be slaves as before." "Den dis chile gwine to die right now."

It is related, but we have not been able to trace the story to its origin, that an elderly gentleman from Iowa, hearing of the calamity, hastened immediately to Chicago to aid his son and his family—perhaps snatch them from their burning house. Hearing at one of the stations that the Water-works had given out, he purchased a cask, filled it with water, and brought it along with great care. It is even said that he was charged forty dollars by an expressman for carrying it to his son's house on the west side, which the old man paid willingly, as it had not yet occurred to him that water was to be had from the lake by going thither.

Some newsboys and bootblacks from Chicago sought refuge in New York right after the fire. Their colleagues of that metropolis were anxious to do something hospitable for them, and so called a meeting at the headquarters of their guild for the reception of the afflicted strangers. One of the leaders of the fraternity, feeling that the eyes of the country were on them, and that a speech, a resolution, or something, was necessary to redeem the occasion, rose to the emergency and to his feet, and remarked, impressively:

"*Gentlemen:* You know about the Chicago fire, and that these gentlemen (pointing to the ten Chicagoans) are sufferers. I now want to tell 'em that we 're sorry for 'em. Our subscription list is making up, and I heard Mr. O'Connor say 't will amount to $8.25, which they will get, though it 's small, and not as much as we 'd like to. That's all I have to say, except that if these gentlemen stay here we 'll post 'em."

Another boy. "Billy, propose a resolution."

Billy. "I move that we 're awful sorry for the sufferings of the newsboys and black-a-boots of the Chicago, and that if they stay we post 'em, and that any thing we can do we will do to help 'em, and that we 're sorry it ain't more than $8.25."

It seems that being "posted," is the *sine qua non* of happiness with the newsboy, and that the intention of Billy's "resolution" was, therefore, to confer the highest honor upon the visiting gentlemen.

Jokes began to peep out in the columns of the daily papers after a few days had elapsed since the fire. It may be set down (though, perhaps, upon rather insufficient *data*) that after a great conflagration conundrums will begin to appear in the local press after twelve days. At any rate the *Tribune*, of the 21st of October, contained this: "The following is, we believe, the first conundrum which was raked up from the ashes of the great Conflagration. It was brought into the local room of the *Tribune* by a suspicious-looking character, whose hair was completely singed off, and whose right cheek was covered with flour to conceal a terrible scar left by the fire. He did not wait to claim any reward:

"*Conundrum.* What is the difference between Theodore Thomas and the Emperor Nero?

"*Answer.* The one fiddled away while his Rome was burning, and the other *roamed* away while his fiddles were burning."

Various squibs soon began to float, having reference to the dire cow of De Koven Street; and what purported to be accurate likenesses of the cow with crumpled horn, that kicked the lamp, that lit the straw, that fired the barn, that burned Chicago up, were published in some of the flash newspapers. The name of the lecturers who presently set out through the country to tell what they knew about the fire, was legion; and the happy thought struck some one, that the notorious bovine would be a good "card," if she could be taken around and exhibited along with somebody's lecture.

No one was allowed to joke about the fire who had not been completely "cleaned out" himself. One of the monthly journals, which had fulfilled this condition, had this squib, *apropos* of the oft-repeated remark that Chicago will rise again:

"We are constantly assured that 'Chicago will rise again.' We hope so, and are inclined to believe it, like the man of whom Hood tells, who, being run over by a heavy wagon, looked up to the frightened neighbors who had gathered about him, and asked if he was flat. On being assured that he was not, he remarked: 'Oh, well, then never fear, boys, I'll come round again.'"

The impression that Chicago would "come round again" was world-wide; and *Punch*, of London, urged Englishmen to hurry up their donations faster than they were doing, or else Chicago would be all built up before their offerings should reach her. The same story was told in the American fashion, at St. Louis, a few days after the fire, thus:

"At the East St. Louis depot, on last Monday evening, considerable confusion occurred among the passengers who were boarding the passenger-train for Chicago, by an individual, carpet-bag in hand, and very much excited, shoving and pushing the crowd in his desperate efforts to reach the cars. He crowded aside and elbowed men, women, and children, making a nuisance of himself generally. Finally a gentleman, whose ribs had been crushed by the excited man's elbows, and his temper ruffled by the unceremonious manner in which he had been hustled, inquired in sharp tones:

"'What the devil is the matter with you, old fellow?'

"*Man in a Hurry.* 'Must get that train.'

"*Other Man.* 'Well, there is plenty of time—the train does not start for ten minutes; and, besides, there are several other people here who want that train.'

"*Man in a Hurry.* 'I *must* get that train, and that's fixed. I'll get that train if it costs me my life.'

"*Other Man.* 'What in thunder is the necessity of your reaching Chicago by this train, any way?'

"*Man in a Hurry.* 'I must get to Chicago to-morrow, on this train, or those people up there will have built up the whole ——— town again, and I won't see them ruins.'"

The way in which the town was built up at first, was more calculated to spoil the picturesqueness of the old Chicago than to inspire admiration for the new. Among the first buildings to "rise phœnix-like from the ashes," as the orators were fond of saying, in those days, was the "Burnt District Restaurant," a stately edifice of rough pine boards, one story high. "Hammer & Smith's Block"—so labelled—was a less imposing structure about 7 x 9 in dimensions, built at an expense of perhaps $40, for a lawyer's office.

We have referred to the effect of the fire in bringing out the salient points of human nature, just as heat brings out the stamp of a piece of coin. The weakness of Boston human nature, as is well known, is for sounding the praises of Boston on all occasions. Some did this under circumstances which were to them doubtless pathetic, while to the unsympathizing they were simply ludicrous. A young pair of parents, for instance—victims of the fire—wrote gushingly to a Boston newspaper how they owed their lives to Boston on that occasion—to a pair of Boston blankets, namely (no other kind would have saved them); also to some Boston crackers, a bundle of baby clothes from Boston, and even a nursing bottle for the little child, who was straightway christened Eva Boston and set to sucking the precious memento. Whether the poor child had abstained from all nourishment until the bottle arrived from BOSTON, we do not know, but are left to infer that she did. A sympathizing poet in Milwaukee was so overcome by the recital of these touching events that he immediately sat down and dashed off the following lullaby for little Eva Boston—to be sung to a flowing accompaniment from the nursing bottle:

Air—Yankee Doodle.

Boston Boston Boston Boston
Boston Boston Boston
Boston Boston Boston Boston
Boston Boston Boston.

CHORUS.—Boston Boston Boston Boston
Boston Boston Boston
Boston Boston Boston Boston
Boston Boston Boston.

A newspaper in southern Illinois tells the following good story of a Mr. Hudson, a railroad superintendent at Macoupin. Whether it is or is not true in all its particulars, it will at least remind many of the readers of this history of their own experience in relieving Chicago:

Upon hearing of the burning of Chicago, his first act was to telegraph to all agents to transport free, all provisions for Chicago, and to receive such articles to the exclusion of freight. He then purchased a number of good hams and sent them home with a request to his wife to cook them as soon as possible, so they might be sent to Chicago. He then ordered the baker to put up fifty loaves of bread. He was kept busy during the day until five o'clock. Just as he was starting for home the baker informed him the hundred loaves of bread were ready.

"But I only ordered fifty," said Ed.

"Mrs. Hudson also ordered fifty," said the baker.

"All right," said Ed., and he inwardly blessed his wife for the generous deed.

Arriving at home he found his little boy, dressed in a fine cloth suit, carrying in wood. He told him that would not do; he must change his clothes.

"But mother sent all my clothes to Chicago," replied the boy.

Entering the house he found his wife, clad in a fine silk dress, superintending the cooking. A remark in regard to the matter elicited the information that she had sent her other dresses to Chicago.

The matter was getting serious. He sat down to a supper without butter, because all that could be purchased had been sent to Chicago. There were no pickles—the poor souls in Chicago would relish them so much.

A little "put out," but not a bit angry or disgusted, Ed. went to the wardrobe to get his overcoat, but it was not there. An interrogatory revealed the fact that it fitted in the box real well, and he needed a new overcoat any way, although he had paid $50 for the one in question only a few days before. An examination revealed the fact that all the rest of his clothes fitted the box real nicely, for not a garment did he possess except those he had on.

While he admitted the generosity of his wife, he thought the matter was getting entirely too personal, and turned to her with the characteristic inquiry:

"Do you think we can stand an *encore* on that Chicago fire?"

There is neat humor, and, at the same time a fine touch of true feeling, in the following verses, by W. H. McElroy, which were printed in the New York *Journal* shortly after the fire, and with which we conclude this chapter:

CHICAGO.

We used to chaff you in other days,
Chicago,
You had such self-asserting ways,
Chicago.
By Jove, but you cut it rather fat,
With your boastful talk of this and that,
As if America's hub was at
Chicago.

We Bohemian boys on the Eastern press,
Chicago,
We *lied* about you, and nothing less;
Chicago.
'T was a way we had—without remorse
To manufacture "another divorce,"
And locate it at—as a matter of course—
Chicago.

The star of empire on its way West,
Chicago,
You said, concluded that it was best,
Chicago,
To fix itself in your special sky,
Unmoved by further claim or cry,
And you hailed the star as "good for high,"
Chicago.

You called New York—so said, at least,
Chicago,
Called it "*Chicago of the East.*"
Chicago,
Now, was n't it cutting it *rather* fat,
To venture on such a speech as that,
As if the hub was certainly at
Chicago.

But we loved you in spite of your many airs,
Chicago,
If it was n't for wheat there would n't be tares,
Chicago,
And so as we heard your trumpets blow,
Loud as theirs were at Jericho,
We said—"Well one thing, she is n't *slow*,"
Chicago.

And when of your terrible trouble we learned,
Chicago,
How your fair young beauty to ashes was turned,
Chicago,
The whole land rose in its love and might,
And swore it would see you through your plight,
And—"Draw by the million on us at sight,
Chicago."

We used to remark, of course with pity,
Chicago,
That you were our champion wickedest city,
Chicago,
And yet, just now, you very well may
Insist with reason we can't gainsay,
That you are *the* power for good to-day,
Chicago.

For if unto Charity it is given,
Chicago,
To hide no end of sins from Heaven,
Chicago,
The Recording Angel his pen may take,
And blot out the record we daily make,
And write on the margin "*for charity's sake,*"
At Chicago.

CHAPTER XXVII.

GOOD OUT OF EVIL.

Some wholesome effects of adversity—Business faults corrected—Aristocracy scotched out—How fire purifies—How individuals may attain improvement—How the body politic—How humanity—The sublimest spectacle of the century.

HENRY WARD BEECHER, whose ready sympathies doubtless entitled him to make such a remark, notwithstanding he lost nothing by the fire, declared in Plymouth Church on the Sunday following, that "we could not afford to do without the Chicago fire"—that it was revealing to us such cheering views of humanity that it was proving a blessing, rather than a calamity. Some caviled at this optimist view of the case, and likened Mr. Beecher to the oriental prince, who, discovering in the ruins of his father's house, which the fire had consumed, the carcass of a pig most exquisitely roasted, was so delighted with the discovery that he kept burning down his subjects' houses, in order that he might enjoy more roast pig.

This moral salvage from the ashes of the great calamity we will leave out of the consideration for the present, and notice some of the unquestioned material advantages to be realized as a partial recompense—perhaps the reader will say a complete recompense—for the manifold evils which our narration has made apparent. These advantages lie mainly in the correction of besetting faults, which it is fair to assume would not have been corrected if the city had not been burned; and their realization depends in some measure upon the willingness of the Chicagoans to receive the lessons of the fire; though not wholly, for there are some corrections which they must receive, whether they will or no.

One of the faults of Chicago business, and one which had long been notorious, was the artificial inflation of the real estate market constantly going on. Hundreds of real estate brokers, agents, and speculators (and the number had been rapidly increasing every year), were striving together to keep prices advancing, to bring into market as city property thousands of wild acres, miles beyond the city limits, and to "turn over" each piece of property as many times a year as possible. To forward these plans, rings were formed and public appropriations secured for the location of parks or public buildings contiguous to the property of the speculators. The course of the market was not left for natural laws to regulate, but was forced by artificial means this way or that; and much capital, and still more business energy, was kept by this means out of channels of enterprise wherein they would have wrought much good to the community. These speculators on margins and operators in what was called "boulevard property," were, like large numbers of the purely speculative operators on 'change, pretty thoroughly scotched out by the flames. Whatever may be said about the expansive effect of heat on most materials, the heat of this conflagration had a decidedly shriveling effect upon suburban real estate; and some "beautiful acre property" in the far suburbs was about as effectually burned up as any merchandise in the center of the town. The destruction of the records of the county, at the Court-house, also gave the fire another effect which few will lament, viz: to wipe out the evidences which made tax titles valid, and land, high and dry, many of the sharks who preyed upon the delinquent tax-payers.

It may also, probably, be scored down to the credit of the fire that it checked the two rapid spread of the city in all directions, which was bound to result in great sacrifices of economy in time and money. The same was true with regard to business, which was scattering broadly over the city, the warehouses and shops of scarcely any line of business being within convenient distance of each other. This made the transaction of business more expensive, both to the jobbers and to the country dealers who favored them with their trade.

The fire is expected to exercise a great reforming effect upon the character of the building done in Chicago after the date of its occurrence. The very inflammable character of the buildings in most parts of the city has been already adverted to. But even in the quarter which has been called "well built" by strangers, as well as by citizens, there was altogether too much regard paid to show, and too little to utility. Chicago, though a mere stripling of a city, already enjoyed the credit of having the most elegant business architecture of any city in the world. The boast was too bold, altogether, though it had many facts for its foundation. Nevertheless, there was scarcely any of the fine buildings of Chicago which were not marred by tawdry ornaments, endangering its safety. Many of them were massive, looking like very Samsons for strength; but they all had the vulnerable heel of Achilles. In the new era it certainly may be expected that this fault will be mended, that public opinion will demand laws compelling the erection of strong, fire-proof buildings only, and forbidding any man to place in jeopardy the lives and property of his fellow-citizens, in order that he may save a few dollars for himself. We must add, in candor, that the outset of the New Chicago is not in the highest degree reassuring on this subject, and that, so far as present appearances go, people are to be left very much to their own devices regarding the style of their building, after the old Chicago fashion, which allows individuals all rights, and the public at large none. But at the writing of this, the new city government, which was elected as a "Fire-proof" government, and upon which the people depend for a more firm, upright, and intelligent conduct of municipal affairs than heretofore, had not assumed its functions.

The charter election, which followed soon after the conflagration, furnishes one of the finest illustrations of the truism that "fire purifies." It was shown in business most unmistakably. The fire assayed the metal of which our merchants were made, purifying the gold from the dross, showing the great importers of the East which was good and which was bad, and leaving the name of many a Chicago merchant, who thought himself bankrupt, shining more brightly than ever in the ledgers and memories of his creditors at the East. It made an invincible Gideon's band of the stanch tradesmen along South Water Street, Lake Street, State Street, etc. But it purified our politics in a still more marked manner. When the fire happened, the city was on the eve of a charter and county election, with an almost certain prospect that the nominations for the offices to be filled would, as usual, be conferred on the class who made it their business to seek those offices for the spoils that are in them.

The citizens felt, however, that this would be too great a misfortune to endure in connection with the grand calamity which they had just undergone. They accordingly set about fortifying themselves against the known advantages of the office-seekers, chiefly in organization and possession of the active ward-politicians. The executive committees of the two political parties were induced to compromise with each other upon a ticket, every member of which, as nominated by one committee was submitted to the scrutiny of the other committee, and of the public, through the press. At length a complete ticket was made out, composed of names of the very best class of citizens—men who had rarely, or never, run for office. An opposition ticket, composed, for the most part, of office-seekers, or "bummers," as they were called, was made up and violently electioneered for until election-day; but the "Fire-proof" ticket was found to be elected by at least five votes to each one of the opposition. Joseph Medill, one of the proprietors of the *Tribune*, was chosen Mayor by this election, and Fred. Gund, one of the Fire Commissioners under whose administration the city burned up, and who had the audacity to run for re-election, was defeated by a five-to-one majority.

Another benefit of the fire was to open people's eyes on the subject of insurance, and enable all to know what was good insurance and what was bogus. The experience which many obtained proved a very dear school to them; but it can not be doubted that the lesson proved worth, in the aggregate, all it cost—that is, Chicago and a few insurance towns paid for the lesson for the whole country. It taught that insurance in companies which were doing a large business on a small margin of paid-up capital, or which insured unlimited amounts in any one city, was no insurance at all; and it taught capitalists to be much more careful than hitherto into what kind of companies they put their funds, and underwriters learned by it to limit their amounts of insurance in any locality, and make more rigid requirements concerning precautions against fire. By this means insurance, which was at first thought to have exploded completely, will become much stronger than it really was before.

But the best work which the fire has wrought has been upon the character and habits of the people, rather than upon their business, political, or other material affairs. The people of Chicago were, before the fire, fast lapsing into luxury—not as yet to any such degree as the people of New York—but still more than was for their good. The fire roused them from this tendency, and made them the same strong men and women, of the same simple, industrious, self-denying habits, which built up Chicago, and pushed her so powerfully along her unparalleled career. All show and frivolity were abandoned, and democracy became the fashion. People found new and rich fields of usefulness open to them. Young men who, in anticipation of a large inheritance, had commenced to lead dawdling lives, now rolled up their sleeves and went to work in the store, or organized a business of their own out of the salvage of their father's capital. Their sisters desisted from the giddy race for pre-eminence in dressing, flirting, and other frivolous pursuits, and became the comfort and consolation of their parents, or the frugal wives of earnest men. Their mothers forsook their brilliant match-making, their incessant "shopping," and their schemes for surpassing their neighbors in the magnitude and absurdity of their assemblies—those nonsensical mobs of snobs and nabobs which abound in high city life during the winter season. Their fathers, who had been lapsing into a chronic state of gout or debility, through lack of nervous stimulus, went back to the office to work, and felt much better for it. Many projected trips to unwholesome haunts of folly and gilded vice were abandoned, and work—work, that sweetener of rest and all legitimate enjoyments—was resumed in earnest. Business men greeted each other gayly in their temporary shanties, and said: "Now, this is something like it; we've got down to the bed rock now"—a miner's phrase, which indicates a poorer yield of metal; but the "bed rock" shall prove, after all, the best rock on which to build the new Chicago—the firm foundation rock of her business, the Plymouth Rock of her society!

The light of the fire revealed the *solidarity* of the nation. It was only by some such great calamity as the Chicago fire that the people of the United States could have been taught how closely bound together they were—not in language merely—not in politics merely—not in race merely, but in interests of apparently the most private and individual nature. This phase of the case has already been treated upon in the chapter on "Sympathy and Relief." Especially along the great lines of railroad and telegraph which connect the East with the West, the union was found to be very complete; so that each wave of disaster which was born upon the western shore died not until it had reached the eastern.

But this solidarity of the nation is one of interest merely. The fire revealed another, more broadly extending and more deeply lying—the solidarity of human sympathy. Never before did the maxim that "blood is thicker than water," rise to such a dignity, or receive such a convincing demonstration. The revelation of brotherhood and intimate fellowship between "man and man, the wide world over," was more sudden and spontaneous, if not more full, than ever before occurred.

Were the reader suddenly asked what is the sublimest spectacle of the century, he might at first answer, a vast city wrapped in flames; mountains of fire stretching to the heavens; a black empyrian of rolling smoke; a crimson river with carnation bridges over-arching it; a sullen, darkened lake surrounding it; a constant thunder of falling walls and exploding element; a constant earthquake shaking the ground; a hundred thousand people rushing, shrieking, struggling, perishing. This was, indeed, it seemed to those who witnessed it, the acme of sublimity, and of terror as well. But there was a sublimer one which followed, and happily blending in its sublimity a world of beauty. It was the sight (too glorious for the physical sense, but none the less clearly brought home to the eye of the mind) of a world uniting simultaneously in one grand act of love to man, and, therefore, worship to God, the source of love. Can any thing more impressive to the mind, more melting to the heart, be conceived? It was felt at Chicago more profoundly far than all our sufferings, or than any common emotion we had ever known. Men tried to speak of it to each other in the streets, and broke down in the midst of the sentence which they would utter. Men who would make a mere jest of their wreched fortunes, and embrace poverty with a shrug and nothing more, wept like children when they came to speak of what the world was doing around them. This is already an old theme. Poets innumerable have sung of it, armies of preachers have built sermons upon it, and hosts of writers in the current press have woven it into their daily discourse; but few of these could have felt it as we did, here in its focus.

And it was wonderful!

The discordant note, announcing sorrow, death, and devastation throughout a fair and prosperous city, went forth in one hour throughout the civilized world, shocking and stunning whom it struck. In another hour it flowed back, resolved into the most delicious chords of love and Christ-like charity. No man who felt that heavenly-sent strain break in upon his senses can but echo in his heart, however grave his sufferings may have been, the words of America's laureate of liberty:

"Ah! not in vain the flames that tossed
Above thy dreadful holocaust;
The Christ again has preached through thee
The Gospel of Humanity

"Then lift once more thy towers on high,
And fret with spires the western sky,
To tell that God is yet with us,
And love is still miraculous!"

CHAPTER XXVIII.

THE NEW CHICAGO.

Five years hence—Why Chicago will keep marching on—Rate of recuperation—Railroads and traffic—Changes in the appearance of the city—Harbor and river—Things which will not be improved—Population in 1876.

LONDON, with a population diminished more than one-third by the plague of the previous year, and demoralized by the licentiousness of the times of the cavaliers, recovered within five years from a destruction quite as complete as that of Chicago. New York was visited in 1835 by a conflagration, much less destructive to be sure than this of ours, but it was preceded by pestilence in 1832 and 1834, and followed by the great commercial revulsion of 1837; in spite of all which disasters, New York grew in that decade from a city of 202,000 people to one of 312,000. The argument from this is, that a general conflagration is not necessarily fatal to a city, nor even a long-continued check upon its forward career. London continued to grow rapidly because it had made itself the center of an immense ocean commerce, and the metropolis of a prosperous country. New York bade defiance to a three-fold disaster for a like reason. Chicago has fastened upon the trade of the great North-west with chains that can not be unbound, and will therefore grow with that rapidly developing country, and without any serious hinderance from what has happened. Individual fortunes have been, in some cases, irretrievably lost, though the way in which these men rebound, even from out the slough of despair, is something wonderful; but the city must still go marching on. The West must have her for uses which no other locality can subserve, and which no other city, even if it had the advantage of location, could prepare itself to subserve in thrice the time it will take Chicago to recuperate. The produce of the West and the capital of the East are alike interested in keeping Chicago the metropolis of the North-west—an empire already vaster, and much more rapidly growing, than that of Great Britain at the time London was destroyed.

People who come to Chicago and take a survey of her present apparent desolation are shocked by it, and go away saying that Chicago can not be rebuilt in less than a generation. They forget that Chicago was a generation in attaining her late magnificence simply because the West was that length of time in growing to its present proportions; and that the question of how long it will take to rebuild Chicago—the West being still intact around her—is simply a question of how long it will require for the country to produce the bricks and the stone to lay up her walls withal. It is estimated by those competent to judge of this that three years will be adequate to the work; in other words, that as soon as the grand buildings of the railway corporations, the city, and the United States Government, can be completed in a solid manner, they will already be surrounded by a complete city, equal in its capacity for the accommodation of business to that which fell in the Great Conflagration. The population will also, by that time, have shot considerably past the mark of September, 1871; but as certain fine theaters, churches, and residences will still be behind, it is better, in order to be within the bounds of moderation, to set the period of Chicago's complete recuperation at five years from the date of her disaster—the eighth of October, 1876.

We have shown in a previous chapter that the average annual rate of increase in the value of property in Chicago, during the ten years preceding 1871, has been 10½ per cent. which compounds at 66½ per cent. in five years. Thus, reckoning only the ordinary growth of the city, and making no allowance for the extraordinary stimulus occasioned by the sudden necessities of the present crisis, the value of property lost by the fire (one-third of the whole) would be more than recovered by the fall of 1876. It may be argued that this ratio of increment will be diminished, owing to the lack of facilities for doing business, and the consequent diversion of trade to competing towns; also that these towns, particularly St. Louis, are sharper competitors than London had in 1666; but this, if true, applies only in a small measure. The country had already elected Chicago as the capital of the North-west, and by converging in her the many railroads which were built for accommodating the traffic of that section, fixed her as the seat of that traffic more firmly far than a State statute and a million or two of dollars in public buildings, fixes the capital of a State in Albany or Springfield. Saying nothing of the $400,000,000 of capital still represented in the buildings, lands, and merchandise of Chicago, there are $300,000,000 invested in her railroads, every dollar of which is vitally interested in keeping the traffic of the North-west upon these roads. New York commercial capital is interested in the same direction, for Chicago is by all odds New York's best customer, and whatever trade should be diverted from Chicago to St. Louis, or Cincinnati, would also be diverted from New York to Philadelphia. With all these artificial influences, and the same powerful natural influences which fixed Chicago where she is, working together for her restoration, it will not be possible for other influences to distract much of her trade or delay her growth in population a single year, or hinder the reconstruction of her edifices beyond the date which we have set down the eighth of October, 1876.

The disaster to Chicago will not probably delay at all the enlargement of the Niagara and St. Lawrence Canals, and the deepening of the channels at each end of Lake Huron, both of which measures for the improvement of navigation and the substitution of larger vessels (and hence cheaper rates) for the grain traffic of the country, are to be undertaken at government expense. These measures, though not at the expense of Chicago, will still benefit Chicago greatly by making the production of grain more profitable to the farmer, who, as a consequence, will not only raise more grain, but have more money to spend in Chicago. At the same time the improvement of this water route will increase Chicago's facilities as an importing city—a function which she had just began to develop extensively at the time the disaster struck her. There are also two or more trunk railways from the East proposing to enter Chicago to compete for the trade of the North-west. These, if completed (and there is no reason why they should be interrupted by what has happened), will still further increase the business of this metropolis, as will also the four or five proposed now routes diverging into the grain and stock producing country, and the route *via* Evansville to Mobile, to be finished early in 1872, which ought to bring in bond all the West India goods consumed in the North-west, the merchants of Chicago deriving from this trade the large profits of the importers, instead of the small ones of the simple jobber.

At the same time that this increase in trade is going on (subject to the drawbacks already mentioned), certain lines of manufactures may be established to increase considerably, for instance, those of all materials used in building and furnishing stores and houses, and those of light articles, the help for making which can be recruited from the ranks of the shop girls and boys thrown out of employment by the fire, or forced by the hard times upon such industrial pursuits.

The city may be expected, then, to make a greater show of railway and shipping warehouses than before the fire. The streets, except a few of them, will not be built up with stores so continuously as before the fire, but the amount of facilities for business—especially for wholesale business, will be greater than it was; while the public buildings, as the Post-office, Custom-house, City Hall, railway passenger depots, Chamber of Commerce, etc., will present an appearance corresponding to a city three or four times as great as that for which the destroyed structures were built. Public libraries and galleries of art will have to wait longer, as will also the park improvements which the citizens were projecting on such a mammoth scale; but the theaters, at the date specified will have just about recovered the number and magnitude which they had attained before the fire, and that, be it recollected, was two-fold greater than one year before, and at least four-fold greater than any other Western city could boast.

Let it not be understood, however, that *fortunes* will be rebuilt within any such period, or that the private luxury and elegance of yesterday will be re-established. The business marts will be humming again simply because they must, but in many cases other men will preside over them, while some who worked with the head yesterday will work with the hands then. The most of the business men of Chicago, however, have too much pluck, and also too much of the quality called *brass* for that. They will make a shift—indeed two-thirds of them have already made a shift to resume their places as proprietors, and get capital from somewhere—the Lord, who tempers the wind to the shorn lamb, knows where. A single case illustrates this. The writer, wandering among the mournful ruins of the North Division, on the day after that quarter was destroyed, met an acquaintance whom he accosted with the usual salutation: "How did you come out?" The answer was: "Yesterday morning I had a warehouse over there with $30,000 worth of wool in it, I had a fine house, well furnished, for my home, and two others to help out my income. To-day, I 've got what I have on my back; my wife the same—that is all." "Are you going to give it up?" we asked. "No, *sir*," he answered. A fortnight later we encountered the same friend dashing down the street at great speed. He had got track of a man who would, he thought, put up a building for him, and was going to have the contract made before night. He was buoyant and enthusiastic.

Probably the reader of this history who visits Chicago five years hence, will find this man in full blast in his new warehouse, not with thirty, but with *sixty* or *ninety* thousand dollars' worth of wool in store, and not with two, but *four* houses to rent; for it is such pluck as this that wins in the West.

This visitor will see, besides the twenty railroads which already converge at Chicago, the six important lines now projected, also entering the heart of the city, probably by sunk tracks, and through viaducts at every street-crossing. He will see, let us hope, a consolidation of all the passenger stations into three at most, and will be told that the system of omnibus tolls upon travelers has been abolished.

He will see the streets of the central portion of the city (the burnt district of the South and part of that of the North Divisions) raised from two to three feet above their present grade, and from ten to fifteen above the original level of the prairie. As a concomitant of this, he will see a good portion of our sewerage reversed in its course, as the river has already been served. The buildings which line these streets he will find to be chiefly of brick, and of soberer appearance than the gay, cream-colored stone (treacherous beauty!) which so delighted his eye in the summer of '71. He will mark, nevertheless, the solidity and substantiality of every thing, and will query if, after all, the painted red brick fronts, relieved at intervals by cream-colored walls from Milwaukee, or rich, natural red from Philadelphia or Baltimore, or light brown sandstone from Cleveland, or gray granite from Duluth, or ruddy brown sandstone from Lake Superior, or the censured, but not entirely tabooed limestone from Joliet, be not, after all, in their endless variety, more cheerful than the stately monotony of the old era. He will see few mansard roofs or ornate cornices, but will, nevertheless, be pleased with the brightness and newness of every thing; and since the beauty of a thing consists, in great part, of its fitness for the place which it occupies, the visitor will be, or, at least should be, inclined to pronounce favorably concerning the beauty of the new Chicago.

He will notice that the pavements are, as in '71, notable for their smoothness and silence under the wheel, being made of wooden blocks, as now, or of the asphalt-rock concrete, in making which we are improving so much every day. He will see sidewalks built of this material, being laid in the filled districts over brick arches; and he will find, on passing under these sidewalks that the vaults, thus formed, are absolutely fireproof receptacles for such articles as may be consigned to them.

He will see upon the lake shore an inclosed harbor of refuge, lined on two sides with slips for the accommodation of vessels of greater draft and tonnage than have ever come to this port hitherto. Passing up the river (that is, *down* it toward the Mississippi), he will find its docks devoted more to the unloading and storing of iron, coal, and heavy merchandise than they now are, much of the merchandise being brought in on lighter scows from the outer harbor. He will look in vain for any yards or depositories for lumber within two and a half miles of the river's mouth.

He will not find the business of the great Union Stock Yards much increased, though he knows that that was almost the only interest which did not suffer by the fire. On asking the reason for this, he will learn that, as the country for grazing has been pushed gradually westward and southward, the cities which sprang up thereaway, particularly Kansas City, had naturally become, to a considerable degree, the distributing points of cattle for the East; but that the increased consumption of meats in Chicago and the district supplied from Chicago, had kept up the demand at about the old figures.

He will see no greater area covered by Chicago than he saw five years before, except at the suburbs along the railroads, whither people of moderate means will go to build wooden houses, and avoid what many will doubtless call the odious fire ordinance, which will prohibit all wooden houses within the city limits. He will see steam or compressed air substituted for horse-power upon the most of the street-railways.

He will see a population greater by nearly one hundred

thousand than that which Uncle Sam's census-taker found in 1870. These people will look hard-worked, and those of the old lot will seem more than five years older than they did on a September morning in 1871. They may well be advised, at that time, to pause a little in their hard chase after material things, and consider those of the heart, the mind, and the immortal soul; and if the visitor be of a missionary turn, he can not throw his subjects into a tender mood more effectually than by reminding them of the night of the 8th of October, '71, and of how the world stood by Chicago in that sad time.

But he will, on the whole, be proud of the new Chicago, from whatever quarter he may hail. He will find her changed from the Chicago of yesterday in such manner as the wild and wanton girl, of luxurious beauty, and generous, free ways, is changed when, becoming a wife, a great bereavement, or the pangs and burdens of maternity overtake her, robbing her cheek of its rich flush, but at the same time ripening her beauty, elevating, deepening, expanding her character, and imbuing her with a susceptibility of feeling, a consciousness of strength, and an earnestness of purpose which she knew not before.

When, thus transformed, the new Chicago shall go, on the centennial of our nation's birth, to join her sisters in laying the laurel wreath upon the mother Columbia's brow, she will be greeted with signal warmth by each and all of them, and welcomed back from out her vale of affliction as one who had suffered that she might be strong.

THE END.

APPENDIX A.

THE GREAT FIRES OF HISTORY.

BURNING OF ROME.

In the year 64, during the reign of the tyrant Nero, the city of Rome, his capital, suffered a terrible conflagration, lasting eight days, and destroying ten of the fourteen wards of the city. Several historians maintain that Nero set the fire himself, but there is considerable doubt about this, as also about the story of the emperor's fiddling (or playing the flute) while the city burned. Either act, however, would have been characteristic of the man.

Nero was liberal to the sufferers by the fire, and rebuilt the city on a new and improved plan, with money which he had extorted from the people. He charged the conflagration upon the Christians, many of whom he put to death by burning. Gibbon writes graphically of this fire in his "Decline and Fall of the Roman Empire." The population of Rome, at the time of its burning, was more than a million souls.

THE GREAT FIRE OF LONDON.

The nearest parallel in history to the Chicago Conflagration is the Great Fire in London, which commenced on the 2d of September, 1666, and continued five days. As in Chicago, the fire was owing to wooden houses, a very dry season, and a high wind; and, as in Chicago, the pumping works which supplied the city with water were very soon destroyed, thereby paralyzing the powers of the fire department, and of all who might, with private engines, have saved their own property, or helped to arrest the progress of the flames. Like the fire at Chicago, it broke out upon a Sunday, though at a different hour—two o'clock in the morning. It originated in a bake-house, kept by a man with the quaint name of Farryner, at Pudding Lane, near the Tower. At that period, the buildings in the English capital were chiefly constructed of wood, with pitched roofs; and in this particular locality, which was immediately adjacent to the water side, the stores were mainly filled with materials employed in the equipment of shipping, mostly, of course, of a highly combustible nature. The vacillation and indecision of the lord mayor aggravated the confusion. For several hours he refused to listen to the counsel given him to call in the aid of the military; and when the probable proportions of the fire were plainly apparent, and when it was clear that the destruction of a block of houses was absolutely necessary to the preservation of the city, he declined to accept the responsibility of destroying them until he could obtain the consent of their owners. He was, evidently, like Governor Palmer, of Illinois, a man of high legal punctilio.

The most graphic and circumstantial account of this fire is that contained in the diary of John Evelyn, in his "Diary," published soon after the event. Commencing on the second day of the fire, it runs thus:

"Sept. 3d.—The fire continuing after dinner, I took coach with my wife and son and went to the Bankside, in Southwark, where we beheld that dreadful spectacle—the whole city in dreadful flames near ye water side; all the houses from the Bridge, all Thames Street, and upwards towards Cheapside, down to the Three Cranes, were now consumed.

"The fire having continued all this night (if I may call that night, which was as light as day for ten miles round about, after a dreadful manner), when conspiring with a fierce eastern wind in a very drie season, I went on foot to the same place and saw the whole south part of ye city burning from Cheapside to the Thames, and all along Cornhill (for it kindled back against the wind as well as forward), Tower Street, Fenchurch Street, Gracious Street, and so along to Bainard's Castle, and was now taking hold of St. Paule's Church, to which the scaffolds contributed exceedingly. The conflagration was so universal and the people so astonished that, from the beginning—I know not from what, despondency or fate—they hardly strived to quench it, so that there was nothing hearde or seene but crying out and lamentation; running about like distracted creatures, without at all attempting to save even their goods, such a strange consternation there was upon them; so, as it burned, both in length and breadth, the churches, public halls, Exchange, hospitals, monuments, and ornaments, leaping after a prodigious manner from house to house and streete to streete, at greate distance one from ye other; for ye heate, with a long set of faire and warme weather, had even ignited the air, and prepared the materials to conceive the fire, which devoured after an incredible manner houses, furniture, and every thing. Here we saw the Thames covered with goods floating, all the barges and boats laden with what some had time and courage to save; as on ye other, ye carts, etc., carrying out to the fields, which for many miles were strewed with moveables of all sorts, and tents erecting to shelter both people and what goods they could get away. Oh, the miserable and calamitous spectacle! such as haply the world had not seene the like since the foundation of it, nor to be outdone till the universal conflagration. All the sky was of a fiery aspect, like the top of a burning oven, the light seene above forty miles round about for many nights. God grant my eyes may never behold the like, now seeing above ten thousand houses all in one flame; the noise, and crackling, and thunder of the impetuous flames, ye shrieking of women and children, the hurry of people, the fall of towers, houses, and churches was like an hideous storme, and the aire all about so hot and inflamed that at last one was not able to approach it, so that they were forced to stand stille and let the flames burn on, which they did for near two miles in length and one in breadth. The clouds of smoke were dismall, and reached, upon computation, near fifty miles in length. Thus I left it in the afternoone burning—a resemblance to Sodom, or the last day. London was, but is no more!

"Sept. 4th.—The burning still rages, and it was now gotten so far as the Inner Temple, Olde Fleete Streete, the Olde Bailey, Ludgate Hill, Warwick Lane, Newgate, Paule's Chain, Watling Streete, now flaming and most of it reduced to ashes; the stones of Paule's flew like granados, ye melting lead running down the streetes in a streame, and the very pavements glowing with fiery rednesse, so as no horse or man was able to tread on them, and the demolition had stopped all the passages, so that no help could be applied. The eastern wind still more impetuously drove the flames forward. Nothing but ye almighty power of God was able to stop them, for vaine was ye helpe of man.

"Sept. 5th.—It crossed towards Whitehalle; oh, the confusion there was then at that Court! It pleased His Majesty to command me among the rest to looke after the quenching of Fetter Lane, and to preserve, if possible, that part of Holborne, while ye rest of ye gentlemen took their several posts and began to consider that nothing was so likely to put a stop but the blowing up of so many houses as might make a wider gap than any had yet been made by the ordinary method of pulling them down by engines."

Then, after a description of the abating of the wind and the gradual dying out of the fire, the quaint old diarist continues:

"The poor inhabitants were dispersed about St. George's Fields and Moorfields, as far as Highgate, and several myles in circle, some under tents, some under miserable huts and hovels, many without a rag or any necessary utensils, bed, or board, who, from delicateness, riches, and easy accommodation in stately and well-furnished houses, were reduced now to extremest misery and poverty."

And again:

"I then went towards Islington and Highgate, where one might have seene 200,000 people, of all ranks and degrees, dispersed and lying along by their heapes of what they could save from the fire, deploring their losse; and, though ready to perish from hunger and destitution, yet not asking one penny for relief, which to me appeared a stranger sight than any I had yet beheld."

Nearly two-thirds of the entire city were destroyed. Thirteen thousand houses, eighty-nine churches, and many public buildings were reduced to charred wood and ashes. Three hundred and seventy-three acres within, and sixty-three acres without, the walls were utterly devastated. The occasion was improved by the preachers of those days, as did the Chicago Conflagration inspire the preachers of our day.

THE BURNING OF MOSCOW, 1812.

The burning of Moscow, by its citizens, in 1812, to prevent its falling into the hands of the notorious Frenchmen, is one of the best known of historical events. The invading army, under Napoleon, had taken possession, and the citizens had fled almost to a man. A few remained behind to fire the city, by order of Count Potapchin, the Governor, who had set the example by firing his own magnificent country palace on the road to the city, and leaving a defiant inscription on its gates.

The conquering army entered the city on the 15th of September, the Emperor taking possession of the Kremlin, the ancient palace of the Czars. The events which followed his solemn entry into the tenantless city are thus described by Sir Archibald Alison: On the night of the 14th a fire broke out in the Bourse, behind the Bazaar, which soon consumed that noble edifice, and spread to a considerable part of the crowded streets in the vicinity. This, however, was but the prelude to more extended calamities. At midnight, on the 15th, a bright light was seen to illuminate the northern and western parts of the city; and the sentinels on watch at the Kremlin soon discovered the splendid edifices in that quarter to be in flames. The wind changed repeatedly during the night, but to whatever quarter it veered the conflagration extended itself; fresh fires were every instant seen breaking out in all directions, and Moscow soon exhibited the spectacle of a sea of flame agitated by the wind. The soldiers, drowned in sleep or overcome by intoxication, were incapable of arresting its progress; and the burning fragments floating through the hot air began to fall on the roofs and courts of the Kremlin. The fury of an autumnal tempest added to the horrors of the scene; it seemed as if the wrath of heaven had combined with the vengeance of man to consume the invaders of the city they had conquered.

But it was chiefly during the nights of the 18th and 19th that the conflagration attained its greatest violence. At that time the whole city was wrapped in flames, and volumes of fire of various colors ascended to the heavens in many places, diffusing a prodigious light on all sides, and attended by an intolerable heat. These balloons of flame were accompanied in their ascent by a frightful hissing noise and loud explosions, the effect of the vast stores of oil, resin, tar, spirits, and other combustible materials with which the greater part of the shops were filled. Large pieces of painted canvas, unrolled from the outside of the buildings by the violence of the heat, floated on fire in the atmosphere, and sent down on all sides a flaming shower, which spread the conflagration in quarters even the most removed from where it originated. The wind, naturally high, was raised, by the sudden rarefaction of the air produced by the heat, to a perfect hurricane. The howling of the tempest drowned even the roar of the conflagration; the whole heavens were filled with the whirl of the volumes of smoke and flame which rose on all sides and made midnight as bright as day; while even the bravest hearts, subdued by the sublimity of the scene, and the feeling of human impotence in the midst of such elemental strife, sank and trembled in silence.

The return of day did not diminish the terrors of the conflagration. An immense crowd of hitherto unseen people, who had taken refuge in the cellars and vaults of their buildings, issued forth as the flames reached their dwellings; the streets were speedily filled with multitudes flying in every direction, with their most precious articles; while the French army, whose discipline this fatal event had entirely dissolved, assembled in drunken crowds and loaded themselves with the spoils of the city. Never in modern times had such a scene been witnessed. The men were loaded with packages charged with their most precious effects, which often took fire as they were carried along, and which they were obliged to throw down to save themselves. The women had often two or three children on their backs, and as many led by the hand, which, with trembling steps and piteous cries, sought their devious way through the labyrinth of flame. Many old men, unable to walk, were drawn on hurdles or wheelbarrows by their children and grandchildren, while their burnt beards and smoking garments showed with what difficulty they had been rescued from the flames. Often the French soldiers, tormented by hunger and thirst, and loosened from all discipline by the horrors which surrounded them, not contented with the booty in the streets, rushed headlong into the burning edifices to ransack their cellars for the stores of wine and spirits which they contained, and beneath the ruins great numbers perished miserably, the victims of intemperance and the surrounding fire. Meanwhile the flames, fanned by the tempestuous gale, advanced with frightful rapidity, devouring alike in their course the palaces of the great, the temples of religion, and the cottages of the poor. For thirty-six hours the conflagration continued at its height, and during that time above nine-tenths of the city was destroyed. The remainder, abandoned to pillage and deserted by its inhabitants, offered no resources to the army. Moscow had been conquered, but the victors had gained only a heap of ruins. It is estimated that 30,800 houses were consumed, and the total value of property destroyed amounted to £30,000,000.

AT NEW YORK, 1835.

At between eight and nine o'clock of the evening above stated, the fire was discovered in the store No. 25 Merchant Street, a narrow street that led from Pearl into Exchange Street, near where the Post-office then was. The flames spread rapidly, and at ten o'clock forty of the most valuable dry goods stores in the city were burned down or on fire. The narrowness of Merchant Street, and the gale which was blowing, aided the spread of the destructive element. It passed from building to building, leaped across the street between the blocks, urged by the gale and in nowise deterred by the feeble forces opposing it. The night was bitterly cold, and, though the firemen were most energetic, the freezing of the hose and the water in their defective engines, combined with their sufferings from the weather, made their efforts of little avail. The flames spread north and south, east and west, until almost every building on the area bounded by Wall, South, and Broad Streets and Coenties slip, was burning, gutted, or leveled to the ground. There was not a building destroyed on Broad Street, nor on the block on Wall Street from William to Broad Street, the fire taking an almost circular course just at the rear of the buildings on the streets named. The scene in the night was one of indescribable grandeur, the glare from the three hundred buildings that were at one time burning brightly lighting up the whole city. In all, five hundred and thirty buildings were destroyed; they were of the largest and most costly description, and were filled with the most valuable goods. The total loss, estimated at about $20,000,000, was afterward found to be about $15,000,000. Of the buildings destroyed the most important were the Merchants' Exchange, the Post-office, the offices of the celebrated bankers, the Josephs, the Allens, and the Livingstons, the Phœnix Bank, and the building owned and occupied by Arthur Tappan, then much despised for his anti-slavery sympathies. The business portion of the city was alone that burned over, so that few poor were rendered otherwise than without employment. The disaster was considered so severe that many predicted that the city would never recover from the fearful blow which it had sustained.

AT CHARLESTON, 1838.

Charleston, S. C., was, on the 27th of April, 1838, visited by one of the most destructive fires that has ever occurred in any city in this country. A territory equal to almost one-half of the entire city was made desolate. The fire broke out at a quarter past eight o'clock on the morning of the day mentioned, in a paint-shop on King Street, corner of Beresford, and raged until about twelve A. M. of the following day. It was then arrested by the blowing up of buildings in its path. There were 1158 buildings destroyed, and the loss occasioned was about $3,000,000. The worst feature of the catastrophe was the loss of life which occurred while the houses were being blown up. Through the careless manner in which the gunpowder was used, four of the most prominent citizens of the city were killed and a number injured.

AT PITTSBURGH, 1845.

Pittsburgh, Pa., was visited by a most destructive conflagration on the 10th of April, 1845. By it a very large portion of the city was laid waste, and a greater number of houses destroyed than by all the fires that had occurred previously to it. Twenty squares, containing about 1100 buildings were burned over. Of these buildings the greater part were business houses containing goods of immense value—grocery, dry goods, and commission houses —and the spring stocks of the latter had just been laid in. The fire commenced in a frame building at the corner of Second and Ferry Streets, and the prevailing strong wind urged it with fearful rapidity through the city. So short was the time between the discovery of the flames and their spread through the city, that many persons were unable to save any of their household goods, while others, having got theirs to the walk, were compelled to flee and leave them to be seized and destroyed by the element. The merchants were equally unsuccessful in saving any thing from their warehouses. The loss was estimated at $10,000,000.

AT ST. LOUIS, 1849.

Flames broke out about ten o'clock on the night of the 17th of May, 1849, on the steamboat *White Cloud*, lying at the leveee between Wash and Cherry Streets, nearly in front of a large lard factory. The wind was blowing stiffly from the north-east, forcing the boats directly into the shore. The *Eudora* and *Edward Bates* soon caught, and the latter, drifting into the stream, carried destruction to nearly all the boats lying south of her. In half an hour after the fire began twenty-three steamboats had fed the fury of the flames, and nearly $500,000 worth of property was destroyed. Spreading to the wharves, where a large quantity of hemp was stored, the whole or part of fifteen blocks were destroyed. The fire lasted till between six and seven o'clock on the morning of the eighteenth. The supply of water had given out early, a strong wind was blowing, and the fire companies, working with hand engines, were entirely powerless. The fire involved a large part of the business portion of the city, and almost every house destroyed was owned by those who were either wealthy enough themselves to build up their property or could readily obtain means to do it. The offices of the Missouri *Republican*, the *Reveille*, the *New Era* and the *Argus* were burned, together with two or three job printing offices. The progress of the devouring element was stayed on Market Street on the blowing up of some buildings with powder, whereby a prominent citizen, T. B. Targee, was instantly killed and two or three others were seriously injured. The number of steamboats destroyed was twenty-three, which, with their cargoes, were valued at $436,-000. The total amount of property lost was about $3,000,000. The value of the stocks of goods burned was about $1,700,000, of which about $500,000 was not covered by insurance. Three of the St. Louis insurance companies were, however, broken up.

PHILADELPHIA, 1850.

A conflagration by which an immense amount of property was destroyed took place in Philadelphia on the 9th of July, 1850. It began about four o'clock on the afternoon of that day, in a store at 78 North Delaware Avenue. The fire was beyond control when discovered, and soon spread, despite the most strenuous efforts to prevent it, to the storehouses adjoining. When the fire had reached the cellar of the building in which it had originated, two explosions occurred which rent the walls of the building and threw flakes of combustible matter in all directions, setting fire to many other buildings. Delaware Avenue and Water Street were covered with persons who exhibited little fear at these evidences of dangerous substances being stored in the building. Suddenly a third and most terrific explosion occurred, by which a number of men, women, and children were killed, and several buildings demolished. This disaster caused a panic among the firemen and spectators, and in the efforts of all to escape from danger many were trampled upon and injured. Some were thrown into the Delaware, and others jumped in to get away from the falling bricks and beams sent up from the burning building by the explosion. The number of persons who lost their lives by the explosion was about thirty; nine persons, who jumped into the river in a fright, were drowned, and about one hundred injured. The area over which the fire spread contained about four hundred buildings. Its locality was one of the most densely populated in the city, and a large number of the residents having been poor people, the suffering caused was immense. The loss was about one million dollars of property.

SAN FRANCISCO, 1851.

The city of San Francisco was retarded in its progress toward its present proud position by many causes, but by nothing more than fire. The most destructive of the many conflagrations which have occurred in that city began on the 3d of May, 1851, at eleven o'clock P. M., and was not overmastered until the 5th inst. The loss that was caused by it amounted to $3,500,000, and it destroyed 2500 buildings. The fire began in a paint-shop on the west side of Portsmouth Square, adjoining the American House. Although but a slight blaze when discovered, the building was within five minutes enwrapped with flames, and before the fire-engines could be got to work, the American House and the building on the other side of the paint shop were also burning. The buildings being all of wood and extremely combustible, the fire spread up Clay Street, back to Sacramento, and down Clay Street toward Kearney with fearful rapidity. Soon the fire department was compelled to give up every attempt to extinguish it, and to confine their work to making its advance less rapid.

Pursuing this plan, they checked the flames on the north side at Dupont Street. But in every other direction it took its own course, and was only arrested at the water's edge and the ruins of the houses that had been blown up. The shipping in the harbor was only protected by the breaking up of the wharves. Thousands of persons were made homeless, and for a long time after lived in tents. The Custom-house, seven hotels, the Post-office, the offices of the Steamship Company, and the banking house of Page, Bacon & Co., were destroyed. During the continuance of the fire a number of persons were burned, and others died from their exertions toward subduing it.

Another large fire devastated a great portion of San Francisco in June, 1851. It occurred on the 22d of that month, and 500 buildings were destroyed by it. The loss was estimated at $3,000,000. The result of these fires has been the rebuilding of the city in a thoroughly fire-proof manner, only second to that of Montreal, which learned wisdom through similar adversity.

AT PHILADELPHIA, 1865.

The most terrible conflagration of which Philadelphia was the theater—after that of July, 1850—occurred there on the morning of February 8, 1865. Like its predecessor, it brought death to many, and in the most horrible and painful manner. The fire originated among several thousand barrels of coal oil, that was stored upon an open lot on Washington Street, near Ninth.

The flames spread through the oil as if it had been gunpowder, and in a very short time 2000 barrels were ablaze, and sending a huge volume of flame and smoke upward. The residents of the vicinity, awakened by the noise of the bells and firemen, and affrighted by the glare and nearness of the fire, rushed in their night garments into the streets that were covered with snow and slush. The most prompt to leave their homes got off with their lives, but those near the spot where the fire commenced, and not prompt to escape, were met by a terrible scene. The blazing oil poured into Ninth Street and down to Federal, making the entire street a lake of fire that ignited the houses on both sides of the street for two blocks. The flames also passed up and down the cross streets, and destroyed a number of houses. The fiery torch was whirled back and forth along the street at the pleasure of the wind, and as it passed destroyed every thing in or near its course. People leaving their blazing homes, hoping to reach a place of safety, were roasted to death by it. Altogether, about twenty persons were roasted in the streets or houses. Firemen making vain endeavors to save the poor creatures from their horrible fate were fearfully burned. The loss of property amounted to about $500,000, and fifty buildings were destroyed. From Washington Street to Federal, on Ninth, every building was burned.

AT CHICAGO, 1857, '59, '66, '68.

On the morning of the 10th of October, 1857, a fire occurred in Chicago which, though notable from the amount of property destroyed by it, was made awful by the loss of human life which it caused. The fire broke out in a large double store in South Water Street, and spread east and west to the buildings adjoining, and across an alley in the rear to a block of new buildings. All these were completely destroyed. When the flames were threatening one of the buildings a number of persons ascended to its roof to there fight against them. Wholly occupied with their work, they did not notice that the wall of the burning building tottered, and when warned of their danger they could not escape ere it fell, crushing through the house on which they were, and carrying them into its cellar. Of the number fourteen were killed and more injured. The loss in property caused by the fire amounted to over $500,000.

A fire, the most disastrous after that of October, 1857, took place on September 15, 1859. It broke out in a stable, and, spreading in different directions, consumed the block bounded by Clinton, North Canal, West Lake, and Fulton Streets, on which the stable was situated. From this block the fire was communicated to Blatchford's lead works and to the hydraulic mills, whence it passed to another block of buildings, all of which were destroyed. The total loss was about $500,000.

Property to the amount of $500,000 was destroyed by fire on the 10th of August, 1866. The fire originated in a wholesale tobacco establishment on South Water Street, and passed to the adjoining buildings, occupied by wholesale grocery and drug firms. The first two buildings and contents were utterly, while the other was but partially, destroyed.

A fire, which destroyed several large business houses on Lake and South Water Streets, took place November 18, 1866. It originated in the tobacco warehouse of Banker & Co., and the loss caused by it was about $500,000.

The fire which occurred on the 28th of January, 1868, was the most destructive by which Chicago had ever been visited. It broke out in a large boot and shoe factory on Lake Street, and destroyed the entire block on which that building was situated. The sparks from those buildings set fire to others distant from them on the same street, and caused their destruction. In all the loss was about $3,000,000.

AT PORTLAND, 1866.

The terrible fire which laid in ruins more than half of the city of Portland, Maine, commenced at five o'clock in the afternoon of the 4th of July, 1866. Beginning in a cooper's shop at the foot of High Street, caused by a fire-cracker being thrown among some wood shavings, it swept through the city with frightful rapidity. With difficulty did the inhabitants of the houses in its path escape with their lives. Little effort was made to save household goods when this saving involved a possibility of death. Every thing in the track of the flames was destroyed, and so completely that, when they had been overcome, even the streets could hardly be traced. For a space of one mile and a half long by a quarter of a mile wide, there seemed a straggling forest of chimneys, with parts of their walls attached. The utmost endeavors of the firemen of the city, aided by those from other cities and towns, were of little avail until the plan of blowing up had been carried out. One-half of the city, and the one which included its business portion, was destroyed. Every bank and all the newspaper offices were burned; and it is somewhat singular to note that all the lawyers' offices in the city were swept away. The splendid city and county building on Congress Street was considered fire-proof and safe, and was filled with furniture from the neighboring houses, and then the flames, catching it, laid it in ruins. All the jewelry establishments, the wholesale dry goods houses, several churches, the telegraph offices, and the majority of other business places were destroyed. The Custom-house, though badly burned, was not destroyed. Most singularly, a building on Middle Street, occupied by a hardware firm, was left unscathed by the sea of flame which surged and devastated all around it.

Two thousand persons were rendered houseless, and were sheltered in churches and tents erected for them. In all, the loss was estimated at $10,000,000, which was but in small part covered by insurance.

VARIOUS DISASTROUS CONFLAGRATIONS.

Norfolk, Va., destroyed by fire and the cannon-balls of the British. Property to the amount of $1,500,000 destroyed. January 1, 1776.

City of New York, soon after passing into possession of the British; 500 buildings consumed. September 20, 21, 1776.

Theater at Richmond, Va. The governor of the State and a large number of the leading inhabitants perished. December 26, 1811.

Washington City. General Post-office and Patent Office, with over ten thousand valuable models, drawings, etc., destroyed. December 15, 1836.

Philadelphia; 52 buildings destroyed. Loss, $500,000. October 4, 1839.

Quebec, Canada; 1500 buildings and many lives destroyed. May 28, 1845.

Quebec, Canada; 1300 buildings destroyed. June 28, 1845.

City of New York; 300 buildings destroyed. Loss, $6,000,000. June 20, 1845.

St. John's, Newfoundland, nearly destroyed; 6000 people made homeless. June 12, 1846.

Quebec, Canada; Theater Royal; 47 persons burned to death. June 14, 1846.

Nantucket; 300 buildings and other property destroyed. Value, $800,000. July 13, 1846.

At Albany; 600 buildings, steamboats, piers, etc., destroyed. Loss, $3,000,000. August 17, 1848.

Brooklyn; 300 buildings destroyed. September 9, 1848.

At St. Louis; 15 blocks of houses and 23 steamboats. Loss estimated at $3,000,000. May 17, 1849.

Frederickton, New Brunswick; about 300 buildings destroyed. November 11, 1850.

Nevada, Cal.; 200 buildings destroyed. Loss, $1,300,000. March 12, 1851.

At Stockton, Cal.; loss, $1,500,000. May 14, 1851.

Concord, N. H.; greater part of the business portion of the town destroyed. August 24, 1850.

Congressional library at Washington; 35,000 volumes, with works of art, destroyed. December 24, 1851.

At Montreal, Canada; 1000 houses destroyed. Loss, $5,000,000. July 8, 1852.

Harper Brothers' establishment, New York. Loss over $1,000,000. December 10, 1853.

Metropolitan Hall and Lafarge House, New York, and Custom House, Portland, Maine. January 8, 1854.

At Jersey City; 30 factories and houses destroyed. July 30, 1854.

More than 100 houses and factories in Troy, N. Y.; and on the same day a large part of Milwaukee, Wis., destroyed. August 25, 1854.

At Syracuse, N. Y.; about 100 buildings destroyed. Loss, $1,000,000. November 8, 1856.

New York Crystal Palace destroyed. October 5, 1858.

City of Charleston, S. C., almost destroyed. February 17, 1856.

Santiago, Chili; Church of the Compara destroyed, with 2,000 worshipers, mostly women. Conflagration caused by fire communicated by candles, used in illumination, to paper decorations about the walls. December 8, 1863.

FOREST FIRES OF WISCONSIN AND MICHIGAN, 1871.

At almost the same moment when the great Chicago fire was breaking out, similar disasters, which proved even more fatal to human life, was setting in in northern Wisconsin. The worst of its horrors centered in the unfortunate village of Peshtigo, a lumbering settlement on Green Bay. The scene which occurred there is thus sketched by a Wisconsin journal:

"Sunday evening, after church, for about half an hour a death-like stillness hung over the doomed town. The smoke from the fires in the region around was so thick as to be stifling, and hung like a funeral pall over every thing, and all was enveloped in Egyptian darkness. Soon light puffs of air were felt; the horizon at the south-east, south, and south-west began to be faintly illuminated; a perceptible trembling of the earth was felt, and a distant roar broke the awful silence. People began to fear that some awful calamity was impending, but as yet no one even dreamed of the danger.

"The illumination soon became intensified into a lurid glare; the roar deepened into a howl, as if all the demons of the infernal pit had been let loose, when the advance gusts of wind from the main body of the tornado struck. Chimneys were blown down, houses were unroofed, and, amid the confusion, terror, and terrible apprehensions of the moment, the fiery element, in tremendous inrolling billows and masses of sheeted flame, enveloped the devoted village. The frenzy of despair seized on all hearts; strong men bowed like reeds before the fiery blast; women and children, like frightened specters flitting through the awful gloom, were swept away like autumn leaves. Crowds rushed for the bridge; but the bridge, like all else, was receiving its baptism of fire. Hundreds crowded into the river; cattle plunged in with them, and being huddled together in the general confusion of the moment, many who had taken to the water to avoid the flames were drowned. A great many were on the blazing bridge when it fell. The debris from the burning town was hurled over and on the heads of those who were in the water, killing many and maiming others, so that they gave up in despair and sank to a watery grave."

The following account, by an intelligent correspondent who traveled over the burnt district after the fires, is the fullest and most circumstantial that has been furnished, and we give it entire:

PESHTIGO, WISCONSIN, *November* 6, 1871.

Some ten days since, I started out for the purpose of writing up the scenes and incidents connected with the recent destruction of this section, and although so much time has elapsed, I now, for the first time, am enabled to send your readers any thing. This was not in consequence of there not being plenty to write about, but because I had previously concluded not to write a line until after personally visiting the scene of devastation, and forming my own conclusions from actual observation.

At Chicago I found the sub-committee from Cincinnati appointed to visit this section and report the condition of things generally; and as we were all bound for one point, we concluded to join forces, and, as much as possible, travel together. A night's travel brought us to Milwaukee, where the committeemen had a very interesting interview with the mayor of that city, Harrison Luddington, Esq., one of the wealthiest and most prominent business men of the North-west, who furnished very much information of importance. From Milwaukee we passed on to Green Bay, a fine city of some five thousand inhabitants, located at the head of Green Bay, a body of water some one hundred and thirty miles long and from fifteen to forty miles wide. At Green Bay your committee, by special request, met Governor Fairchild, Hon. Mr. Sawyer, member of Congress from this district, General Bailey, and other prominent persons. The governor could not find words to express, in behalf of his people, the gratitude they all felt for the solid evidences of sympathy shown for the sufferers, and assured your committee that the gifts of Cincinnati were fully as large as from any other section. The interview with the governor ended by your committee concluding to take the several car-loads of goods they had with them right on through to Peshtigo, and know for themselves that the sufferers were supplied as rapidly as possible, and not have the much-needed supplies remain in the various warehouses of different cities until all the forms of red tape could be gone through with; for if the goods were needed at all, it was to relieve the more pressing demands of the moment. Taking the good steamer Geo. L. Dunlap (I believe that is the way bills of lading read), after a very pleasant ride of sixty miles on the bay, we reached Menominee, the point from which all persons start out to visit the burnt region. Crossing over the Menominee River, we reach Marinette and Menekaune, or, rather, what is left of the latter place, as the fire almost blotted it out of existence. The fire came sweeping through the forests toward these towns, threatening destruction to every thing in its path. At this point Mr. A. C. Brown, the resident partner of one of the large mills here, ordered out all his men and teams to a point where a street had been cut through the timber a short time previously. The teams hauled water, which the men dashed on the ground and trees; thus for fourteen hours successfully keeping back the flames from Marinette, until all danger was over. While the men were working here the fire quickly passed to the left, and in a few minutes almost every house in Menekaune was in flames. These included two large mills, a fine Catholic and Methodist Churches, a school-house, and, in fact, almost every house in the town. When the flames reached the river, not finding any thing else to devour, with one bound the fire jumped over the water, which is fully as wide as the Ohio at Cincinnati, and consumed a very fine mill. The wind now abated, to which fact alone can be attributed the saving of Menominee.

SCENES IN THE HOSPITAL.

The main hospitals for the wounded are located are Marinette, and through the kindness of Dr. Wright, the surgeon in charge, I visited the premises, and saw the many sad sights to be seen. The buildings are made of rough boards, very much similar in appearance to the barracks of the army. The interior arrangements were made as comfortable as could be expected under the circumstances. The first patient on the right as you enter is an American, who has with him his wife, babe, and five other children. Three of the latter are half-breeds, by a former wife, a squaw of the Stockbridge tribe, whose reservation is located in the burnt district. The story of this man is the same in substance as that of a score of others. The fire ap proached them so unexpectedly that they had to run for their lives without saving any thing but the clothes they had on. They reached a small pool of water, where they sat for many hours, or until the fury of the fire had passed, when, terribly burned as they were, they managed to reach help, and were brought to town and properly cared for. Strange as it may seem, that while the half-breed children of this family were the worst burned, they exhibited the stoical indifference to pain of their people, while the other children, all white, moaned loud enough to be heard all over the room. The next patient—an old German, seventy-six years of age—was from the lower bush country. He lost his wife, daughter, son, and eight grandchildren. The old man bore up with wonderful fortitude under all his afflictions, and would tell you, in his own quiet way, all about the fire, until he came to where his aged partner lost her life, when the tears would roll down his furrowed cheeks, and, with clasped hands, he would say, "Mine Got! is my poor frau dead?" We pass on to another bed, where an aged lady is writhing in the greatest pain, undoubtedly in a dying condition. She is the only one left of a family of ten, and she, too, must go, blotting out from existence one large family which, so short time ago, had cause to feel so much promise for the future. The next three beds are occupied by the Hoyt family, or, at least, what is left of it, some half a dozen of them having perished. Those here are all badly burned, one or two past recovery. On the next bed is one of the half-breed boys before referred to. He is burned on the abdomen until his bowels almost protrude, yet he never complains, and answers your questions as indifferently as if he was a disinterested spectator of the scene. The next is a double bed, occupied by two full grown men, former members of a Wisconsin regiment. One of them, Lovett Reed, started to run for a clearing, but finding he could not reach it, took out his pocket-knife and deliberately attempted to commit suicide by stabbing himself to the heart. After inflicting several severe, though not fatal, wounds, he accidentally dropped his weapon, which, owing to the darkness, he could not recover, and his design was frustrated. The fire passed over, he was only slightly burned, and next day was brought into the hospital, where he is slowly recovering. The next three beds are occupied by a German family, or, at least, what is left of it, the mother and one child having died since they reached the hospital, and one more little fellow will go before many hours. These children are quite bright, polite, and intelligent, plainly showing that when their mother passed over into the dark valley they lost their best earthly friend. But why particularize the different individual cases where there are so many? There are now nearly three hundred of the burned in Marinette and Menominee. Most of them, however, are quartered in private houses. The people of these towns were very prompt in offering relief, opening wide their doors to all who came for quarters or assistance. The proprietor of the leading hotel, the Dunlap House, at once vacated all his rooms, and filled his hotel with the sick and wounded, and I had the not pleasant lot of sleeping in a bed which the night before was occupied by one of the wounded, and which was still covered with blood. As these were the best quarters to be had, I was even glad to get in here. This morning, a fine team, the property of Mr. Brown, was at the door ready to take us down to Peshtigo, a town which, through its misfortunes, now has a national notoriety. A short distance out we reach the inner limit of the fire district, and from there to this place every thing is gone; nothing left, not even the soil, which was a sort of peat. The tornado took the great forests of gigantic pines and leveled them to the ground, as if they had only been blades of grass. In their fall the ground around their roots was torn up, presenting on every hand great barriers of earth, forcibly reminding an old soldier of earthworks in the army. Along the road where, before the fire, you could only see half a rod to the right or left, you can now see for miles in either direction. The trees, uprooted and twisted by the terrible wind, in falling have so interlocked that it would cost much more to clear the charred trunks away and level the roots than the land is worth, which fact adds to the general gloom. Passing ahead, on every side witnessing as sad sights as the human mind could picture, we finally reached Peshtigo, or, at least, where it once stood. The town was located on both banks of a river, from which it took its name; the stream being about one-half as wide as the Ohio. As you enter, on the left, a few pieces of charcoal, a handful of ashes, and a few bricks show all that remains of what was once a very fine church; three rods away marks the spot where Ogden, one of the millionaires of Chicago, and the president of the rich Peshtigo Lumber Company, had his country palace, where he spent his summers.

The street where we now pass along was lined with the best houses of the town. Here stood the fire-engine house, a small frame structure just large enough to hold a steam fire engine. The cupola was of open wood-work, but so intense was the heat that the bell, weighing several hundred pounds, was melted up. A little further along we are shown where a train of platform cars loaded with green lumber stood at the time of the fire, all of which was destroyed excepting the iron wheels, which are partly melted. The force of the tornado was so great that one car load of the lumber was carried more than one hundred feet, where it burned. Here to the right was the company store-house, which was an immense building. In the debris we find spoons by the dozen, all melted together, stove-pipes melted into balls not larger than your fist, crockery, china, glass and hardware all run together, showing the great intensity of the heat. Some hundreds of feet to the right and rear of the last building, stands the only house left of the once flourishing town. The house had a gable end fronting the river, with an ell on the upper side, and was not finished. The fire struck the ell, which was destroyed in almost the time it takes me to tell of it, but such was the velocity of the wind that after the wing was burned off the fire was actually blown off, passing into the timber a few feet away, and the main house was saved. The wooden-ware factory is also on this side of the river, and was the largest of the kind in the world. It was some five hundred feet long, by half as great a width, and five stories high. The section of the house in which the engine, boilers, and machinery were located, was of heavy stones, with stone and grouted floors, and was constructed with the idea that it was positively fire-proof. The little remaining of it is conclusive proof that it went up in smoke, like a tinder-box. Among the ruins can be found thousands of dozens of pail and tub hoops, melted together like so much lead.

A few rods down the river from this building were a number of boards in the river, forming a platform some twelve feet square, upon which twenty-eight persons got for safety. After the fire was over, they discovered that their platform was buoyed up by seventeen barrels of benzine, which, fortunately, did not burst and ignite, or the destruction of life would have been frightful, as only a few hundred feet below, on the same side of the river, were five hundred people in the water, and the benzine on fire would have floated right down among them, and it is my judgment that every one of them would have been destroyed. The company had erected a fine bridge across the river, which was destroyed, fortunately after most of the people had crossed over safely. There is a temporary structure in its place, over which we pass, and stop at the barracks, where we find Mr. Burns, the company's agent, who extended every favor in his power. Being a man of fine culture, his description of the fire was very interesting. I suppose that he took more trouble to describe things minutely to me, as I was the first correspondent from a distance who had personally visited the town; the other vivid descriptions in other papers having been written by writers of great imagination, while snugly stowed away in hotels at either Chicago, Milwaukee, or Green Bay. In this number, of course, are not be included the writers for the two or three weekly papers published in this section of the State. Mr. Burns, as soon as the fire commenced, put on the hose, and had the water thrown all around the factories, stores, and boarding-houses belonging to the company. This was soon abandoned, as the brass couplings of the hose were actually melting with the intense heat. Then it was the order was given for every man to look out for himself, and Burns ran down to the river's edge, and got into the water. Just before doing so he met a friend who was hatless, and almost at the same moment Burns' dog came up with a hat in his mouth, which was given to the needy one. The strange part of this incident is the fact that the dog, a water spaniel, had been locked up in the house, and how he escaped, or what induced him at this particular moment to take a hat with him, none could tell.

Burns said the fire came creeping slowly up the main street on the side of the town first reached by fire, went up the front door of the Congregational Church, hesitated a moment at the door knob, then quickly reached the spire, and in three minutes every house in town was on fire, and in one hour all that remained of the town was the unfinished house before alluded to. The feelings of the hundreds of men, women, and children during the seven fearful hours they remained in the water, watching the terrific progress of the flames, almost perishing from the heat and smoke, can better be imagined than described. When the fury of the tempest had passed by, and the heat moderated enough to allow a human being to live, it was found that almost all of those in the water were so benumbed as to be powerless, and it took the few who had nerve enough left a considerable length of time to assist the others to land. Their situation was little better now than while they were in the water, for they were without any food or clothing, with the roads in every direction so blockaded with fallen timber that it was impossible for any of those who were able, to go out for help. Here they remained all that night and the next day; yet still they did not lose confidence. They felt that if any had been spared they would surely come to their assistance,—and their hopes were not groundless, for toward evening one of the ladies asserted that she could hear the sound of axes, and although none others could hear the welcome noise, still the woman with her keen sense would not give up. After awhile others heard the noise, and before an hour had elapsed a few of the more daring of the noble men of Menominee and Marinette had cut their way through the terrible six miles of devastation, carrying with them a few provisions and some clothing, and before the sun went down wagons of stores arrived with sufficient to make all comfortable. The burned were taken back to the last two towns in the empty wagons, and were as well cared for as the sudden emergency would permit. The next day the balance of the population went to the different towns on the bay, where they were kindly attended to. To-morrow I go down to the Sugar Bush country, and you may then expect another letter. W. L.

NEWBERRY'S FARM, *November* 7, 1871.

My letter yesterday described the situation at Peshtigo, and to-day I write you from the Lower Sugar Bush country, the most desolate part of the burnt region.

After a hearty lunch at Peshtigo we again started on our tour of observation, our objective point being what is known as the Lower Sugar Bush, where the loss of life was far greater than in any other place. A few hundred yards out from the town, on the right hand side of the road, is the village graveyard, where we had the privilege of seeing an

INDIAN BURIAL.

There were quite a number of the red faces present, all of whom joined in the solemn orgies. The deceased was a leading man of the Stockbridge tribe, and had passed over to the beautiful hunting-grounds of his forefathers after a lingering illness. The body was placed in a plain box coffin, which also contained all the little articles belonging to the deceased during lifetime, such as the pipe, knife, clothes, etc. The coffin was carried by three braves and a like number of squaws, who, with heads uncovered, were constantly repeating short Catholic prayers, as all aborigines of the Stockbridge tribe belong to that church. After passing around the grave several times, the coffin was finally lowered, the grave filled up, and the spectators departed, the squaws to the left and the men in the opposite direction.

It is impossible for the most graphic writer to attempt to picture the utter desolation of the scene before us. It was our good fortune to have in company with us as our guide Mr. W. P. Newberry, one of the greatest sufferers by the fire, who, being thoroughly acquainted with every foot of the ground over which we traveled, could point out to us every object of interest, of which there are any number.

SCHWARTZ, THE HERMIT.

About the first farm out from Peshtigo is owned by a one-eyed German, who is known the country round as Schwartz, the Hermit. Some twenty years since, when this region was an unbroken wilderness, occupied almost exclusively by Indians, this man Schwartz came here, built a cabin, and ever since has lived entirely alone, apparently caring very little for the outside world, or for what other people thought of him. At that time, with the exception of the blind eye, Schwartz was a splendid-looking man, and blessed with a very superior education. The story of the cause of his abandoning the world and adopting the life of a recluse is the same as has been told thousands of times before. He fell in love with a handsome girl—the story would be spoiled if she was not beautiful—was engaged to be married, when she, like too many others of her sex, proved false, and married another fellow, a major in the Prussian army. This was too much for our hero, who forthwith fled to America, and found consolation for his blighted affections in the solitude of these pine forests. He dug, or, rather, burrowed, in the ground, where he lived with his chickens, geese, cats, hogs, and dogs, presenting as happy a family as can be found in any managerie in the country. Schwartz has been very thrifty and industrious since he came here, and was considered very wealthy, many even asserting that he had gold stored away in every corner of his filthy abode. When the fire came, Schwartz and his family ran down to Trout Brook, into which they plunged, and remained until the fire had spent its fury. The hermit has already commenced building another hut, where he will doubtless spend the balance of his days, little heeding what takes place elsewhere.

DOWN IN THE WELL.

About half a mile beyond Schwartz, on the right, and about two hundred yards from the road, are the remains of a dwelling which was occupied by a family named Hill. The family were all in the house at evening prayers, when they were suddenly startled by a loud noise, much resembling continuous thunder. On going to the door they found themselves entirely surrounded by fire, and, as the only means of escape, the whole of them, eight in number, went down into the well. Here they remained in safety until the wooden house covering the well caught fire, fell in, and burned the entire party to death. Another case exactly similar to the last was that of the Davis family in Peshtigo, who were all smothered to death in their well, into which they had descended in the vain hope of saving their lives. I have heard of quite a number of such cases, but as the facts were not definitely given, I make no mention of them.

THE LAMP FAMILY.

A short distance on, we come to a low stone wall, the foundation of a house, the former residence of a family named Lawrence, all of whom perished. Immediately in front of this place was the iron-work of a wagon, which once belonged to Chas. Lamp. Lamp lived about a mile beyond, and when he found the fire approaching his house so rapidly, he hitched up his team, and, with his wife and five children, drove with all speed toward Peshtigo. In a very few minutes after starting he heard screams in the wagon, and looking back, found that the clothes of his wife and children were all ablaze; it was certain death to stop, and he therefore urged his horses to still greater speed; but before moving many rods one of the horses fell, and finding that he could not get him up, and seeing that all of his family were dead, Lamp started to save his life, which he did after being most horribly burned. He is now in the hospital at Green Bay, and is slowly recovering. When at the latter place, I saw him, and had a full narrative of the bloody tragedy from himself. What little was found of the charred remains of the wife and five children were buried in a field not far off. Of the wagon not a speck was to be seen, excepting the half-melted iron-work.

We next come to the Lawrence farm, one of the best on the whole route, showing a very high state of cultivation, on which every thing had been swept away. Lawrence, with his wife and four children, ran to the center of an immense clearing, several hundred yards from any house or timber, with the idea that they would be entirely safe there. The fire came, and rushed along on every side of them, yet they remained unharmed; at this moment one of the great balloons dropped in their midst, and in an instant they were burned up, hardly any thing being left of them.

FIRE BALLOONS.

Your readers may wonder what I mean by fire balloons, and I confess that I hardly know myself, and only use the term because it was so frequently used by others in conversation with me. All of the survivors with whom I conversed said that the whole sky seemed filled with dark, round masses of smoke, about the size of a large balloon, which traveled with fearful rapidity. These balloons would fall to the ground, burst, and send forth a most brilliant blaze of fire, which would instantly consume every thing in the neighborhood. An eye-witness, who was in a pool of water not far off, told us about the balloon falling right down on the Lawrence family, and burning them up.

Passing on a mile or more, we reach the edge of a very small stream, on the bank of which stood the stately residence of Nathaniel May, one of the best farmers of Northern Wisconsin, a man held in the highest estimation by all. At the time of the fire a man named William Aldous, with his wife and three children, residents of Western New York, were visiting at May's. The first intimation that any of them had of the danger was the roaring of the flames in the woods, not more than five hundred feet away. They all rushed out, but before they could reach the water, fifty feet off, the flames struck them, and they all instantly perished. Mr. Newberry, of our party, with his family, were in the water, not more than one hundred feet from May's, and all they heard was Mrs. May crying out to her daughter: "Lola, come this way; come with mother." A couple of days afterward the burial party from Marinette visited the May farm, and found the remains of them all close together, with the exception of the little girl, who was some distance off, showing that in the darkness she had accidentally been separated. I will have more to say about the brook near May's house, but will defer until I visit the Newberry farms, which are about one mile further on.

Henry Newberry, a citizen of Connecticut, came to Wisconsin some fifteen years ago, with his family, consisting of a wife and six children. The whole of them having the thrift and industry for which the Yankees are so famous, they were very prosperous, and soon acquired nearly a thousand acres of land, a considerable portion of which they cleared, and had under cultivation. As the children grew up, they married, and had allotted to them, for their own use, their portions of the farm. In addition to this, they had joined forces and built a very good mill, where all of them were employed. The only son saved, William P. Newberry, was one of our party, and from his own lips I had the story of the great disaster. This gentleman was formerly a teacher, for which position, by education and habits, he is eminently fitted. Mr. Newberry being a man of unusual nerve and sound judgment, I concluded to give his statement of the fire as most reliable.

The fire had been burning down in the swamps, some miles to the west, for two or three weeks. But little was thought of it, as it traveled only a few feet in a day, and all felt confident that whenever desirable it could be "fought out" in a few hours.

On Sunday night, about 9 o'clock (the same day and hour the Chicago fire commenced), they heard a great roaring, and, on going out, Mr. Newberry found the smoke so suffocating as to be almost unbearable. He started over to his brother's house, a few rods off, to see what must be done, but before he had gone far, was forced to return to his house. The noise was now of the most appalling character, like one long peal of thunder, or rapid discharge of heavy parks of artillery. The rear door was open, and it was only by the greatest exertion that it was closed, which was no sooner done than the flames blew through the cracks underneath, clear across the room. Mr. Newberry now knew that the only safety was in flight, so, taking their only child in his arms, and accompanied by his wife and her sister, they all fled, but where, they knew not. At last, coming to the creek known as Little Trout, they found a pool of water some six inches deep, about twelve feet wide and as many long; and being totally exhausted, here they sat down, with their backs toward the fire. In an almost incredible short space of time the fire was on all sides of them, the flames from May's barn, and a heavy log bridge which spanned the creek, in which they were sitting, almost reaching them. Here they were expecting every moment to perish either by being burned to death, or suffocated. Once in a while they would feel a pleasant breeze from the bay, when they would inflate their lungs to their fullest capacity, and then breathe as little as possible while the hot air was passing. They constantly threw water over themselves to keep their clothing from burning, which proved effectual. Strange as it may seem, the babe, which was resting in its father's arms in the water, slept the entire time, over six hours, that they were there. When the fire had passed, the party crawled up on the side of the creek, and, almost chilled to death, awaited the approach of daylight. A little later they heard a man calling for help, who, on coming to them, proved to be Charles Lamp, their neighbor, mention of whose family burning to death in the wagon has already been made. Lamp was blind and powerless, but with help reached the creek bank. As soon as it was light enough, Mr. Newberry started out to see what had become of his father, brothers, and sisters. A short distance off the bank of the creek were the bodies of two men, and a few feet further on the carcasses of several hogs and cows. Finding that he was too blind to go on, he cut off some meat from one of the cows, and took it back to his family, when they cooked and ate it.

Some time during the day a wagon came out and took the family down to Peshtigo, where they received attentions from the Marinette people. The same party that helped this gentleman went to look after the other branches of the family. One brother they found near a barn wall, a hundred yards away, curled up around a stake, dead. Two hundred yards off, to the left, in the creek, under a bridge, they found Walter Newberry, his wife, and three children, and some distance on, alongside the road, they found several other members of the family. The father was also lost, but his remains thus far have not been found, and it is not improbable that they were entirely consumed. Thus, out of a family of seventeen persons, twelve perished. The mother was on a visit to her daughter at Menominee, or she also would have been one of the number lost. Near the ruins of Walter Newberry's house could be seen the iron-work of a wagon, remnants of a trunk, with daguerreotype frames, buttons, beads, parts of breast-pins, etc., showing conclusively that when the danger was discerned the family had loaded their trunks into their wagon and started off, but had only proceeded a few feet when they were forced to abandon the wagon, and flee down the road to the spot where their bodies were found.

As we went around with Mr. Newberry, and he pointed out to us the various places on the farm—spots which now have a holy remembrance to him—we could not but feel how sad must be his thoughts. All the bodies of his family are buried on the farm, six in one place, and ten in another, four of the latter belonging to another family. In this place I can not forbear mentioning a singular fact which our party noticed while standing and looking at the little pool of water where the Newberry family were saved. All over it were small dead trout floating, which had been boiled to death by the action of the heat on the water. We secured some of these boiled fish for the purpose of showing them to our citizens.

THE CHURCH FAMILY.

Opposite where the Newberry house stood could be seen the *debris* marking the spot where had stood the residence of John Church, the village blacksmith, a man respected by all. His household consisted of himself, wife, and son, the latter a young man just of age. When the hurricane of fire came, the old man and wife appeared to despair, but the son started on the race for life to save himself. He had only ran about ten rods, when, finding escape impossible, he deliberately took out his knife and cut his throat from ear to ear, dying, as was supposed, almost instantly. The only living tree or plant to be seen in all this region are two or three strawberry plants, on Mr. Newberry's farm, which, on account of the direction of the wind, or from some other cause, were not burned. Mr. Newberry, in describing the fire, said that it seemed to him that the elements were on fire with fervent heat. The flames were rolling along hundreds of feet high above the tops of the highest trees, and seemed to travel with lightning speed. I am not surprised at any opinion, however exaggerated, but for my own part concluded that there was not any outside influence at work. The fire, which had been burning for weeks in the marshes, suddenly fanned into power by the force of the tornado, reached the heavy pine timber, which, as is well known, contains a large percentage of resinous matter. and as it was carried along, gained such a momentum that it doubtless did appear that the very heavens were being consumed, causing many, even intelligent persons, to conclude that the day of judgment, the hour of complete, total destruction was at hand.

To the west of the Newberry settlement were many very fine farms, and of all the persons who lived in that direction, for about five miles, hardly one was saved. It seemed to matter little whether they lived near the timber or in the center of large clearings, their doom was the same.

In the westerly and southerly direction, or the point from which the fire started, every thing is burned up for some twelve miles in length, and as far in breadth.

A PATH THROUGH THE FIRE.

In returning, about a mile to the north we came to Adnah Newton's farm, where sixteen persons were burned to death. As soon as Newton saw the fire he started out to see what was best to be done. Running down to the road, he found himself headed off by the flames. Turning back, he saw his family and workmen in the yard coming toward him, but when they noticed him turn back they also changed their course; in an instant more they were all on fire, and must have perished in a moment. Newton happened to notice on his right what proved to be a path through the flames, about fifty yards wide, for which he rushed, and continued for three-fourths of a mile, when he came to a house still occupied by several persons. They all invited him to come into the house, but he declined, saying he would rather trust to being saved in a small pool of water close by. In another instant the house was on fire, and before the inmates could get to him they were all burned to death, while Newton escaped pretty well singed. I had a long conversation with Newton, and he declared that he had no hankering after another such race. The second day after the fire thirty-three remains were found on these three farms.

Not far from where Newton saved himself was a field, into which two bears and several deer had fled for safety; but they exhibited very little of the instinct of self-preservation, as they all smothered to death together, the bears not even taking time to take a lunch of deer meat before their departure.

The Doyle family consisted of the husband and father, Patrick, the wife, and seven children. The fire came, and not one single trace of any of them could be found, excepting a Catholic medal, some nails out of a pair of shoes, and some hooks and eyes. Of their bodies not one single thing was left, not even the ashes of their bones. Next to the Doyles lived the Pratt family, all of whom perished, excepting a small boy, who saved himself by jumping into the well. When the burial party arrived, they found the large Newfoundland dog watching by the body of his mistress, and it was only by force that they could drive him away long enough to bury the corpse. The Hill family, consisting of ten persons, lived near by. They had working for them a half-grown Indian boy, who was ordered down to hitch up the team. The barn getting on fire, the master ordered him to return. Not coming as fast as Hill desired, the order was repeated in a more peremptory manner, when the Indian looked up, and said: "It's every body for himself now," and off he started with the speed of a deer. Rushing through the fire, he reached a clearing half a mile away, and was saved, while the entire Hill family perished.

THE ONLY HOUSE LEFT.

In the entire Upper Bush country there is only one house left, the home of "old man" Place. Many years ago this man settled here, soon afterward marrying a squaw, by whom he has had many children. He has always engaged in trading with the Indians, who have had his house as their headquarters. When the fire came about twenty Indians covered his house with their blankets, which they kept wet down, thus saving the house. One great big fellow stood at the pump for nine hours, showing an endurance possessed by very few white men. Strange as it may seem, that while there are about as many Indians as whites in this section, at least one thousand of the latter perished and not a single Indian. This may seem strange, but was vouched for by the very best persons here. Whether the Indians could smell the fire sooner than their more refined white brethren and escaped in time, I know not; but I do know that they were all saved. And the only ones I heard of being injured were the half-breed children I spoke of in my last letter. To-morrow I travel in the further Bush region.

W. L.

SPEARS' PLACE, WISCONSIN, *November* 9, 1871.

Yesterday, when I wrote from Newberry's Farm, the weather was as pleasant as could be desired, and to-day a cold norwester makes a heavy overcoat very acceptable. As many of your readers may not understand why this is called the Sugar Bush country, it may not be out of place to say that there are many Swedes and Norwegians residing in this section, who give the name "Sugar Bush" on account of the large forests of maples to be found here, while in every other direction are only pines and cedars. At Peshtigo center three roads; the left hand one leads to the Lower Sugar Bush, the center one to the Middle, and the third to the Upper Sugar Bush, and it is from the latter that I now write.

This farm was owned by a Mr. Louis E. Spear, an excellent citizen, who, with his wife and two children, perished while attempting to escape from the fearful blast. They only reached a point a few hundred yards from their house, when they fell to rise no more, while two Indians, who were at the house when the fire commenced, saved themselves by getting into a small creek, which is to be seen a short distance off on the opposite side. They had their woolen blankets, which they threw over their heads and kept wetted down. That this would preserve them seems very strange, as the fire in the timber was not more than twenty feet off from where they sat, and the intensity of the heat was so great that a stove in a house not more than three rods away was melted.

The Penegree farm was the next one we visited, where the destruction is fully as great as in every other quarter—every thing is gone, one total wreck—not a house, barn, fence, or tree, nay, not even the soil itself being left. The Upper Sugar Bush was not so thickly populated as the Lower, but the farms were fully as well cultivated, and as much thrift shown as elsewhere, but now all the people are gone, the scene one picture of desolation, not a shrub, not even a blade of grass growing. We now come to a farm that was occupied by Philip Weinhardt, wife, and five children, a real good, solid, substantial German family. The first warning any of them had, was the low, rumbling noise heretofore described. The wife went to the door, found fire on every side of them, and believing the day of judgment was at hand, without an effort to save themselves, they all perished. This idea of final dissolution was entertained, not by the ignorant only, as the most intelligent thought that the noise they heard was the echo of Gabriel's trumpet. Mr. Beebe, the Peshtigo Company's Agent, as soon as he saw the fire, declared that the last hour had come, and, although repeatedly requested to save himself, refused to do so, and perished without an effort to get away. The last seen of him, he was in his front door, with hands clasped, exclaiming: "Great God, Thy will be done; to Thee I intrust my soul." In the center of a large sandy field, hundreds of yards from any timber or house, stood a stump, which was entirely destroyed, down even into the roots, leaving the ground like just so much honey-comb. A few rods off was the carcass of a cow, with the bell which had been around her neck lying near by, in a half-melted condition. All of your readers have undoubtedly visited houses which have been totally destroyed, and noticed the stoves and other articles of iron in the cellars, all of which were in good condition, excepting they were, perhaps, warped or discolored, but I doubt whether they ever saw such things melted—a sight to be seen here, wherever the *debris* of a house is to be found, the iron of the stoves, and even the wrought-iron pipe, being melted up. In one cellar, I think that of a house formerly occupied by the Carrough family, I found three smoothing-irons melted together, so as to all lift out and adhere together; this was one of the finest specimens to be found anywhere.

DUTCH PLUCK.

We next come to a farm, the property of a real honest-looking German, who had the good fortune to save all of his family, and his team, but every thing else was gone. Leaving his wife and family to live on the roasted potatoes to be found in the cellar, after two days' extraordinary exertions, he made his way down to Menominee, where he purchased a saw, hatchet, nails, and some lumber, and made his way back home, where he arrived in one day, the road having been partially cleared by the workmen of the Peshtigo Company. He at once made a cabin about the size of a common pig-pen, where that night the good *frau* gave birth to another son. This did not deter Hans from traveling on in the even tenor of his way, for he has already a good comfortable house nearly built, and with the clothing and provisions furnished by the committee, he says he can keep his head afloat until next harvest. The innocent little Teuton which last made his entry into the world, has a fiery red head, which might be attributed to the action of the heat, were it not that both the father and mother have heads as red as little Myers' face.

A LONELY FUNERAL.

Passing around the road, we come to a country cemetery, where we see a half-grown boy busily engaged in digging some graves. Going up to him, we enter into conversation, and find that he is the only survivor of a family of ten, all the rest having perished in the fire, the boy having saved himself by getting down a deep well, and covering his head with a blanket which he kept wet. The Marinette burial party had buried this family in rude boxes, on the spot where the bodies were found, but this son, with a devotion rarely equaled, disinterred the bodies, and put them into good plain coffins, which he made himself, and then carried them, one at a time, on his shoulder to the cemetery, a distance of nearly one mile. When the young fellow mentioned the names of his family his eyes would fill with tears, and he would say, "What am I to do in the world all alone?"

In this Bush lived a great many French families, all of whom were in comfortable circumstances, and hardly one of them escaped from the fury of the blast. Just beyond the cemetery was a stone wall, at least one full mile from the nearest timber in the direction from which the fire came, yet so intense was the heat that the stones cracked into minute pieces, and in many places the sandstones actually melted, leaving a glazed surface, something like pottery ware. Near here the road is quite sandy, and the surface melted down, leaving a crust on the face of a glassy nature. Wherever the sand was blown against the trees, the wood presented a smooth appearance, just as if it had been covered with melted glass. As we ride along we are greeted with the sight of a fine buck which crossed the road only a short distance ahead of us, and when about five rods from the road quietly stopped, and stood eyeing us as we passed by. I did not wish the lonesome fellow any harm, but I must confess that I said to myself that I would willingly pay for the champagne if Joseph Glenn, the partner of the "truly good man," could have been with us with his pups and gun. Perhaps the deer would then have been in as little danger as he was from us.

Leaving the "hard wood" country, we enter where only a short time ago were vast forests of huge pines, fully as large as any I have ever seen excepting in Oregon. The trees are now mostly uprooted, and leveled with the ground, presenting as complete an *abattis* as could be desired by the most skillful military commander. I could go on and give any number of sights to be seen in this desolated country, but as they are only repetitions of what has already been written, therefore content myself by saying that after passing through many miles of barren territory, where all was once prosperous, we return to Menominee, ready to visit the Peninsula and Michigan, where the fires were fully as severe as in this section.

WHAT SUPPLIES ARE NEEDED.

I know not of any better place to speak of the supply question than the present. When the first cry for assistance went forth the people all over the land, in their excitement, sent here whatever came first. This fact is noticeable in any of the general supply rooms, such as the one at Green Bay. When we visited them, we found some twenty of the first ladies of the town, headed by Mrs. Colonel Chas. D. Robinson, their Chairman, busily engaged assorting the clothing; and such an assortment. Did the world ever see the like? There was Horace Greeley's famous hat, without crown or rim, several cartloads of odd, worn-out shoes, an unlimited quantity of antique, used-up summer clothing, just the thing for people where the thermometer often falls to fifteen and twenty degrees below zero. One of the beautiful ladies engaged in matching the odd shoes, said that "it reminded her of playing 'Old Maid' with one of the cards gone." I wondered at the time whether the card she referred to was the wedding card.

Of such useless stuff enough has already been sent to start all the "Cheap Johns" in business to be found throughout the country. And whenever second-hand clothing is sent, it is advisable to have it washed first, as it has to be handled by ladies, who, not being accustomed to the work, are not partial to the effluvia arising from aged perspiration. What is really needed is good, warm, serviceable underwear for the ladies and children, and gloves and underwear for the men, who have to work out in the forests chopping timber and hauling logs. So far as money is concerned, it is better to keep it home, and save it until spring time, when farming implements, provisions, seed, grain, etc., will be wanted, none of which any of the farmers now have. In fact, the real suffering is yet to come, after the first rush of sympathy has gone by and the real substantials are needed.

TOO MUCH COMMITTEE.

I have had the pleasure of meeting many of the leading citizens of all the places in the North-west where committees have been formed for the purpose of relieving the sufferers by the fire, and I must say that, after a full investigation, I have come to the conclusion that there is too much committee entirely, and that the work would have been pushed through more rapidly had fewer persons been held responsible for the task.

As it was, boxes and bundles from every section of the land came pouring in, directed to almost every town in the State, just as if Wisconsin was the size of "Little Rhody," instead of a vast State. To distribute these gifts, committees of the eminently respectable gentlemen were organized, who went to work in their old-fashioned, even-tempered way, while the poor sufferers were shivering with cold and empty in stomach. The snap, the fire, the energy having long since left these gentlemen, it was soon found that things were not working smoothly and forcibly as desirable, and in many instances new men of undoubted "push-aheaditiveness" were selected, and went to work right at the marrow of the question, cutting red tape; and when a poor wretch came pleading for clothing to keep him warm, at once giving it to him. This new deal has been productive of much good, and saved a vast quantity of suffering. For my part, I can not see any sense in directing any supplies for the Wisconsin sufferers to any point south of Green Bay, which is on the southern border of the burnt region, and whose citizens, with one will, are doing all they can to alleviate the misfortunes of the unfortunates. They are a whole-soul people, who, without compensation, are doing a grand work. All they need are the goods, and they will see that only the deserving get any thing. As an evidence of the good work they are doing, it will only be necessary to say that the noble-hearted ladies have already made preparations for the taking care of the one hundred and seventy-five children made orphans by the fire. This will save these children from being cuffed about in the cold and cruel world, and be the means of making them good, useful, and educated people. I hope that the charitable every-where will assist these ladies in their commendable enterprise—an undertaking of the noblest character. To-morrow I go over to the peninsula, and, if not too much occupied with other things, may write again.

W. L.

Another account says:

"You can imagine a beautiful and thriving village, with its immense manufactories and busy life, now a waste of sand, deserted. The carcasses of fifty horses lay in regular rows as they had stood in their stalls, with scarcely a vestige of the building remaining. The people only had ten minutes' warning of the hurricane of fire, and no time to comprehend the situation. They rushed into the streets and started for the river, but were overtaken by the storm of fire, and fell in the middle of the streets. One man, carrying his wife, approached the river, but the blast drove him over some obstruction, and, falling, he was separated from her. He picked up a woman, supposing her to be his wife, carried her into the river and saved her. It proved to be another man's wife and his own was lost. One man was sick with the typhoid fever; a young man stopping with him took the sick man out back of the house and buried him in the sand. He was saved, and is rapidly gaining his health.

The half has not been told; the whole will never be known. The loss of life increases every hour. On Friday last twenty-six dead bodies were found in the woods, and, on Saturday, thirty-six. The woods and fields are literally full of dead bodies, and many were burned entirely up. We found some teeth, a jack-knife and a slate pencil. It must have been all that remained of a promising boy. Truly in this case the darkness preceded the light. On Sunday night, October 9th, just after the churches were closed, for half an hour there reigned the stillness of death. The smoke settled down so thickly that the darkness, like Egyptian, could be felt. Then came light gusts of wind, and in the south was seen, through the smoke and darkness, faint glimmers of light. The earth trembled, and the roar of the approaching tornado, and the shock of the falling trees broke the awful stillness. No one could realize the approaching danger, when, in almost a moment, the holocaust was upon them. The fire, in its maddening rage, could not keep pace with the wind, and trees, and houses, and men were blown down that they might be more rapidly consumed. Men, women, and children rose again to rush like specters through the flames, and fell separated from each other. In this terrible moment men thought the final day had come when the earth should be burnt, and they bowed themselves to offer their last prayer. More might have been saved if this conviction had not seized them.

The drouth and tornado which brought disaster to Chicago brought this also. These forest fires prevailed the most destructively in Door, Kewannee, and Oconto counties, Wisconsin, nearly all of which were so completely devastated as to leave no vestige of property remaining to its owners except the bare land. In open fields the destruction was more complete than in the Pine forests, where the trunks of green trees are still standing, though nearly worthless. In each of a dozen or more townships from twenty to eighty dead bodies were found. Only those who had time and presence of mind enough to escape to a freshly plowed area escaped a fiery death. The fatalities were increased greatly by the suddenness with which the tornado of fire swept upon them, and the impression which it made on a majority of the people that the day of judgment had arrived, from which there was no escape. The loss of life in Wisconsin is estimated at one thousand. On the east shore of Lake Michigan the City of Manista and Town of Holland were almost entirely destroyed. The same fires prevailed throughout all the pine country bordering on Lake Michigan, Green Bay, and the southern shore of Lake Huron. Governor Baldwin, of Michigan, estimates that at least 15,000 people in his state lost homes, clothing, crops, farm stock, and all their provisions by the fire. The devastation in Wisconsin was still greater. Very extensive and disastrous prairie fires occurred in Western and Central Minnesota, just before these calamities set in, thus making the first fortnight of October, A. D. 1871, a period wholly without a parallel in the history of the world for the extent of the fiery devastations which it witnessed.

It should be added that a goodly portion of the world's charity, which would otherwise have been bestowed upon Chicago, went to relieve the equal or greater distress in these country places, and it poured in so bountifully on all that the Governor of Wisconsin issued a proclamation, early in November, addressed to the charitable every-where, the purport of which was, "*Enough!*"

APPENDIX B.

DOCUMENTARY HISTORY OF THE FIRE.

I. PROCLAMATIONS, ORDERS, AND CORRESPONDENCE.

THE FIRST NOTE FROM THE MAYOR AND GOVERNMENT.

(*Issued early on Monday, 9th.*)

WHEREAS, in the Providence of God, to whose will we humbly submit, a terrible calamity has befallen our city, which demands of us our best efforts for the preservation of order, and the relief of the suffering;

BE IT KNOWN that the faith and credit of the city of Chicago is hereby pledged for the necessary expenses for the relief of the suffering. Public order will be preserved. The Police and Special Police now being appointed, will be responsible for the maintenance of the peace and the protection of property. All officers and men of the Fire Department and Health Department will act as Special Policemen without further notice. The Mayor and Comptroller will give vouchers for all supplies furnished by the different Relief Committees. The head-quarters of the City Government will be at the Congregational Church, corner of West Washington and Ann Sts. All persons are warned against any acts tending to endanger property. All persons caught in any depredation will be immediately arrested.

With the help of God, order and peace and private property shall be preserved. The City Government and committees of citizens pledge themselves to the community to protect them, and prepare the way for a restoration of public and private welfare.

It is believed the fire has spent its force, and all will soon be well.

R. B. MASON, *Mayor.*

GEO. TAYLOR, *Comptroller.*

CHAS. C. P. HOLDEN, *President Common Council.*

T. B. BROWN, *President Board of Police.*

CHICAGO, *October 9th,* 1871.

BREAD ORDINANCE—NOTICE.

CHICAGO, *October* 10, 1871.

The following Ordinance was passed at a meeting of the Common Council of the City of Chicago, on the 10th day of October, A. D. 1871:

An Ordinance.

Be it ordained by the Common Council of the City of Chicago:

SECTION 1.—That the Price of Bread in the City of Chicago for the next 10 days is hereby fixed and established at *Eight* (8) *Cents per Loaf* of 12 ounces, and at the same rate for all Loaves of less or greater weight.

SECTION 2.—Any person selling or attempting to sell any bread within the City of Chicago, within said 10 days, at a greater price than is fixed in this Ordinance, shall be liable to a penalty of ten (10) dollars for each and every offense, to be collected as other penalties for violation of City Ordinances.

SECTION 3.—This Ordinance shall be in full force and effect from and after its passage.

Approved October 10th, 1871.

Attest: R. B. MASON, *Mayor.*

N. [C. T.] HOTCHKISS, *City Clerk.*

MAYOR'S PROCLAMATION—ADVISORY AND PRECAUTIONARY.

1. All citizens are requested to exercise great caution in the use of fire in their dwellings, and not to use kerosene lights at present, as the city will be without a full supply of water for probably two or three days.

2. The following bridges are passable, to-wit: All bridges (except Van Buren and Adams Streets) from Lake Street south, and all bridges over the North Branch of the Chicago River.

3. All good citizens who are willing to serve are requested to report at the corner of Ann and Washington Streets, to be sworn in as special policemen.

Citizens are requested to organize a police for each block in the city, and to send reports of such organization to the police head-quarters, corner of Union and West Madison Streets.

All persons needing food will be relieved by applying at the following places:

At the corner of Ann and Washington; Illinois Central Railroad round-house.

M. S. R. R.—Twenty-second Street Station.

C. B. & Q. R. R.—Canal Street Depot.

St. L. & A. R. R.—Near Sixteenth Street.

C. & N. W. R. R.—Corner of Kinzie and Canal Streets.

All the public school-houses, and at nearly all the churches.

4. Citizens are requested to avoid passing through the burnt districts until the dangerous walls left standing can be leveled.

5. All saloons are ordered to be closed by 8 P. M. every day for one week, under a penalty of forfeiture of license.

6. The Common Council have this day, by ordinance, fixed the price of bread at eight (8) cents per loaf of 12 ounces, and at the same rate for loaves of a greater or less weight, and affixed a penalty of ten dollars for selling or attempting to sell, bread at a greater rate within the next ten days.

7. Any hackman, expressman, drayman, or teamster charging more than the regular fees, will have his license revoked.

8. All citizens are requested to aid in preserving the peace, good order, and good name of our city.

R. B. MASON, *Mayor.*

October 10, 1871.

ORGANIZING FOR SAFETY.

[The following is not dated. It appeared upon the 10th of October.]

Let us Organize for Safety in Chicago.

1. The Mayor's headquarters will be at the corner of Ann and Washington Streets.

2. Police headquarters at the corner of Union and Madison Streets.

3. Every special policeman will be subject to the orders of the sergeant for the district in which he performs duty. The sergeants of districts will be appointed by the police superintendent.

4. Five hundred citizens for each of the districts will be sworn in as special policemen.

5. The sergeant of each district will procure from police headquarters rations and supplies for special policemen in his district.

6. Orders to the police will be issued by the superintendent of police.

7. The military will co-operate with the police organization and the city government in the preservation of order.

8. The military are invested with full police power, and will be respected and obeyed in their efforts to preserve order.

Health department corner of Ann and Washington.

R. B. MASON, *Mayor.*

[The above are here printed from the original fly sheets, having been issued before the journals got under way again.—ED.]

Distribution of Relief.

1. All supplies of provisions will be received and distributed by the Special Relief Committee, of which O. E. Moore is Chairman and C. G. Hotchkiss Secretary. Headquarters of committee on Ann and West Washington Streets.

2. All contributions of money will be delivered to the City Treasurer, David A. Gage, who will receipt and keep the same as a Special Relief Fund.

3. All moneys deposited at other places for the relief of the city will be drawn for only by the mayor of this city.

4. No moneys will be paid out of the Special Relief Fund except upon the order of the Auditing Committee.

George Taylor, City Comptroller, Mancell Tallcott, Esq., of the West Division, and Brock McVicker, of the South Divison, are hereby appointed such Auditing Committee.

5. Railroad passes from the city will be issued under direction of the Relief Committee, corner of Ann and West Washington Streets, until further orders.

Given under my hand this 11th day of October, 1871.

R. B. Mason, *Mayor.*

Location of City Offices.

From and after the 12th day of October, 1871, the Mayor's Office, City Comptroller's, City Treasurer's, and other City Offices, will be at the corner of Hubbard Court and Wabash Avenue.

The Department of the Board of Public Works and other departments of the City Government will be located in the immediate vicinity of the other city offices.

Given under my hand this 11th day of October, 1871.

Attest: R. B. Mason, *Mayor.*

C. T. Hotchkiss, *City Clerk.*

Turning Affairs over to General Sheridan.

The preservation of the good order and peace of the city is hereby intrusted to Lieutenant-General Philip H. Sheridan, United States Army.

The police will act in conjunction with the lieutenant-general in the preservation of the peace and quiet of the city, and the superintendent of the police will consult with him to that end. The intent being to preserve the peace of the city without interfering with the functions of the city government.

Given under my seal this October 11, A. D. 1871.

R. B. Mason, *Mayor.*

Ordered by the full Board of Police that all powers granted to special police since Sunday, October 8th, be and hereby are revoked.

The large military force now in the city, under the command of Lieutenant-General Sheridan, co-operating with the regular police organization, is now deemed sufficient to maintain good and quietude for the future.

T. B. BROWN,
F. GUND,
MARK SHERIDAN, } Commissioners.

SHERIDAN'S FIRST REPORT.

HEADQUARTERS MIL. DIV. OF THE MISSOURI,
CHICAGO, *October* 12, 1871.

To His Honor the Mayor:

The preservation of peace and good order of the city having been intrusted to me by Your Honor, I am happy to state that no case of outbreak or disorder has been reported. No authenticated attempt at incendiarism has reached me, and that the people of the city are calm, quiet, and well disposed.

The force at my disposal is ample to maintain order, should it be necessary, and protect the district devastated by fire. Still, I would suggest to citizens not to relax in their watchfulness until the smoldering fires of the burnt buildings are entirely extinguished.

P. H. SHERIDAN, *Lieutenant-General.*

SHERIDAN ON THE ROMANCERS.

HEADQUARTERS MIL. DIV. OF THE MISSOURI,
CHICAGO, *October* 17, 1871.

To His Honor Mayor Mason, Chicago, Ill.:

I respectfully report to Your Honor the continued peace and quiet of the city. There has been no case of violence since the disaster of Sunday night and Monday morning.

The reports in the public press of violence and disorder here are without the slightest foundation. There has not been a single case of arson, hanging, or shooting—not even a case of riot or a street fight. I have seen no reason for the circulation of such reports.

It gives me pleasure to bring to the notice of Your Honor the cheerful spirit with which the population of this city have met their losses and suffering.

Very respectfully, your obedient servant,

P. H. SHERIDAN, *Lieutenant-General.*

Dismissing City Employés.

To the Heads of all Departments of the City Government:

The late fire has, of necessity, caused the suspension of public improvements, and of much work heretofore done in various departments of the city government. It therefore becomes necessary to discharge all employés of the city government whose services are not absolutely required. I respectfully request that you, in your several departments, immediately give notice of discharge to all such, with a view to the most rigid economy which must now be observed in all departments.

R. B. Mason, *Mayor.*

[Not dated. Issued the 19th.]

Fast Day Recommended.

In view of the recent appalling public calamity, the undersigned, Mayor of Chicago, hereby earnestly recommends that all the inhabitants of this city do observe Sunday, October 29, as a special day of humiliation and prayer; of humiliation for those past offenses against Almighty God, to which these severe afflictions were doubtless intended to lead our minds; of prayer for the relief and comfort of the suffering thousands in our midst; for the restoration of our material prosperity, especially for our lasting improvement as a people in reverence and obedience to God. Nor should we even, amidst our losses and sorrows, forget to render thanks to Him for the arrest of the devouring fires in time to save so many homes, and for the unexampled sympathy and aid which has flowed in upon us from every quarter of our land, and even from beyond the seas.

Given under my hand this 20th day of October, 1871.

R. B. Mason, *Mayor.*

Sheridan Steps Out.

The Mayor to General Sheridan.

Lieutenant-General P. H. Sheridan, U. S. A.:

Permit me to tender you the thanks of the city of Chicago and its whole people for the very efficient aid which you have rendered, in protecting the lives and property of the citizens, and in the preservation of the general peace and good order of the community. I would like your opinion as to whether there is any longer a necessity for the continued aid of the military in that behalf. Very respectfully,

R. B. Mason, *Mayor.*

Chicago, *Oct.* 22.

General Sheridan to the Mayor.

CHICAGO, Ill., *Oct.* 23.

To His Honor, R. B. Mason, Mayor of Chicago:

SIR: I have the honor to acknowledge the receipt of your kind note of the date of yesterday, and in reply I beg leave to report a good condition of affairs in the city. If Your Honor deem it best, I will disband the volunteer organization of military on duty since the fire, and will consider myself relieved from the responsibility of your proclamation of the 11th instant. With my sincere thanks for your kindness and courtesy in my intercourse with you, I am respectfully your obedient servant,

P. H. SHERIDAN, *Lieutenant-General.*

The Mayor to General Sheridan.

Lieutenant-General P. H. Sheridan, U. S. A.:

Upon consultation with the Board of Police Commissioners, I am satisfied that the continuance of the efficient aid in the preservation of order in this city which has been rendered by the forces under your command in pursuance of my proclamation is no longer required. I will therefore fix the hour of 6 P. M. of this day as the hour at which the aid requested of you shall cease. Allow me again to tender you the assurance of my high appreciation of the great and efficient service which you have rendered in the preservation of order and the protection of property in this city, and to again thank you in the name of the city of Chicago and its citizens therefor. I am respectfully yours,

R. B. MASON, *Mayor.*

CHICAGO, *Oct.* 23.

Orders of Disbandment.

HEADQUARTERS MIL. DIV. OF THE MISSOURI,
CHICAGO, Ill., *Oct.* 24, 1871.

Special Orders No. 76.

1. The companies of the Fourth, Fifth, Sixth, Ninth, and Sixteenth United States Infantry, on duty in this city, are hereby relieved, and will proceed to their respective stations as follows:

Companies F, H, and K, of the Fourth, and E, of the Sixteenth, to Louisville, Ky.

Companies A, H, and K, of the Fifth, to Fort Leavenworth.

Company I, of the Sixth, to Fort Hays.

Companies A and K, of the Ninth, to Omaha.

The Quartermaster's Department will furnish the necessary transportation.

By command of Lieutenant-General Sheridan.

JAMES B. FRY, *A. A. G.*

Official:

M. V. SHERIDAN, *Lt. Col. A. D. C.*

HEADQUARTERS MIL. DIV. OF THE MISSOURI,
CHICAGO, Ill., *Oct.* 24, 1871.

General Orders No. 5.

The First Regiment Chicago Volunteers, raised with the approbation of the Mayor, and in pursuance of orders dated October 11, 1871, from these headquarters, is hereby honorably mustered out of service and discharged. . . . . These troops were suddenly called from civil pursuits to aid Lieutenant-General Sheridan in preserving peace and good order, and in protecting the property in the unburnt portion of the city, a duty intrusted to him during the emergency resulting from the late fire. They came forward promptly and cheerfully at a time rendered critical by the unparalleled disaster which visited the city on the 8th and 9th insts., a calamity producing general distrust and distress, leaving a large part of the city in smoldering ruins, a large part in darkness by the destruction of the gas-works, and the whole of it without water; and this with a fire department crippled and exhausted by the struggle it had gone through. They have performed the arduous and delicate duties falling to them under these circumstances with marked industry, fidelity, and intelligence. The Lietenant-General thanks officers and men of the command for the services rendered, and commends them to the kind consideration of their fellow-citizens; and he makes special acknowledgment of the valuable aid received from their commander, General Frank T. Sherman—distinguished upon the battle-fields of the late war—as well as from his efficient staff, Major C. H. Dyer, Adjutant, and Major Charles T. Scammon, Aide-de-camp.

By command of Lieutenant-General Sheridan.

JAMES B. FRY, *Assistant Adjutant-General.*

SHERIDAN'S REPORT TO SHERMAN.

HEADQUARTERS MILITARY DIVISION OF THE MISSOURI,
CHICAGO, *October* 25, 1871.

To the Adjutant General of the Army, Washington D. C.:

SIR: The disorganized condition of affairs in this city, produced by and immediately following the late fire, induced the city authorities to ask for assistance from the military forces, as shown by the Mayor's proclamation of October 11, 1871. [Copy herewith, marked A.] To protect the public interests intrusted to me by the Mayor's proclamation, I called to this city companies A and K of the Ninth Infantry, from Omaha; companies A, H and K of the Fifth Infantry, from Fort Leavenworth; company I, Sixth Infantry, from Fort Scott, and accepted the kind offer of Major-General Halleck to send to me companies F, H and K of the Fourth, and company E of the Sixteenth Infantry, from Kentucky. I also, with the approbation of the

Mayor, called into the service of the city of Chicago, a regiment of volunteers for twenty days. [Copy of this call inclosed herewith, marked B.] These troops, both regulars and volunteers, were actively engaged during their service here in protecting the treasure in the burnt district, guarding the unburnt district from disorders and danger by further fires, and in protecting the store-houses, depots, and sub-depots of supplies established for the relief of the sufferers from the fire. These duties were terminated on the 23d inst., as shown by letters herewith [marked C, D, and E], and on the 24th inst. the regulars started to their respective stations, and the volunteers were discharged, as shown by special order No. 76, and general order No. 5, from these headquarters. [Copies herewith.] It is proper to mention that these volunteers were not taken into the service of the United States, and no orders, agreements, or promises were made giving them any claims against the United States for services rendered.

I am, very respectfully, your obedient servant,

P. H. SHERIDAN,
Lieutenant-General United States Army, Commanding.

SHERMAN'S APPROVAL.

General Sherman submitted the foregoing report to the Secretary of War, with the following emphatic endorsement:

The extraordinary circumstances attending the great fire in Chicago made it eminently proper that General Sheridan should exercise the influence, authority, and power he did on the universal appeal of a ruined and distressed people, backed by their civil agents, who were powerless for good. The very moment that the civil authorities felt able to resume their functions General Sheridan ceased to exercise authority, and the United States troops returned to their respective stations. General Sheridan's course is fully approved.

W. T. SHERMAN, General.

II. OFFICIAL EXPRESSIONS OF SYMPATHY FROM ABROAD.

PROCLAMATION BY THE GOVERNOR OF ILLINOIS.

STATE OF ILLINOIS,
EXECUTIVE DEPARTMENT.

John M. Palmer, Governor of Illinois, To all whom these presents shall come, greeting:

Whereas, in my judgment, the great calamity that has overtaken Chicago, the largest city of the State; that has deprived many thousands of our citizens of homes and rendered them destitute; that has destroyed many millions in value of property, and thereby disturbing the business of the people and deranging the finances of the State, and interrupting the execution of the laws, is and constitutes "an extraordinary occasion" within the true intent and meaning of the eighth section of the fifth article of the Constitution.

Now, therefore, I, John M. Palmer, Governor of the State of Illinois, do by this, my proclamation, convene and invite the two Houses of the General Assembly in session in the city of Springfield, on Friday, the 13th day of the month of October, in the year of our Lord 1871, at 12 o'clock noon of said day, to take into consideration the following subjects:

1. To appropriate such sum or sums of money, or adopt such other legislative measures as may be thought judicious, necessary, or proper, for the relief of the people of the city of Chicago.

2. To make provision, by amending the revenue laws or otherwise, for the proper and just assessment and collection of taxes within the city of Chicago.

3. To enact such other laws and to adopt such other measures as may be necessary for the relief of the city of Chicago and the people of said city, and for the execution and enforcement of the laws of the State.

4. To make appropriations for the expenses of the General Assembly, and such other appropriations as may be necessary to carry on the State Government.

[SEAL.] In testimony whereof I have hereunto set my hand and caused the great seal of the State to be affixed. Done at the city of Springfield, this 10th day of October, A. D. 1871.

JOHN M. PALMER.

By the Governor,

EDWARD RUMMELL, *Secretary of State.*

BY THE GOVERNOR OF WISCONSIN.

To the People of Wisconsin:

Throughout the northern part of this State fires have been raging in the woods for many days, spreading desolation on every side. It is reported that hundreds of families have been rendered homeless by this devouring element, and reduced to utter destitution, their entire crops having been consumed. Their stock has been destroyed, and their farms are but a blackened desert. Unless they receive instant aid from portions not visited by this dreadful calamity, they must perish.

The telegraph also brings the terrible news that a large portion of the city of Chicago is destroyed by a conflagration, which is still raging. Many thousands of people are thus reduced to penury, stripped of their all, and are now destitute of shelter and food. Their sufferings will be intense, and many may perish unless provisions are at once sent to them from the surrounding country. They must be assisted now.

In the awful presence of such calamities the people of Wisconsin will not be backward in giving assistance to their afflicted fellow-men.

I, therefore, recommend that immediate organized effort be made in every locality to forward provisions and money to the sufferers by this visitation, and suggest to Mayors of cities, Presidents of villages, Town Supervisors, Pastors of Churches, and to the various benevolent societies, that they devote themselves immediately to the work of organizing effort, collecting contributions, and sending forward supplies for distribution.

And I entreat all to give their abundance to help those in such sore distress

Given under my hand, at the Capitol, at Madison, this 9th day of October, A. D. 1871. LUCIUS FAIRCHILD.

BY THE GOVERNOR OF MICHIGAN.

STATE OF MICHIGAN, EXECUTIVE OFFICE,
LANSING, *October 9th.*

The city of Chicago, in the neighboring State of Illinois, has been visited, in the providence of Almighty God, with a calamity almost unequaled in the annals of history. A large portion of that beautiful and most prosperous city has been reduced to ashes and is now in ruins. Many millions of dollars in property, the accumulation of years of industry and toil, have been swept away in a moment. The rich have been reduced to penury, the poor have lost the little they possessed, and many thousands of people rendered homeless and houseless, and are now without the absolute necessaries of life. I, therefore, earnestly call upon the citizens of every portion of Michigan to take immediate measures for alleviating the pressing wants of that fearfully afflicted city by collecting and forwarding to the Mayor or proper authorities of Chicago supplies of food as well as liberal collections of money. Let this sore calamity of our neighbors remind us of the uncertainty of earthly possessions, and that when one member suffers all the members should suffer with it. I can not doubt that the whole people of the State will most gladly, and most promptly, and most liberally respond to this urgent demand upon their sympathy, but no words of mine can plead so strongly as the calamity itself. HENRY P. BALDWIN.

Governor of Michigan.

BY THE GOVERNOR OF MISSOURI.

JEFFERSON CITY, *October* 9, 1871.

To the People of Missouri:

A calamity unparalleled in the history of our country has befallen the great city of our sister State. Half of the houses of the people of Chicago

43

are in ashes, and all of its business portion is destroyed. Every bank, railroad depot, insurance office, newspaper establishment, every wholesale house, all its accumulated products and food supply, and nearly every trade appliance and the elevators are reported as utterly consumed. Such disaster will move the hearts of our citizens with the profoundest sympathy. Let us unite likewise in the most generous emulation, and extend the largest possible aid to them in this, the hour of misfortune. I, therefore, recommend all counties, cities, towns, and other corporations, to all business and charitable associations, and to the community at large, to take immediate steps to organize relief committees to express the deep sorrow which Missouri feels at this overwhelming affliction. It was only yesterday that they were united with you in congratulating you on your own soil and in your own chief city, whilst their own homes were being destroyed. Let us respond by throwing open wide our own doors to those who are without shelter, by sending bread and raiment at once, and by such contributions ward off further distress, as the generous heart of our own great State will be proud to transmit, in recognition, too, of the warm and intimate feeling that has heretofore so closely bound our citizens together. I can not forbear to extend to all who have been thus stricken down in the midst of an unbounded prosperity the sincerest sympathy of Missouri's sons and daughters in their distress.

Done at the City of Jefferson, this 9th day of October, A. D. 1871.

B. GRATZ BROWN, *Governor of Missouri.*

BY THE GOVERNOR OF IOWA.

To the People of Iowa:

An appalling calamity has befallen our sister State. Her metropolis, the great city of Chicago, is in ruins. Over 100,000 people are without shelter or food, except as supplied by others. A helping hand let us now promptly give. Let the liberality of our people, so lavishly displayed during the long period of national peril, come again to the front, to lend succor in this hour of distress. I would urge the appointment at once of relief committees in every city, town, and township, and I respectfully ask the local authorities to call meetings of the citizens to devise ways and means to render efficient aid. I would also ask the pastors of the various churches throughout the State to take up collections on Sunday morning next, or at such other time as they may deem proper, for the relief of the sufferers. Let us not be satisfied with any spasmodic effort. There will be need of relief of a substantial character to aid the many thousands to prepare for the rigors of the coming winter. The magnificent public charities of that city, now paralyzed, can do little to this end. Those who live in homes of comfort and plenty must furnish this help, or misery and suffering will be the fate of many thousands of our neighbors.

SAMUEL MERRILL, *Governor.*

DES MOINES, *October* 10, 1871.

BY THE GOVERNOR OF OHIO.

CHICAGO, *October* 12*th.*

To the People of Ohio:

It is believed by the best informed citizens here that many thousands of the sufferers must be provided with the necessaries of life during the cold winter. Let the efforts to raise contributions be energetically pushed. Money, fuel, flour, pork, clothing, and other articles not perishable, should be collected as rapidly as possible—especially money, fuel, and flour. Mr. Joseph Medill, of *The Tribune,* estimates the number of those who will need assistance at about 70,000.

R. B. HAYES, *Governor of Ohio.*

[Governor Randolph, of New Jersey, and perhaps other Governors of States, issued a similar appeal to his people in behalf of the stricken city.]

LETTER FROM THE PRESIDENT.

EXECUTIVE MANSION, WASHINGTON,
October 11, 1871.

To Hon. Samuel Hooper, Boston, Mass.:

Would it not be well for the good people of Boston to dispense with the ceremony and expense of a public reception on the occasion of my visit to your city, and appropriate such portion of the fund set apart for that purpose, as is deemed advisable, for the relief of the sufferers by the Chicago disaster? I am sure such a course would please me.

U. S. GRANT.

PROCLAMATION OF THE MAYOR OF SALT LAKE CITY.

The news having been confirmed of the terrible conflagration by which a great portion of the city of Chicago has been reduced to ashes, and one hundred thousand people have been stripped of their homes, clothing, and means of subsistence, therefore,

I, Daniel H. Wells, Mayor of Salt Lake City, by the wish and authority of the City Council of said city, call upon all classes of the people to assemble in mass meeting, to-morrow, Wednesday, October 11th, at 1 o'clock, P. M., at the Old Tabernacle, in this city, for the purpose of making subscriptions and taking such measures as are demanded for the relief of our fellow-citizens who are sufferers by this dreadful visitation.

DANIEL H. WELLS, *Mayor of Salt Lake City.*

October 10, 1871.

THE MASONS OF NEW YORK STATE.

To the Worshipful Masters, Wardens, and Brethren of all Lodges of Free and Accepted Masons in the State of New York:

Brethren, a calamity, one of the most appalling either of ancient or modern times, has befallen one of the fairest and hitherto most prosperous cities of our Union. Within a brief space of time the devastating element has swept out of existence the public and private edifices of Chicago, destroying millions of dollars' worth of property, and leaving homeless and penniless thousands of its people, among whom are many of our brethren and their families. The cry of distress and the prayer for relief, speedy and sufficient, reaches our ears; our hearts should not be shut to the appeal, nor our hands be idle in extending aid. We should show that our ancient order is founded upon brotherly love, and that we are ever willing to extend relief to suffering humanity.

Therefore, I, John H. Anthon, Grand Master of Masons of the State of New York, desire to lay before the Masons of the State of New York the appeal of our suffering brethren in Chicago, and all the desolate and oppressed of that afflicted city, in order that a fund may be raised for their immediate relief; and I do fraternally and most earnestly beseech my brethren to give toward this object as liberally as their means will allow. I suggest contributions in money, knowing that relief committees will be organized, and that such sums as may be raised will be disbursed by them in a proper and efficient manner. Contributions, sent in drafts on New York to the order of the Grand Master, at his office, No. 271 Broadway, will be by him forwarded to Chicago.

J. H. ANTHON.

Grand Master's Office, *October* 9, 1871.

GENERAL SHERIDAN TO SECRETARY BELKNAP.

CHICAGO, *October 9th.*

General Belknap, Secretary of War:

The city of Chicago is almost utterly destroyed by fire. There is now no reasonable hope of arresting it, as the wind, which is yet blowing a gale, does not change. I ordered, on your authority, rations from St. Louis, tents from

Jeffersonville, and two companies from Omaha. There will be many houseless people and much distress.

(Signed) P. H. SHERIDAN, *Lieutenant-General.*

CHICAGO, *October 9th.*

W. W. Belknap, Secretary of War:

The fire here last night and to-day has destroyed almost all that was very valuable in this city. There is not a business house, bank, or hotel, left. Most of the best part of the city is gone. Without exaggeration, all the valuable portion of the city is in ruins. I think that not less than one hundred thousand persons are houseless, and those who have had the most wealth are now poor. It seems to me to be such a terrible misfortune that it may with propriety be considered a national calamity.

(Signed) P. H. SHERIDAN, *Lieutenant-General.*

THE SECRETARY'S RESPONSE.

WASHINGTON, *October 10th.*

Lieutenant-General Sheridan, Chicago:

I agree with you that the fire is a national calamity. The sufferers have the sincere sympathy of the nation. The officers at the depots at St. Louis, Jeffersonville, and elsewhere have been ordered to forward supplies liberally and promptly.

(Signed) WILLIAM W. BELKNAP, *Secretary of War.*

To the Mayor of Chicago:

General Sheridan has been authorized to supply clothing, tools, and provisions from the depots at Jeffersonville and St. Louis to the extent and ability of the Department.

(Signed) WILLIAM W. BELKNAP, *Secretary of War.*

APPENDIX C.

CONTEMPORARY OPINION CONCERNING THE CITY AND THE EVENT.

REBUILDING THE CITY.

SHE WILL RISE AGAIN.

[From the New York World, October 11.]

The appalling calamity which has so suddenly overtaken Chicago like a thief in the night, and which fills all imaginations with horror and all hearts with oppressive, agonizing pity, has, nevertheless, a hopeful side. It is not as if that great city and its inhabitants had been ingulfed by an earthquake. The greater part of the people are spared, and although there will be much suffering for want of shelter, this will be but temporary, and contributions of food are already reaching them from sources of generous, commiserating cities. None of these sufferers will die of starvation, and those of them who remain during the winter will have such protection from cold as can be given by tents and abundant clothing. By close overcrowding of the unconsumed dwellings in the city and suburbs, by the emigration of manufacturing laborers, by the placing of women and children with distant friends, or procuring them board in the country, it will not be necessary for any but the hardier class of laborers to pass the winter in tents. The stress of the suffering will not extend beyond the ensuing ten days, and will consist chiefly in exposure (especially if there should be cold, pelting rain storms), and in the desolating sense of the utter loss of property by people whom lives of toil had rendered comfortable. Many individuals are hopelessly ruined, but a very few years will restore the city.

The growth of Chicago, a city which has risen like an exhalation on the south-western shore of Lake Michigan, has been regarded by travelers and economists as one of the chief marvels of recent times. It is a phenomenon which never had a parallel, but which will be eclipsed and outdone by the more astonishing miracle of the reconstruction of the burnt city out of its ashes. Forty and two years was this city in building, and yet it will be reconstructed in three years. It will rise again from its ruins as if by magic, and the wonder of its original growth will be forgotten in the greater wonder of its sudden new creation.

There is not the slightest danger of the transfer of her grain trade and her various business to other lake cities. At present the other lake cities have not facilities to accommodate it; their elevators, warehouses, mercantile establishments, banks, etc., being proportioned to the business they already possess. To transact in addition the business of Chicago, they would need an enormous increase of structures, accommodations, and capital. But these can be replaced in Chicago as quickly as they could be built at Milwaukee and other lake ports; and nobody will invest money for them elsewhere with the certainty that Chicago will be rebuilt as speedily as multitudes of busy hands can do the work. The lake commerce will always tend to one great center, and there is no other center which possesses such natural advantages as Chicago. These have been increased by costly artificial advantages which it has required thirty years of persistent industry to create. All the great railroad lines have been constructed with a view to Chicago as a starting point and a terminus. It might be easy to build a new town, if that were all; but not easy to reconstruct the railroad system of the West with a new point of convergence.

Chicago has still all the elements of a great city, except the mere buildings. She has her river harbor, which has been dredged and enlarged, and her piers and breakwaters, which have been constructed at enormous expense. These can not be extemporized in any other place. She has her light-houses for the security of navigation. She has her expensive tunnel under Lake Michigan for supplying a city thrice her recent magnitude with pure water. She has her entensive system of sewerage, which, being under ground and constructed of incombustible materials, has not been consumed. She has the grading of her streets and the excavation of her cellars and vaults. She has the outlying vegetable gardens and milk dairies for supplying her tables. Her vast cattle-yards were untouched by the flames. The destruction of her great railroad depots will scarcely obstruct travel and traffic, as passengers can be received and landed, and freight taken and delivered, in the open air, until the depots are rebuilt.

And what is, perhaps, the most important of all her remaining advantages and sources of resuscitation, Chicago has not lost her shrewd, enterprising, energetic, indomitable men of business. They can more easily re-establish themselves in Chicago than they can form new connections elsewhere. They will not break from their creditors in the East, nor from their customers in the West. The vast, magnificent North-west must still be supplied with goods, and they will continue to furnish the supply. New men in new cities have not their business acquaintances, and can not build stores and collect stocks as quickly as the Chicago merchants can build and renew them. Chicago will restore herself before competitors can come into the field.

She Will Rise Quickly.

[From the New York Commercial Advertiser, October 14.]

Chicago will recover, not by gradual steps, but with a bound. The calamity that befell her, appalling as it is, has only destroyed the results, not the causes of her prosperity. Chicago has still all the natural advantages that made her what she was. Her position in reference to the great chain of lakes, and the great grain-producing, stock-raising, and lumber regions of the North-west, with the network of railways connecting her with the Atlantic, the Pacific, and the Gulf, made Chicago a great commercial center, and must continue to make her so still. The ground on which the city stands, the lakes, the rivers, the fields, the prairies, the forest, and the railways, which gave her greatness, are all there to give it to her again. Commerce must continue to flow through its natural channels and through the artificial ones provided for it. It would be more difficult to stop or divert it now than it would be to build a dozen cities. Chicago grew, from four thousand people in 1840, to thirty thousand in 1850, then to a hundred thousand in 1860, and then to three hundred thousand in 1870. The channels that poured population and wealth into the great city of the West at this astonishing rate still exist, and there is no reason to doubt that they will produce the same result in the future as in the past.

St. Louis' Opinion.

[From the St. Louis Republican, Oct. 13.]

That Chicago will be rebuilt, and that with wonderful rapidity, is a truth too manifest to be denied. The necessities that led to the erection of a great city at the end of Lake Michigan, demand its reconstruction. The destruction of that city creates an immense vacuum, and the first instinctive efforts of the great North-west will be directed to filling it. The vast traffic that was wont to flow into Chicago will, for a time, be turned aside from it, for want of accommodations, and Milwaukee and St. Louis will temporarily profit by this diversion; Milwaukee and St. Louis merchants will be called on to do the business which Chicago merchants did; the great Northwest, that sent its blood through the Lake City, is untouched, and possesses all its blood unimpaired. It needs only new channels and new reservoirs to supply those which have been destroyed; and it will turn spontaneously to St. Louis and Milwaukee to find them. But Chicago was a necessity, and a great city on the site where it stood is a necessity now. Things in this country have not reached that decayed condition which makes wastes, desolations, and the permanent ruin of ancient splendor, possible. The very convergence of railroads at Chicago proves the need of a great city there, and tells us that the rebuilding of the one which we have seen destroyed will be witnessed. The noise of the ax, the hammer, and the saw will shortly be heard in the borders of the smitten city as it was never heard before; its palaces and temples will rise again from the seared and blackened earth, and in a few years the burnt district will be hidden by fair and stately buildings revealing no vestige of the great calamity. The sad feature in this bright picture of future glory and greatness is that the victims of the calamity will not largely participate in the enjoyment of it. The ruined great men of Chicago will have given place to others; those of them who have managed to save something from the wreck of their fortunes will have these fragments to begin with again, and will thus be able to keep abreast with competitors in the new race about to commence; but the capital to rebuild the city and to control its commerce must come from elsewhere, and be directed by other men; and when the reconstruction shall have been completed, and a towering city reared on the site of the destroyed one, we shall find that the new city is in the hands of a new generation.

It will be some years to come before Chicago can again be a center of opulence, luxury, and extravagance, but it will be a good place for an industrious man to go to, if he desires to find profitable employment, and to grow up with its growth.

Milwaukee Opinion.

[From the Milwaukee News, October 16.]

The year 1880, now less than nine years distant, will find Chicago with more than her late greatness, and with scarcely a scar of her present calamity remaining. Chicago was not an accident, nor the creature of speculation, nor a mushroom growth. It was brought into existence by the development and necessities of the great North-west, and at the time of its destruction no more than fairly represented that development and ministered to those necessities. It was forty years in its growth, just because the North-west was forty years in its growth. But it is now cut off, with all its growth, and all these necessities which created it remaining in active existence. These necessities represent an omnipotent power. All the difficulties you can cite are but flax in the fire or mist in the sun compared with the concentrated vigor which must inevitably and necessarily center on this spot for recuperation and reconstruction. Where there is a will there is a way; and here there is a will which can not flag, because it proceeds from precisely the same causes which have already lifted the city from the prairie marsh, and which causes are not obliged to pass again through a forty years' growth, inasmuch as they exist now in all the power and vigor pertaining to them before this destruction.

Nine or ten years at farthest will witness the complete restoration of the city, but even this time may be shortened by an energetic grasping and wise application of the agencies which would hasten the result.

Of one thing, let us disabuse ourselves, if we entertain such ideas—that we can ever be permanently benefited by this disaster remaining without remedy. As well hope that one part of the human body can be benefited by an unhealed sore on another part. Individual fortunes have been swallowed up, and many of the sufferers will know no recuperation; but the time is not distant when Chicago, in greatness and wealth, will exceed her late condition.

C. L. SHOLES.

New Orleans Opinion.—"Chicago delenda est."

[From a New Orleans Paper.]

Now that the first shock with which the Chicago calamity was received has passed away, we are enabled to estimate its magnitude more deliberately, and the hopeful promise which pierced the consuming flames of her speedy restoration seems to be now dying in the smoke of her smoldering embers. The magical growth and stupendous wealth of this great interior metropolis was, in the main, due to geographical, commercial, and other causes, which no longer exist in their original force.

The center of a net-work of railroads, all immediately tributary, their gradual extension and multiplication, have since brought rivals into nearer competition, while the completion of the great national highway to the Pacific has materially lessened the importance of her location in trade channels.

Despite the remarkable boldness and dash manifested by Chicago in her outward evidences of prosperity, maintained in great newspapers, marvelous hotels, magnificent buildings, and speedy fortunes acquired, it was all seen through a glamour of unsubstantiality. The rampant spirit of speculation haunted all her operations, and a gloss of *doré* covered all her enterprises. The growth of St. Louis, on the other hand, though slower, was more sure and solid. Although its buildings extended less rapidly, the value of real estate had advanced in a greater comparative proportion. Gradually the trade of Chicago was being diverted toward the nearer, the more accessible and larger market, and already several prominent Chicago business houses had sought footing in the better field. This was the condition of affairs when the fire fiend came to sweep the Lake City with his besom of destruction, inflicting a blow from which she will scarcely recover in the present generation.

Already a large portion of her population has deserted; some, through the stress of poverty, have been driven to other localities, while no limited number of the more fortunate have seized upon the opportunity of transferring their business to St. Louis.

No doubt, the people of Chicago will struggle earnestly against their adverse fate, and that a new city will arise speedily from the ashes of the old one; but it will never be the Carthage of old. Its prestige has passed away, like that of a man who turns the downward hill of life; its glory will be of the past, not the present; while its hopes, once so bright and cloudless, will be to the end marred and blackened by the smoke of its fiery fate.

GENERAL EXPRESSIONS FROM OUTSIDERS.

Human Nature at its Best.

[From the St. Paul Press, October 15.]

This supreme tragedy, in which a hundred thousand human beings passed, in a single awful night, by one terrible stroke of Providence, from the extreme of human prosperity to the extreme of human misery, has melted the heart of Christendom as no other catastrophe of human woe has melted it within the memory of man.

Such a calamity as this tests the quality of our civilization, and the result proves, as all great calamities prove, that men every-where are better and nobler than they seem, and that under all the sordid selfishness of trade there pulses a fine and sweet humanity, and through all the coarse ties which bind together the material interests of States, and cities, and villages, there run sensitive electric nerves of fraternal love and sympathy which weave mankind together in a universal kinship.

Such a magnificent outburst of human sympathy was never witnessed in this country as that which was evoked by the Chicago fire. The whole country leaped spontaneously to the rescue, and all its cities and villages rose up as if by a common impulse of generosity to relieve the victims of this sudden and overwhelming blow. Every telegraph line was subsidized to convey messages that instant relief was on the way, and thirty railroad lines were burdened the same day with the offerings of money, food, clothes, and other necessaries forwarded to the sufferers. In presence of this stupendous catastrophe, human nature rose to its most heroic and exalted mood, and never has it shone more brightly since the dark days of our civil war, than in the glare of the great Chicago conflagration. The aggregate contributions to the relief of the Chicago sufferers must already have reached millions. But the generosity of the sympathizing world is outdone by the heroism of the sufferers. So great a calamity was never so nobly endured. Thousands of men who have been toiling a lifetime for wealth or a competence, have seen the accumulations of years swept away in a single night, and yet, reduced to beggary, as they are, there is no despair—not even despondency. The fire has conquered their houses, but not their hearts. Their warehouses are low in the dust, but their courage and their hopes are still as high as ever—and the marvelous energy which built Chicago is now already busy clearing away the ashes of its ruins to rebuild it, as if it was not much of a fire after all.

Ramifications of the Disaster.

[From the N. Y. Commercial Advertiser, October 20.]

It is not one of the least effects of the Chicago disaster that it reaches deep strata in our social life, as well as in our moneyed circles.

The bankruptcy of many companies in New York and Chicago has involved in heavy losses hundreds of private citizens, to whom insurance dividends gave a handsome and constant income, but now their stock is worth nothing. A case in point occurred in this city last week—a young lady, inheriting a large fortune, not long ago, invested the bulk of it in insurance stocks, attracted by the large profits of that method of investment, but the failure of the companies since the Chicago disaster has reduced her to comparative poverty. Merchants in New York, Boston, and elsewhere, who had ventures in Chicago, safe in ordinary times, can now look for only partial payments, and in many cases must submit to total loss. Private capitalists, who had large resources a month since, and were eager to begin new enterprises, have been compelled, by this disaster, to alter their plans, and promising projects are set aside. Those who had money out on call have been forced to take it up, and the borrowers in all branches of business have come to grief accordingly. The sudden and serious blow to the business of the Stock Exchange has embarrassed a very large number, and all investments are less valuable now than they were when the month opened. And, to crown all, the terrible shaking up of the insurance companies in every part of the country has inspired a feeling of distrust in regard to the safety of the risks held upon property as yet untouched by fire. So it is not in one or two circles alone that the Chicago blow is felt, but in every community in the Union a direct effect is visible.

New York's Need of Chicago.

To the Editor of the N. Y. Journal of Commerce:

I was well pleased with the remarks of Governor Bross, of Chicago, before the Chamber of Commerce; but there is one point which might well be added for the consideration of New York.

It is this: New York can not afford to have Chicago ruined, or seriously injured. Some one well remarked that New York and Chicago were members of a firm, and it would not do to have the junior member ruined. It might well be said that the two cities are like the Siamese twins—when one is sick the other is sick also, so intimately are the interests of the two connected.

What Cincinnati is to Baltimore, Chicago is to New York. Blot out Chicago, and the trade she now has would be divided between St. Louis, Cincinnati, and Milwaukee. That part of it which St. Louis got would go largely to New Orleans and Baltimore. The part which Cincinnati got would largely go to Baltimore also, while the part which fell to the lot of Milwaukee would be divided between New York and Boston.

It will readily be seen from the foregoing that the most serious blow which New York could receive would be the destruction of Chicago.

I am speaking more particularly of grocery goods, such as sugar, coffee, etc. A careful estimate, based upon established facts, shows us that Chicago bought last year nine hundred thousand (900,000) barrels of sugar, or an average of three thousand (3000) barrels daily for every working day in the year. I have not the data for the amount of coffee bought, but it was as large in proportion.

Already a large part of that trade has been diverted to Baltimore and Boston, and with the ruin of Chicago, they, with New Orleans, would get the lion's share of it. New York is doing nobly in giving to the sufferers, but she must do something to keep up the credit of the junior partner, or the *firm* of New York and Chicago will suffer badly.

Lessons from the Fire.

[From the New York Times, October, 23.]

When the great fire in London occurred, we can not doubt that public joy was expressed in Holland and Spain. The calamity of one great power was then thought the gain of all others. Now, political economy has taught, and religion sanctions the axiom, that the losses of one nation are the misfortune of all. Chicago herself feels this great generosity and sympathy of the world far more even than the money contributions, rich as those are. They seem to have given her new life and hope in her hard struggle. Now, too, for the first time, men have appreciated the precious value of that best feature in America—a pure family life. In the utter beggary of all worldly goods, with years of penury and sacrifice opening before them, and all their hard-earned wealth suddenly turned to ashes, they have found a new treasure in the love of wife and child, which has shone brighter and purer the more utter and crushing the calamity. We hear of one wealthy merchant stripped of every thing, who sends his children away to his relatives, while his wife becomes his book-keeper, and they start in life anew in a single room. But the innumerable instances of woman's generosity and sympathy in this hour of man's misfortune, will never be known except on the records of heaven.

It can not but be, also, that a profound moral lesson will reach both the West and the whole country from this tremendous calamity. The two cities which will suffer from it most have been the centers of national gambling and the wildest speculation. New York and Chicago have the evil reputation of containing the most insane and untiring hunters for wealth, the most unscrupulous speculators in grain and stocks, and the most extravagant spendthrifts of wealth suddenly made, who have ever been known under modern civilization. This awful misfortune suddenly falling on these classes, must touch those sentiments which are never utterly dried up in the human breast—the desire for other goods than the things seen and temporal, and the sense of the nothingness of all worldly wealth, compared with the riches unseen and eternal.

Chicago and St. Louis.

[From the St. Louis Democrat, October 21.]

That the annihilation of hundreds of millions of wealth in one city can absolutely benefit another city, is impossible. Wealth, in its broadest meaning, is the material for supplying human needs, and is the product of human toil. Its exchangeable character imparts to it a fluid nature, so that every important increase of it in one place is sooner or later an actual increase in other places, and every material diminution of it in one locality is sooner or later an actual diminution of it in others. If ten thousand houses are destroyed, all their occupants are not only made houseless, but temporarily cease to be producers, buyers, and consumers, to the extent that they were, and a blow is given to universal trade. As far as they can rebuild, so far the prices of materials and labor are raised, and so far the loss falls upon all who need such materials or labor. If active industries are paralyzed, so much production is withdrawn from the total production, and every consumer ultimately suffers. This line of thought may be continued indefinitely, and will show that not even St. Louis, the rival of Chicago, can be actually benefited by the prostration of the latter. In a thousand unimaginable ways this disaster will act and react, directly and indirectly, upon the essential thrift of some three hundred and forty thousand people of our city, and if it brings more money into some men's coffers, it will at last take still more money from the pockets of the masses. It is a blow to this whole agricultural region, and through it to the cities which that region sustains. That business will seek a level, like water, is an old and true adage. Subtract vastly from capital in one locality by sending it up in flames and smoke to the atmosphere, and the main level is lowered, and the prime sources of metropolitan growth every-where are reduced. Were it possible for any human being worthy of the name to exult in the ruin of a great city, this consideration alone, had he intelligence enough to pursue it, would prevent such a sentiment.

Suddenness of Chicago's Growth.

[From the London Times, October 11.]

When Mr. Cobden complained that English schoolboys were taught all about a trumpery Attic stream called the Ilissus, but nothing of Chicago, it should have been remembered in fairness that at that time Chicago had hardly existed long enough to be known by any but merchants. It will now not soon be forgotten. We may be confident, however, that the natural resources of the place, and the native energy of the Americans, will more than repeat the marvels of the original development of the city. The novelty and rapid growth of American civilization render the people far more indifferent to such calamities than dwellers in older countries who are conscious that their possessions are the accumulation of centuries. At the same time with the news of the fire the telegraph informed us that its mercantile effects were already being discounted in New York, and we have no doubt there are numbers of enterprising speculators who see their way to fortune through the speedy reconstruction of the city. The most cordial sympathy will be felt in this country with individual sufferers, and we can only wish the great mercantile community of the West the prompt recovery which their energy deserves.

"Resurgam."

[From the London Telegraph, October 11.]

It is idle to suppose that such a city is destined to become a Tadmor in the wilderness, or to sink into the chronic decadence of Sebastopol after the bombardment. "Resurgam" might be written upon every brick of the burnt-up houses of Chicago. It will rise again, and with a vengeance. Luckily no venerable cathedrals, no historic palaces, no monuments of art, no hoary relics of antiquity have perished in the colossal fire. Chicago has blazed away with the rapidity of lace curtains, or of "ornaments" in a drawing-room grate. The articles were handsome and expensive, but they can be replaced. To repair the injury done, all that is wanted is a certain amount of resources, energy, and pluck; and in pluck, energy, and resources the American people will never be bankrupt.

A swift steamer, laden with warm clothing and body linen, for both sexes and for all ages, would be the immediate testimony of our recognition that blood is thicker than water, and that, when Americans are in distress, we have not forgotten our common parentage.

Chicago's Magnificence—A London Opinion.

[From the London News, October 11.]

Nowhere in the world—not in Manchester, not in London, not in New York—were busier streets to be found. A river, hardly better than the Irwell, flowing through part of the business quarter of the city, and spanned by innumerable drawbridges, did, indeed, make hideous some of the city scenes, which showed like an uproarious Rotterdam or a great commercial Konigsberg. But the streets of shops and banks and theaters and hotels might stand a rivalry with those of any city in the world. Enormous piles of warehouses, with handsome and costly fronts; huge "stores," compared with which Schoolbred's or Tarn's seem diminutive; hotels as large as the Langham or the Louvre; bookshops which are unsurpassed in London or Paris; and theaters where Christine Nilsson found a fortune awaiting her such as the Old World could not offer—such were the principal features of that wonderful quarter which has just been reduced to ashes. Nor was Chicago wholly given up to business. Her avenues of private residences were—some, we trust, still are—as beautiful as any city can show. Michigan Avenue and Wabash Avenue were the streets where her merchant princes lived; and there is nothing to be seen in Paris, London, or New York to surpass either avenue in situation or in beauty. Michigan Avenue is a sort of Piccadilly, with a lake instead of a park under its drawing-room windows. The other great avenue was distinguished from almost any street of the kind in Europe or the United States by the variety of its architecture. Mr. Ruskin himself might have acknowledged that in this civilized and modern street, at least, the curse of monotony did not prevail, and the yoke of the Italian style was not accepted. Let it be added that Chicago, having the advantage of newness, and the warning of all the world before her, had but few narrow streets and lanes. The thoroughfares were, as a rule, nearly all of the same width. The inexperienced traveler often found himself sadly perplexed as he wandered through a city of broad white streets, each looking just like another, and any one seeming as well entitled as its neighbor to claim the leadership in business or fashion.

Chicago will not remain in her ruins as an ancient city might have done. Already in the thick of all the wreck and misery we may be sure that active and undaunted minds are planning the reconstruction of many a gutted and blackened building, the restoration of many shattered fortunes. It is only a few years since the city of Portland, in Maine, was destroyed by fire; and the traveler to-day sees there, a new, busy, and solid town, where the story of the conflagration has already become a tradition. The people of Illinois are still more energetic and fertile of expedient than the people of Maine, and they will not long leave the city, which was their pride, to lie in her smoldering ruins. The claims which Chicago used at one time to urge for the transference of the National Capital to the shore of her lake, are, indeed, put out of court for the present; and her rival, St. Louis, will, for some time to come, have the advantage of her in the race for commerce, wealth, and population. But the city whose rate of growth distanced that of any other on the earth, will not be long in recovering the effects even of the present calamity. So much at least of consolation may be found. Before the widows and orphans whom this catastrophe bereaves, shall have put aside the robes of mourning, Chicago will be rising from her ruins, perhaps more magnificent than ever. Her restoration, we may feel assured, will be in keeping with the marvelous rapidity of her rise, and the awful suddenness of her fall.

Why she was Burned—A Rebel View.

[From the Rushville, Ind., American.]

Near one-half the city has been laid in ashes, and a hundred and fifty thousand people rendered homeless.

The announcement, at first, seemed incredible. When the telegraph confirmed the facts, a thrill of horror and sympathy pervaded the universal heart. This fact presents a palliative for many of the outrages and cruelties of the past ten years, and shows that human nature has, after all, some redeeming traits. It was far different when Sherman's army desolated and destroyed the fairest region of the South, robbing and plundering, and burning as they went, leaving the people to starve; or, when Sheridan, a monster of cruelty, overran and destroyed the valley of Virginia, afterward boasting that a crow would have to carry its provisions under its wings, if it should attempt to fly over it; and thus he brought starvation on the old men, women, and children of that region, so that thousands perished of famine. More property, and more lives were destroyed in these raids than all Chicago put together, and what was the sentiment of the North? One of exultation and rejoicing. These acts of vandalism were paraded as victories, and the heroes were met on their return with ovations of men and oblations of kisses from many of the gentle damsels of the North, carried away by the military glory that settled around the heads of these vandal chiefs, that was degrading, sickening, disgusting! What cared these women for the homeless, houseless, starving mothers and children of the South? Nothing. They exulted in their sufferings; laughed at the story of the ravishment of the daughters of the South, the burning and robberies of their dwellings, and slaughter of her strong men; shouted hosannahs and threw from the tips of their fingers kisses to the perpetrators of these acts of vandalism.

That was then! Now, that which is not half so horrible, thrills their bosom with sympathy, and their hand is quick and liberal to the relief of the sufferers. These things prove that man is a good deal lower than the angels, and sometimes, at least, a little higher than the devils. Chicago has lost, perhaps, three hundred million dollars by the fire. The property destroyed in the South is estimated at over one thousand millions. The fire in Chicago was the result of accident. The destruction of property in the South was done purposely, by Northern soldiers, and compares exactly with the acts of the Goths and Vandals, savages that overran and subjugated the Roman Empire. But we are living under a higher civilization. Chicago did her full share in the destruction of the South. God adjusts balances. Maybe with Chicago the books are now squared.

Chicago Suffering for the World's Sins.

The Rev. Dr. Bellows gave an eloquent sermon, in his church in New York, on Chicago, on the Sunday following the fire, after which a liberal collection was made. He said the real Chicago was not burned at all. Ten years will not leave one cinder-mark on her robes. Her wealth was visibly represented in her great warehouses, but her wealth is in the souls, breasts, and irrepressible elasticity of her citizens. She has gained a stimulant in activity, and a name which will realize all it has lost. The great lesson which Chicago presented is that humanity is loosened from its selfishness and shocked into a sense of the nobleness of true riches. God has not stirred Chicago for its sins. It is now punished for the sins of the world.

No, for her own!

[From the N. Y. Tribune, October 20.]

The Rev. Granville Moody, of the Methodist Church in Cincinnati, has been preaching an occasional sermon on "Fire," in his preliminary prayer alluding to the calamity which had befallen Chicago, and attributing it to the fact that the city recently gave a majority vote against Sunday and the Liquor Laws. The Rev. Mr. Moody likewise found in the fire "a retributive judgment on a city which has shown such a devotion in its worship to the Golden Calf." The Rev. Mr. Moody is clearly of the opinion that when cities sink to a certain depth of iniquity, the Almighty makes it his particular business to destroy them; and the following are cited as instances of those which either have been destroyed, or may expect to be destroyed, on account of their sins:

Cincinnati,	Babylon,	Sodom,	Zeboim,
New York,	Jerusalem,	Gomorrah,	Herculaneum,
Boston,	Tyre,	Zoar,	Pompeii,

Chicago.

Mr. Beecher on the Calamity.

[From a "Lecture Room Talk" of Rev. H. W. Beecher, Oct. 13.]

It has become a matter of remark to those who study the interior of history that events move in cycles. In certain years there are riots, or commercial troubles, and so it would seem that there are years of catastrophes, and this might be called the year of fire. In the burning of town after town, of men, women, and children by the scores, there would seem to be enough to terrify us, even if it were not for the greater disaster of Chicago. This last disaster can be measured by the way in which it dwarfs other calamities. I am utterly unable to take in the calamity of Chicago. As it is in the case of mountains when first seen, I can not adjust my sight to take it in. It was so during the war. I could feel only so much, and then I was full, but the events went on. So with this disaster. The desolation of a house is as much as you can feel, but take a street of houses, and then a ward, and from that to miles, and tens of thousands, and fifty thousand, and two hundred thousand people homeless, and it is wholly immeasurable. The mass and magnitude of suffering can not be estimated. Yet, though we can not measure it and take it in, every individual goes on suffering. Chicago is not destroyed; like another Phœnix, it will rise again. The strong will take care of themselves; but O, for the poor, the women and children, the aged and the stranger, my heart goes out.

Next to the greatness of the calamity is the admirableness of the sympathy. The whole northern part of the nation has uprisen and stretched out its arms and taken that great city to its heart. We know no Catholic, no Protestant, no Democrat, no Republican, and the hand of the charity of this nation is like God's hand, that sendeth rain upon the just and the unjust. It is sublime, and when you add that across the sea the kingdom of Great Britain and the German nation are sending their gifts, it shows how the great element of Christian sympathy has unitized the world. It is one of the auspicious signs of the times. There is one danger, and that is that our sympathy will be merely emotive, and that as the weary winter months move on we shall get tired. Suffering never gets tired. Mr. Beecher remarked, further on: "I have been struck with the indifference of some men to the terrific suffering. Some say there can't be a devil. I have only to say that if there is n't a devil there is very good material to make one of, and if God is too good to have a devil in chief, He is n't too good to have one in detail. Nothing can exceed the wickedness and inhumanity of those men who have taken this occasion to prey upon their fellow-men."

A Poet's Tribute.

Men said at vespers: All is well!
In one wild night the city fell;
Fell shrines of prayer and marts of gain
Before the fiery hurricane.

On threescore spires had sunset shone,
Where ghastly sunrise looked on none;
Men clasped each other's hands and said:
The City of the West is dead!

Brave hearts who fought, in slow retreat,
The fiends of fire from street to street,
Turned, powerless, to the blinding glare,
The dumb defiance of despair.

A sudden impulse thrilled each wire
That signaled round that sea of fire;
Swift words of cheer, warm heart-throbs came;
In tears of pity died the flame!

From East, from West, from South, from North,
The messages of hope shot forth,
And, underneath the severing wave,
The world, full-handed, reached to save.

Fair seemed the old; but fairer still
The new the dreary void shall fill,
With dearer homes than those o'erthrown,
For love shall lay each corner-stone.

Rise, stricken city!—from thee throw
The ashen sackcloth of thy woe;
And build, as Thebes to Amphion's strain,
To songs of cheer thy walls again!

How shriveled, in thy hot distress,
The primal sin of selfishness!
How instant rose, to take thy part,
The angel in the human heart!

Ah! not in vain the flames that tossed
Above thy dreadful holocaust;
The Christ again has preached through thee
The gospel of humanity!

Then lift once more thy towers on high,
And fret with spires the Western sky,
To tell that God is yet with us,
And love is still miraculous!

[John G. Whittier.

APPENDIX D.

THE WORK OF RELIEF.

REPORT OF THE PHILADELPHIA COMMITTEE.

The following extracts from a report, made by a committee of the Philadelphia benevolent organizations to their constituents, are given, as affording not only a clear sketch of the operations of the Chicago Relief Society, but as showing how its work was regarded from an outside standpoint. The account of the Committee is correct, except in two minor respects; the money given out by the Bureau of Special Relief is intended as a downright gift, and the recipients of houses from the Shelter Committee are not asked to give even their notes in payment, except where their circumstances and prospects are such as to justify the expectation of their being able to pay.

The committee, after enumerating the various departments of the Society's business, each in charge of a committee, proceeds:

"To these committees a ninth was added during a visit of your committee, entitled the Bureau of Special Counsel and Assistance, to take charge of cases which could not be readily disposed of by either of the others, its principal functions being to aid those who were suffering in silence because they had not made their wants known, and by supplying small sums of money, either as donations or as advances in the nature of loans, to be repaid if the recipients shall be able to do so in the future, so as to aid the beneficiaries in their efforts to take care of themselves.

"Each of these committees is employed throughout the whole of the day in the discharge of its special duties, and the Chairmen of all of them meet every night as an Executive Board. At these nightly meetings all the proceedings of the various committees are reported, and all information of the progress and developments of the work of relief is concentrated. Your committee, by invitation, attended one of these meetings of the Executive Board, where they had ample opportunity to observe its proceedings; and they were also invited to examine the whole work of relief critically, and to make suggestions in the way of improvement.

"The business of your committee mainly concerned the Executive Board, and the subjects of food, clothing, fuel, and shelter. Having been fully and satisfactorily advised of the general plan of operations, by the Chairman of the Executive Board, your committee next inquired into the faithful, intelligent, and impartial execution of the work in its details by the subordinate agencies. To this end they visited the office of the General

Superintendent of Distribution of Supplies, Mr. O. C. Gibbs. This gentleman has been for a long time the Agent of the Relief and Aid Society. Here we found that under the general direction of the Executive Committee, of which Wirt Dexter, Esq., is the Chairman, the work of relief was in operation under a thoughtfully-conceived and well-regulated and methodized system. The city had been divided into districts and sub-districts, in each of which there was a carefully selected Superintendent of Distribution, aided by citizens in whom the people of the districts have confidence, and by corps of visitors. Books had been opened and blank forms printed, so as to carry on the work with system and accuracy, as well as dispatch. Copies of all these printed forms were furnished your committee. They could easily see that the system adopted was well calculated to prevent imposition on the part of the applicants not entitled to relief, to prevent to a great degree the duplication of aid by "repeating," to prevent wasteful and improvident application of supplies, and above all to make it certain that that meritorious class who suffer patiently, and who are reluctant to make their wants known, shall not be overlooked or neglected.

"Each of the districts and sub-districts has headquarters where applications for relief are received, where the claims of the applicants are examined according to a printed form of instructions, and where the results are filed and recorded. Each one of the districts is also furnished with a depot for the storage and distribution of supplies. After an application is approved and supplies are issued, the "visitor" for the particular locality in which the applicant is lodged, makes a further examination to verify the statements of the applicants. If they are found to be correct, a report to that effect is made; if otherwise, no further supplies are issued. In addition to this duty the visitors are charged with another important service. In order to find *all* who need or deserve aid, they have been instructed to go from house to house, until the whole of the city has been covered. By these means a full registry of all who are either in the receipt of aid, or who need it, had been very nearly completed before your committee left Chicago. In the examination of applicants for relief according to the printed instructions, every thing essential to the identification of the applicant and the verification of his or her necessities are set down in writing on the printed forms referred to, and filed for reference at the headquarters of the district; and in every case where any person or head of a family is recommended for relief, and supplies of any kind are issued, a regular account is opened under the name of the beneficiary in a large ledger specially prepared for the purpose.

"In this account all the particulars concerning the relief granted, what the supplies consisted of, the date when they were issued, how many persons they were to maintain, and how many days the supplies furnished ought to last with care and economy, are all noted, and can be understood at a glance. By interchange of these recorded sources of information among the several districts, there is a reasonable approach to certainty, that no persons entitled to relief can procure supplies at more than one place.

"Thus far your committee had 'ascertained the mode of distribution' of food, clothing, and fuel, according to the general plan, and in the details of its execution. It remained to them to pursue their inquiries as to the subject of shelter. The subject of providing shelter for the hundred thousand people whose houses had been destroyed was one of the most difficult with which the Relief and Aid Society had to grapple, and the way in which it has been dealt with, affords an opportunity to illustrate the intelligence, energy, business-like economy, and prompt dispatch with which its executive board does its work. Immediately after the fire, and before the Aid Society was intrusted with the work of relief, some of the homeless sufferers were taken into the houses of the unburned districts among their acquaintances, but the great body of them were housed temporarily in church buildings, school buildings, empty warehouses, &c. There was, of course, intense discomfort, and great risk of disease and death from privation, exposure, and overcrowding. Then the authorities commenced the hasty construction of barracks in long, close and inconvenient rows on vacant ground. These, although better than the crowded churches and other large buildings, were still very objectionable; and the Aid Society, immediately upon coming into control of the relief funds, adopted a very different and much more effective plan. They procured estimates in minute detail for the construction of cheap *separate* dwellings of two kinds, one for families of not more than three persons, and one for families of four or five persons. These were immediately printed, with diagrams and schedules of particulars embracing all the necessary materials. A copy is annexed to this report. The dimensions of the house for five persons are 16 feet by 20, one story high. The house contains two rooms, one 12 feet by 16, and one 8 by 16. Wherever a sufferer by the fire owned or had a lease upon the lot on which his or her house was situated, or could procure the use of a lot, an order was at once issued by the Committee on Shelter for all the materials for the construction of the house. Every thing was so well arranged in this business that three mechanics could put up such a house in two days. It is estimated that eight thousand of them in all will be required; and of these not less than three thousand had been erected before your committee left Chicago, and the materials had been issued for at least one thousand more. The total cost of the house for five persons, including a cook-stove, a mattress, bedding, and half a ton of coal, is $110! The house is not furnished to the beneficiary as a gift, but in order to stimulate thrift, to cultivate the sentiment of self-respect, and to guard against imposition, a note for the amount without interest is taken, payable in one year.

"This plan has worked admirably, and that it has been carried out with wonderful dispatch and economy, the facts your committee have recited fully prove. In further illustration of the forethought, energy, and economy of the Aid Society's movements, it is worthy of mention that immediately upon the adoption of the plan of furnishing separate dwellings for the homeless sufferers, and before the plan was made public, apprehending a possible rise in the price of lumber, a member of the Executive Committee, under authority of the committee, mounted his horse, visited the great lumber depots, and in three hours made contracts for all the lumber required, at six dollars per thousand feet less than the rise which immediately followed.

"After an examination of all these matters, both in their general direction and the administration of their details, and after considering information obtained from other trustworthy sources, your committee came to the conclusion that 'the mode of distributing' the relief money and supplies contributed to the suffering people of Chicago, as at present administered under the auspices of the 'Aid and Relief Society' of that city, is admirably adapted to the purpose, and that its direction is intrusted to able, experienced and eminently trustworthy hands. They were strongly impressed with the superior intelligence, large administrative capacity, and high character of the men who plan, direct, and give impulse to the work.

"More than a hundred thousand people were left without the shelter of a roof, most of them without a change of clothes, and at least half of them utterly destitute. When your committee reached Chicago, they were grateful to hear the assurance that all of those who remained in Chicago and who need assistance were housed in some way, and were supplied with clothes sufficient for present emergencies. About forty thousand persons were being supplied with food on Thursday last, October 26, but the number was in course of reduction through the vigilance of the visitors and the exertions of the Committee on Employment. It is expected, however, that not less than twenty-five to thirty thousand of the destitute will have to be carried through the winter and early spring months. The severest part of the trial, and the period of greatest distress for all these, are yet to come. These considerations suggest continued exercise of the benevolence already so generously expressed, and such encouragement and support to the excellent society charged with the administration of the world's bounty to the ruined city, as will strengthen its purpose to check all tendency toward profuse and wasteful distribution, so that its stores and resources may be husbanded to meet the wants of the trying season yet to come.

"Jos. Patterson, Geo. G. Meade,
Wm. V. McKean, Geo. H. Stuart."

www.ingramcontent.com/pod-product-compliance
Lightning Source LLC
LaVergne TN
LVHW021242110826
845150LV00002B/384

9781425561031